LANDFALL PRESS:

TWENTY-FIVE YEARS
OF PRINTMAKING

1. Claes Oldenburg saluting as Jack Lemon fans (or in printer's parlance, flags) a lithographic plate for Oldenburg's *Picasso Cufflink*, 1974, in the West Ontario Street shop.

LANDFALL PRESS:

TWENTY-FIVE YEARS OF PRINTMAKING

Joseph Ruzicka

With contributions by
Jack Lemon, Vernon Fisher, Mark Pascale

MILWAUKEE ART MUSEUM

Exhibition Itinerary

Milwaukee Art Museum, Milwaukee, Wisconsin	September 13-November 10, 1996
Chicago Cultural Center, Chicago, Illinois	March 15-May 18, 1997
Davenport Museum of Art, Davenport, Iowa	September 14-November 17, 1997
Springfield Museum of Art, Springfield, Ohio	March 13-May 9, 1999

Support for this exhibition is provided by the John Porter Retzer and Florence Horn Retzer Fund.

Published by the Milwaukee Art Museum, Milwaukee, Wisconsin
First edition

Available through D.A.P./Distributed Art Publishers, 636 Broadway, 12th Floor, New York, New York 10012.
Tel: (212)473-5119, Fax: (212)673-2887.

ISBN: 0-944110-69-X (cloth)
      0-944110-68-1 (paper)

Library of Congress Catalog Card Number: 96-77356

Edited by Sheila Schwartz
Design and production by Michael Dooley, Milwaukee Art Museum
Films, color separations, and printing by Zimmermann Printing Company, Sheboygan, Wisconsin

Note: All works of art reproduced in black-and-white are in the Landfall Press Archive, Milwaukee Art Museum, unless otherwise noted. Captions for works in the exhibition reproduced in black-and-white appear in short form; full data is given in the listing of exhibited works, beginning on p. 204. Captions for works reproduced in the color plate section appear in short form; full data is given in the listing of exhibited works.

Cover: Robert Cottingham, *Art*, 1992, lithograph, (detail of Pl. 20)

CONTENTS

FOREWORD

This volume is published on the occasion of the retrospective exhibition, "Landfall Press: Twenty-Five Years of Printmaking," held to honor a printer who has played a critical role in American art during the last quarter of a century. This catalogue and exhibition celebrate the singular achievements of Jack Lemon and Landfall Press, founded in Chicago in 1970. Lemon possesses a keen eye and unshakable convictions, and, in many ways, the history of Landfall Press is also his history, and it is important that it be told. This whole project also extends a long tradition of the Milwaukee Art Museum's exhibition program: to offer to the public and to our peers the most challenging and significant contemporary art.

One of the crucial defining moments in postwar American art was the establishment and growth of the great fine-art printing houses: Universal Limited Art Editions (ULAE), West Islip, New York, founded in 1957; Tamarind Lithography Workshop, Los Angeles, in 1960; Gemini G.E.L., Los Angeles, in 1966; Graphicstudio U.S.F., Tampa, Florida, in 1969; Landfall Press, Chicago, in 1970; Tyler Graphics, Bedford Village, New York, in 1974; Solo Press (today, Solo Impression), New York, in 1975, among many others. The net result of all this activity was an unprecedented flourishing of the graphic arts in this country, which continues unabated to this day. The establishment of this network of printer-publishers has given major artists of our time an important outlet for their creative energies, among them, at Landfall Press, Vito Acconci, Christo, Chuck Close, Jim Dine, Nancy Graves, and Pat Steir. The list could go on for pages.

Since my years as a graduate student at the University of Chicago, I avidly followed and deeply admired the ground-breaking work that Jack Lemon was publishing at Landfall Press. From the time I arrived at the Milwaukee Art Museum in 1980, my enthusiasm was shared by Christopher and Janet Graf, who have generously given important gifts of Landfall prints to the Museum for many years, and by the Print Forum, the Museum's support group for the Department of Prints and Drawings, which has also purchased major gifts of Landfall publications for the Museum's collection. The Milwaukee Art Museum had also organized a traveling retrospective of the work of Philip Pearlstein, who did a number of his earlier prints at Landfall, and the collection included major paintings and sculptures by a number of artists, such as Robert Arneson, Roger Brown, Alfred Leslie, Claes Oldenburg, Ed Paschke, William T. Wiley, and others, who had frequently worked at Landfall.

In the late 1980s, it therefore seemed entirely appropriate to approach Jack Lemon with the idea of establishing a Landfall archive at the Milwaukee Art Museum. Talks progressed, and in 1992 an agreement was reached and the Landfall Press Archive was established. As in the best of such agreements, both sides benefited. The whole of Landfall's oeuvre would be preserved as a unit, cared for in a scholarly manner, and made available to the public; in this way, the reputation and history of the Press would be secured. It is much easier to write history if all the relevant material is accessible in one location. The Museum, in its turn, benefited by acquiring a most significant body of contemporary work, expanding our presentation of artists already in the collection, while adding work by artists hitherto absent, such as Terry Allen, Lesley Dill, Nancy Dwyer, and Vernon Fisher. It also meant that the Milwaukee Art Museum joined an elite group of institutions across the nation that care for the archives of major print shops, such as The Art Institute of Chicago (ULAE), the National Gallery of Art, Washington, D.C. (Gemini G.E.L. and Graphicstudio), and the Walker Art Center, Minneapolis (Tyler Graphics). This is a most important responsibility because it means making the material of such a press available to both scholars and the general public, furthering historical and critical studies of each press and of printmaking in general.

A project of this magnitude necessarily requires the hard work and vision of many people. My deepest thanks go to Jack Lemon for working with the Milwaukee Art Museum to establish the Landfall Press Archive and to make this whole project such a success. He has been most generous with his time, knowledge, and energy. His major gift and continued donations of works of art are the foundations of the Archive. I am also sincerely grateful to the artists in the Archive, for they have warmly and enthusiastically responded whenever the Museum has asked (sometimes at length) for information regarding their printmaking philosophies and practices, and they have made gifts of their drawings, proofs, and other material related to their tenure at Landfall, so that we might have as thorough an Archive as possible. Dick and Sue Pieper enthusiastically shared our vision of establishing this Archive and provided crucial support at precisely the time when it was needed. Without them, the Landfall Press Archive would not have been created; its ongoing role as a major educational function within the

Museum's permanent collection will continue to mark the Piepers' extraordinary generosity. Support for this project has also been provided by the John Porter Retzer and Florence Horn Retzer Fund.

Generous support for the initial cataloguing and organization of the Archive was provided through a grant from the National Endowment for the Arts, continuing its admirable history of assisting significant programs.

Thanks should also be extended to the staff of the Milwaukee Art Museum, almost all of whom contributed in some degree to the realization of a project of this magnitude. Several people, in particular, played significant roles. In the early stages, Verna Posever Curtis, Curator of Prints, Drawings and Photographs, made important contributions to the conception of the project. During the negotiations for the Archive and in the formative stages of its organization and cataloguing, Sue Taylor, Curator of Prints and Drawings, played a central role. For the last two years, Joseph Ruzicka, present Curator of Prints and Drawings, has conceived and shaped both the exhibition and the catalogue, supervising every detail of their organization. Since 1992, Marty Stewart Huff has served as Project Coordinator, overseeing the day-to-day operation of the Archive and the cataloguing of the collection. Both Joseph Ruzicka and Marty Stewart Huff have worked tirelessly, creatively, and most effectively to plan and accomplish this exhibition and publication.

Russell Bowman
Director
Milwaukee Art Museum

INTRODUCTION
AND ACKNOWLEDGMENTS

2. John Rios graining a stone to remove an old image and prepare the surface for the next, in the West Ontario Street shop.

The primary purpose of this quarter-century retrospective is to set forth, on the walls and in print, the history of Jack Lemon's Landfall Press. Founded by Lemon in Chicago in 1970, Landfall established itself as one of the leading printer-publishers in the United States, and played a critical formative role in the early decades of the American print renaissance. In 1966, Lemon trained at the ground-breaking Tamarind Lithography Workshop in Los Angeles, founded by June Wayne six years earlier. After establishing shops at the Kansas City Art Institute and the Nova Scotia College of Art and Design, Lemon opened his Landfall Press in Chicago.

Today, the Press remains active, continuing both long-term collaborations and initiating first-time projects with new artists. Surveying the prints published over the last twenty-five years, it is clear that a broad and varied group of artists created signature images at Landfall. It is especially significant that many female and minority artists, such as Lesley Dill, Nancy Graves,

Richard Hunt, Luis Jiménez, Roberto Juarez, Marilyn Minter, Martin Puryear, Pat Steir, and Kara Walker, have worked at Landfall, and this is but one aspect of the Press that distinguishes it from the other major presses. Lemon's openness has resulted in a strong body of work diverse in its imagery, techniques, and conceptual range.

While figurative work, for instance—by artists such as Jim Dine, Claes Oldenburg, and Philip Pearlstein—has long been understood as the Press' strong suit, much abstract work has also been made there—by Freya Hansell, Sol LeWitt, Jack Tworkov, Duane Zaloudek, and others. Lemon has also worked on projects with many Conceptual artists, such as Terry Allen, Nancy Dwyer, Ronald Jones, and Dennis Oppenheim. There is a very clear interest in story-telling, seen in the work of Phyllis Bramson, Vernon Fisher, Ellen Lanyon, and William T. Wiley. And there are strong political currents running through many of the prints, such as those by Robert Arneson, Roger Brown, Ed Paschke, and Peter Saul. In shaping the visual and intellectual personality of Landfall Press, Lemon has made ample use of the diverse currents that characterize contemporary American art.

Sitting down to write a twenty-five-year history of any institution is a daunting task, but especially so when confronted with an organization whose personality is as rich and varied as that of Landfall Press. Early in the course of preparing the exhibition and catalogue, I made the astounding discovery that very little historical and critical work had ever been done on Landfall—a remarkably anomalous situation given the great range of issues and ideas embodied in the Press' output. I hope that this volume will spawn the investigations that Landfall so clearly merits.

To fulfill this function, the catalogue would, I realized, have to provide the basic history of the Press, and this idea shaped the table of contents. Jack Lemon has contributed an aesthetic statement, outlining the salient features he looks for in the work and the life of the artists with whom he collaborates. Vernon Fisher,

a key Landfall collaborator, has written an appreciation of Lemon and the Press. Mark Pascale, Assistant Curator of Prints and Drawings at The Art Institute of Chicago, has written an essay treating Lemon's long involvement with Conceptual art, which will, it is hoped, be the first of many specialized articles dealing with Landfall's history. As Pascale points out, Landfall's consistent commitment to Conceptual issues may be one of the most unexpected and underappreciated aspects of its history. I offer a broad aesthetic history of Landfall, its intellectual and visual development, through a chronological discussion of the work of artists who have played instrumental, defining roles. Finally, there is a selected bibliography and exhibition history, the first ever published for Landfall.

While preparing my essay, I became acutely aware of the seemingly countless issues raised by Landfall's work, and it soon became apparent that it would be impossible to treat them all. Indeed, for every idea I discussed, another was left unmentioned. So while I wrote about the work at Landfall that has a distinct narrative quality to it, I left virtually untouched the large body of related work, such as that by Terry Allen, Nancy Dwyer, and Pat Steir, in which words can transcend their narrative or descriptive roles to become objects or images in and of themselves. The whole issue of sculptors working at the Press also deserves a fuller treatment than it is accorded here. And I only obliquely touched on the distinct urban sensibility that informs the work of Vito Acconci and Robert Cottingham; in that discussion, however, I did not include the work of John Baeder, Christo, and Richard Haas. I hope these lacunae will serve as a spur for other historians and that my essay in general will provide a source of topics for future specialized investigations into Landfall's history.

The rich history of the Press is easily accessible, now that the Landfall Press Archive has been established at the Milwaukee Art Museum. Founded in 1992, the Archive has more than six hundred editioned prints and some three thousand drawings, proofs, plates, stones, and other related process material. All these objects have been catalogued and stored in a dedicated print room, and all the editioned prints have been photographed. Other resources include the Press' documentation, correspondence between this curator and the artists in the Archive, and ephemera related to the Press, such as exhibition pamphlets, sales catalogues, and newsletters. Also available for consultation are documents and lists created during the course of preparing this exhibition and catalogue. This material includes a listing, alphabetical by artist, of all of the prints—published and contract—made at Landfall Press since 1970, a chronological listing of the published prints, and a listing of the portfolios issued by Landfall.

The Landfall Press Archive is not a static collection. With great foresight, Jack Lemon has most generously agreed to send to the Museum each year's publications, with related material, as long as he remains proprietor of Landfall. We will, moreover, continue to correspond with the artists in order to get the clearest possible picture of their ideas and attitudes regarding printmaking in general and working at Landfall in particular. Ongoing research on the production and history of the Press will generate, for example, a checklist of the monoprints published by Landfall and a catalogue documenting Lemon's deep commitment to music.

Because the Archive is an organic entity and Lemon remains active as a printer, the Museum and the Press decided not to publish a catalogue raisonné at this time. Although such a catalogue has become standard practice when a museum assumes the custodianship of an archive, it seemed that we would be writing the final chapter on an organization that is still charging into the future. This, of course, does not preclude the publication of a comprehensive catalogue at some later date—which we fully intend to do. In the meantime, all our resources are available to interested scholars and the public.

The present catalogue provides a twenty-five-year overview of the Press' achievements. In addition to the essays, we felt that it was important to reproduce all the work in the exhibition, *and* as many images as possible of equally important pieces that we could not fit into the show, along with photographs of shop life. This format offered us a partial solution to the thorny problem of how to give an accurate visual impression of the aesthetic and intellectual breadth and excellence marking Landfall's quarter century. Getting the exhibition checklist down to its present size was a painful exercise, because there was simply not enough gallery space to include all important works. Thus, one way to make up the shortfall was to include as many reproductions as possible in the catalogue.

An exhibition of this magnitude and complexity necessarily requires the involvement and cooperation of many people. Foremost, we are indebted to Jack Lemon, who has given so very generously of his time, vast knowledge, and deep concern for his artists and their art. He has bravely and cordially entertained endless requests for information and survived small-scale invasions at the Press by Museum staff members, who searched through his library, photo collection, filing cabinets, documentation folders, and forgotten boxes on high shelves. I hope that he does not anticipate a reprieve anytime soon, for there is still much information that he has and we need.

My deepest personal thanks must be extended to all the artists in the Archive for their kind patience and generosity in answering my queries about their ideas regarding printmaking and their experiences at Landfall, sometimes for hours on end. This project has allowed me to further some old friendships and to make new ones, and this is the most rewarding experience for any curator. Special thanks are owed to those artists and their families who donated their work—editioned prints, drawings, proofs, etc.—helping us in our quest to make the Archive comprehensive: Vito Acconci, Lorraine and Gregory Dean, Lesley Dill, Jim Dine, Nancy Dwyer, Freya Hansell, Ronald Jones,

Ellen Lanyon, Don Nice, Claes Oldenburg, Dennis Oppenheim, Philip Pearlstein, Allen Ruppersberg, Jeanette Pasin Sloan, William T. Wiley, and Karl Wirsum.

Jack Lemon, Vernon Fisher, and Mark Pascale made essential contributions to this volume, and the catalogue is immeasurably better because they had a hand in it. Thanks, too, must be extended to Sheila Schwartz for her sensitive and insightful editing. Marc Sapir provided much valuable advice and encouragement.

For their patience and dedication to the project, I am also grateful to colleagues at the institutions that will be showing this exhibition: Gregory G. Knight, Director of Visual Arts/Chief Curator, Chicago Cultural Center; Bradey Roberts, Curator of Collections/Exhibitions, Davenport Museum of Art, Iowa; and Mark Chepp, Director, Springfield Museum of Art, Ohio. Special thanks go to Wendy Weitman, Associate Curator of Prints and Illustrated Books, The Museum of Modern Art, New York, for making a crucial loan to the exhibition, and for advice and wisdom.

The preparation of this entire project has necessarily touched every department in the Milwaukee Art Museum. My foremost thanks go to the Museum's Director, Russell Bowman, and Executive Director, Christopher Goldsmith, without whose support this project could never have been realized. I am indebted to my colleagues in the curatorial department. Dean Sobel, Curator of Contemporary Art and Coordinator of Curatorial Affairs, helped guide the project through various administrative stages. Terry Marvel, Curatorial Assistant of Prints, Drawings and Photographs, provided much support and advice at crucial times in the production of this manuscript, including rewriting the artists' biographies. Marty Stewart Huff, Project Coordinator, has catalogued and cared for the Archive since it arrived at the Museum in 1992, coordinated the activities of many interns and volunteers, gathered much of the basic research material and put it into usable form, and served as a most effective liaison between the Museum and Landfall Press. She has accomplished a huge task. Jane O'Meara, Administrative Assistant, oversaw and coordinated the many difficult details in a timely and professional manner, and put in long hours at critical moments. I extend special thanks to my two predecessors, Verna Curtis and Sue Taylor, who played essential roles in the creation and organization of this whole project. Claire Fox, former Curatorial Assistant, and Megan Powell, former Administrative Assistant, also contributed in key ways in the early stages of the exhibition. I am also grateful to Cheryl Robertson, former Curator of Decorative Arts, for her wise counsel.

This exhibition could not have happened without the efforts of Lucia Petrie, Director of Development, and Marcia Prokupek. I am particularly indebted to Donna Kempf, former Grants Coordinator, and to Ray Kehm, former Director of Planned Giving, for their wisdom and timely help.

A whole marine corps of interns and volunteers assisted in the cataloguing of the Archive and the preparation of certain parts of this catalogue. Many of them were students at the Milwaukee Institute of Art and Design or the University of Wisconsin—Milwaukee, and I owe a debt to the intern advisers at these schools, Duane Seidensticker and Barry Wind, respectively. Shary Costello, Leslie Dutton, Jodi Hanel, Ariana Huggett, Annik Lott, and Helen Weber all contributed to the artists' biographies for the catalogue. Grace Jankowski undertook the huge task of organizing and researching the bibliography and exhibition history of Landfall. Other interns who so ably assisted with the complex tasks of organizing the Archive and preparing material for the catalogue include Irene Bialobrzeski, Lauren James, Kim Loewe, Jean Mross, Jennifer Olsen, Patti Pagelsdorf, Elaine Palmer, and Amy Westpfahl. I am particularly grateful to Linda Polzin and to Project Assistants Mark Baltzley and Steve Burnham for their hard work, patience, and camaraderie.

Leigh Albritton, Registrar, expertly arranged the

3. Landfall Press Curator Judy Freilich, in the West Ontario Street Shop, embossing the
Landfall chopmark on a print by John Himmelfarb.

shipping of the more than three thousand items of the Archive over a span of four years, a very complex task. Dawnmarie Frank, Assistant to the Registrar, coordinated the photography of the Archive's six hundred editioned prints. Efraim Lev-er and Larry Sanders took the photographs. Jim deYoung, Senior Conservator, answered many vexing questions regarding technique and media and oversaw the conservation and storage arrangements for the Archive with his customary efficiency and intelligence. He was ably assisted by Mark Dombek, Chris Niver, Paula Schultz, and Terry White. Michael Dooley, Director of Design and Publications, designed this marvelous publication and John Irion, Exhibition Designer, produced yet another beautiful exhibition. Larry Stadler, Facilities Manager, and his crew of Jo-Bob Boblick, John Dreckmann, Joe Kavanaugh, Dave Moynihan, John Nicholson, and Scott Radtke assisted with the construction of the special Archive room, and hung and lit the exhibition in their usual efficient manner.

This project served as a testing ground for the Museum's new computer cataloguing program, and I am grateful to John Gee and Sarah Nesbitt for their advice, skill, and above all, their patience.

Alerting the public to such an exhibition is a large and complicated task that Polly Scott, Director of Communications, handled in an expert manner. Fran Serlin, Director of Audience Development, devised ingenious ways to bring this exhibition to the public. Barbara Brown-Lee, Director of Education, marshaled her dedicated corps of docents to do their usual marvelous job of teaching and interpreting the material for groups of visitors to the Museum. Dedra Walls, Coordinator of Media, wrote perceptive and informative text panels for the show and also worked out the arrangements for our guest lecturers.

A research project of this scope is possible only with a dedicated library staff. For all of their efforts and patience, I am grateful to Rebecca Schultz, Librarian, and Suzy Weisman and Lynn Hagen, former Librarians.

Finally, very special thanks are due to Susan Fancher, who now knows as much about Landfall Press as anyone. Without her, this project would not have been completed.

Joseph Ruzicka
Curator of Prints and Drawings
Milwaukee Art Museum

LANDFALL PRESS:
A PERSONAL VIEW

Jack Lemon

4. Close-up of an ink roller, with an assistant mixing ink in the background.

Landfall Press has never been associated with an artistic movement or style; it's my own aesthetic that explains or unites twenty-five years of its publications. There is no preconceived agenda. I encourage the highly individualistic quality of each artist who comes to Landfall. My personal art collection is full of unique, even strange expressions of individual ideas, often put forth by people who do not set out to make

Art but who do so in spite of themselves. The artists I've invited to Landfall have an honesty about them, like Cliff Westermann, who was a folk artist—an acrobat, a carpenter, a really good craftsman just weird and wacky enough to make a knot out of plywood and sand it till it gleamed. I knew that the Milwaukee Art Museum would be the right home for the Archive not only because the galleries are filled with works by people who have made prints at Landfall over the years, but also because the Museum appreciates authentic, self-taught artists and "outsiders."

The artists whose prints I publish integrate their work and their lives. It is this integration, more than any technique, subject, or point of view, that defines the art produced at Landfall. William T. Wiley is someone whose whole life is of a piece with his art. His material is everything around him, and to watch him work is to see his thoughts just coming right out the ends of his fingers. He is elusive and totally free-thinking. I like artwork that speaks spontaneously and directly, work that is smart and has a sense of humor. Sometimes, too, there is a political edge to an artist that I really enjoy, as in the case of Robert Arneson and Roger Brown, who are satirists of great candor and wit.

I value genuineness in artists, of the sort one sees in certain authors, like Ernest Hemingway, whose work reflects their lives. For the same reasons, I like the novels of Cormac McCarthy and Larry McMurtry. My preference is for a kind of minimalism or plainness, which reminds me of the experience of driving at night through Kansas, say, when there's essentially nothing there but the land, and the moon is like a fireball in a million miles of sky. It's amazing, but at the same time it's all pretty simple. I respect artists who, like John Wayne, are not primitive, folksy, or uneducated, but seem to be in touch with everyday reality.

Writing is important to me and I'm interested in narrative, which I've explored in many Landfall prints, including Wiley's book, *Suite of Daze*. Terry Allen, one of the quickest wits I've ever known, and his fellow flatlander Vernon Fisher are both fine writers. I think of Kara Walker, too, as a storyteller. Her series of silhouetted figures register like panoramic dramas arranged across the wall; they're great human stories, stories no one else would ever tell. Lesley Dill, who grew up in Maine, used to be a schoolteacher; she inscribes Emily Dickinson poems on surfaces that are surrogates for the body—armatures and dresses.

There is something appealing to me as well about Lesley's use of words as formal objects on paper (or cloth). And I remember how Nancy Graves' *Lunar Maps* grew out of a set of calculations she was working on at the time, which fascinated me on account of their resemblance to handwriting. This interest in "calligraphy," in mark-making, relates to my funda-mental love of drawing; it's a concept that ties together much of the work, however apparently eclectic, that Landfall has produced through the years.

Landfall Press has survived because of my deep per-sonal commitment and maniacal work habits. The artists I collaborate with are in some way as obsessed as I am, and that intensity comes out in their drawing. What I respect so much in Christo, for instance, aside from his confident and expressive mark-making, is his complete devotion to a project. My own commitment is such that I couldn't stop working, even if I wanted to, because artists need printers who are not only technically skilled and proficient problem-solvers but who understand them. In the collaborative situation, the artist relies on the printer not just for technical information but for essential judgments. Artists *want* honest input; they need help, encouragement, and advice. Communicating with artists is something I know how to do. Getting to the truth of the artist's vision and keeping to that truth has always been my goal with Landfall Press.

This exhibition catalogue is dedicated to
Allan Frumkin.
J.L.

LANDFALL JACK

Vernon Fisher

5. Vernon Fisher working on *Genetic Variations/Natural Selections*, 1983,
with Jack Lemon looking on in the West Superior Street shop.

FORT WORTH

I open the studio door and there's this stocky guy with a barrel chest and Popeye forearms. His curly salt-and-pepper hair is receding slightly, and with the very uncool eyeglasses he's wearing he might be mistaken for a public school teacher were it not for the tattoos. There's one of a bluebird, one of a big red rose with the word "Mother." Another one says simply "Jack."

"Hi," he says. This brief introduction is followed by a whole lot of awkward silence—what radio calls dead air. I realize pretty soon that if there's going to be a conversation, it's all going to have to come from my end. We wander around the studio, I show him my stuff and finally enough words are said that I put together the idea he wants me to come to Chicago and make prints.

CHICAGO

Jack drops me off at his apartment downtown; he's staying at Jeanette's out in River Forest. In the apartment, prints and drawings are everywhere, double and triple hung, leaning in stacks against the walls. Stuff I like. None of what Jack calls "mushy stuff" (corporate art?). Jack says he hates mushy stuff and though I'm not exactly sure what it is, I'm prepared to hate it too.

The work is from all over. I spot a Chuck Close that I especially like: a portrait-sequence of four variations, the first and largest composed of several hundred little spray-dots, the others gradually becoming smaller and more simplified, the smallest only a half-dozen dots or so. And over in a corner there's a nice Pat Steir with a rainbow roll, and several of the Chicago guys. A lot of the work is from out West. Funky stuff from Bill Wiley and Robert Arneson. John Buck. Outlaw types like Terry Allen and Luis Jiménez. I notice that a lot of the drawings are inscribed to Jack. Then there's a wall of Westermanns. In one featuring Jesus and the disciples, Jack's head appears bouncing on a spring. Westermann was a jarhead in WWII, Jack in Korea, kids who ran away from home to join the Marines. Semper Fi, I guess.

That evening, after pizza you can only get in Chicago, I'm bored but tired of the streets. I sort through the shelves of tapes under Jack's VCR. There is *The Sands of Iwo Jima*, *The Fighting Seabees*, *Flying Leathernecks*, *Back to Bataan*, *The Green Berets*, *The War Wagon*, *The Sons of Katie Elder*, *Stagecoach*, *Red River*, *Rio Grande*, *Circus World...Circus World?* There are seventy to eighty movies on the shelf and they're all John Wayne. I pick out *Rio Lobo*. "John Wayne plays a tough ex-soldier who, no matter what the odds, will fight to see justice is done."

THE SANDS OF IWO JIMA

Jack picks me up in the morning for breakfast. "It's still dark outside," I complain. Jack gives me a withering look and edges the van into the morning traffic. Years later I recall this when I see the scene in *City Slickers* where Billy Crystal asks Jack Palance if he's killed anybody today and Palance replies, "Day ain't over yet," before riding on.

At the shop the first thing I see is a life-size poster of John Wayne, legs apart, gun blazing. Over at the sink, Steve's energetically grinding a stone (stone on stone, the old fashioned way), Barb is at the press sponging a plate at lightning speed, a Terry Allen song is blaring from what appears to be a stadium-scaled sound system. It's clear that everybody is fast and efficient and *on time*. Will Jack expect me to know what I'm doing? Everyone's heard the stories. How Jack threw Peter Plagens out of the shop for making a smart-ass remark about one of the artists. (Terry, who told me the story, thought it was way cool, by the way.) How Jack tore up somebody's edition, whose was it? Pearlstein's? Roger Brown's? Like many of the other stories, the details are obscure, shrouded in mystery, or legend. How one day Jack came into the shop all pissed off, fired everybody and had to start Landfall over from scratch. Steve, who's worked with Jack for a long time, has been canned twice and has quit once just on *my* visits to Chicago. "I never fire anybody unless they need it," Jack says.

Soon I'm equipped with a stone, some strange looking drawing materials and a minimum of instructions. I smile wryly, Jack nods. I wonder—do any artists ever just turn up missing? I mentally run through the admonitions of Sergeant Stryker in *The Sands of Iwo Jima*: "You're a professional. You've got a job to do. (Take that hill.) You don't whine; you don't bitch and moan; you saddle up and move out." Something like that.

TRUE GRIT

Well, eventually I did think of something and the print came out okay, as have a number of others I did at Landfall over the years. I don't know if I've ever managed to have a truly two-sided conversation with Jack, but I think I've come to know him pretty well. You may never know what he's thinking, but you know

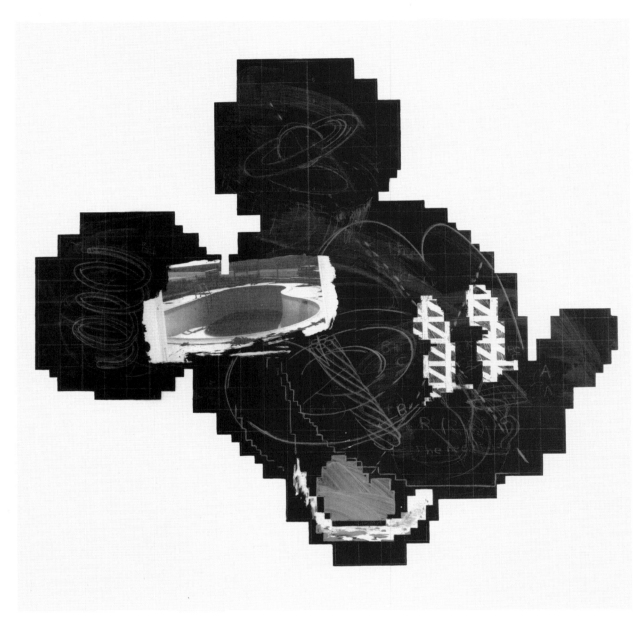

6. Vernon Fisher, *Mickey Mouse/Scenes from the American West*, 1990,
lithograph, printed in color, 36 1/8 X 40 1/4 (91.4 X 108.3)

where he stands, where *you* stand, and where his heart is. You see it in how he runs the shop, in the kinds of prints he continues to publish. Artists who know Jack from the early years say Jack has mellowed. Comparing my experiences with the stories I've heard, I suspect that's probably true. How tough can a guy be who reads Ian Frazier, goes roller-blading, and cooks *spaghettini alla carrettiera* for you?

I sometimes wish I *had* been at Landfall in the crazy, early days when the artists stayed in an apartment above the shop and would come in at all hours of the day and night to work on their prints. To have met Westermann and Arneson. To have been there for Terry's *Juarez* project, the suite of prints boxed with the first LP of Terry's songs, or Vito Acconci's *Stones for a Wall*, or Wiley's bound book of etchings, *Suite of Daze*.

Ambitious stuff that was sometimes hard to take and still harder to sell (hard to sell stuff you can't hang on the wall). Jack, it seems, was always finding some project to do that was also a sure way to lose money. There have been a lot of projects like that and I think that counts for something. Someone's got to fight to see justice is done. When he published *Navigating by the Stars*, a collection of my fiction, I got to make my own contribution to Jack's being perpetually in the hole. Even before I came up to Landfall for the first time, Luis had clued me into this: "Say you want to do something that is maybe a little crazy," Luis said. "Don't confront him directly. Just say, 'whatever you think, Jack, I just thought it would make a better print.' He'll fall for it every time." You were right, Luis, he will.

PRINTMAKING (on everything) APOLOGY TO TERRY ALLEN*

Mark Pascale

For many connoisseurs of contemporary prints, the mention of Landfall Press conjures a material notion akin to the mythic nickname for Chicago—City of Big Shoulders—where Jack Lemon founded his Press in 1970. As an art student in the 1970s, I was most aware of Landfall's brawny publications by artists working in a representational mode. Philip Pearlstein, Robert Cottingham, Claes Oldenburg (Fig. 7), and Alfred Leslie's lithographic output at Landfall was informed by Lemon's signature lush printing of fat blacks and generously applied luminous colors. However, twenty-five years later, the one aspect of Lemon's publishing that remains consistent is his penchant for publishing artists whose work could loosely be described as Conceptually based.[1]

There is no doubt that Lemon's reasons for engaging these artists are as multifaceted as are their individual modes of making art. It also seems true that, with the exception of Cirrus Editions and Crown Point Press, both in California, no other American printer-publisher has committed itself to publishing multiples for Conceptual or Neo-Conceptual artists as has Jack Lemon.[2] In this essay, I will attempt to provide an overdue examination of the roots of Lemon's publishing choices, and for several of the artists, of the links between their prints and other works.

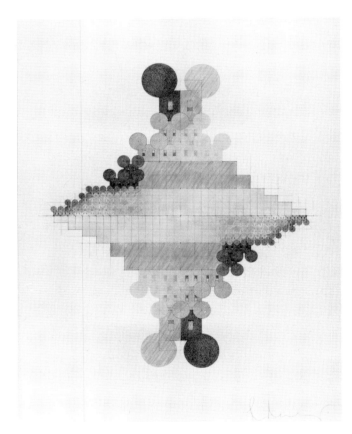

7. Claes Oldenburg, *Geometric Mouse Pyramid Doubled*, 1976, lithograph, printed in color

Lemon's personal background, training as an artist, and apprenticeship as a printer provide some clues about his diverse choices as a publisher, which are exemplified by his first two publications at Landfall (Philip Pearlstein's *Six Lithographs Drawn from Life* and

*The title is a play on Terry Allen's 1978 recording *Lubbock (on everything)*.

Sol LeWitt's *Lines of One Inch, Four Directions, Four Colors (Set of 16)*; Pls. 63, 48). In interviews, he has maintained his admiration for great draftsmanship, an appreciation he developed as an undergraduate art student. His understanding of artistic process and decision-making have also surely informed his choices of artists to publish. More recently, Lemon commented on his empathy for those artists who steadfastly pursue complex projects to completion:

> *What attracted me to Christo's work, in addition to his confident and expressive mark-making, was his complete commitment to his project. This integration between the work and everything else in the person's life is what I find admirable in all the artists whose prints I publish. More than anything else, more than any particular style, subject, or point of view, that's what defines Landfall Press.*[3]

Moreover, from Landfall's early publications, we can easily discern Lemon's propensity for finding creative solutions to unorthodox artistic practice (e.g., Christo's collaged lithographs of 1971 or William T. Wiley's chamois hides and wood veneer papers of 1972-74). With these publications, Lemon extended a practice within print publishing of breaking the rule that required exactly repeatable editions made strictly on flat paper supports.[4] Ironically, traditional printing also is a constant within Lemon's overall publishing oeuvre. The ways in which Landfall's artists have broken with traditional notions of printed multiples defines the special aesthetic contribution of the workshop's output. The contribution is difficult to name precisely, but it embraces a notion not dissimilar from an idea of recharged residue, or the by-products of artists' performances, earthworks, and installations, which cannot be reproduced or even preserved. Many of these publications were created using traditional print techniques, but their resonance as objects goes beyond our received assumptions about printed pictures.

The publications that speak to this idea—Christo's *(Some) Not Realized Projects*, Dennis Oppenheim's *Projects* portfolio, Terry Allen's *Juarez Suite*, and subsequent recordings "co-published" by Lemon under the name Fate Records, Vito Acconci's *Stones for a Wall* and *Wav(er)ing Flag*, Allen Ruppersberg's *Preview Suite*, and Lesley Dill's recent projects—will be discussed later in this essay. For now, we need only point out that these artists share several qualities. First and foremost, they are all sculptors, and their printed work tends to challenge our traditional notions of the painter-printmaker aesthetic.[5] It follows that they must conceive of the print as an object or material presence more than as a picture. Therefore, the wall, floor, or container in their printed work is considered as an important component, rather than as a mere surface on which to situate a picture.

LEMON'S JOURNEYMAN PERIOD

From 1966 until 1970—when he opened Landfall in Chicago—Lemon experienced firsthand the radical changes in art production then sweeping the US, particularly the newer uses of photography and notational schemes that artists had devised to expand the quality and role of the art object.[6] The Tamarind Lithography Workshop was still in Los Angeles when Lemon arrived for his printer fellowship in 1966. Several artists with whom he eventually worked—Terry Allen, Allen Ruppersberg, and Alexis Smith—were educated in Southern California's hotbed of developing aesthetics. Peter Plagens has described the tenor of those years:

> *Since the late 1950s, considerable parody of art and the artist's role, as well as exterior subject matter ha[d] permeated Southern California art. The artist's role in Los Angeles is schizophrenic because it's constantly measured not against ingrained "fine*

8. Bruce Conner, *Thumb Print*, 1965, lithograph,
41 5/8 X 29 7/8 (105.7 X 75.9), private collection

art" tradition, but against the most salient facets of California culture: pop architecture and music, movies, and the garment industry.[7]

The art produced during this period began to include manipulated texts and photographs and was produced in large installations or in the new format of the artist's book. Ed Ruscha pioneered the artist's book as early as 1962 with his release of *Twenty-six Gasoline Stations*. Although Lemon's training at Tamarind was focused on traditional methods of lithography, as well as business practices for operating a commercial print shop, he was no doubt a witness to the scene in Los Angeles.[8] More significant for Lemon was his awareness of Bruce Conner's stormy Tamarind fellowship in 1965, which yielded two lithographs that predicted the kind of twist on traditional print projects that would become a staple of Landfall's output. One of these, Conner's *Thumb Print* (Fig. 8), a lithographed impression of the artist's thumb which he had applied to an enormous stone, printed on a large sheet of paper, and signed with his thumbprint, may well be the first formal example of Conceptual printmaking in the US. By this I mean that Conner's idea was of greater importance than the pictorial qualities of the print. Moreover, Conner's playfulness with the process and the printers—he insisted on signing with a thumbprint, which the workshop scrupulously kept off of finished editions, because it was more autographic than a signature, so that one could compare reality (the original thumbprint) to art (the printed copy)[9]—underscores the importance of the joke as a strategy of early West Coast Conceptualism.

Upon his return to Kansas City, Lemon worked on prints with H.C. Westermann, a California native who had studied at the School of The Art Institute of Chicago. Although not strictly a Conceptual artist, Westermann had a pungent visual wit firmly rooted in the tradition of the rugged American individualist, as opposed to that of a European-based academic.

Lemon's preferences in literature and other cultural pursuits are decidedly American, heavily favoring writers like Larry McMurtry, the authentic visions of self-taught artists, folk heroes, and country-western music. Within his aesthetic sense there is a deep empathy for Westermann, as well as other artists whose art evolves from the American work ethic and is charged by exterior subject matter. In this sense, Westermann provided a link between Lemon's apprenticeship period and journeyman phase, which lasted through his brief tenure at the Nova Scotia College of Art and Design from 1968 to 1970.

It was Lemon's experience in Nova Scotia that prepared him for the more Conceptual aspects of his publications at Landfall Press. The Lithography Workshop he set up in Halifax—which lasted from 1969 until 1976—was part of the overall educational stimulus: a professional facility where students could engage visiting artists who were working with a master printer. Lemon had been invited by NSCAD's President Garry Kennedy to become the first director of the workshop, specifically because of his previous experience at Tamarind. The hope was to introduce to Canada the print renaissance that had been launched ten years earlier in the United States, largely because of Tamarind's program. However, Kennedy's plan for NSCAD was to create an environment conducive to advanced art practice by instituting a progressive visiting artist program that could be served by the Lithography Workshop, and later, The Press of NSCAD.[10] The Lithography Workshop's position within this expanded educational notion was augmented by the idea that "Tamarind's [contribution to the American print renaissance] like all renaissances was essentially a revival of past values, while, in the meantime, the development of art on a broader front had called into question the presuppositions on which those values were based."[11] Therefore, the workshop's production was tailored specifically to that of a laboratory environment congruent with the school's curriculum; it was not driven by market pressures.[12]

As Lemon understood it, Kennedy's program was designed to turn the school around, to make it more than a traditional art academy. As artists, Kennedy and the other faculty had been associated with the ideas of Postminimal and Conceptual artists, who were frequently invited for conferences, lectures, and short-term teaching positions.[13] There was so much money available for visits by out-of-town artists that Lemon—who often went to New York City to scout for artists and to arrange contacts—was "meeting himself coming and going." Although his tenure at Nova Scotia was short-lived, he made contact with many of the most important Conceptualists then working, several of whom would eventually make prints at Landfall Press.[14] To underscore the importance of these relationships to Lemon's foundations as a publisher-collaborator, I should also point out that in 1970, Seth Siegelaub organized at NSCAD the "Halifax Conference," a two-day event that brought together some of the most radical artists then working (including Joseph Beuys and Robert Smithson). Although this event took place as Lemon was phasing out his relationship with NSCAD and setting up Landfall, it represents the denouement of his participation in the program.

In this phase of Lemon's career, the seeds were sown for some of his signature approaches to making prints. First, there is Lemon's propensity for tightly controlled feats of technical bravura, exemplified by two of his collaborations at the Lithography Workshop. Gordon Rayner's *Untitled* and Gene Davis' *Halifax*, both of 1970, were extravagant productions. Bob Rogers, Master Printer, and Lemon together devised the complex blended inking and press procedure for Rayner's print, and perfectly matched registration for the twenty-two individually printed vertical bands of color in Davis' print. More significant for the argument here, Lemon worked with Canadian artist Joyce Wieland to produce her 1970 print *O Canada* (Fig. 9), in which she applied her lips to the stone, leaving imprints of the shape of the mouth for each syllable of the Canadian national anthem (Fig. 10). Embedded within this print is an early example of editioned performance documentation, as well as a highly unconventional method of applying marks, or "drawing," on the lithography stone. We could say that the "drawing" literally was performed on the stone for subsequent printing (or fixing). It is possible that Vito Acconci discovered in *O Canada* a resolution to the problem of

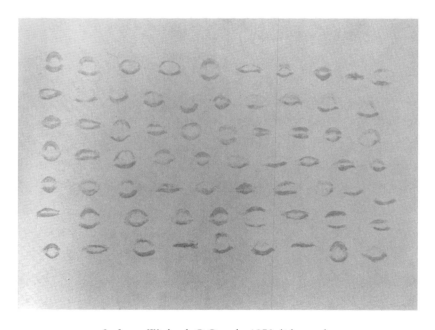

9. Joyce Wieland, *O Canada*, 1970, lithograph,
22 X 30 (55.8 X 76.2), private collection

10. Joyce Wieland in the Lithography Workshop, NSCAD, Halifax, creating her lithograph *O Canada*, 1970, by pressing her greased lips against the stone.

accommodating his performance art to the format of prints; his first two prints at the shop, *Trademarks* and *Kiss-Off* (Fig. 11), both center on the mouth of the artist (Fig. 12).[15] In addition, as much as one third of the total output of the NSCAD shop involved the use of photographs and methods of photographic transfer.[16] Notable among these—for comparison to Landfall's publications—are Dennis Oppenheim's three prints, all of which used photographs from his performances and, in one case, added text (Fig. 13).

While these methods by no means represent a complete inventory of Landfall's history of workshop procedures, considered along with Lemon's earlier connection to the anecdotal art that emerged in the late 1960s, they help us better understand his diverse publishing choices after 1970. This is summed up best by his colleague (and replacement as director of the Lithography Workshop) Gerald Ferguson:

> *I regard lithography as an open circumstance with a rich historic tradition, but no more or less valuable than any other medium for the demonstration of an idea by an artist.*[17]

ALLOGAMY

The projects to be discussed in this last section were chosen because they represent the notions about print publishing as practiced by Jack Lemon that I have sketched out. Central to all this work is the concept of reproducing in multiples ideas or projects that were ephemeral to begin with, even in cases where some object or installation was produced. All these prints therefore bear an allogamous relationship to another work by the artist. As objects, they are enriched by our knowledge of this related work, but they should also stand alone as complete expressions within the artist's oeuvre. Lemon's participation in bringing them to life ranges widely, from his willingness to make literal what previously existed only as a series of proposals (Christo's *(Some) Not Realized Projects*, 1971), to the financing of a series of recordings (Terry Allen's six records published and released on the Fate Records label between 1975 and 1983).

Christo had produced wrapped multiples earlier in his career, which thus existed as concrete or hermetic objects.[18] His *(Some) Not Realized Projects* provided an early test of Lemon's capacity to coax into existence a

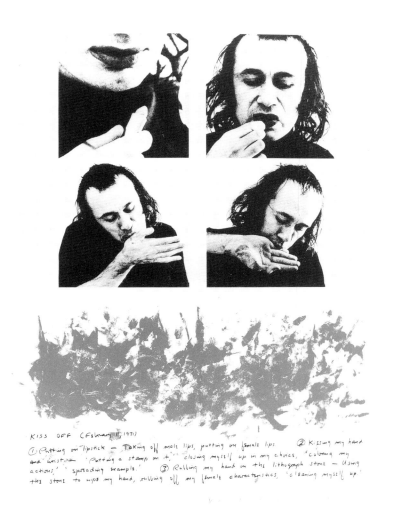

KISS OFF (February 11, 1971)

① Putting on lipstick — Taking off male lips, putting on female lips   ② Kissing my hand and wrist — "Putting a stamp on it," "closing myself up in my choice," "coloring my actions," "spreading example."   ③ Rubbing my hand on the lithograph stone — Using the stone to wipe my hand, rubbing off my female characteristics, "cleaning myself up."

11. Vito Acconci, *Kiss Off*, 1971, lithograph,
printed in color, 30 1/8 X 22 3/8 (76.5 X 56.8), private collection

12. Vito Acconci in the Lithography Workshop,
NSCAD, Halifax, making his lithograph *Kiss Off*, 1971.

13. Dennis Oppenheim during the production of his first prints executed at NSCAD, *Stills from Projects*, 1970.

work that had not succeeded as intended. Although Christo previously had produced models or proposals for each of the three projects, for a variety of reasons none was realized.[19] The resulting portfolio contains a lexicon of procedures to which Lemon would return for subsequent projects by Christo, as well as for many others who have worked at Landfall. The first print in the set, *The Whitney Museum, New York, Packed* (Pl. 15), is one of the icons of postwar printmaking. The print makes use of several collage methods—fabric and plastic wrapped with twine and thread, stapled and glued—that Christo had employed in earlier objects. What is different about this lithograph is the deft overlaying of printed, drawn, and photographic elements. The resulting richness makes for an allomorphic transition of Christo's idea, so that the object satisfies perhaps as much as the actual transformation of the Whitney might have.

The remaining prints in the set, *MoMA (Front)* and *MoMA (Rear)*, and *Times Square (Front)* and *Times Square (Rear)*, respectively, document in multiple form Christo's ideas modeled on the language of his drawings. However, the graphic language Christo employed here brings to mind the deadpan photolithography being practiced then at Nova Scotia, for the prints are enhanced by hand-lithographed photo-reproductions. In one case, *MoMA (Rear)*, a reproduced street map and an actual black-and-white photograph of the rear of The Museum of Modern Art, New York, are integrated at the bottom of the composition for reference. *MoMA (Front)*, as well as *Times Square (Front)*, also based on a photomontage, are composed dramatically, tightly framed and printed to the edge of the sheet in a way that makes the image surprisingly real, even though we can see from the editing of sky details that the image is conflated. The suite represents an altogether impressive print-publishing accomplishment, dependent in equal measure on the artist's skill, on Lemon's sensitivity to traditional lithography, and on his expanded view of what constitutes an original print. Lemon's use of a wrapped, printed collage element that was manufactured by another hand, but based on the artist's template, both broke with tradition and embraced it.[20] This portfolio subtly repudiated the autographic notions about original prints that Lemon had learned at Tamarind.

Dennis Oppenheim, like Christo, is another pioneer Conceptualist with whom Lemon worked during Landfall's first few years of operation. Although they had met in Nova Scotia, it took a few years before

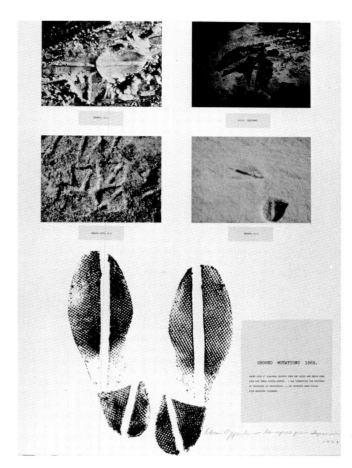

14. Dennis Oppenheim, *Annual Rings*,
from the portfolio *Projects*, 1973,
lithograph, printed in color

15. Dennis Oppenheim, *Ground Mutations*,
from the portfolio *Projects*, 1973,
lithograph, printed in color

Lemon had the opportunity to print Oppenheim's 1973 portfolio *Projects* as a contract job initiated by the artist's dealer, John Gibson, in collaboration with Marian Goodman at Multiples, Inc. The ten lithographs in *Projects* provide a printed retrospective of the projects the artist made between 1968 and 1972 (Figs. 14-16). Because Oppenheim regularly used photography in a casual way to record his site-specific sculptures and temporary performances, making the lithographs was not an extraordinary act. But as Eric Cameron succinctly observed in describing Oppenheim's first lithographs made at Nova Scotia:

> *The content of the works becomes the multiple layering of transference that distances the print from the events it purports to record; from paper to plate to photographic positive to photographic negative to video monitor (from which some of the shots are taken) to the altered time and place of the artist's original performance, and all made more alien by their intermediate transposition through chemical and electronic states, unshown and unshowable.[21]*

This project—and others from the period—helped to establish the idea that prints could be more than beautiful or decorative objects. And as a way of preserving Oppenheim's concepts and actions and making them available to a more general audience, the prints helped fulfill the artist's interest in democratizing the art object—just as prints have done for centuries.

Vito Acconci has likewise made frequent use of photographs and electronic media in his work, as sources and the principal medium. Coming from his concept of poetry— "he had viewed the page as an

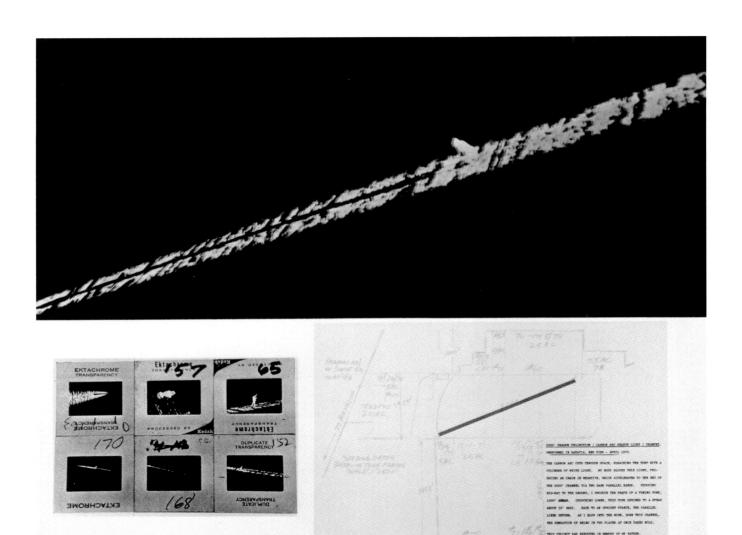

16. Dennis Oppenheim, *2000 Foot Shadow Projection*,
from the portfolio *Projects*, 1973, lithograph, printed in color

area in which to act and defined words as props for movement and the page as a thing, a container, a map, and a field for movement"[22]—it may seem natural that Acconci made the leap into prints. But because he prefers to create art as "a kind of instrument in the world,"[23] no medium would provide an easy translation of his actions. In 1977, Acconci created several print projects at Crown Point Press in Oakland, as well as his *Stones for a Wall* portfolio at Landfall (Pl. 1). These prints were created during the transition from what he called floor-based art to wall-based art. If his earlier work was about the dichotomy between public and private space and actions, the subject matter of his prints tended to focus more on the political ramifications of actions and symbols.

As he had with his Nova Scotia prints,[24] Acconci made printing part of the subject of his *Stones* portfolio. A photographic matrix of a stone wall (printed with an irregular edge like a litho stone) was used as a beginning or imprint on all ten sheets in the suite. Over each of the final nine prints, the artist incorporated images of blood (*Approved—Sometimes You Can Get Blood from a Stone…*), a gun (*Approved—There's Always Another Secret Behind the Wall)*, violent graffiti reading "HELP CAN'T STOP KILL" (*Approved—But Don't Be Fooled, This is a Message from the American Lover)*, and an explosion (*Approved—Finally It's Blowing Up in my Hands)*. The set reads as a kind of forbidding drama played out against a backdrop of political intrigue. At this time, with American involvement in Vietnam ended, the political rhetoric of democracy versus communism was directed to several developing "third-world" regions. We could scarcely imagine the détente that would arrive ten years later, not to mention the breakup of the USSR.

Wav(er)ing Flag (Fig. 73) of 1990 echoes the terse political content of Acconci's projects from the 1970s, but its printed Pledge of Allegiance marks a return to a subtle and cunning use of language, which had been an important component of his earlier performances and sound- and videotapes. Another important element of the piece is Acconci's skillful use of the portfolio form to create a sculptural work that rests against the wall—the individual sheets are conceived as parts of a whole that must be seen together to understand the artist's message. In the work's assembled form, the recitation of the Pledge in a prosaic typeface stutters along, contracting to illegibility where the undulating flag reaches the end of each panel. Taken together, the Pledge, pasty colors, and saccharine drawing of the flag, all ring hollow. Acconci has here managed to create a printed art multiple that recalls the broadsheets of Benjamin Franklin and Thomas Paine, but without succumbing to simple propaganda. It is an image that serves to remind us that potent visual symbols and words carry relative meanings.

Terry Allen is a kind of bridge figure within this group of artists. He is not specifically a Conceptualist in the manner of the East Coast-based artists discussed here. Rather, he represents an all-purpose artist, as he navigates media as diverse as drawing and printmaking, painting, sculptural installation, video, sound, and performance. Allen's art practice, like that of Allen Ruppersberg and others who came out of art school in the late 1960s, is primarily the domain of the popular, not the fine arts. As recently noted by Gary Kornblau:

> In the late 1960s, some artists began to accept the fact that art is a part of leisure culture….how the tricks of the conceptual art trade were not learned in a textbook, but experienced by all of us first outside of art—in the often absurd, profound humor of a fledgling, democratic civilization.[25]

Allen came out of the honky-tonk culture of Lubbock, Texas, where he was raised and to which he returns from time to time. One of his earliest prints, *Yellow Man's Revenge* of 1974, formally set the stage for the magnificent *Juarez Suite*, completed in 1976. The format of *Yellow Man's Revenge* resembles a notebook—as if several pages of a diary, text and image,

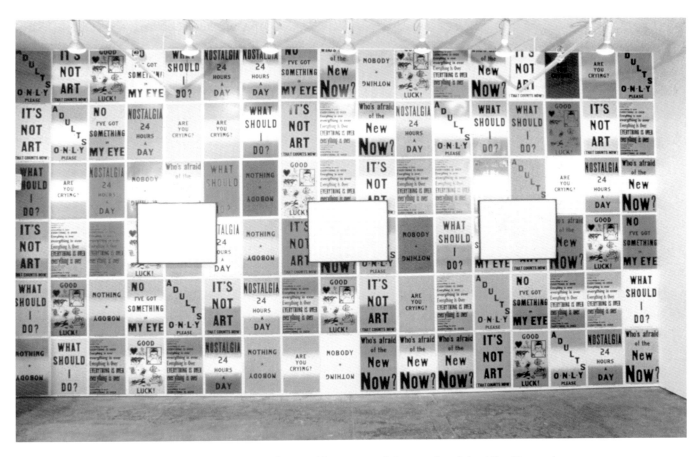

17. Installation view of *A Collection of Letters*, an exhibition of work by Allen Ruppersberg
at the Christine Burgin Gallery, New York, January 21-February 13, 1988.

were conflated in a stream-of-conscious manner—with literal perforations in the paper. In fact, *Juarez Suite* developed from the format of song-drawings, Allen's self-described method of using drawing as a catalyst for his song-writing. In *Yellow Man's Revenge,* there are allusions to locations, characters, and lyrics that would eventually appear in the performance Juarez, which has its origins in the late 1960s, but was not performed until 1975. The completed Juarez installation consisted of thirty-five two- and three-dimensional works and thirteen songs with two narrative segments.[26] The portfolio contains a record album, a printed cast of characters, and six color lithographs that depict vignettes from the installation, as well as portions of the text, which enlarge upon the drawn images (Pl. 3). With *Juarez Suite,* Lemon had found a way to produce a multiple object that translated Allen's difficult method of art production, and which used printmaking as an important component. Although Allen and

Lemon made additional prints together, none surpasses the complex achievement of *Juarez Suite,* nor equals what may be their most impressive joint publication, Allen's 1978 recording with his Panhandle Mystery Band, *Lubbock (on everything),* which became somewhat of an underground hit.[27]

Allen Ruppersberg's only Landfall publication, *Preview Suite* (Pl. 69), derives from his 1988 installation, *A Collection of Letters* (Fig. 17), at the Christine Burgin Gallery. As with the print projects by Christo, Oppenheim, and Allen, Ruppersberg isolates an aspect of one work in order to create a variant of it. The Landfall portfolio consists of ten color lithograph signs that duplicate what the artist originally had had made in a commercial sign shop for the gallery exhibition. The signs had provided a background—literally papering the gallery walls—for a series of seven drawings of personal letters by famous authors that Ruppersberg had painstakingly copied from original documents and arranged in frames over the signs. The effect, as Ken Johnson has noted, was "a conceptually intricate, multilayered mix of public and private, personally refined and commercially gross, verbal and graphic modes of address."[28]

When I asked how he came to engage Ruppersberg, Lemon noted that he had known the artist for several years, but that his response to the installation was so visceral that he immediately envisioned a collaboration. Knowing that Lemon collects early circus posters and lobby cards for John Wayne movies points us to his obvious motivation for the Ruppersberg project. The signs Ruppersberg created are modeled after the kind of garishly hued posters that announce neighborhood carnivals and boxing matches; these are the contemporary equivalent to Lemon's beloved commercial lithography. We can imagine the subversive delight with which Lemon re-created by hand the ubiquitous properties of the commercial

blend-roll. And by releasing a set of the background posters extracted from their original context, Ruppersberg completed the cycle implied by his initial exhibition of the drawings alone in the late 1970s.

Finally, we come to Lesley Dill, who started working at Landfall in 1992. All Dill's projects have used printing and the receiving surfaces as integrated sculptural elements. Her second print, the tiny 1993 lithographed object *Poem Dress "The Soul Selects Her Own Society"* (Fig. 84), set the stage for her most involved project, conceived as an installation in late 1995 (Fig. 18).[29] For *Poem Dress*, Dill used found paper—a different piece of an Indian newspaper for each impression—to create a small dress onto which was lithographed an Emily Dickinson poem. Subsequently, the artist created a series of works on prepared paper and muslin grounds, which also used printed Dickinson poems over photographic images of bodies, limbs, and heads (Fig. 19).[30] This last group makes

18. Installation view of *Voices in My Head*, an exhibition of work by Lesley Dill
at the George Adams Gallery, New York, September 21-October 28, 1995.

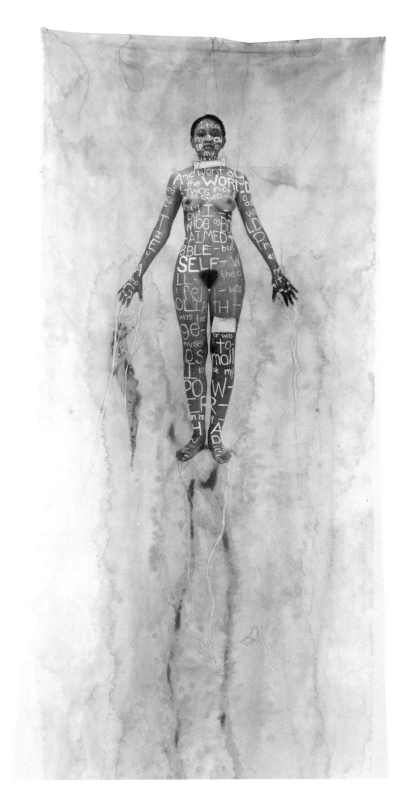

19. Lesley Dill, *Rolled Up Poem Girl*, 1995,
serigraph, with acrylic, oil, thread, and wire,
156 X 45 (396.2 X 114.3), private collection

extensive use of applied thread and muslin, which serve as metaphors for nerves and skin. Coincidentally, Dill's methods and materials are quite similar to those employed by Christo for his printed collage elements, although Dill's work achieves a more spontaneous effect (Fig. 20).

It is Dill's Landfall projects, more than any of the others, in which the print is finally and completely released from the realm of a discretely boxed or framed print. The prints used as a part of her "Voices in My Head" installation were both suspended from the ceiling and hung on the wall. They functioned more like banners or scrims, and they alluded as much to public (open) as to private (intimate) spaces.[31]

CONCLUSION

Throughout Landfall's history, Jack Lemon has demonstrated an affinity for translating the work of sculptors into prints. Lemon's special feeling for the material dimension, coupled with a playful spirit of informed production, has yielded what are arguably the most forceful of the workshop's publications, and those which have contributed the most to print aesthetics overall. This essay is not meant to be a definitive reading of Landfall's output, but I do hope that I have provided enough background history, personal reflection, and print analysis to pique the reader's curiosity. I was delighted to undertake this project because, as a student in the mid-1970s, Jack Lemon was my first printer-hero. Figuratively, we now share the same backyard. I have come to know Jack and Landfall more intimately and to study with appreciation the creatively idiosyncratic tendencies of his publishing.

20. Lesley Dill consulting with printer Steve Campbell at Landfall Press,
June 1995, in the West 18th Street Shop.

NOTES

While I have not addressed Vernon Fisher's prints, our conversation during my recent studio visit with him was a major catalyst for this essay. He suggested that Jack shared an interest with those artists discussed here, for whom rigorous ideas and a deliberate tactility are combined to form a kind of Post-Conceptual ideology. It is this notion that forms my thesis. I am grateful to Vernon and to Jack Lemon for their time and their thoughts. Thanks also to Joe Ruzicka for affording me the opportunity to contribute this essay to help celebrate Jack's publishing achievements. Finally, I must acknowledge my deepest appreciation for Keith Hatcher, my first lithography teacher and the first person who told me great stories about Jack, Landfall Press, and the City of Big Shoulders.

1. By Conceptual, I mean a broad range of artistic processes that include language, process, idea, performance, narrative, and variations. The Landfall artists who fit into this category are Vito Acconci, Terry Allen, Christo, Jessica Diamond, Lesley Dill, Nancy Dwyer, Vernon Fisher, Ronald Jones, Sol LeWitt, Marilyn Minter, Dennis Oppenheim, Allen Ruppersberg, Alexis Smith, and William T. Wiley.

2. Among those who are just publishers, Bob Feldman at Parasol Press, and Marian Goodman at Multiples, Inc., have also committed themselves to Conceptual art.

3. Jack Lemon, "Inside Landfall Press," unpublished manuscript, 1995, Landfall Press Archive, Milwaukee Art Museum, p. 10.

4. There were precedents for this kind of work, particularly Fluxus multiples such as *Fluxkit* (1964) and, later, the editioned Pop multiples of *Seven Objects in a Box* (1966), Roy Lichtenstein's *Ten Landscapes* (1967), and his earlier manipulations of sheet plastics as a receptacle for printing, as well as the highly manufactured sculptural editions produced at Gemini G.E.L., especially those by Claes Oldenburg, who would eventually work at Landfall Press.

5. By this I mean that their way of working does not rely so firmly on principles of autographic draftsmanship, even though all of them do draw in the traditional sense of drawing, that is, they make marks.

6. For a recent discussion of this phenomenon, see Ann Goldstein and Anne Rorimer, Reconsidering the Object of Art: 1965–1975, exh. cat. (Los Angeles: The Museum of Contemporary Art, 1995), and Elizabeth Armstrong, Joan Rothfuss, et al., In the Spirit of Fluxus, exh. cat. (Minneapolis: Walker Art Center, 1993).

7. Peter Plagens, *Sunshine Muse: Contemporary Art on the West Coast* (New York: Praeger Publishers, 1974), p. 30.

8. In conversation with Lemon, he confirmed that he was very aware of the developing trends and that he had met Terry Allen through a fellow Tamarind printer.

9. See Elizabeth Armstrong, *First Impressions: Early Prints by Forty-Six Contemporary Artists*, exh. cat. (Minneapolis: Walker Art Center, 1989), pp. 54-57.

10. See Garry N. Kennedy et al., *NSCAD: The Nova Scotia College of Art and Design: Prints and Books*, exh. cat. (Halifax: Nova Scotia College of Art and Design, 1982).

11. Eric Cameron, "The Lithography Workshop," ibid., p. 10.

12. For instance, John Baldessari's 1971 lithograph *I Will Not Make Any More Boring Art* was instigated by his encounter with NSCAD students. For an exhibition at the college he invited them to write the print's eventual title over and over on the gallery walls. The print is made—somewhat inelegantly—from a photographic plate reproducing his sample instructions in horizontal rows, flush with the edges of the paper.

13. Benjamin H.D. Buchloh, "The Press of NSCAD: A Brief Incomplete History and Its Future Books," in *NSCAD*, p. 65.

14. Vito Acconci, Sol LeWitt, and Dennis Opppenheim are among the Landfall artists Lemon met during his Nova Scotia tenure. Other artists whose work during the Lithography Workshop's early years may have contributed significantly to Lemon's development as a publisher are John Baldessari, Dan Graham, Michael Snow, and Joyce Wieland.

15. Cameron, "The Lithography Workshop," p. 20.

16. Ibid., p. 17.

17. Ibid., p. 13.

18. See, most recently, Judith Goldman, *The Pop Image: Prints and Multiples*, exh. cat. (New York: Marlborough Graphics), 1994.

19. For a brief explanation, see Jörg Schellmann and Joséphine Benecke, eds., *Christo: Prints and Objects, 1963-1987* (Munich and New York: Edition Schellmann, 1988), p. 56.

20. For instance, the front view of the wrapped MoMA is similar to a tint lithograph (a black element to delineate value, a tone element to extend the range of atmosphere). In addition, Lemon knew that there was a time-honored tradition of the artisan's participation in the print process, which included the actual cutting of blocks—in the case of Dürer—and other acts of an allographic rather than an autographic nature.

21. Cameron, "The Lithography Workshop," pp. 17-18.

22. Rorimer, "Vito Acconci," in *Reconsidering the Object of Art*, p. 42.

23. Robin White, "Vito Acconci," *View*, 2 (October-November 1979), p. 1.

24. Ibid., pp. 19-20, 43.

25. Gary Kornblau, "1965–1975: Reconsidering the Object of Art," *Art Issues*, no. 41 (January-February 1996), p. 37.

26. The songs were recorded and issued as an album and a component part of the Landfall publication; see Robert McDonald, "Terry Allen: The Plain Story, An Introduction," in *Rooms and Stories: Recent Work by Terry Allen*, exh. cat. (La Jolla, California: La Jolla Museum of Contemporary Art, 1983), p. 11.

27. As noted earlier, Lemon incorporated under the name Fate Records in order to produce, from 1975 until 1983, four long-playing albums and two 45 rpm records for Allen.

28. Ken Johnson, "Allen Ruppersberg at Christine Burgin," *Art in America*, 76 (April 1988), p. 205.

29. "Voices in My Head," installed at the George Adams Gallery, New York, September 21 - October 28, 1995.

30. These include the 1994 suite, *A Word Made Flesh*, of four collaged prints entitled *Arms*, *Back*, *Front*, and *Throat*, and several monoprints, including the screenprinted pieces that comprised the bulk of Dill's recent exhibition at the George Adams Gallery.

31. As has been noted by the artist, the format of these prints was inspired by Buddhist prayer flags she observed while living in India.

LANDFALL PRESS:
TWENTY-FIVE YEARS

Joseph Ruzicka

21. Roger Brown working on a drawing for his lithograph,
Hank Williams, Honky Tonk Man, 1991,
in the West 18th Street shop (see Pl. 10).

A PLACE TO MAKE ART

Jack Lemon pulled the first editions at his newly founded Landfall Press in 1970: Philip Pearlstein's *Six Lithographs Drawn from Life* (Pl. 63) inaugurated one of the most important printing-publishing establishments in postwar America. Not only has Lemon's Chicago-based Landfall Press made prints, but it has also published music, poetry, fiction, and exhibition catalogues.

Indeed, for a full quarter century, Landfall has operated as a sanctuary for art-making for a wide array of artists, representing a broad range of intellectual and aesthetic interests all across the United States. Lemon, of course, made ample use of artists in and around the Chicago area, printing important work for Phyllis Bramson, Roger Brown (Fig. 21), Richard Hunt, Ellen Lanyon, Ed Paschke, Barbara Rossi (Fig. 22), Jeanette Pasin Sloan, Karl Wirsum, and others. He cultivated the heartland, working with Keith Jacobshagen, James McGarrell and T.L. Solien, all the way down to Texas and the Southwest, where he enlisted Terry Allen, Vernon Fisher, Luis Jiménez, and Randy Twaddle. Lemon also looked to both coasts, to Christo, Lesley Dill, Jim Dine, Nancy Graves, Denise Green, Ronald Jones, Sol LeWitt, Marilyn Minter, Claes Oldenburg, and Pat Steir (Figs. 23-29) on the East Coast, and Robert Arneson, Laddie John Dill, David Ligare, and William T. Wiley on the West Coast.

The result of Lemon's voracious visual appetite is an output ranging from figurative to abstract art, from color-filled to black-and-white, from purely formal concerns to the densely theoretical and Conceptual. No other major press in this country can claim such an inclusive and far-ranging aesthetic, one that exploits all the currents flowing through American art of the last twenty-five years. In the late 1970s, when asked if he saw Landfall "as part of the Chicago art scene," Lemon answered, "This is a printing establishment that just happens to be in Chicago. We could operate anywhere."[1] Looking back over Landfall's quarter century, it might be said that the shop operated every-

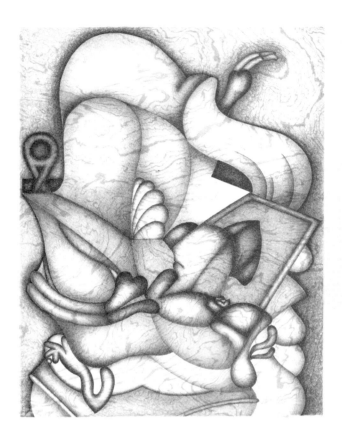

22. Barbara Rossi, *Eye Deal*, 1973,
lithograph, printed in color, with chine collé

where. What follows in this essay is an outline of the basic intellectual and stylistic threads that help define the character of Landfall Press. It begins with an overview of Lemon's artistic training and intellectual grounding, then continues with a broad, chronological discussion of some of the artists and works that define Landfall Press.

BASIC TRAINING

After four years in the Marines, Jack Lemon attended the Kansas City Art Institute in the late 1950s and early 1960s with aspirations of becoming a painter. Although he took no formal classes in printmaking, there was a lithography shop in the school's basement, where he received his first exposure to the medium, guided by William McKim, a member of the faculty. Graduating in 1962, Lemon toyed with the idea of opening up his own printshop in Kansas City, but instead opted to do graduate work in painting at the University of Nebraska.[2]

In 1964, frustrated by the politics and bureaucracy of the academic system, Lemon returned to Kansas City to work as a preparator at The Nelson-Atkins Museum and to teach a night course in lithography at the Art Institute. It was during this time that McKim asked him to collaborate as printer for a portfolio with members of the Art Institute faculty.[3] This set into motion the chain of events that led Lemon to train as a master printer.

While working on this faculty portfolio, Lemon corresponded with Garo Antreasian, the first master printer at the Tamarind Lithography Workshop in Los Angeles. Antreasian talked Lemon through the technical problems with various pieces in the portfolio, and when the project was finished, asked Lemon to send him a copy. Antreasian was so impressed with the

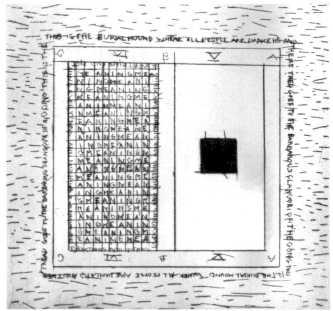

23. Pat Steir, *Introduction*, from the *Burial Mound Series*, 1976,
drypoint, soft-ground etching, spit-bite etching

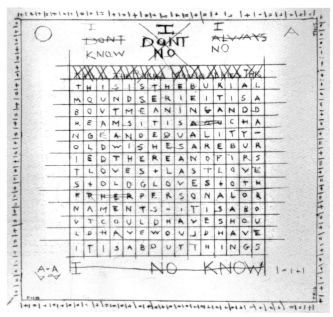

24. Pat Steir, *Meaning*, from the *Burial Mound Series*, 1976,
drypoint

25. Pat Steir, *I Don't Know*, from the *Burial Mound Series*, 1976,
drypoint

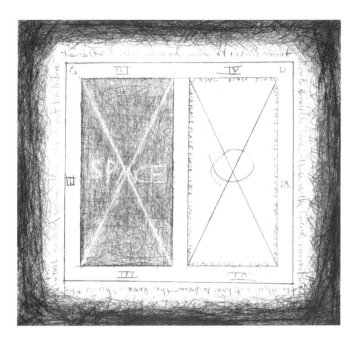

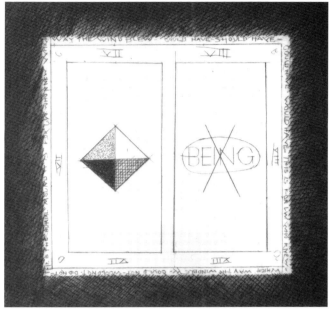

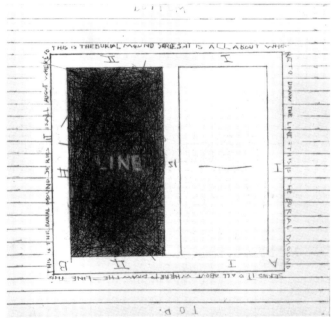

26. Pat Steir, *Space*, from the *Burial Mound Series*, 1976, drypoint

27. Pat Steir, *Little Line*, from the *Burial Mound Series*, 1976, drypoint

28. Pat Steir, *Being*, from the *Burial Mound Series*, 1976, drypoint

29. Pat Steir, *Identity*, from the *Burial Mound Series*, 1976, drypoint

results that in 1965 he invited Lemon to attend a summer training course in lithography that he had established as professor of art at the University of New Mexico (Fig. 30).[4]

Between March and September of the following year, Lemon won consecutive Ford Foundation grants to train at Tamarind directly under the master printers in residence there—first, Kenneth Tyler, then Clifford Smith.[5] In addition to increasing his technical knowledge of printmaking, Lemon was exposed to a wide range of prominent artists for the first time, working with the likes of Bruce Conner, Richard Diebenkorn, Sam Francis, Allen Jones, Nathan Oliveira, George Ortman, and Jesse Reichek.[6] The collaborative relationship between artist and printer was an essential innovation of Tamarind's approach and would prove to be crucial to formation of the character of Landfall Press.

After this intensive and innovative training, Lemon returned to Kansas City to direct the Art Institute's gallery, where he also established his own lithography shop[7] (one of the first university-affiliated workshops in the United States),[8] and to teach lithography at the University of Kansas in Lawrence (Fig. 31). In Tamarind's mission to reestablish lithography's prestige as a fine-art medium, it trained master printers in both the technical aspects of making prints and the more subtle issues of collaboration. Lemon, therefore, was very much a pioneer in the American print renaissance, among the first wave of Tamarind alumni to venture forth from Los Angeles.[9]

In 1968, Garry Kennedy, President of the Nova Scotia College of Art and Design in Halifax, invited Lemon to organize a printmaking curriculum and to establish and direct the Lithography Workshop, modeled on his Kansas City Art Institute shop, with Robert Rogers, another Tamarind-trained printer, serving as master printer.[10] Lemon established the shop, and it continued well into the next decade, even after he left for Chicago in 1970. From the beginning, it had a

30. Tom Minkler (left) and Jack Lemon at Garo Antreasian's summer course in lithography at the University of New Mexico, Albuquerque, 1965.

31. Peter Saul (left) and Jack Lemon conferring in Lemon's Kansas City Art Institute shop, c. 1966.

Conceptual, highly experimental character. While in Nova Scotia, Lemon collaborated with Dan Christensen, Greg Curnoe, Gene Davis, Dan Graham, Art Green, Philip Pearlstein and Joyce Wieland, among others; these relationships provide important insights into Lemon's subsequent intellectual development at Landfall Press (see Mark Pascale's essay, pp. 20-35 above).

MINDSET OF A MASTER PRINTER

Changing from a studio artist to a master printer, as Jack Lemon did, requires a basic change in a person's role in a project and approach to the work. A painter works alone in the studio on every step of a project, makes all the aesthetic and technical decisions, and accepts all the consequences, good or bad. A master printer, however, must subordinate personal aesthetic preferences to the agenda of the artist working in the shop, acting instead as a sort of facilitator who helps the artist finish a project successfully. The printer can suggest technical solutions or alternatives that will help an artist achieve a certain goal, but these suggestions should always accord with the artist's wishes. A good master printer, like a good curator, must have a

32. Jack Lemon and Christo (right) conferring on *The Whitney Museum, New York, Packed*, early one morning in the West Ontario Street shop, 1971 (see Plate 15).

supple mind and eye in order to adapt to and understand the varying demands of the work of each artist.

A stellar example of Lemon's flexibility is his work with Christo (Fig. 32). Before Christo first went to Landfall in 1971, all his prints were two-dimensional.[11] He had wanted, however, to make his prints relieflike, in the manner of his photocollaged drawings, in which the wrapped object is actually wrapped. Lemon understood this when he worked with Christo on their first collaboration, the portfolio *(Some) Not Realized Projects*.[12] Among the prints was *The Whitney Museum, New York, Packed* (Pl. 15), in which a cutout of the facade of the museum is actually wrapped with cloth and string and affixed to a lithograph of the museum's urban surroundings.

This is not to say that the master printer abandons personal aesthetic judgments. The conscious selection of which artists to work with constitutes a very real visual and intellectual agenda on the part of a shop. But determining the underlying aesthetic of the variety of work printed at Landfall is difficult—the artists themselves have not been able to discern any dominant aesthetic governing the "look" of Landfall's output.[13]

There are more important issues, however, than a dominant look. The first is that Lemon was schooled as a painter at a university and had not considered becoming a master printer until his taste and his intellectual character were well formed. He therefore had clear aesthetic preferences that determined which avenues he chose to explore. He carried this deeply personal taste with him and sharpened it each time he set up his various shops. In a certain practical way, being a master printer allows him to indulge in far more aesthetic directions—abstract, figurative, Conceptual, political—than he could possibly pursue if he were a painter in his studio; to this day, he remains remarkably open to new ideas and trends.

Lemon once made a remark which at first seems to belie the heterogeneous output of Landfall Press that others perceive: "Every shop seems to have a 'look' to it. I think [my] shop has the look of drawing....I choose artists whose work deals with drawing, the use of the hand. I'm interested in drawing and I feel that this is the basis of my choice."[14] This method of choosing, however, is precisely what underlies Landfall's diversity. Drawing can encompass any number of styles, and it enabled Lemon to fully indulge his catholic taste, rather than pursue one given theoretical or stylistic issue. He simply sought out those artists he felt were most accomplished at making marks and who displayed a strong intellectual rigor. Lemon traces his deep commitment to drawing to his student days, in drawing classes taught by Wilber Newald at the Kansas City Art Institute. He also attributes to Newald his early interest in lithography, the medium in which "the immediacy of mark-making is preserved as an integral part of making the print."[15]

Another facet of Landfall is clearly the result of Lemon's early training in the studio, where he learned to think creatively, rather than in terms of technical issues or production concerns.[16] He thus wants to abet the artist's creativity—he is not interested in "making prints over the phone,"[17] meaning that the intense personal involvement of the collaboration is always crucial to him.

LANDFALL: A REAL ESTATE OVERVIEW

In 1970, Lemon decided to leave Nova Scotia, intending to set up his own independent workshop. He had once again tired of teaching, and of the whole academic environment in general, and longed for the greater autonomy that his own shop would offer.[18] So he was most receptive when the Chicago gallery owner Allan Frumkin approached him with ideas for print projects with several artists. He offered financial backing if Lemon would establish his own workshop.[19] Lemon served out his term at Nova Scotia, then left for Chicago in June 1970. Before leaving, however, he printed and published the first Landfall editions there, Pearlstein's *Six Lithographs Drawn from Life*. The first prints pulled in Landfall's Chicago shop were the two

33. Claes Oldenburg in the artist's work room, West Ontario Street shop, with a proof of *Hats Vesuvius*, 1973 (see Fig. 51).

34. Proofs from the *Landfall Press Etching Portfolio*, 1975, tacked to the wall of the curating room in the West Ontario Street shop. From left to right: William Allan, *Tamales*; Christo, *Wrapped Statue, Villa Borghese, 1963*; Robert Cottingham, *F.W.*; Claes Oldenburg, *Spoon Pier*; Philip Pearlstein, *Nude on Iron Bench*; William T. Wiley, *Seasonall Gate*.

35. Demolition of the shop on West Ontario Street, 1979.

36. William T. Wiley, *Mr. Unpopular*, 1980, lithograph, printed in color, 38 X 27 3/4 (96.5 X 70.5)

Sol LeWitt portfolios, *Lines of One Inch, Four Directions, Four Colors (Set of 16)* (Pl. 48) and *Lines of One Inch in Four Directions and All Combinations (Set of 16)*, both published in 1971.

Lemon settled in Chicago because it had greater potential than other art centers. New York City and California already had a number of well-established shops, with several new ones just beginning. At that time, Chicago had no printing ateliers to complement its fine museums, art schools, and strong, rambunctious art tradition. This lack, along with Chicago's situation on Lake Michigan, prompted Lemon to christen his shop Landfall: "Landfall is a nautical term, meaning 'first sight of.' There's a huge body of water sitting out there, so I thought the name was very appropriate. When I opened Landfall in 1970, there were few printing shops in Chicago, so Landfall meant first sight of a printing establishment."[20]

Landfall's first shop was in a three-story building at 63 West Ontario Street. A narrow space, the first floor had lithography presses, stones and a small room where the visiting artists worked (Fig. 33). The second floor had a curating room (Fig. 136), a gallery, and office space. The third floor was for photography and, beginning in 1975, etching.[21] For the first several years, Landfall was dedicated solely to lithography, but in 1975, with the publication of the *Landfall Press Etching Portfolio*, the shop expanded into other media (Fig. 34).[22]

The Press had to move in 1979 to make way for a Hard Rock Café restaurant (Fig. 35), an event commemorated by Wiley in his *Mr. Unpopular* (Fig. 36), across the top of which he wrote "R.I.P. 63 W. ONTARIO." The new shop was located in a sprawling loft at 215 West Superior Street (Fig. 37), with a large gallery in front, a long, narrow shop

37. Nighttime view of the West Superior Street shop, with the skyline of Chicago in the background. Visible on the wall are proofs of John Buck's woodcut, *Untitled (La Grande Eclipse)*, 1982 (see Pl. 12).

(Fig. 38), and a separate curating room. Landfall continued to make lithographs and etchings and, in 1982, produced its first woodcut, John Buck's *Untitled (La Grande Eclipse)* (Pl. 12).

In 1984, Landfall moved for a third time, to 329 West 18th Street (Fig. 39), its present location, and in 1987 doubled its floor space. There is now a small gallery in the front, a large, rectangular shop behind and, to the side of the shop, a large curating, packing, and storage area. In 1989, Landfall once again expanded its range of media with Marilyn Minter's serigraphs, *Hands Folding*, *Hands Dumping*, and *Hands Washing* (Pls. 51-53).

THE EARLY YEARS

From the beginning, Landfall exhibited a strong interest in artists who were engaged in the formal issues of art-making, and it seemed not to matter if the work was abstract or figurative. Because abstract work at that time was *de rigueur* among New York avant-garde artists, it was those working with the figure, Philip Pearlstein in particular, who were in a certain sense making some of the more defiant statements of the time.[23]

Pearlstein, a consistent participant in Landfall's early history (Fig. 40), consciously turned to the figure at a time when such behavior could be seen as blasphemous, even though he was deeply concerned with the same formal issues with which many of the Pop and Minimal artists were dealing. He started depicting nudes in the early 1960s with the sole intention of exploring formal issues, which he could do in the carefully circumscribed environment he defined—that of professional models posing in his studio.[24] "I have usu-

38. Tom Blackman (left) and Jack Lemon working on a lithograph in the West Superior Street shop.

39. Exterior of the West 18th Street shop building, c. 1990.

40. Philip Pearlstein in the artist's work room, West Ontario Street shop, drawing on the stone for the lithograph *Nude Standing by Easel*, 1974.

ally dismissed subject matter as such, and have relied on stylistic motivation instead. That is, I have paid little attention to content or the psychological aspects of content, letting the chips of interpretation fall where they will. I have concentrated instead on the formal problems of realist painting as I became aware of them in succession."[25] Clearly, there are tensions and charges that these very individualized, large-scale nudes carry, but these were, by the artist's own admission, beyond his control. So he concentrated on perspective, composition, color, and form. And when he entered the Landfall shop to create his *Six Lithographs Drawn from Life* in 1970 (Pl. 63), he brought along his studio painting technique of working directly from models.

Chuck Close also approaches the human figure in a dispassionate manner, adhering to an even narrower range of subject matter than Pearlstein by focusing on portrait heads of friends and family and working almost exclusively from photographs. In *Keith/Four Times* (Fig. 41), his first lithograph, Close set up a number of technical and perceptual problems that, in fact, were intertwined.[26] In an attempt to push the limits of the medium, he wanted to make a huge print of four images of Keith, each larger than the last, on a single sheet of paper.[27] The challenge to him was to make the same image in different sizes legible independently and within the ensemble.[28] The challenge to the printer was to print these four separate images—which required eleven different stones—on a single 88-inch wide sheet of paper.[29]

The emotional detachment exhibited by these two figurative artists as they pursued formal problems has much in common with the abstract and Minimal art that Landfall helped produce in its early years, such as the late Color Field lithographs by Dan Christensen (Pl. 14), Kenneth Showell (Pl. 72), and Jim Dine (Pl. 25). In retrospect, Lemon's interest in this movement seems most logical because Color Field imagery was concerned primarily with formal issues such as the clear identity of the support surface and the interrelationship of large areas of color—the same issues that engaged Pearlstein and Close, albeit within a figurative framework. Christensen's untitled 1972 lithograph, with its flat, adjacent rectangles of color, is the most uncompromising piece in this Color Field group. Showell's *Terni* of 1970 is an abstract composition of subtle color gradations, yet the shading and patterning permits a reading of shape—the suggestion of crumpled paper—so that the literal flatness of the support is not predominant. In fact, there is a clear element of humor in this piece, a Color Field print deliberately depicting a less than flat surface.

Dine, too, approached the whole Color Field movement with a sense of humor. *The Red Bandana* and his *Wall Chart* prints (Fig. 42), all from 1974, clearly focus on Color Field issues, such as the flatness of the support (a handkerchief and color tiles being flat objects) and the interrelationship of colors. Yet Dine's address of high-minded, theoretical concerns using common objects was a deeply subversive strategy, undermining critical opinion in circles where abstraction held sway.[30]

Many of Landfall's initial projects in Conceptual art were ambitious wall-sized ensembles, designed to make a major impact. Sol LeWitt created two related portfolios of sixteen lithographs, one in color, *Lines of One Inch, Four Directions, Four Colors (Set of 16)* (Pl. 48) and one in black-and-white, *Lines of One Inch in Four Directions and All Combinations (Set of 16)*. When installed, each ensemble forms an 8-foot square.

42. Jim Dine, *Wall Chart II*, 1974, lithograph, printed in color, 48 3/8 X 34 7/8 (122.9 X 88.6)

41. Chuck Close, *Keith/Four Times*, 1975, lithograph

43. David Ligare, *Sand Drawing #23*, from the suite
Sand Drawings, 1973, lithograph

Lemon was once asked why he was interested in print-ing LeWitt's work, and he replied that it is always about drawing, "LeWitt's drawings, especially his *Wall Drawings* [sic], are magnificent. He's a fine drafts-man."[31] Indeed, close inspection of LeWitt's Landfall prints reveals that the marks for each sheet were drawn individually; for example, LeWitt did not draw a single red-line stone to be reused each time red appeared in the various sheets, but rather redrew it for each occur-rence.

In the early 1970s, LeWitt's prints were closely related to concepts in his wall drawings and drawings on paper.[32] In fact, LeWitt's 1971 Landfall prints are intimately related to two wall drawings—one in color, the other in black-and-white—executed at the Milwaukee Art Center in the summer of that year.[33] They not only share a similarly ambitious scale, but they treat a similar problem, that of drawing one of four kinds of straight lines—vertical, horizontal, diag-onal left, diagonal right—in a grid of squares. So, in a

sense, LeWitt's early prints have a certain documen-tary aspect to them, since they are the tangible representations of no longer extant installation work from that period.

A number of other early publications at Landfall also have a certain retrospective character. The most important was Dennis Oppenheim's *Projects* of 1973, the documentation of ten site-specific, ephemeral Earth or Body works that he executed between 1968 and 1972 (Figs. 14-16). Each lithograph documents a project through diagrams, maps, and photographs. The ten projects recorded at Landfall plot Oppenheim's changing focus, from manipulating the earth to concentrating on issues of the body. Oppenheim has commented that he was exploring and discarding ideas and issues with such speed that he felt the need to document the works, lest they be forgot-ten; even at such a short temporal remove, therefore, he understood the necessary retrospective function that this portfolio served.[34]

David Ligare also documented transient Earth art, though of a much more modest and delicate character, in his suite of *Sand Drawings* (Fig. 43).[35] Gestural strokes drawn in the sand will soon be erased by the wind and by the surf looming in the background, so this series serves to fix the ephemeral for posterity.[36]

In the 1970s, Landfall prints also provided records of transient Pop art works. Claes Oldenburg's 1973 *Store Window: Bow, Hats, Heart, Shirt, 29¢* (Pl. 57) documents, though not literally, *The Store*, a perfor-mance-installation of twelve years earlier, in which the artist made papier-mâché replicas of food, clothing, and furniture and sold them for one month in a store-front on New York's Lower East Side.[37] In this litho-graph, Oldenburg reconstructs in his mind's eye a mosaic of some of the objects that filled the store— themselves reconstructions of common, everyday objects.

In most of these works, there is an intense desire to save and document, an impulse perhaps at odds with some of the broader aims of Performance and

Conceptual art, in which the action or idea is more important than its physical record. But the artists seem to have understood that an era had passed, or at least that a chapter had closed, and that it should be visually documented before the next era was in full swing.

Christo, who has been making prints at Landfall for nearly its entire quarter century, has produced documentary work of a different nature. As in most of his two-dimensional work, including his drawings, he predicts in his prints what a certain project will look like, including maps, technical specifications, and the final realization.[38] Christo's prints look to the future rather than the past. They function both as sketchpad and presentation piece, announcing to a broad audience how his wrapped projects will appear, given funding and permissions. These prints also allow him to work on certain projects that would never otherwise reach fruition, as he explicitly stated in his first portfolio of five prints at Landfall, (Some) Not Realized Projects, including *The Whitney Museum, New York, Packed*.

The idea that prints could create imposing installation art, as in LeWitt's *Lines of One Inch, Four Directions, Four Colors (Set of 16)*, was an important aspect of Landfall's production in the early years.[39] Both sets of LeWitt lithographs come beautifully presented in a special box and each 23-inch-square sheet can be handled individually and admired, much as prints have been for centuries. However, the reasoning behind the whole group of sixteen lithographs is clearest only when the entire portfolio is viewed as an ensemble filling a wall, so that all the combinations and permutations of line and color can be understood. At this point, the 8-foot square installation passes very much into the public realm and exerts a strong impact on the space around it. This dramatically alters the traditional relationship between viewer and print, for the viewer must stand back from the wall in order to understand the artist's intentions.

Vito Acconci's ten-sheet lithographic portfolio *Stones for a Wall*, made in 1977 (Fig. 44), also must be installed to be understood (Pl. 1). The title itself

44. Vito Acconci in the West Ontario Street shop working on a drawing for
Approved—You Know Where You Are, You Sucker, from the portfolio, *Stones for a Wall*, 1977 (see Pl. 1).

45. Peter Saul, *Amboosh*, 1972, lithograph,
printed in color, 30 X 40 (76.2 X 101.6)

underlines the architectural implications of the portfolio, the necessity of placing all ten pieces next to each other on the wall, in order to create a new wall.[40] As separate prints, there is little about them that encourages individual handling and scrutiny. Together, however, they form a most forceful and direct unit—a tough section of urban masonry—that affects space in the challenging way familiar in Acconci's work in other media.

Terry Allen's *Juarez Suite* of lithographs was issued as a boxed set of six prints, each available for individual perusal. However, the written narrative accompanying the six scenes from the lives of the four characters—Sailor, Alice, Jabo, Chic—asks that the pieces be hung together on the wall (Pl. 3). Allen creates an additional layer of complexity by including a record album with music and narration intimately related to the story that unfolds in figures and words in the

prints, an altogether multimedia project.[41]

As the work of Dine, Allen, and Acconci indicates, not all of Landfall's production in the 1970s was concerned only with theoretical and formal issues. Indeed, in prints by other artists, we find the entire spectrum of human emotion and experience, including strains of humor and irony, political anger, domestic discovery, personal mythology, introspection and self-examination, catharsis, and visual and verbal punning. The artists who explored these issues worked primarily with the human figure, but in a wide range of styles, although most employed broad areas of flat color as an expressive vehicle.

Peter Saul made the most direct, biting political images during the early years of Landfall. *Amboosh* (Fig. 45) is a sort of morality play without heroes that confronts the insanity, uncertain goals and camouflaged dangers of the Vietnam war. The complicated

46. Alfred Leslie, *Alfred Leslie*, 1974, lithograph

cast of characters—friend, foe, and otherwise—keeps turning back in on itself, the beginning and end of the chain of events unclear and, after a certain point, unimportant, since the deceit and destruction will continue no matter what. *Angela Davis* (Pl. 70) is a most direct and viscerally disturbing composition, whose large acidic colors and tortured, flailing figure unambiguously convey Saul's anger about the United States government's ruthless impalement of Davis.

In certain ways, H.C. Westermann's complicated and deeply personal narratives are just as emotionally intense as Saul's public tirades, as Westermann tries to come to grips with the horrors he survived in an earlier war.[42] In *Death Ship in a Port* (Pl. 83), his two-dimensional art confronts a brutally senseless kamikaze attack and its charred result. Throughout his career, Westermann reenacted the bombing over and again, or transfigured the horror into an elaborate jungle stage set in which various dangers lie in wait for the unsuspecting protagonists.

In 1974, Alfred Leslie also made a suite of three very forceful, frontal bust portraits, in which he exploited dramatic lighting effects to underscore the personality of the sitters (Fig. 46).[43] In a touching

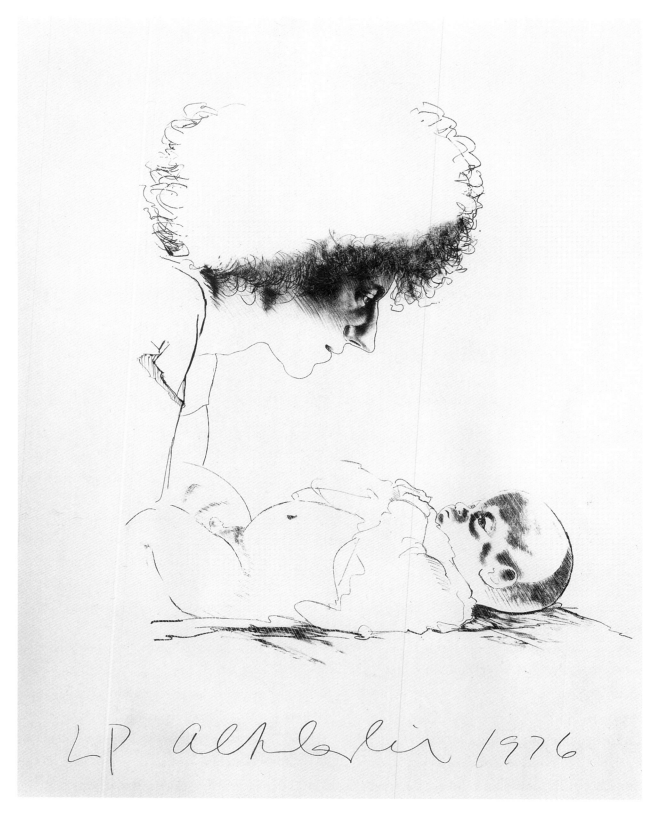

47. Alfred Leslie, *Connie with Baby*, 1976, lithograph

2/5   W B 88

48. William Beckman, *Self-Portrait with Black Shirt*, 1988,
lithograph

series made two years later, he explored tranquil domestic life, centering on the intimate bonding between a parent and an infant. Leslie here worked in an unusually lyrical manner to record the gentle rituals basic to the formation of a family (Fig. 47).

Portraiture, as practiced by Leslie, Close, William Beckman (Fig. 48), and others, was an important part of Landfall's identity during these early years, and it continues to characterize the Press today. In the realm of self-portraiture, we find interesting variations on the theme, such as the use of an object or an alternate character to stand in for the actual likeness of the artist.

For Robert Arneson, it was a brick (Pl. 5), for Jim Dine, a bathrobe. The Arneson-as-brick analogy developed from his deep involvement with ceramic art, the brick being one of the most ancient and ubiquitous ceramic objects.[44] While Arneson excelled at making literal likenesses of himself and his sitters, his self-portrait as a brick declares his inviolable identification with his profession. In the context of Landfall,

the device dovetails with the practice of visual punning that is a distinguishing feature of the Press' output. In fact, Arneson did a whole series of prints on the subject, dressing the brick up, as it were, in various roles—as a literary character, *Moby Brick* (Fig. 49), sinking in the ocean, as bricks do,[45] and as *California Brick* (Fig. 50), an earthquake-damaged object, earthquakes being a crucial geographic reality for this West Coast artist.[46]

The artist-as-bathrobe motif appeared in Jim Dine's art as early as 1963, when, as a young artist, he wanted to paint himself but felt inhibited because figurative art of such a personal nature was frowned upon by those in his advanced circle. So he substituted a robe, taken from an advertisement, a robe he felt looked as though he were in it.[47] Even after Dine fully embraced the figure, bathrobes frequently appear in his work in the guise of self-portraits (Pl. 26).[48]

William T. Wiley, on the other hand, created alter egos that permitted him to view himself with a kind of detachment: *Mr. Unatural* (Pl. 87) and, a bit later,

49. Robert Arneson, *Moby Brick*, from the *Brick Suite*, 1976,
lithograph, printed in color, 16 X 16 1/2 (40.6 X 41.9)

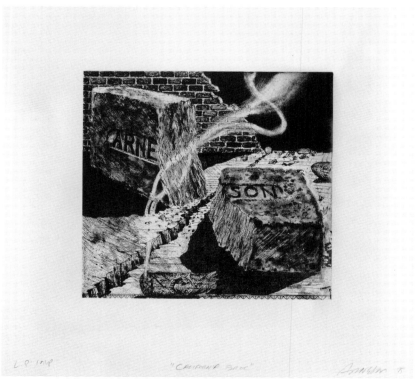

50. Robert Arneson, *California Brick*, from the *Brick Suite*, 1976, spit-bite etching,
soft-ground etching, and aquatint, printed in color

Mr. Unpopular. In these thinly disguised self-portraits, Wiley dresses himself up as characters who act out complex, often self-effacing dramas on stage. In other prints, Wiley uses objects as autobiographical memory devices. *Green Shoes*, in two states (Pls. 88, 89), has a particularly complex genesis, and was in part an apology to his cat, Gabby, whom he had recently run over; hence the dedication, "Good-by Gabby I wasn't always nice to you and now your gone." Wiley conceived the title and the idea of an elaborate dance in Chicago in 1977, when for days he watched a pimp wearing a flashy suit and green platform shoes do an elaborate curbside dance.[49] This is typical of the way in which Wiley seizes a seemingly minor event and turns it into a masterful composition.

Claes Oldenburg also employed irony and wry humor in his work at Landfall, but in a less personal sense than Arneson and Wiley. Common objects assume a new and unusual scale, and their original function and identity are subverted and transformed by their placement in highly improbable environments—in one lithograph, Vesuvius spews forth fedoras (Fig. 51). Oldenburg's giant downtown Chicago landmark, *Bat Column*, starts spinning in motion in its two-dimensional lithographic incarnation (Fig. 52); a monumental, robust sculpture by Picasso (another Chicago landmark) mutates into a dainty piece of men's jewelry (Pl. 58); a common spoon is aggrandized into a gargantuan pier (Pl. 59).

THE MIDDLE YEARS

From the late seventies to the mid-eighties, Landfall matured as a press. A core group of artists became closely identified with it, the Press set a predominantly figurative course while maintaining close ties with abstract art and Conceptual issues, and it actively continued to seek new movements and ideas. Among those artists who became practically synonymous with Landfall at this time are Terry Allen, Robert Arneson, Christo, Robert Cottingham, Martha Erlebacher, Denise Green, Luis Jiménez, Ellen Lanyon, Ed

51. Claes Oldenburg, *Hats Vesuvius*, 1973, lithograph, printed in color, 19 7/8 X 26 3/8 (50.5 X 67)

52. Claes Oldenburg, *Bat Spinning at the Speed of Light*, 1975, lithograph, printed in color, 36 7/8 X 25 (93.7 X 63.5)

53. Robert Cottingham, *F.W.*, from the *Landfall Press Etching Portfolio*, 1975, etching and aquatint, with chine collé

Paschke, Philip Pearlstein, Jeanette Pasin Sloan, Jack Tworkov, and William T. Wiley. Cool, analytical abstraction nevertheless continued to interest Lemon until about 1980, as he worked with Charles Gaines (Pl. 33), James Juszczyk (Pl. 46), and Jack Tworkov (Pls. 77-79)—all artists involved with a geometric, grid-derived compositional structure and a general interest in color progressions and interrelationships.

Pearlstein continued to work at Landfall well into the eighties and Cottingham still works there, using the city as a framework for exploring formal problems. But just as Pearlstein's nudes can never be completely neutral, neither is Cottingham's subject matter. Lemon was attracted to Cottingham's ability to draw and compose, and the two first collaborated in 1973 (Pl. 19). Cottingham typically focuses on second-story architectural details and signage while ignoring the bustle of the street below (Fig. 53). Yet the way he angles and crops his compositions generates a tilting energy; rarely does he offer a frontal, self-contained

view. "I like to think of these prints, and of my work in general, as a celebration of the signs and urban iconography that have given American cities their peculiar energy. Monumental, poignant, absurd and surreal, these structures stand as a vivid testimony to the vitality and variety of contemporary life."[50]

Jeanette Pasin Sloan first collaborated at Landfall in 1978 and continues to produce significant work there to this day (Fig. 54). She focuses on highly reflective domestic objects (Pl. 73), creating pristine, precise still lifes to articulate her concerns with color, depth, and composition. Yet, like the prints of Cottingham, the subject matter of her work has a deep personal resonance, in her case stemming directly from her experience as a housewife and mother: "The objects I used were domestic things familiar to me; and I was able to arrange them formally so that their relationships were controlled, harmonious and ordered. Over the next twenty years of my life...I learned that relationships are complicated and always changing— that a life must be recomposed continuously, day-by-day. My work has grown to express these issues."[51]

During this period, Martha Erlebacher established her standing among Landfall's figurative ranks, with her placid nudes (Fig. 98) and still lifes (Pl. 29). Erlebacher is an accomplished draftsperson and has been a key exponent of realist art since the 1970s.[52] Her works invite a slow contemplation, revealing a subtle sensuousness tinged with a certain edginess. If the composition and execution of these lithographs are restrained, the psychological intentions are not. The sexual overtones are clear, particularly in the suggestive arrangements of turgid fruit.

The figurative nature of Landfall's output guarantees that some sort of narrative structure can be found in many of the prints produced by the Press. Terry Allen's *Juarez Suite*, for example, combines a multipaneled picture story with text relating specifically to each scene. Allen is one of the great storytellers to have worked at Landfall, often operating on the fringes of society. In his four-lithograph *Debris from the Text*

(Fig. 101), he tells of the excruciating failure of a doomed marriage.

Surprisingly, there has been little storytelling using a book format at Landfall.[53] Ellen Lanyon, one of the first artists to work at Landfall, published her *Wonder Book* there in 1971 (Pl. 47). Through images of the magic and brutality of the animal world, it unfolds the mysteries of life and death. As the reader turns each page, the life cycle is revealed slowly and unflinchingly. Six years later, William T. Wiley wrote and illustrated his book *Suite of Daze* (Pl. 90), in which he recounts the creative block that he overcame to make the book while he was in residence at Landfall.

In general, however, artists working at Landfall have produced prints with a more open-ended sense of narrative, often within a cinematic or stagelike setting, as in William T. Wiley's prints (Pls. 88, 89). Laddie

John Dill constructed theatrical spaces from heavy, brooding marks and dark colors, stages sinister in their lack of actors. Dill specifically addressed the space and lighting of the stage in a number of prints from the early 1980s, such as *Stage Left* (Fig. 55). Speaking in general of his work of that period, he said, "Now they look like stages to me, like theatrical sets....I thought, 'If these are stages and I am concerned with the light, why not deal with it as theatrical lighting.'"[54]

Phyllis Bramson, interested in the theater since she was a young girl,[55] uses proscenium spaces in a diptych format to explore the polarities of life and society (Pl. 9; Figs. 61, 62). In these dreamy, evocative compositions, contorted, voluptuous figures try to reach out to each other in an elaborate, wordless, and endless dance.[56]

54. Jeanette Pasin Sloan in the West 18th Street shop drawing on a metal plate for her print *Binary*, from the portfolio *Jeanette Pasin Sloan*, 1986.

55. Laddie John Dill, *Stage Left*, 1981, lithograph, printed in color, 25 1/4 X 49 (64.1 X 124.5)

56. Ed Paschke, *Klaus*, 1976, lithograph,
printed in color, 34 7/8 X 28 1/8 (88.6 X 71.4)

By 1980, even as these artists were continuing their formal investigations and quiet dramas, another current, hotter and more expressive both emotionally and stylistically, appeared on the horizon. An edgy subject matter and gestural handling had been present earlier in the work of Vito Acconci, Ed Paschke (Fig. 56), Peter Saul, and Pat Steir (Pl. 75), but it now came to the fore at Landfall, as it did throughout American art.

Laddie John Dill indulged in gestural mark-making in his numerous Landfall lithographs,[57] and as early as 1977, was one of the first artists to exploit such a bold, expressive style at the Press. In 1982, these marks— deep furrows and high ridges—were translated into bronze relief sculptures, the only cast-metal pieces published by Landfall (Fig. 57).[58]

Another manifestation of this expressiveness is a furious, all-over line found, for example, in Freya Hansell's *Center* (Fig. 58), a composition freely filled with an endlessly snaking line. Wiley often exploited a similar type of line throughout his career at Landfall (Figs. 59, 60), and Richard Hull did the same in 1986 (Pl. 39). In all these works, the whiplike growth of the line endows the surface with a visual crackle and energy, while challenging us to see what is beneath. In most cases, the line obscures, almost like a fog, portions of the underlying design and requires a more concentrated effort on the part of the viewer.

During the 1980s, a sort of fragmented, nervous surface became common in work of the artists printing at Landfall, as opposed to the more smooth, pristine planes of the previous decade. There was a general trend in the shop away from broad unbroken areas of color to a much more aggressive surface, whether in a lithograph, intaglio, or in the woodcut medium adopted by Landfall in 1982.[59] Indeed, the woodcut, with its characteristic bold, raw strokes and more fragmented planar structure, quickly became a crucial facet of the Press' production. Among the important practitioners of the woodcut in these years were Phyllis Bramson (Figs. 61, 62), John Buck (Pls. 12, 13), Maurie Kerrigan (Fig. 63), Lance Kiland (Fig. 64), Martin

57. Laddie John Dill, *Sioux Portal*, 1982, bronze, 23 1/2 X 15 3/4 X 2 (59.7 X 40 X 5.1)

Puryear (Pl. 68) and T.L. Solien (Pl. 74).

In 1982, Buck began his ten-year relationship with the Press by editioning *Untitled (La Grande Eclipse)* (Pl. 12), one of eight woodcuts that he executed at Landfall—the largest number of woodcuts made there by a single artist. Found in this piece, and typical of his work at Landfall throughout the decade, is a dominant central image supported by a grid of smaller images, within a large-scale format.[60] The direct and vigorous rendering of the images is afforded by the pliability and subtlety of the wood.[61] The energetic handling underscores the sort of agitation and unease evoked by the ambiguous relationship between the various objects and figures in their squares. As in many of Buck's prints, questions are raised, but no clear answers are offered.

Puryear, another sculptor who works in wood, executed his only Landfall print in 1982. The woodcut

58. Freya Hansell, *Center*, 1979, from the portfolio *N.A.M.E.*, 1980, etching, 22 X 30 (55.9 X 76.2), sheet trimmed to plate

59. William T. Wiley, *Down the Line with Ol' Sir Rot*, from the book, *Suite of Daze*, 1976, etching, 10 X 13 3/4 (25.4 X 34.9), 14 1/2 X 18 1/2 (36.8 X 47)

60. William T. Wiley, *Thickening Heir*, 1989, lithograph, 50 1/8 X 35 1/2 (127.3 X 90.2)

Dark Loop is dominated by a black brooding sculptural shape that appears about to burst out of the confines of the composition. Puryear's piece reminds us that for twenty-five years Landfall has printed the work of a large number of sculptors. Early on, Acconci, Arneson, Christo, Graves (Pl. 34), Richard Hunt (Fig. 65), LeWitt, Oldenburg, Oppenheim, and Westermann printed with Landfall, in a variety of styles and conceptual forms. In the middle years of the Press, there was Lynda Benglis (Fig. 66), Buck, Luis Jiménez (Pls. 40, 41), Puryear, and Bernar Venet (Pl. 81), and more recently Buck, Lesley Dill (Fig. 84), Jiménez, Ronald Jones (Pls. 42, 43), Venet, and Karl Wirsum (Pl. 93). As this roll call makes clear, the work of these sculptors played a large role in defining the character of Landfall's production. Their prints fall into three categories. There are ambitious works (installations, really), such as those portfolios by LeWitt, Acconci, and Graves that, by their sheer presence, dominate the space as a sculpture would. Then there are the high relief or literally three-dimensional works by Arneson, Don Baum (Pl. 8), Christo, Lesley Dill, and Wirsum. The last group is best characterized by a robust drawing style, seen in prints by Arneson (Fig. 67), Benglis, Hunt, Jiménez, Oldenburg, Puryear, and Venet. It is this large, muscular style that is a

noted feature of Landfall work, and it is a characteristic that made Lemon receptive to the boldness of Neo-Expressionist art.

Not only woodcut, but lithographic and intaglio media as well can yield vigorous, even violent work. In the highly charged lithograph *Hear No Evil* of 1984, Peter Dean offers an up-to-date version of the death-and-the-maiden theme, a particularly poignant subject in the early years of AIDS (Pl. 22). Peter Julian uses the edges of the paper to literally sever the heads of victims in his 1982 diptych-lithograph (Pl. 45).

Although Neo-Expressionism clearly became the dominant mode at Landfall in the eighties, not all of it was so violent. Arneson set aside the brick and faced himself in a series of animated self-portraits. Humor and punning remained his primary interests (Pl. 8), sometimes colored by the poignancy of his effort to laugh during his losing battle with cancer (Fig. 67). In all these works, Arneson loosened his line and drew more freely than he had in his earlier work at Landfall, with a more experimental use of vivid color. This stylistic direction intensified to his very last Landfall prints, in which seething political outrage poured directly from his fingers onto the page, here matching the furor of Dean and Julian (Pl. 7).

Jiménez also employed a muscular drawing style in

61, 62. Phyllis Bramson, *The Psychology of Fire #1 (Man)*, *The Psychology of Fire #2 (Woman)*, 1984, woodcut, printed in color, diptych, 24 3/8 X 32 (61.9 X 81.3) each

"Oxidation"

63. Maurie Kerrigan, *Oxidation*, 1985, woodcut,
printed in color, 23 3/4 X 31 1/2 (60.3 X 80)

his work at Landfall, a style that clearly paralleled the full, rounded forms of his sculpture. His art deals specifically with the experience of the Mexican-American Southwest: its heroes and villains, play and work, joys and hardships. Jiménez's monumental and heroic presentation of his world addresses issues and ideas not normally dealt with in mainstream American art (Fig. 68). While not aggressively political— Jiménez depicts his world because it is his world—the artist is aware of the edge and sense of defiance that his subject matter carries.[62] Jiménez's work, therefore, represents one facet of Landfall's long-standing interest, the publication of political art, which increased significantly in the past decade.

THE SECOND HALF

Since 1985, Landfall has maintained strong relationships with familiar faces, such as Christo, Cottingham, Vernon Fisher, Jiménez, Paschke, and Pasin Sloan; renewed some lapsed ties—with Acconci, Roger Brown, and Denise Green; and forged new relationships with younger artists, among them Lesley Dill, Tony Fitzpatrick, Ronald Jones, and Randy Twaddle. In more recent years, the Press has refocused on some of its earlier concerns, among them political and Conceptual art.

A reinvigorated, more strident political focus became manifest at Landfall during the early to mid-1980s and continued into the 1990s, encompassing a

64. Lance Kiland, *A Sharp Eye*, 1988, lithograph and woodcut, printed in color, 20 X 17 (50.8 X 43.2)

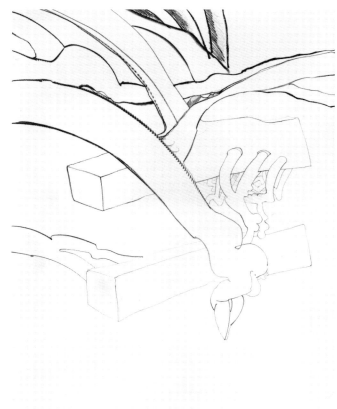

65. Richard Hunt, *Untitled*, 1971, lithograph

wide array of controversial issues: gender, war, the environment, AIDS, American national politics, race relations, and the art world. Initially, the wrath of the artists was most often aimed at the Republican goings-on in Washington. Ed Larson set the tenor with his 1983 *Ronald Radiation*, offering a plea for the curtailment of the proliferation nuclear energy and weaponry (Fig. 69). In 1985, Peter Saul, after a hiatus of more than ten years from Landfall, picked up where he had left off in 1972. His lithograph *Politics* offers a grotesque vision of a dazed Ronald Reagan "who becomes a logolike sign of overwhelming confusion. A close look at the details reveals a grasping hand of power and a tongue licking the world" (Pl. 71).[63] In the early 1990s, Roger Brown was targeting Jesse Helms, one of the most vocal and least-informed opponents of contemporary art and progressive attitudes in general (Fig. 70).

The military establishment also came under critical scrutiny during these years. Ed Paschke offered a

66. Lynda Benglis, *Untitled*, 1979, from the portfolio *N.A.M.E.*, 1980, lithograph, printed in color, 22 1/2 X 30 1/8 (57.2 X 76.5)

vision of a generic military strongman, at a time when repressive authoritarian regimes were particularly active around the world (Fig. 71).[64] The extreme close-up of the face, coupled with Paschke's signature video-influenced distortions, make this a particularly poignant image for 1984. Robert Arneson raged uncontrollably at the inhumanity of the worldwide

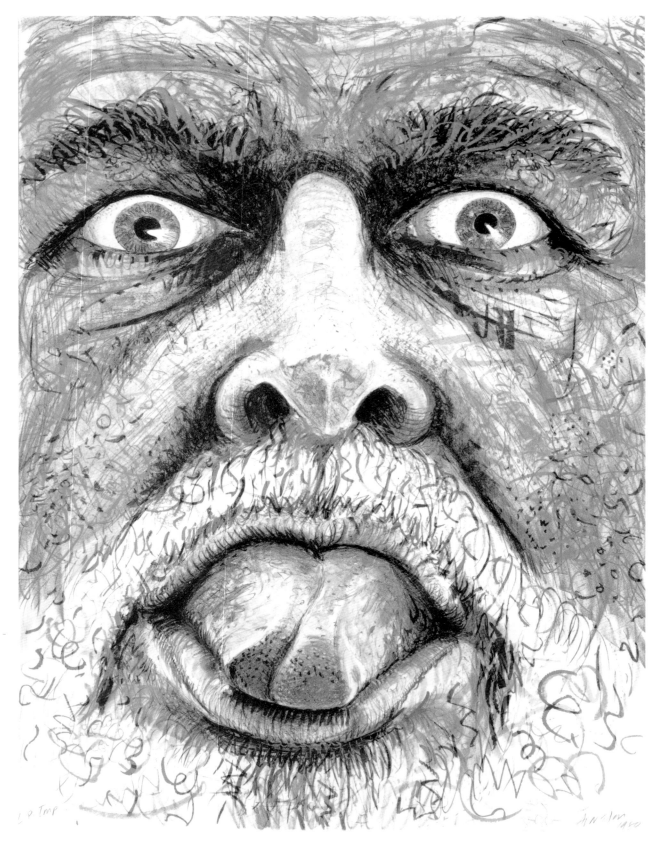

67. Robert Arneson, *A Hollow Gesture*, 1980,
lithograph, printed in color, 40 X 30 (101.6 X 76.2)

68. Luis Jiménez working on his lithograph *Honky Tonk*, 1981, in the Superior Street shop (see Pl. 41).

69. Edward Larson, *Ronald Radiation*, 1983, woodcut, printed in color, 23 7/8 X 18 (60.6 X 45.7)

military complex, an entire culture whose sole business is death (Pl. 7).

Also under attack by the artists was the corporate-industrial complex. William T. Wiley performed a postmortem on the Three Mile Island nuclear reactor disaster, in the guise of an obscure, mutant life form that grew out of the contaminated aftermath (Fig. 72).[65] Paschke set down the grotesque face of the greedy corporate executive structure, *Execo*, the "'shifty-eyed'...look of dissipation [that] suggests too many three-martini business lunches" (Fig. 102).[66]

Vito Acconci questioned the habit of blind allegiance to the American political system in his multipart *Wav(er)ing Flag* (Fig. 73). Stretching an excerpt from the Pledge of Allegiance across an elongated flag, pulling letters up and down out of the central line of text, Acconci creates a sort of visual noise or interference that highlights the fragmented, confused nature of contemporary American political life, as society increasingly breaks down into contentious special interest groups.

70. Roger Brown, *Fear No Evil*, 1991, lithograph

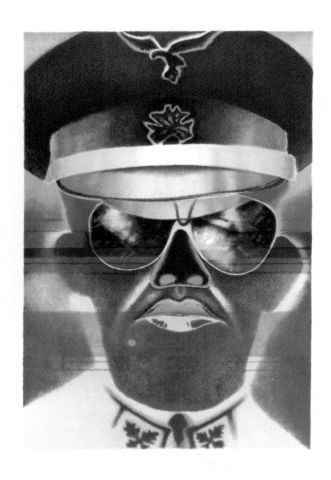

71. Ed Paschke, *Kontato*, 1984, lithograph,
printed in color, 34 1/4 X 24 (87 X 61)

72. William T. Wiley, *Three Mile Island Three Years Later*, 1983,
lithograph, printed in color, 38 1/4 X 26 7/8 (97.2 X 68.3)

Acconci's piece is part of a genre of political art that deals with broader issues, including gender and human rights positions, in a more conceptual, highly intellectual manner, quite different from the immediate, specific grievances of Larson or Saul. In a set of three serigraphs on aluminum sheets (Pls. 51-53), Marilyn Minter deals with traditional notions of woman's work and a woman's role in the art world. *Hands Dumping* is a close-up of a female hand disposing of coffee grounds; in *Hands Folding*, two hands fold laundry. Both images elicit a sort of passive, perhaps unconscious, acceptance that these are suitable tasks for women. However, in the third panel, *Hands Washing*, a hand is washing a paintbrush, a traditionally unfeminine activity. The assumptions reinforced by the images and titles of the first two panels are confirmed by the title of the third, but thoroughly under-mined by the latter's imagery. "There were all these women's hands painting...and you don't think of women's hands as painting, you think of them as cleaning."[67]

In two biting, cynical pieces, Roger Brown addresses internal art-world politics, offering a gloomy assessment of the industry. *One Share Art Stock* (Fig. 74) reduces a work of art to its basic monetary unit to be traded in the market, regardless of its intellectual and aesthetic worth. *Museum of What's Happening Now* (Fig. 75) sums up the sort of shallow, hip trendiness endemic to the programming in many contemporary art museums.

Ronald Jones made a pair of large, geometric, seemingly abstract woodcuts that appear to deal with formal issues of color, shape, and design (Pls. 42, 43). Yet upon learning the full elaborate title, the viewer

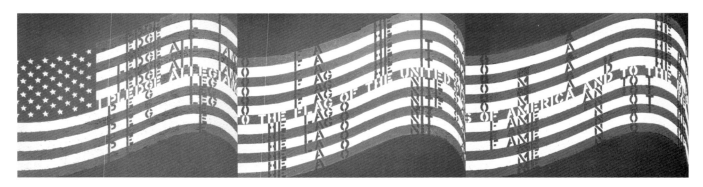

73. Vito Acconci, *Wav(er)ing Flag*, 1990, lithograph, printed in color, 6 sheets, 18 X 24 (45.7 X 61) each

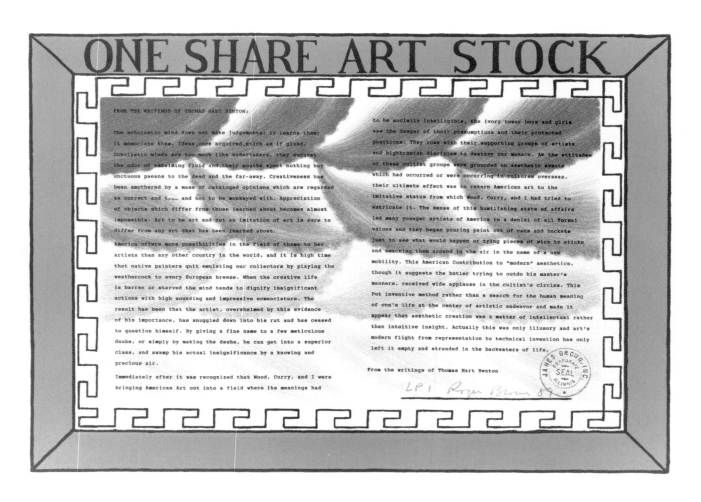

74. Roger Brown, *One Share Art Stock*, 1989, lithograph,
printed in color, 22 1/4 X 30 (56.5 X 76.2)

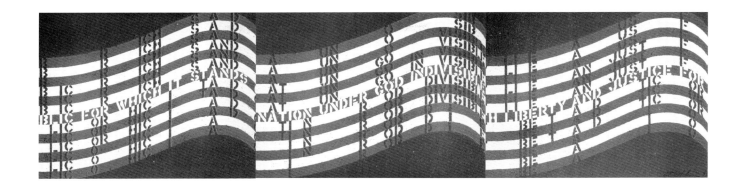

understands these are representations of collapse boards, life-size wooden boards sometimes used in hanging executions in Washington State.[68] Knowing the horrific, inhumane reality of the real objects forever colors and complicates the viewing of the prints; in this way, the verbal, conceptual side of the work is as important as the visual.

This intellectual vein of political art formed part of Landfall's general return to Conceptual art, signaled by the work of a new generation of artists such as Minter and Jones. Allen Ruppersberg directly translated ten of the many different mass-produced offset posters he had used in installations into fine-art lithographs (Pl. 69). Their models are the garish and eye-catching events posters ubiquitous in the Los Angeles landscape.[69] But here, instead of here announcing concerts and sporting events, they pose grim and ambiguous questions and pronouncements. In these terse statements, Ruppersberg raises disquieting issues about art, society, emotions, and relationships in a public forum.

Nancy Dwyer, too, was an important contributor to the Conceptual tradition at Landfall with her 1991 lithographs *Mayhem* and *Out of My Mind* (Pls. 27, 28). Relying on words—their design on the page and the meaning that they carry—Dwyer set two charged statements across vertiginous backgrounds. These two pieces clearly embody her interest in the various, and sometimes uncontrollable, meanings that words carry.[70] When working at the Press, Dwyer was aware of an "atmosphere of dark quietness," a mood that seems to have been pervasive in most of Landfall's work from the late eighties and early nineties. In retrospect, she thinks that this mood contributed to Lemon's decision to publish these two works, rather than others that she could have done.[71]

75. Roger Brown, *Museum of What's Happening Now*, 1992, serigraph and lithograph, printed in color, 20 X 16 (50.8 X 40.6)

76. Robert Yarber, *The Corruption of Ecstasy*, 1989, lithograph, printed in color

A BUMPY ROAD

Most appropriately, the first unmistakable manifestation of this whole emotional and psychological shift was Robert Yarber's *The Corruption of Ecstasy* of 1989 (Fig. 76), in which the burly Neo-Expressionist style so central to the 1980s takes a literal death plunge from its pinnacle to unseen depths.[72] Here was a clear acknowledgment that the party was over; that the giddy, heady art world of the eighties, in which things only got bigger and better, was no more. In its stead was exhaustion, collapse, and despair, unfamiliar and disturbing terrain. This global turn of events—a shrinking audience and the dwindling certainty of sales—could not but strongly color Lemon's whole outlook on the survival of his Press and affect the mood and psychology of the work that he chose to print and publish.[73]

Surprisingly, the normally inscrutable Roger Brown played an important role in defining this new atmosphere. An experienced art-world and Landfall veteran, Brown usually maintained a distinct emotional reserve in his work, typically composed of large forms defined by broad areas of color (Pl. 10) During these years, however, his anger rose to the surface, at first in the pointed messages conveyed by *One Share Art Stock* and *Fear No Evil*. In these works, he maintained at least his signature formal calm. The same cannot be said about *Museum of What's Happening Now*, in which Brown was so clearly irritated by the shallowness of many cultural establishments that he was driven to atomize his normally smooth and pristine surfaces.

Dennis Oppenheim returned to Chicago to create a dark technological world filled with fantastic, dangerous machines run amok; strange, illogical, tremoring contraptions endlessly engaged in senseless, menacing acts (Fig. 77). At this time, Oppenheim was thinking of the objects in his art "according to their physiological and psychological conditions, encom-

Text within the artwork:

WHEEL-
BARROWS
6'X12'X12'

STUDY FOR: OBJECTS DREAM
OF FLYING TERMINATED
BY COLLISION.- WOOD
SILK SCREENED VIDEO STATIC
FIBERGLASS-ALUMINUM ARCS.

11/40   Dennis Oppenheim   1992

77. Dennis Oppenheim, *Study for: Objects Dream of Flying Terminated by Collision*, edition printed in 1991, signed in 1992, lithograph, printed in color, 34 X 48 (86.4 X 121.9)

78. Randy Twaddle, *Untitled*, 1985, lithograph, printed in color, 29 X 40 1/2 (73.7 X 102.9)

79. Randy Twaddle, *Untitled*, 1991,
aquatint, soft-ground etching, and spit-bite etching

80. Keith Jacobshagen, *Missouri Valley*, 1987, hard-ground etching,
4 X 4 1/2 (10.2 X 11.4), 15 7/8 X 16 3/8 (40.3 X 41.6)

passing stress, trauma, and the tremor of synthesis....There is something natural about how things fall apart, the conflicts, the abandonment, the despair."[74]

In his Landfall prints, Randy Twaddle has often made images of familiar objects: crutches, city skylines, eagles, lunar landers. In his early work (Fig. 78), he offered silhouettes of these things in a diptych or triptych format "that would imply a comparative and possibly evolutionary...relationship."[75] By 1991, Twaddle's work had shed its previous intellectual comparisons of objects and had become much more confrontational, as if the whole equilibrium of the situation had spun out of control (Fig. 79). A single, weighty image now fills the whole composition, poised in front of a sky streaked by hazy black residue. Twaddle shares with Oppenheim a vision of an intimidating, sinister technological-industrial world.[76]

Even nature offered no refuge during these years. The broad, life-nurturing expanses in Keith Jacobshagen's idyllic vision of the American heartland of the mid-1980s (Fig. 80) gave way to Leonard Koscianski's bloodthirsty animals locked in vicious combat (Fig. 81). Wolf and eagle, pressed tight against the foreground plane, engage in a struggle that neither will win, as the fire advances ever closer.

Yet within this damaged nature lay the hope that this dark period would soon end. John Buck's 1991 *Fireweed* (Pl. 13) centers on the first plant to grow after a forest fire, making a phoenixlike appearance that offers the possibility of rebirth and renewal.[77] The red and yellow fireweed stretches up and across and tries to cover a black and gray grid of dismal imagery that evokes assassinations, war, and deceit.

As the shock of the new conditions of a radically altered art world waned, new work and a new calm slowly emerged. Duane Zaloudek offered his white-on-white etchings, in which boldly stroked X's printed in white are visible on the white page only if the viewer has great patience.[78] Only time and concentration reveal the subtleties of the composition, and this slowing down of the viewing experience creates a tranquil, contemplative environment.[79] For Zaloudek, his lengthy, thoughtful creation process engenders a similar viewing process, for which a direct physical encounter with the work is absolutely necessary.

In *Domus* (Pl. 8), Don Baum constructed a literal haven—a miniature, house-shaped object—that might symbolically shelter this new sense of tranquility. Baum's "edifices release and nourish the daydreams...of contentment made impossible by the cold realities of our modern, frequently peripatetic lives."[80]

81. Leonard Koscianski, *Fire-Eaters*, 1991, lithograph, printed in color

82. Ed Paschke, *Compassion*, 1992,
lithograph, printed in color, 18 1/8 X 20 (46 X 50.8)

A NEW ERA

1992 witnessed a strengthening of this process, a sort of reorientation, leaving a good clean edge to the work done at Landfall; gone was the sense of being buffeted by uncontrollable events. Essential to this most recent work is humor, a sense of purpose, and hope, no matter how thorny an issue the work addresses. And Landfall continues to refuse, up to the present day, to shy away from controversial subjects, such as race relations and politics. It is as if, having survived the trauma of the preceding years, the Press emerged stronger to renew its mission of risk taking.

Several artists from Chicago (including Baum) helped set the tone of this new era. Karl Wirsum made one of his infrequent visits to Landfall to create the freestanding *Blue Burger Quartet à la Carte*, a dinosaur pushing a food cart, which perfectly balances whimsical and dark humor (Pl. 93). The very sight of a carnivorous reptile offering up edibles gives the viewer pause. In Ed Paschke's *Compassion* (Fig. 82), two distorted mutants protect and offer solace to each other. This is a more lyrical subject than Paschke usually offers, but he maintains the edge through his signature acid-colored distortions that mask the features of his figures. This balance of the humane and the uncertain runs through much of Landfall's work.

Tony Fitzpatrick created a number of similarly double-edged images, dealing with boxers, baseball

83. Tony Fitzpatrick, *Black-Eyed Fight Dog*, 1991,
hard-ground etching, soft-ground etching, spit-bite etching,
with chine collé

84. Lesley Dill, *Poem Dress "The Souls Selects Her Own Society,"*
1993, lithograph, with thread

85. Kara Walker, *The Means to an End…A Shadow Drama in Five Acts*, 1995, hard-ground etching and aquatint, 5 sheets

players, circus performers, and bizarre mutants in general (Fig. 83). Like Paschke, Fitzpatrick does not sentimentalize or otherwise trivialize the inhabitants of his work. Instead, this ex-boxer unflinchingly evokes the deep pain and the grim reality of the street life that he knows so well. Yet his characters, even the animals, carry themselves with a certain dignity, maintaining a sense of humor and hope in all situations. This balancing act of hope and despair appeared in Fitzpatrick's art only after the birth of his son in 1992, the year in which he did most of his work at Landfall.[81]

Some of the strongest work of recent years has been made by two younger artists, Lesley Dill and Kara Walker. Since 1992, Dill has created a compelling range of paper sculptures (Fig. 84), high reliefs, and sewn and collaged flat pieces (Pls. 23, 24). Paper is the ideal material for Dill because it allows her to create objects of sensuous beauty, while its fragile nature is a poignant metaphor for the general human emotional condition.[82] She uses the dual nature of the nude, too, both as something very beautiful and as something exposed and unprotected. Dill recently stressed that she is not interested in grotesque imagery of extreme emotions such as hate or anger; she instead wants to get at "the emotions that we live with most of the time, such as hope, sorrow or apprehension."[83]

Overprinting her images and constructions with excerpts from the poetry of Emily Dickinson,[84] Dill explores a number of complex issues, such as how we use language to clothe, define and protect ourselves,

and how vulnerable we become when these layers are stripped away. Dill's work clearly brings together Landfall's long-standing interest in Conceptual art, narrative, and the figure in one coherent group of works.

Kara Walker subversively adapts the old-fashioned medium of the paper cut-out silhouette to produce works that deal in startling ways with race relations, past and present (Fig. 85). She takes a genteel parlor diversion, revels in its inherent exquisiteness, and then turns it on its head by using it to illustrate a shocking narrative of domination and murder. We are drawn to the charm and whimsy of the design, and it is only after this initial seduction that the violence is thrust upon us.[85] This double edge of beauty and horror is precisely the source of her work's stunning power. A recent reviewer of Walker's work observed: "But for all of their grace, spirit and humor, none of these images are simply pleasant to look at. How could they be?"[86]

Landfall is charging bravely into the future with the formula that has brought it so successfully to the present. The basis of this success has been Lemon's ability to maintain long-lasting, productive relationships with certain artists, while simultaneously having the open mind and willingness to seek out and nuture the younger generations.

One vital new relationship is between the Press and the Milwaukee Art Museum. The whole process of cataloguing the Museum's Landfall Press Archive has clarified many aspects of the Press' history, and recent American printmaking in general, and has pulled much information out of dark corners and forgotten boxes. And this process will continue indefinitely, as the Museum continues to research the history of the Press, as Lemon donates new publications and other material, and artists offer more information and insights about their work. This is a far-reaching collaboration that holds many exciting possibilities—and that bodes well for scholars and connoisseurs.

NOTES

1. "A Conversation with Jack Lemon and Pauline Saliga," in Judith Kirshner, *Landfall Press: A Survey of Prints (1970-1977)*, exh. brochure (Chicago: Museum of Contemporary Art, 1977), p. 5.

2. Recalling his experience at Nebraska, Lemon once said, "I would never have gotten a degree in printmaking....I liked printmaking, I loved it, but not enough to get involved in it to where it was going to become my [profession]." Unpublished interview with Sue Taylor, October 9, 1993, Landfall Press Archive, Milwaukee Art Museum.

3. The title of the 1965 portfolio, the first Lemon ever printed, was *Kansas City Art Institute Impressions*. It contained lithographs by Rick van Benton, Harold Bruder, Dale Eldred, Lemon, Rosalie Lovell, William Lovell, William McKim, and Wilbur Newald.

4. June Wayne established the Tamarind Lithography Workshop in 1960 in Los Angeles. It was a non-profit organization created and sustained with financial support from the Ford Foundation. Tamarind Lithography Workshop operated as a professional studio, independent of any university system, until 1970, when it became the Tamarind Institute of the University of New Mexico.
Tamarind was founded to revive the high standards of fine-art lithographic printing in the United States and to train master printers and assistants in the art of lithography. Those trained at Tamarind generally opened up their own shops across the country, based on the Tamarind model. The Tamarind Institute was established by Garo Antreasian (the first master printer at the Workshop) to maintain the Tamarind philosophy and to continue research into the medium of lithography. See June Wayne, "Preface," and Garo Antreasian, "Introduction," in Garo Antreasian and Clinton Adams, *The Tamarind Book of Lithography: Art & Techniques* (Los Angeles: Tamarind Lithography Workshops; New York: Harry N. Abrams, [1976]).

5. For a history of the Ford Foundation's involvement with the establishment of the Tamarind Lithography Workshop, see David Mickenberg, "Multiple Purposes: Collaboration and Education in University and Non-Profit Workshops," in Trudy V. Hansen, David Mickenberg, Joann Moser, and Barry Walker, *Printmaking in America: Collaborative Prints and Presses, 1960-1990* (New York: Harry N. Abrams in association with the Mary and Leigh Block Gallery, Northwestern University, Evanston, Illinois, 1995), pp. 96-111.

6. Conversation with Jack Lemon, October 1995.

7. Among the artists with whom Lemon worked at the Kansas City Art Institute were Richard Diebenkorn, Rosalind Drexler, Sam Francis, Peter Saul, Ernest Trova, and H.C. Westermann; see Jack Lemon, "Inside Landfall Press," unpublished manuscript, 1995, Landfall Press Archive, Milwaukee Art Museum, pp. 5-6.

8. A rare early precedent was the affiliation in 1956 of the Contemporaries Gallery, later renamed the Pratt Graphic Art Center, with Pratt University, Brooklyn, New York; see Mickenberg, "Multiple Purposes," pp. 100-02.

9. Acting on the Tamarind model, Landfall Press has helped launch the careers of a number of master printers, including David Keister of Echo Press, formerly at the University of Indiana; the late Fred Gude of the defunct Four Brothers Press, Chicago; Steve Britko (who also trained at Tamarind Institute of the University of New Mexico) of the Naravisa Press, Santa Fe; and David Jones of Anchor Graphics, Chicago.

10. Michael Knigin and Murray Zimiles, *The Contemporary Lithographic Workshop Around the World* (New York: Van Nostrand Reinhold Co., 1974), pp. 117-18.

For an interesting critical history of the Lithography Workshop, see Garry N. Kennedy et al., *NSCAD: The Nova Scotia College of Art and Design: Prints and Books*, exh. cat. (Halifax: Nova Scotia College of Art and Design, 1982).

11. See Per Hovdenakk, *Christo: Complete Editions 1964-1982* (Munich: Verlag Schellmann and Klüser; New York: New York University Press, 1982), nos. 5, 6, 10-12, 14-17, 20-22.

12. Ibid., no. 25.

13. In conversations with various artists in 1994 and 1995, I asked if they could discern any underlying aesthetic that tied together Landfall's output. No one could pinpoint any definitive visual character. Some mentioned Lemon's concern for mark-making, others, his concern for the placement of elements on a page.

14. "A Conversation with Jack Lemon and Pauline Saliga," p. 4.

15. "[Wilber Newald] taught his students incredible discipline along with life drawing, and above all introduced us to the possibilities of *seeing* through the very process of drawing. Hour after hour was spent before a model....Professor Newald's rigorous and demanding instruction instilled in me a deep love of drawing..."; Jack Lemon, "Inside Landfall Press," p. 2.

16. "I'm not especially interested in making multiples. I'm instead interested in what the artist draws in the plate or stone and what is put on the paper"; "A Conversation with Jack Lemon and Pauline Saliga," p. 2.

17. Ibid.

18. For a discussion of the differences between independent and university printshops, specifically a comparison between Tamarind Lithography Workshop and Pratt Graphic Art Center, see Mickenberg, "Multiple Purposes," passim.

19. Lemon, "Inside Landfall Press," pp. 7-8. Over the years, Lemon and Frumkin have had a most productive relationship and they share similar interests in art. Artists who have both shown at Frumkin's galleries in Chicago and New York and printed at Landfall include Robert Arneson, Lesley Dill, Alfred Leslie, James McGarrell, Philip Pearlstein, Peter Saul, H.C. Westermann, and William T. Wiley.

20. "A Conversation with Jack Lemon and Pauline Saliga," p. 1.

21. Ibid., p. 2.

22. The *Landfall Press Etching Portfolio* comprises William Allan's etching, *Tamales*; Christo's etching with collage, *Wrapped Venus, Villa Borghese, 1963*; Robert Cottingham's etching and aquatint, *F.W.*; Claes Oldenburg's etching and aquatint, *Spoon Pier*; Philip Pearlstein's etching, *Nude on an Iron Bench*; and William T. Wiley's lithograph and hard-ground etching, *Seasonall Gate*. Lemon invited the printer Timothy Berry and his Teaberry Press to set up an etching press in Landfall in 1975. Berry printed intaglio prints for several years for Lemon before moving to the San Francisco Bay Area in 1978. He continued to print for Lemon until 1981.

Lemon was motivated to move into etching after seeing an exhibition of Thomas Gainsborough's etchings at The Tate Gallery, London, in the early 1970s. The show featured the plates and impressions by Gainsborough himself, and the quality and beauty of the work caught Lemon's eye.

23. Irving Sandler, "Philip Pearlstein and the New Realism," in *Philip Pearlstein: A Retrospective*, exh. cat. (Milwaukee: Milwaukee Art Museum, 1983), p. 19.

24. Philip Pearlstein, "A Realist Artist in an Abstract World," ibid., p. 13.

25. Ibid.

26. Jim Pernotto, *Chuck Close Editions: A Catalogue Raisonné and Exhibition*, exh. cat. (Youngstown, Ohio: The Butler Institute of American Art, 1989), n.p. In 1972, Close made his first print, *Keith/Mezzotint*, at Crown Point Press. In 1975, he traveled to Landfall to work on his second print, his first lithograph, *Keith/Four Times*.

27. Close has commented on his intentional search for difficult technical issues when collaborating with printers: "I didn't want to go somewhere where they had all the expertise, and you had none. If I was going to do a print, I wanted to do something where I didn't know how to do it. And the printer didn't know how to do it either. We could be in it together, a real collaborative experience"; quoted in Pernotto, *Chuck Close Editions*, n.p.

28. Conversation with the author, January 26, 1995.

29. "Close was using an airbrush to spray tiny dots of touche onto a lithographic limestone. One mistake in the volume of spray made it necessary for the entire drawing to be redone. In addition, several stones were broken under the pressure of printing, again requiring redrawing and reprinting. But the artist and the printer persevered..."; Pernotto, *Chuck Close Editions*, n.p.

"In order to see the results of his drawing on stone, Close had to use separate stones for different tones and separate stones for each figure and each background, thus accounting for the large number of stones required for the printing, eleven in all for the final edition. Two stones each were used for the largest, second and third largest figures, and only one stone for the smallest figure. A separate stone was used for each background. The huge piece of paper presented another problem, because it could not pass through a conventional lithography press. We rolled the paper up at both ends, like a typewriter ribbon, using large bobby pins to hold the curled paper in place"; conversation with Jack Lemon, December 7, 1995.

30. For Dine's energetic yet ambivalent dialogue with the various

currents of the New York avant-garde during the 1960s and early 1970s, see Joseph Ruzicka, "Jim Dine and Performance," *Studies in Modern Art*, 1 (1991), pp. 96-121.

For the only appearances of bandanas in Dine's art, see *The Red Bandana*, 1961, oil on canvas, repr. in David Shapiro, *Jim Dine* (New York: Harry N. Abrams, 1981), pl. 65; *Throat* (from the portfolio *11 Pop Artists: A New Image*), 1965, serigraph, repr. in *Jim Dine: Complete Graphics*, exh. cat. (Berlin: Galerie Mikro, 1970), pl. 36.

For gridded color charts in Dine's paintings, see *Red Devil Color Chart No. Two*, 1963, oil on canvas and collage; *A Color Chart*, 1963, oil on canvas; *Self-Portrait Next to Colored Window*, 1964, charcoal on canvas, oil on glass and wood; *A Thin Kindergarten Painting*, 1974, oil on canvas with objects.

Dine's four wall chart prints from Landfall Press are part of a larger series of works, including a painting now in the Louisiana Museum, Humlebaek, Denmark, and bathroom tiles that he made in his kiln on his farm in Putney, Vermont; conversation with the author, December 24, 1995.

31. "A Conversation with Jack Lemon and Pauline Saliga," p. 4.

32. Jeremy Lewison, *Sol LeWitt Prints 1970-1986*, exh. cat. (London: The Tate Gallery, 1986), p. 12.

33. LeWitt worked on his two Landfall Press projects from October 1970 to March 1971.

The Milwaukee Art Center wall drawings were part of the exhibition, "Directions 3: Eight Artists," June 19-August 8, 1971. The drawings were executed on either side of an 11-foot by 10-foot, 6-inch temporary wall in the middle of a gallery: *Using a hard pencil draw a 6" x 6" grid covering the wall. Within the square draw freehand lines horizontally, vertically, diagonally left to right and diagonally right to left. Draw only one kind of line within each square, as many lines as desired but with at least one line within each square* (drawn by William Torphy); *Using a hard black pencil draw a 6" x 6" grid covering the wall. Within the squares draw freehand lines horizontally using the black pencil, vertically using yellow, diagonally left to right using red, and diagonally right to left using blue. Draw as many lines in as many colors as desired with at least one line in each square* (drawn by Kaye Roseneck).

34. Conversation with the author, January 27, 1995. When he was making the portfolio, Oppenheim was quite aware of the irony of documenting and preserving transient, non-commercial art. However, the need to remember was foremost in his mind.

35. For a review of related paintings and drawings, see Jane Bell, "David Ligare," *Arts Magazine*, 48 (April 1974), p. 70.

36. Conversation with Jack Lemon, December 7, 1995. Ligare first drew the marks with his fingers in the sandy beach, then photographed them from overhead. These photos were then transferred to the stones, and he drew in the seascape. Much of the tension in Ligare's *Sand Drawing* prints derive from the competing perspectives, the sand drawing seen from directly above and the landscape in a more traditional one-point perspective.

37. *The Store*, December 1-31, 1961, at Ray-Gun Manufacturing Co., 107 East 2nd Street, New York, New York. For Oldenburg's contemporaneous writings on the store and various designs, posters, and photographs, see *Claes Oldenburg: An Anthology*, exh. cat. (New York: The Solomon R. Guggenheim Museum, 1985), pp. 104-30.

38. Once a project has been realized, Christo then records the results on film; conversation with the author, August 30, 1995.

39. For the change in the character of prints that began to occur in the 1960s—from objects of private delectation to works with an imposing public presence, see Barry Walker, *Public and Private: American Prints Today*, exh. cat. (New York: The Brooklyn Museum, 1986).

40. Acconci thinks of *Stones for a Wall* as a "group of works that make a wall—two-dimensional stones that make a new wall. There is also a literal stone interpretation in all of this—using a litho stone to make two-dimensional paper stones....These stones are from an active building, a building from any American city. These are stones that you build with, that you write graffiti on, that you hide things—like the gun—between, that you can use as a weapon"; conversation with the author, August 27, 1995.

41. Talking about *Juarez Suite*, Lemon said that Allen "was very involved with *Juarez*, an exhibition he had been working on for quite a while. *Juarez* was a performance and an exhibition of actual objects with music and words and visual images working closely together. The record that accompanies the *Juarez* suite of prints was a way of preserving the music that Terry brought together for the *Juarez* exhibition"; "A Conversation with Jack Lemon and Pauline Saliga," p. 5.

42. About the traumas that Westermann suffered during World War II and their indelible effect, see Bill Barrette, ed., and Joanna Beall Westermann, *Letters from H.C. Westermann* (New York: Timken Publishers, 1988), pp. 149-63.

43. The three portraits are of himself, Richard Bellamy, his dealer at the time, and his friend Frank Fata, an English professor. Leslie also worked on, but never editioned, a similiar portrait of his wife Constance. When Leslie was working on these four lithographs, he was particularly interested in the dramatic lighting effects employed by Caravaggio; conversation with Jack Lemon, December 7, 1995.

44. For Arneson's connection to the ancient traditions of ceramic and brick relief figurative work, see Neal Benezra, *Robert Arneson: A Retrospective*, exh. cat. (Des Moines, Iowa: Des Moines Art Center, 1986), pp. 33-43.

Commenting on the *Brick Suite* (of five prints and one terracotta) that Arneson executed at Landfall in 1976, Lemon said, "The reason we did the brick project was that the brick has been a part of Arneson's work....Actually the three-dimensional brick is the main object in the suite and the prints are portraits of the brick..."; "A Conversation with Jack Lemon and Pauline Saliga," p. 5.

45. Arneson was working at Landfall on his 1976 *Brick Suite* at the same time that Terry Allen was there working on his *Juarez Suite*.

The titles of Arneson's prints, e.g., *Moby Brick*, evolved from the verbal interchange between the two artists while they worked; conversation with Jack Lemon, December 7, 1995.

46. For Arneson's self-identification as an artist working in California, see Benezra, *Robert Arneson*, pp. 63-64, 67, 70.

47. Barbaralee Diamonstein, *Inside New York's Art World* (New York: Rizzoli, [1979]), p. 99; Constance Glenn, *Jim Dine: Drawings* (New York: Harry N. Abrams, 1985), p. 37; John Gruen, "Jim Dine and the Life of Objects," *Art News*, 76 (September 1977), p. 38.

48. Conversation with the author, August 29, 1995.

49. Conversation with Jack Lemon, December 7, 1995. For a time in the 1970s, Landfall rented a small apartment for visiting artists in the Three Trees building in Chicago. Across the street was the Ohio Street Bar, in front of which the pimp in the green shoes did his dance.

50. Statement written in 1986, quoted in William C. Landwehr and John Arthur, *Robert Cottingham: A Print Retrospective, 1972-1986*, exh. cat. (Springfield, Missouri: Springfield Art Museum, 1986), p. 34.

51. Artist's statement, April 1995, published in *Jeanette Pasin Sloan*, exh. cat. (New York: Tatistcheff and Co., 1995), n.p.

For some of the broader issues of domesticity and feminism in Pasin Sloan's art, see Marty Stewart Huff, *Jeanette Pasin Sloan*, exh. cat. (Milwaukee: UWM Art Museum, Art History Gallery, 1995), pp. 2-12.

52. For two reviews by Hilton Kramer placing Erlebacher squarely in the forefront of the realist revival, see Hilton Kramer, "Martha Mayer Erlebacher," *The New York Times*, May 10, 1975; idem, "Art: A Realist with a Touch of Fantasy," *The New York Times*, January 4, 1980.

53. While Landfall published only two artist's books in its first twenty-five years, there are now plans to publish three in near future, by Lesley Dill, Ed Paschke, and Kara Walker.

Landfall has published a number of commercial books. These include a veneer-bound book by Wiley, *Ships Log*, an inexpensive version of his *Suite of Daze*, a book of stories by Vernon Fisher, and various exhibition catalogues (see Selected Bibliography and Exhibition History).

54. Quoted in "Laddie John Dill," clipping in Landfall Press Archive, Milwaukee Art Museum, p. 38.

55. "I've always been an artist, there was never anything else I was going to be. If there had been anything else, it would have been the theater. I dabbled in that, but as a child. I could never discipline myself to remember my lines properly. Nor could I rid myself of a feeling of inadequacy while acting. I did a lot of strange things when I was on the stage, so I set myself up not to go into theater. It took me a long time to realize that I was still dealing with theater in my art." About the content of her work, Bramson has remarked: "These [images] are not just about male/female relationships. They are more about the male and female within each one of us, about yin and yang, intelligence and emotion, rational and irrational thought." Both passages are quoted in an undated press release, Printworks, Chicago, copy in the artist's file, Milwaukee Art Museum.

56. For a perceptive review of Bramson's work in the mid-1980s, see Colin Westerbeck, "Chicago, Phyllis Bramson," *Artforum*, 24 (Summer 1986), p. 131.

57. In the late 1960s, Laddie John Dill was at Gemini G.E.L., Los Angeles, as an apprentice printer, working on the prints of Jasper Johns and Claes Oldenburg, among others; see Laura Stevenson Maslas, "Laddie John Dill," *Arttalk*, (April-May 1989), p. 20.

Lemon first saw Dill's work at the Sonnabend Gallery in New York in the early 1970s. In these large sand, glass, and neon tube installations, Lemon saw "a strong ability to draw in the way that Dill used the tubing and the edge of the glass"; conversation with the author, December 7, 1995.

58. Throughout his career, Dill has been making sculptures, paintings, and room-sized installations in a variety of media, notably neon and cement. His bronze Landfall sculptures represent a rare use of such a high-art material.

59. By 1977, Lemon had contemplated working with woodcuts, but did not set up operations for them until 1982; "A Conversation with Jack Lemon and Pauline Saliga," p. 2.

60. Buck's compositional device of arranging a number of small images of ambiguously related objects is an early manifestation of a composition where objects float in a field, a type that later became quite prevalent at Landfall. See, for instance, the work of Vernon Fisher, Tony Fitzpatrick, Roberto Juarez, and Greg Murdock, among others.

61. Buck's stylistic treatment of the woodcut print is closely related to his equally direct and strong handling of the wood in his sculpture. Whereas John Yau has argued that Buck's prints and sculptures are "distinct though interrelated," I find an equivalent sensibility in the handling of the wood. See John Yau, "Of, With, and Against Nature," in Robert Flynn Johnson and John Yau, *John Buck: Woodblock Prints*, exh. cat. (San Francisco: The Fine Arts Museums of San Francisco, 1993), p. 11.

62. For the most recent and complete assessment of Jiménez's work and subject matter, and its political implications, see *Man on Fire: Luis Jiménez*, exh. cat. (Albuquerque: The Albuquerque Museum, 1994).

63. Deborah Wye, *Committed to Print: Social and Political Themes in Recent American Printed Art*, exh. cat. (New York: The Museum of Modern Art, 1988), p. 27.

64. Ibid., p. 77.

65. Ibid., p. 62, for Wiley's print and his particular sensitivity to the issue of nuclear contamination.

66. Ibid., p. 85. Wye noted the irony that "this lithograph was commissioned by the Business Committee for the Arts and *Forbes* magazine, for the seventeenth annual Business in the Arts awards, in 1983. Examples of it were presented to the corporations that

had played the most important roles in the arts for the year."

67. "Marilyn Minter" (interview with John Zinsser), *Journal of Contemporary Art*, 3 (Spring-Summer, 1990), p. 28. The artist was commenting on a 1988 exhibition of her paintings at White Columns, New York. The three Landfall prints of the following year were closely based on paintings from that show. For the gender issues that these paintings, and by extension, prints, raise, see Pat McCoy, "Disrupted Narrative: Recent Works by Marilyn Minter," *Arts Magazine*, 65 (January 1989), pp. 32-35; Stephen Westfall, "Marilyn Minter at White Columns," *Art in America*, 77 (June 1989), p. 170; Susan Tallman, "Prints and Editions, Reproductive Arts," *Arts Magazine*, 64 (September 1989), pp. 21-22.

68. According to the artist, original wood matrices for the prints were constructed at Landfall Press. These matrices are now in the Landfall Press Archive, Milwaukee Art Museum. Collapse boards provided the inspiration for the whole project, but were not used, as has been reported, to print from; conversation with the author, January 27, 1995. For the report that the prints were from actual collapse boards, see Nancy Princethal, "Good Vibrations: Ronald Jones' 'Petrarch's Air' and Multiples," *The Print Collector's Newsletter*, 25 (March-April 1994), p. 3.

69. Conversation with the author, August 1995. The Landfall lithographs are precise copies of the offset posters that the Colby Poster Printing Company, Los Angeles, ran off for Ruppersberg; hence, the company's name, address, phone number, and union seal at the bottom of the Landfall edition.

Ruppersberg used these offset posters as wallpaper, entirely covering two walls in his 1988 exhibition at the Christine Burgin Gallery, New York; see Michael Kimmelman, "Allen Ruppersberg," *The New York Times*, February 5, 1988, and Ken Johnson, "Allen Ruppersberg at Christine Burgin," *Art in America* 76 (April 1988), p. 205.

70. For Dwyer's use of words and their multilevel meanings, see Marcia Tucker, "Nancy Dwyer Makes Trubble," *Artforum*, 28 (November 1989), pp. 140-44.

By the summer of 1985, Dwyer was dealing exclusively with words as images, "as a new version of pictures." The artist has commented that she is "not interested in telling the viewer what to think. They must come to their own conclusions"; conversation with the author, August 30, 1995.

71. Lemon went to Dwyer's studio to look at her paintings and watercolors. He then invited her to come work at the Press, to develop the themes of the *Mayhem* and *Out of My Mind* watercolors and paintings that he had seen in her studio.

While Dwyer's Landfall lithographs have their roots in earlier work, she recently stressed that she had not wanted to merely make a small version of something she had done before. She was interested in exploring the possibilities offered by paper and the printing process, hence features like the die-cuts used in the prints; conversation with the author, August 30, 1995.

72. See Edward F. Fry, "Artifice and Escapes: The Recent Paintings of Robert Yarber," in *Robert Yarber: Artifice and Escapes*, exh. cat. (Allentown, Pennsylvania: The Frank Martin Gallery, Muhlenberg College, 1991), n.p.: "Thus, the quality of Yarber's Baroque finally emerges clearly. It is a negative, almost parodic Baroque, driven by the force of a myth become dogma but also by the collapse of that dogma into despair and tragedy. Amidst scenes of supposed glamour and high consumption individuals bankrupt themselves, kill themselves or each other, and experience moments of blissful escape before their dead lives come to an end."

73. In a recent comment about the broad changes that swept through the art world in the late 1980s and the implications that they held for his operation, Lemon agreed with this reading of the mood of Landfall's work. "There was a darkness and terror that gripped almost every corner of the art world at that time. That had to have had an impact on the work that I was publishing"; conversation with the author, March 19, 1996.

74. "Behind the Eight Ball with Dennis Oppenheim," in *Dennis Oppenheim: Recent Works*, exh. cat. (Brussels: Liverpool Gallery, 1990), pp. 6, 7. See also Alanna Heiss, "Another Point of Entry: An Interview with Dennis Oppenheim," in Alanna Heiss, *Dennis Oppenheim: Selected Works, 1967-90*, exh. cat. (New York: The Institute for Contemporary Art, P.S. 1 Museum, 1992), pp. 137-83.

75. "Artist's Statement," in *Awards in the Visual Arts 9*, exh. cat. (Winston-Salem, North Carolina: Southeastern Center for Contemporary Art, 1990), n.p.

76. For this increased emphasis on the sinister in Twaddle's art, beginning around 1989, and in particular regarding his 1990 series of ten charcoal drawings of electrical transformers, directly related to Fig. 79, see Jock Reynolds, *Drawn to Scale: Cynthia Carlson, Michael Glier and Randy Twaddle*, exh. cat. (Andover, Massachusetts: Addison Gallery of American Art, Phillips Academy, 1990), n.p.

77. See Jack Lemon, "Working with John Buck, Landfall Press, Chicago, 1982," in Johnson and Yau, *John Buck: Woodblock Prints*, p. 21.

78. Zaloudek has commented that these X shapes are to his mind neutral images. He suggested that they may derive in part from such equally balanced shapes as a Greek cross or the cardinal points on a compass; conversation with the author, August 28, 1995.

79. Because of the exquisite subtlety of Zaloudek's white-on-white prints, they are all but impossible to photograph. Zaloudek's work is not reproduced in this catalogue at the request of the artist, who felt that any attempt to do so would require such manipulation of the image as to render it totally unrelated to his intentions. The artist also intends that the viewer experience the work firsthand and develop a specific language to describe his pieces—a process that he feels is analogous Sol LeWitt's precise use of language for the creation of his art work; conversation with author, August 28, 1995.

80. For a thorough and insightful discussion of the issues of shelter and domesticity embodied in Baum's houses, see Sue Taylor, "Don Baum: Domus," in René Paul Barilleaux, *Don Baum: Domus*, exh.

cat (Madison, Wisconsin: Madison Art Center, 1988). The passage quoted is on p. 10.

81. Commenting on the effect that the birth of his son, Max, has had on his work since 1992, Fitzpatrick said, "What removed all of the cynicism was being there when my son was born....Now there are elements of hope and some humor in my work. You get to the point where you get sick of playing in the mud"; quoted in Harlene Ellin, "Mr. Outsider," *Chicago Tribune Magazine*, March 26, 1995, p. 20.

For some of the more nightmarish aspects of Fitzpatrick's earlier work, see Carlo McCormick, "Tony Fitzpatrick," *Artforum*, 27 (December 1988), p. 123, and Jennifer Crohn, "Tony Fitzpatrick," *New Art Examiner*, 16 (March 1989), p. 51.

82. Conversation with the author, March 20, 1996. Dill has commented that she is interested in pushing beyond traditional ideas and methods of printmaking, and that Lemon is very supportive of her ideas.

In an exhibition review, Douglas Dreishpoon remarked on Dill's ability to coax a feeling of vulnerability out of almost any material. "Bronze usually brings with it associations of permanence and durability. Leslie [sic] Dill's *Man...* is intriguing, therefore, for the way in which bronze is cast to suggest a more vulnerable and fragile condition"; Dreishpoon, "New Bronze Sculpture," *Art News*, 91 (March 1992), p. 136.

83. Conversation with the author, March 20, 1996. Dill went on to say, "I will do some confrontational images, but nothing too despairing or too down. I'll destroy a piece if it goes too far."

The author is deeply grateful to Dill for helping to pinpoint some of the salient features of work done at Landfall in the 1990s, both by herself and by other artists.

84. An English major in college, Dill received her first book of Dickinson's poetry in 1990. She has commented that the work "hit me like a bullet. Now I feel her works are basically blood to me"; see Sue Scott, *Lesley Dill: The Poetic Body*, exh. brochure (Orlando, Florida: Orlando Museum of Art, 1996), n.p.

85. Walker issued a statement in conjunction with the publication of this, her first Landfall print, *The Means to an End...A Shadow Drama in Five Acts*: "Presents a panoramic view of an Antebellum swampland wherein mythic and stereotypic characters, Negro and otherwise, respond to outrageous demands with benign passivity. Illicit sex and violence are suggested as the means by which freedom is attained. The Master/slave narrative is expanded and inverted to include authoritarian control over children, the landscape and the self. From left to right this suite of aquatints reads like the table of contents in a romantic novel: The Beginning, The Hunt, The Chase, The Plunge, The End. The remainder of the story is couched in polite silence—the kind of silence which harbors racism, distrust, fear and intense and obsessive love."

86. Roberta Smith, "Slavery in Black and White," *The New York Times*, May 5, 1995. For an interview with the artist, see Sydney Jenkins, *Look Away! Look Away! Look Away!: Kara Elizabeth Walker*, exh. brochure (Annandale-on-Hudson, New York: Center for Curatorial Studies, Bard College, 1995), pp. 11-26.

SELECTED BIBLIOGRAPHY

Following is a selected bibliography of books, exhibition catalogues, articles, and ephemeral material that specifically deal with Landfall Press, books published by Landfall (exhibition catalogues, short stories, and poetry), publications that treat Landfall's place in the broad history of recent printmaking or have relevant discussions about the Press, and monographs on Landfall artists (notably, catalogues raisonnés) that offer a fundamental understanding of the artist's print-making oeuvre.

Adams, Clinton. *Fifty Artists/Fifty Printers* (exhibition catalogue). Albuquerque: University Art Museum, University of New Mexico, 1985.

Adrian, Dennis. *Master Prints from Landfall Press* (exhibition brochure). Chicago: The David and Alfred Smart Gallery, University of Chicago, 1980.

_____. *Robert Arneson: Masks and Portraits* (exhibition catalogue). Chicago: Landfall Press, 1984.

_____. *Sight Out of Mind: Essays and Criticism on Art.* Ann Arbor: University of Michigan Research Press, 1986.

_____. *Visions/Painting and Sculpture/Distinguished Alumni, 1945 to the Present* (exhibition catalogue). Chicago: School of The Art Institute of Chicago, 1976.

Adrian, Dennis, and Richard A. Born. *The Chicago Imagist Print: Ten Artists' Works, 1958-1987* (exhibition catalogue). Chicago: The David and Alfred Smart Gallery, University of Chicago, 1987.

Adrian, Dennis, and Whitney Halstead. *Made in Chicago.* (exhibition catalogue). Washington, D.C.: National Collection of Fine Arts, Smithsonian Institution, 1974.

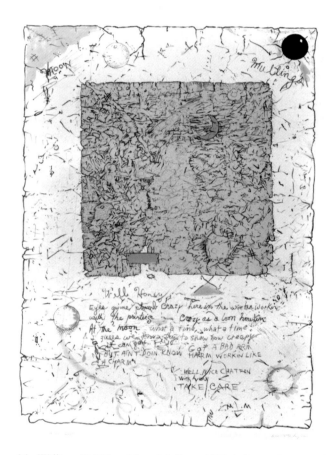

86. William T. Wiley, *Moon Mullings*, 1972, lithograph, printed in color, 30 X 21 7/8 (76.2 X 55.6). This print was one of several by Wiley in the exhibition catalogue by Elizabeth Armstrong, *First Impressions*, 1989.

"Alfred Leslie, *Richard Bellamy, Frank Fata, Alfred Leslie* (1974)." *The Print Collector's Newsletter*, 5 (January-February 1975), p. 151.

"Allen Ruppersberg, *Barrio L.A.* (1988)." *The Print Collector's Newsletter*, 20 (May-June 1989), p. 64.

Anderson, Don J. "A 3-in-1 Exhibit of Man's Noninvolvement." *Chicago Today*, January 31, 1971.

Andries, Dorothy. "North Shore Arts." *Winnetka Talk*, July 1, 1971.

Antreasian, Garo Z. "Some Thoughts about Printmaking and Print Collaborations." *Art Journal*, 39 (Spring 1980), pp. 180-88.

Armstrong, Elizabeth. *First Impressions: Early Prints by Forty-Six Contemporary Artists* (exhibition catalogue). Minneapolis: Walker Art Center, 1989.

Artner, Alan G. "Landfall Windfall." *Chicago Tribune*, February 14, 1993.

Axsom, Richard, and David Platzker. *Claes Oldenburg: Printed Stuff*. New York: Hudson Hills Press, forthcoming.

Baro, Gene. *Thirty Years of American Printmaking* (exhibition catalogue). New York: The Brooklyn Museum, 1976.

87. Robert Cottingham, *Hot*, 1973, lithograph, printed in color, 22 7/8 X 22 3/4 (58.1 X 57.8). This print was included in the exhibition catalogue by Gene Baro, *Thirty Years of American Printmaking*, 1976.

Barry, Edward. "The Art of Lithography." *Chicago Tribune Magazine*, March 28, 1971.

Beasley, James M., and Greg G. Thielen. *The Graphic Works of Philip Pearlstein, 1978-1994* (exhibition catalogue). Springfield, Missouri: Springfield Art Museum, 1995.

Brody, Jacqueline, ed. "Printing Today: Eight Views." *The Print Collector's Newsletter*, 13 (January-February 1983), pp. 180-200.

Broun, Elizabeth, with the assistance of Jan Howard. *Form, Illusion, Myth: Prints and Drawings of Pat Steir* (exhibition catalogue). Lawrence, Kansas: Helen Foresman Spencer Museum of Art, University of Kansas, 1983.

88. James McGarrell in the West Ontario Street shop drawing on a stone for his lithograph, *V*, from the portfolio, *The Quincy Inventions*, 1970.

Canaday, John. "Art: Symbolism of 'Quincy Inventions.'" *The New York Times*, May 15, 1971.

"Charles Gaines, *Untitled* (1979)." *The Print Collector's Newsletter*, 10 (July-August 1979), p. 93.

"Christo, '(Some) Not Realized Projects': Whitney Museum Wrapped, Moma (Rear), Moma (Front), Times Square (Front), Times Square (Rear) (1971)." *The Print Collector's Newsletter*, 3 (March-April 1972), p. 9.

"Christo, *Wrapped Floors* (1982)." *The Print Collector's Newsletter*, 13 (January-February 1983), p. 217.

"Claes Oldenburg, *Geometric Mouse Pyramid Doubled* (1976)." *The Print Collector's Newsletter*, 8 (March-April 1977), p. 17.

"Claes Oldenburg, *Study for Standing Mitt with Ball* (1973)." *The Print Collector's Newsletter*, 5 (March-April 1974), p. 13.

Cohen, Ronny. "Jumbo Prints: Artists Who Paint Big Want to Print Big." *Art News*, 83 (October 1984), p. 87.

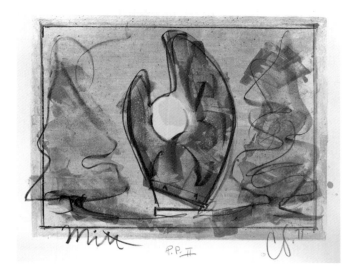

89. Claes Oldenburg, *Study for Standing Mitt with Ball*, 1974, lithograph, printed in color, 19 1/2 X 21 3/8 (49.5 X 54.3)

90. Richard Florsheim (left) conferring with Jack Lemon in the artist's work room, West Ontario Street shop, 1973.

Cole, Sylvan, and Domenic J. Iacono. *A Catalogue Raisonné of the Graphic Work of Richard Florsheim* (exhibition catalogue). Syracuse: The Syracuse University Art Collection, in cooperation with The Richard A. Florsheim Art Fund, 1988.

D'Oench, Ellen G., and Jean E. Feinberg. *Jim Dine Prints: 1977-1985* (exhibition catalogue). Middletown, Connecticut: Davison Art Center and the Ezra and Cecile Zilkha Gallery, Wesleyen University, 1987.

"Denise Green, *Circle Invaded by a Square* (1982)." *The Print Collector's Newsletter*, 13 (January-February 1983), p. 218.

91. Don Nice, *Buffalo*, 1976, lithograph, printed in color, 31 5/8 X 47 3/4 (80.3 X 121.3)

"Dennis Oppenheim, *Projects* (1973)." *The Print Collector's Newsletter*, 4 (July-August 1973), p. 63.

"Don Nice, *Buffalo* (1977)." *The Print Collector's Newsletter*, 8 (July-August 1977), p. 79.

"Don Nice, *Bull Durham* (1976)." *The Print Collector's Newsletter*, 8 (May-June 1977), p. 44.

"Ellen Lanyon, *Black Egret, Eagle Beak* (1984)." *The Print Collector's Newsletter*, 15 (September-October 1984), p. 144.

Eng, Rosemary T. "Landfall Press." *SAIC [School of The Art Institute of Chicago] Quarterly*, no. 10C (Fall 1975), p. 8.

"Eric Bulatov, *New York* (1989)." *The Print Collector's Newsletter*, 21 (July-August 1990), p. 108.

"Establishment of Landfall Press Archive: Milwaukee Art Museum." *Journal of the Print World*, 16 (Spring 1993), p. 19.

92. Ellen Lanyon, *Black Egret*, 1985, lithograph, printed in color, 44 1/2 X 30 3/8 (113 X 77.2)

93. Eric Bulatov in the West 18th Street shop drawing on a stone for his lithograph *New York*, 1989.

Fisher, Vernon. *Navigating by the Stars*. Chicago: Landfall Press; and Kansas City, Missouri: The Karl Oskar Group, 1989.

"The Gift That Keeps on Giving." *Art Muscle*, 7 (February-March 1993), p. 5.

Gordon, Peter, with Sidney Waller and Paul Weinman, eds. *Diamonds Are Forever: Artists and Writers on Baseball* (exhibition catalogue). Albany, New York: New York State Museum, 1987.

Green, Laura. "Turning Out Fine Prints in 'Boot Camp.'" *Chicago Sun Times*, August 29, 1973.

"Grisha Bruskin, *Untitled* (1988)." *The Print Collector's Newsletter*, 20 (July-August 1989), p. 102.

"H.C. Westermann, *Six Lithographs* (1972-73)." *The Print Collector's Newsletter*, 4 (May-June 1973), p. 38.

Hansen, Trudy V., David Mickenberg, Joann Moser, and Barry Walker. *Printmaking in America: Collaborative Prints and Presses, 1960-1990* (exhibition catalogue). Evanston, Illinois: Mary and Leigh Block Gallery, Northwestern University, 1995.

Hanson, Henry. "Back Talk." *Chicago*, 43 (February 1993), p. 144.

_____. "Our Jack Lemon: Fit to Print." *Chicago Daily News*, November 27, 1975.

Hoffmann, Donald. "From the Press or Darkroom." *The Kansas City Star*, September 12, 1976.

Hopkins, Marilyn. "Printmaking in Chicago." *Saver*, (Winter 1971), pp. 14-18.

Hovdenakk, Per. *Christo: Complete Editions, 1964-1982*. Translated by Jörg Schellmann. Munich: Verlag Schellmann and Klüser; New York: New York University Press, 1982.

"Jack Tworkov, *L.P. No. 3—Q2—75* (1975)." *The Print Collector's Newsletter*, 6 (January-February 1976), p. 162.

"Jeanette Pasin Sloan, *Cup with Blue Rim* (1980)." *The Print Collector's Newsletter*, 11 (January-February 1981), p. 211.

"Jeanette Pasin Sloan, *Jeanette Pasin Sloan* (1986)." *The Print Collector's Newsletter*, 17 (September-October 1986), p. 144.

"Jeanette Pasin Sloan, *Silver Bowls* (1978)." *The Print Collector's Newsletter*, 9 (January-February 1979), p. 195.

"Jessica Diamond, *Commemorative Gold Pieces* (1990)." *The Print Collector's Newsletter*, 22 (March-April 1991), p. 17.

"Jim Dine, *Wall Chart I, Wall Chart II, Wall Chart III, Wall Chart IV* (1974)." *The Print Collector's Newsletter*, 5 (November-December 1974), p. 116.

94. Ed Paschke, *Hubert—State I*, 1976, lithograph, printed in color, 34 3/4 X 28 (88.3 X 71.1). This was one of the Landfall editions included in the exhibition catalogue by Trudy Hansen et al., *Printmaking in America*, 1995.

95. Jeanette Pasin Sloan, *Silver Bowls*, 1978, lithograph, printed in color, 32 3/8 X 42 3/4 (82.2 X 108.6)

96. Allen Jones, *Magician 2*, from the *Magician Suite*, 1976, lithograph, printed in color, 32 1/4 X 22 1/2 (81.9 X 57.2). This print was included in the exhibition brochure by Judith Kirshner, *Landfall Press*, 1977.

"John Buck, *Untitled* (1982)." *The Print Collector's Newsletter*, 14 (May-June 1983), p. 63.

"John Himmelfarb, *Words Cannot Describe* (1979)." *The Print Collector's Newsletter*, 11 (March-April 1980), p. 17.

Johnson, Flora. "Art for Art's Sake." *Chicago*, 25 (May 1975), p. 21.

Johnson, Robert Flynn, and John Yau. *John Buck: Woodblock Prints* (exhibition catalogue). San Francisco: The Fine Arts Museums of San Francisco, 1993.

Johnson, Una. *American Prints and Printmakers*. Garden City, New York: Doubleday & Co., 1980.

"Kara Walker, *The Means to an End...A Shadow Drama in Five Acts* (1995)." *The Print Collector's Newsletter*, 26 (July-August 1995), pp. 103, 107.

Keefe, Katharine Lee. *Some Recent Art from Chicago* (exhibition catalogue). Chapel Hill, North Carolina: Ackland Art Museum, University of North Carolina, 1980.

Kennedy, Garry N., et al. *NSCAD: The Nova Scotia College of Art and Design: Prints and Books* (exhibition catalogue). Halifax: Nova Scotia College of Art and Design, 1982.

"Ken Showell, *Aldan, Terni*." *The Print Collector's Newsletter*, 1 (January-February 1971), p. 133.

Kirshner, Judith. *Landfall Press: A Survey of Prints (1970-1977)* (exhibition brochure). Chicago: Museum of Contemporary Art, 1977.

Knigin, Michael, and Murray Zimilies. *The Contemporary Lithographic Workshop Around the World*. New York: Van Nostrand Reinhold Co., 1974.

Kramer, Hilton. "What's Missing from Today's Art World." *The Kansas City Star*, September 5, 1976.

Krens, Thomas. *Jim Dine Prints: 1970-1977* (exhibition catalogue). Williamstown, Massachusetts: Williams College Museum of Art, 1977.

"Laddie John Dill, *Portal #1, Portal #2, Portal #3, Portal #4* (1978)." *The Print Collector's Newsletter*, 9 (July-August 1978), p. 90.

"Laddie John Dill, *Stage Left* (1981)." *The Print Collector's Newsletter*, 14 (May-June 1983), p. 64.

"Landfall Press." *The New Art Examiner*, 1 (October 1973), p. 6.

"Landfall Press Etchings." *The Print Collector's Newsletter*, 6 (March-April 1975), p. 15.

97. Laddie John Dill, *Portal #1*, 1977, lithograph, printed in color, 20 7/8 X 40 1/8 (53 X 101.9)

"Landfall Press Makes an Impression." *Printing Views*, 42 (April 1976), pp. 26-27.

Landfall Press Newsletter, 1984-present (irregular).

Landfall Press Slide Portfolio Catalogue. Chicago: Landfall Press, 1976.

"Landfall Windfall." *The Print Collector's Newsletter*, 23 (January-February 1993), p. 221.

Landwehr, William C., and John Arthur. *Robert Cottingham: A Print Retrospective, 1972-1986* (exhibition catalogue). Springfield, Missouri: Springfield Art Museum, 1986.

Landwehr, William C., and Richard S. Field. *The Lithographs and Etchings of Philip Pearlstein* (exhibition catalogue). Springfield, Missouri: Springfield Art Museum, 1978.

"Lesley Dill, *Poem Dress: The Soul Selects Her Own Society* (1993)." *The Print Collector's Newsletter*, 25 (March-April 1994), p. 25.

"Lesley Dill, *A Word Made Flesh* (1994)." *The Print Collector's Newsletter*, 25 (July-August 1994), p. 106.

Lithographs from a New Workshop: Landfall Press (exhibition catalogue). Washington, D.C.: National Collection of Fine Arts, Smithsonian Institution, 1973.

Mahin, Bill. "Landfall Press Puts Emphasis on Artists." *Chicago Sun Times*, May 10, 1991.

98. Martha Erlebacher, *Shawl*, 1984, lithograph, printed in color, 23 X 20 (58.4 X 50.8)

"Martha Erlebacher, *Shawl* (1984)." *The Print Collector's Newsletter*, 15 (September-October 1984), p. 143.

"Martha Mayer Erlebacher, *Still Lifes 1978* (1978)." *The Print Collector's Newsletter*, 9 (September-October 1978), p. 122.

99. Pat Steir, *Wish #1*, 1974, lithograph, printed in color, 31 3/4 X 32 (80.6 X 81.3)

McCracken, David. "Words Speak Louder Than Images Alone." *Chicago Tribune*, May 10, 1991.

Moser, Joann. *The Landfall Press, 1970-1980* (exhibition catalogue). Washington, D.C.: United States International Communication Agency, 1981.

100. Philip Pearlstein, *Canyon de Chelly*, 1979, lithograph, printed in color, 28 X 22 1/2 (71.1 X 57.2)

"Pat Steir, *The Burial Mound Series* (1976)." *The Print Collector's Newsletter*, 7 (July-August 1976), p. 88.

"Pat Steir, *Wish #1, Wish #2—Breadfruit, Wish #3—Transformation* (1973)." *The Print Collector's Newsletter*, 5 (March-April 1974), p. 14.

Pernotto, Jim. *Chuck Close Editions: A Catalogue Raisonné and Exhibition* (exhibition catalogue). Youngstown, Ohio: The Butler Institute of American Art, 1989.

"Peter Dean, *Summer Interior* (1983)." *The Print Collector's Newsletter*, 15 (May-June 1984), p. 63.

"Philip Pearlstein, *Girl on Orange and Black Mexican Rug* (1973)." *The Print Collector's Newsletter*, 4 (January-February 1974), p. 141.

"Philip Pearlstein, *Mummy Cave: Canyon de Chelly* (1978-79)." *The Print Collector's Newsletter*, 10 (July-August 1979), p. 94.

"Philip Pearlstein, *Nude on Eames Stool* (1977)." *The Print Collector's Newsletter*, 8 (January-February 1978), p. 183.

"Philip Pearlstein, *Six Lithographs Drawn from Life*." *The Print Collector's Newsletter*, 1 (November-December 1970), p. 109.

Princethal, Nancy. "Good Vibrations: Ronald Jones' 'Petrarch's Air' and Multiples." *The Print Collector's Newsletter*, 25 (March-April 1994), pp. 1-5.

"Ravinia Sets Print, Sculpture Exhibits." *Chicago Daily News*, February 13-14, 1971.

"Robert Arneson, *General Nuke* (1986)." *The Print Collector's Newsletter*, 17 (May-June 1986), p. 58.

"Robert Arneson, *A Hollow Gesture, Pic, Up Against It* (1980)." *The Print Collector's Newsletter*, 12 (July-August 1981), p. 82.

"Robert Arneson, *Untitled* (1975)." *The Print Collector's Newsletter* 6 (July-August 1975), p. 72.

"Robert Cottingham, *Cottingham Suite* (1978)." *The Print Collector's Newsletter*, 9 (July-August 1978), p. 90.

"Robert Cottingham, *Ice* (1975)." *The Print Collector's Newsletter*, 7 (March-April 1976), p. 23.

"Roberto Juarez, *March Law* (1994)." *The Print Collector's Newsletter*, 25 (January-February 1995), p.225.

Schimmel, Paul, and Marcia Tucker. *American Narrative/Story Art, 1976-77* (exhibition catalogue). Houston: Contemporary Arts Museum, 1976.

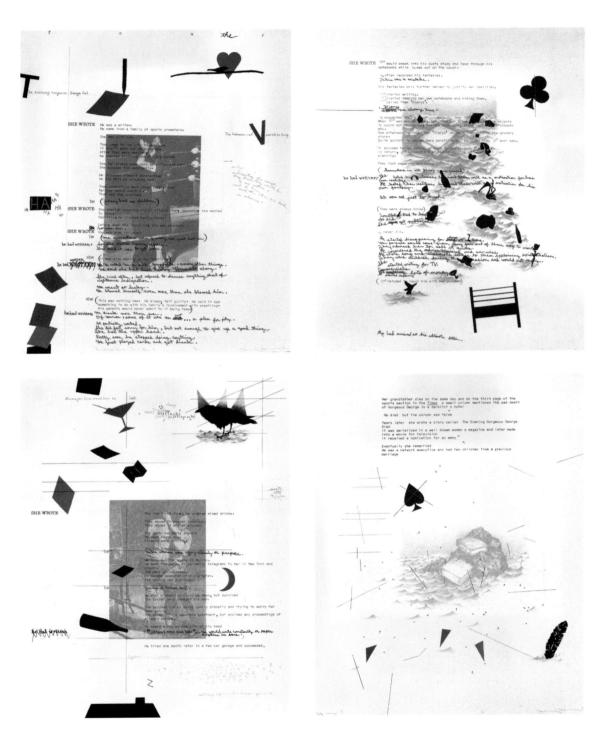

101. Terry Allen, *Debris from the Text*, 1981,
lithographs, printed in color, 30 1/4 X 23 1/2 (76.8 X 59.7) each
Top row, left to right: *R, I*;
Bottom row, left to right: *N, G*

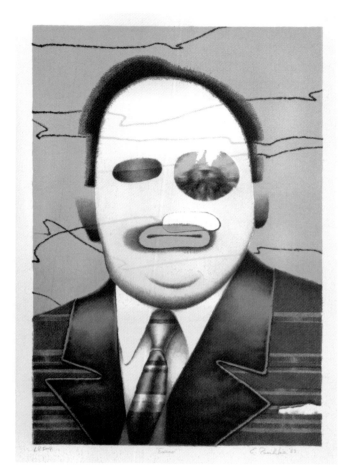

102. Ed Paschke, *Execo*, 1983, lithograph, printed in color, 34 1/4 X 24 (87 X 61). This print was included in Deborah Wye's exhibition catalogue, *Committed to Print*, 1988.

Schimmel, Paul, Michael Walls, and Dave Hickey. *Juarez Series: Terry Allen* (exhibition catalogue). Houston: Contemporary Arts Museum, 1975.

Schleifer, Kristen Brooke. "On View Chicago." *The New Art Examiner*, 21 (September 1993), pp. 27-28.

Schulze, Franz. "Landfall Press: 'Making Marks' in Chicago." *Art News*, 75 (September 1976), pp. 60-62.

_____. "Printmaking: In Praise of Stone and Ink." *Chicago Daily News*, July 10-11, 1971.

Shaman, Sanford Sivitz. *Contemporary Chicago Painters* (exhibition catalogue). Cedar Falls: University of Northern Iowa Gallery of Art, 1978.

Sheehan, Susan, with Poppy Gandler Orchier and Catherine Mennega. *Robert Indiana Prints: A Catalogue Raisonné, 1951-1991* (exhibition catalogue). New York: Susan Sheehan Gallery, 1991.

Sol LeWitt Graphics 1970-75 (exhibition catalogue). Basel: Kunsthalle Basel, 1975.

"Sol LeWitt, *Sixteen Lithographs: Black and White, Sixteen Lithographs: Color*." *The Print Collector's Newsletter*, 1 (January-February 1971), p. 132.

Sparks, Esther. *Jeanette Pasin Sloan, Graphics 1977-1986* (exhibition catalogue). Chicago: Landfall Press, 1986.

Sparks, Esther. "*Suite of Daze*: A Book of Etchings by William T. Wiley." *Bulletin of The Art Institute [of Chicago]*, 71 (September-October 1977), p. 8.

Spies, Werner. Jörg Schellmann and Joséphine Benecke, eds. *Christo: Prints and Objects, 1963-1987*. Translated by Nancy Grubb and Amy Handy. Munich: Edition Schellmann; New York: Abbeville Press, 1988.

Spies, Werner. Jörg Schellmann and Joséphine Benecke, eds. *Christo and Jeanne-Claude: Prints and Objects*. Translated by John Gabriel. Munich and New York: Edition Schellmann, 1995.

Stevens, Elizabeth. "The Graphics Boom: Craftsmen at Work." *The Wall Street Journal*, February 19, 1971.

Stone, Bob, "An Interview with Jack Lemon." *The Magazine of the Kansas City Art Institute* (Spring 1982), pp. 17-19.

Strand, Mark. *James McGarrell: The Quincy Inventions* (exhibition brochure). Quincy, Illinois: The Quincy Art Club, 1970.

Tallman, Susan. "Prints and Editions, Reproductive Acts." *Arts Magazine*, 64 (September 1989), pp. 21-22.

"Terry Allen, *Juarez* (1975-76)." *The Print Collector's Newsletter*, 7 (September-October 1976), p. 115.

"Tony Fitzpatrick, *My Snake Bitten Heart* (1993)." *The Print Collector's Newsletter*, 24 (July-August 1993), p. 108.

Tucker, Marcia, and Sherry Cromwell-Lacy. *Ring: Terry Allen* (exhibition catalogue). Kansas City, Missouri: The Nelson-Atkins Museum of Art, 1981.

"Vernon Fisher, *Dark Night Full of Stars* (1985)." *Art News*, 84 (October 1985), pp. 96-97.

"Vernon Fisher, *Genetic Variations/Natural Selections* (1983)." *The Print Collector's Newsletter*, 15 (March-April 1984), p. 25.

"Vito Acconci, *Stones for a Wall* (1977)." *The Print Collector's Newsletter*, 9 (September-October 1978), p. 120.

Wiley, William T. *Ships Log*. Chicago: Landfall Press, 1971.

Wiley, William T. *Suite of Daze*. Chicago: Landfall Press, 1977.

"William Allan, *Trout* (1973)." *The Print Collector's Newsletter*, 4 (September-October 1973), p. 85.

"William Wiley, *Coast Reverse* (1972)." *The Print Collector's Newsletter*, 3 (November-December 1972), p. 108.

William T. Wiley Graphics 1967-1979 (exhibition catalogue). Chicago: Landfall Press Gallery, 1980.

"William T. Wiley, *Once Upon a Time When All Is Flawless* (1982)." *The Print Collector's Newsletter*, 14 (July-August 1983), p. 106.

"William T. Wiley, *Suite of Daze* (1977)." *The Print Collector's Newsletter*, 8 (September-October 1977), p. 117.

"William T. Wiley, *Thank You Hide* (1972)." *The Print Collector's Newsletter*, 4 (May-June 1973), p. 38.

Witt, Linda. "The Lemons of Landfall Press: They'll Sacrifice Anything for Art But Their Family." *People*, October 27, 1975, pp. 66-69.

Wye, Deborah. *Committed to Print: Social and Political Themes in Recent American Printed Art* (exhibition catalogue). New York: The Museum of Modern Art, 1988.

_____. *Thinking Prints: Books to Billboards, 1980-95* (exhibition catalogue). New York: The Museum of Modern Art, 1996.

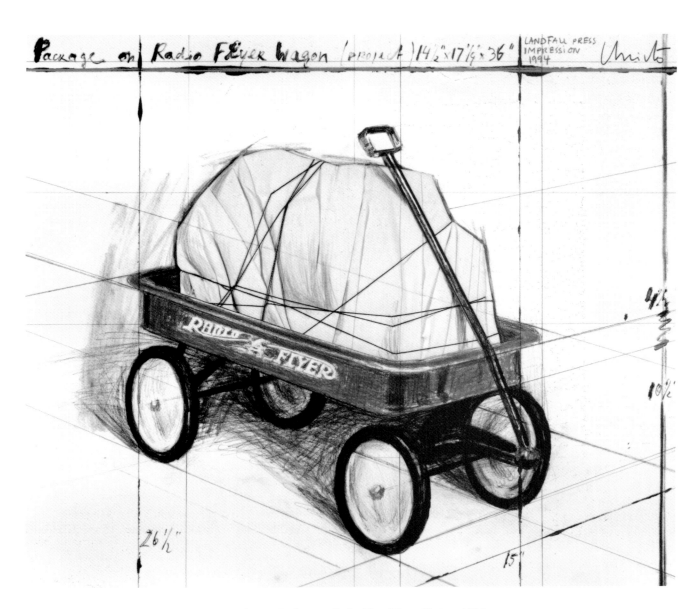

103. Christo, *Package on Radio Flyer Wagon/Project*, 1994,
lithograph and serigraph, printed in color, with collage, 19 3/8 X 22 (49.2 X 55.9)

EXHIBITION HISTORY

Following is a selected chronological listing of exhibitions specifically about Landfall Press, organized by Landfall Press (usually for the Chicago and/or New York galleries that the Press has operated over time, although periodically it has organized exhibitions for other venues), and exhibitions in which Landfall prints had a significant presence.

Publications accompanying exhibitions are so noted at the end of entries. Those that provide essential material or interpretations about the Press itself or its place in the recent history of printmaking are also included in the Selected Bibliography.

Every effort has been made to provide complete information for the exhibitions cited. However, due to the passage of time and the difficulty of locating certain records, some entries are incomplete.

1970
Quincy, Illinois, The Quincy Art Club, "James McGarrell: The Quincy Inventions," 1970 (brochure).

1971
Ravinia, Illinois, Casino Gallery, "Landfall Press," June 26-August 15, 1971 (brochure).

1972
Madison, Wisconsin, Madison Art Center, "Wonder Production Volume #1: A Magic Book by Ellen Lanyon," March 10-April 9, 1972 (brochure).

1973
Peoria, Illinois, Bradley University and The Peoria Art Guild, "Fourteenth Bradley National Print Show," March-April 1973 (brochure).

104. James McGarrell, *I*, from the portfolio *The Quincy Inventions*, 1970, lithograph, printed in color, 30 X 22 (76.2 X 55.9)

Smithsonian Institution Traveling Exhibitions Service, Washington, D.C. (organizer), "Lithographs from a New Workshop: Landfall Press." Traveled to: The Baltimore Museum of Art, June 20-July 15, 1973; Ella Sharp Museum, Jackson, Michigan, May 4-June 1, 1975.

The David and Alfred Smart Gallery, University of Chicago, "The Chicago Style: Prints," November 11-December 15, 1973 (catalogue).

THE LOST PLANET

105. H.C. Westermann, *The Lost Planet*, 1972, lithograph, printed in color, 25 X 33 1/8 (63.5 X 84.1). This print was included in the traveling exhibition "Lithographs from the Landfall Press," 1974

1974
Bruce Gallery, Edinboro University of Pennsylvania, "Second Edinboro Invitational Exhibition of Prints," March 19-April 5, 1974 (brochure).

Landfall Press, Chicago (organizer), "Lithographs from the Landfall Press." Traveled to: Center for the Visual Arts Gallery, Illinois State University, Normal, October 10-November 17, 1974; Joslyn Art Museum, Omaha, December 8, 1974-January 5, 1975; Davis Art Gallery, Stephens College, Columbia, Missouri, January 13-31, 1975; University of Nebraska Art Gallery, Omaha, February 10-28, 1975; The Haggerty Art Center, University of Dallas, Irving, Texas, March 4-21, 1975; Ball State Museum of Art, Muncie, Indiana, October 1-31, 1975; Kalamazoo Institute of Arts, Michigan, November 4-30, 1975; Wright Museum of Art, Beloit College, Beloit, Wisconsin, December 2-31, 1975; Scheaffer Gallery, Grinnell College, Grinnell, Iowa, January 30-February 19, 1976; Marvin Cohn Gallery, Coe College, Cedar Rapids, Iowa, February 23-March 26, 1976; Madison Art Center, Wisconsin, May 3-31, 1976; Albrecht Art Museum, St. Joseph, Missouri, June 2-30, 1976.

1975
University of South Dakota Print Making Department, Vermillion. "Exhibition and Symposium of Prints and Printmakers," March 1-30, 1975 (brochure).

106. Garo Antreasian (left) and Jack Lemon demonstrating printing technique at the March 1975 symposium sponsored by the University of South Dakota Print Making Department, "Exhibition and Symposium of Prints and Printmakers."

107. Robert Cottingham, *Carl's*, 1977, etching and aquatint, 17 1/8 X 17 3/8 (43.5 X 44.1)

Davidson Art Center, Wesleyan University, Middletown, Connecticut, "Recent American Etching," October 10-November 23, 1975. Traveled to: National Collection of Fine Arts, Smithsonian Institution, Washington, D.C., January 21-March 27, 1976; and various locations abroad during the Bicentennial year.

Rubicon Gallery, Los Altos, California, "Philip Pearlstein Lithographs," November 10-December 7, 1975.

1976
The Contemporary Gallery, Dallas, "Philip Pearlstein," March-May 1976.

Charlotte Crosby Kemper Gallery, Kansas City Art Institute, Missouri, "Lithographs and Etchings from the Landfall Press," September 1-30, 1976.

The Brooklyn Museum, New York, "Thirty Years of American Printmaking," November 20, 1976-January 30, 1977 (catalogue).

1977
Landfall Press Gallery, Chicago, "Robert Cottingham," 1977.

University of Wisconsin Art Gallery, University of Wisconsin–Lacrosse, "Contemporary American Graphics," February-March 1977.

Allan Frumkin Gallery, New York and Chicago, "William T. Wiley," March-April 1977.

108. Philip Pearlstein, *Girl on Empire Sofa*, 1971, lithograph, printed in color, 32 1/4 X 24 (81.9 X 61). This print was included in the exhibition "Landfall Press," 1977.

Marion Locks Gallery, Philadelphia, "Philip Pearlstein," April-May 1977.

The Art Institute of Chicago, "*Suite of Daze:* A Book of Etchings by William T. Wiley," September 6-October 6, 1977.

Landfall Press Gallery, Chicago, "Philip Pearlstein," September-October 1977.

Museum of Contemporary Art, Chicago, "Landfall Press: A Survey of Prints (1970-1977)," November 18, 1977-January 8, 1978 (brochure).

1978
Landfall Press Gallery, Chicago, "Pasin Sloan," 1978.

Annmary Brown Memorial Gallery, Brown University, Providence, Rhode Island, "Group Exhibition," January-February 1978.

Ball State University Museum of Art, Muncie, Indiana, "William T. Wiley, *Suite of Daze,*" February 1-26, 1978.

Springfield Art Museum, Springfield, Missouri, "The Lithographs and Etchings of Philip Pearlstein," February 25-March 26, 1978 (catalogue).

The New Harmony Gallery of Contemporary Art, New Harmony, Indiana, "Prints from Landfall Press," June 4-July 7, 1978.

G.W. Einstein Gallery, New York, "New Editions From Landfall Press, Inc.," November 11-December 9, 1978.

The Baltimore Museum of Art, "William T. Wiley: Prints," November 28, 1978-February 4, 1979.

1979
Landfall Press Gallery, Chicago, "Group Exhibition," 1979.

Landfall Press Gallery, Chicago, "Robert Cottingham," 1979.

Aspen Center for the Visual Arts, Colorado, "William T. Wiley and Alfred Leslie," June-August 1979.

Springfield Art Museum, Springfield, Missouri, "William T. Wiley," October-November 1979.

United States International Communications Agency (organizer), "Print Publishing in America," October 1979-October 1980. Traveled to: Alexandria, Egypt; Tel Aviv, Israel; Paris, France.

1980
Landfall Press Gallery, Chicago, "William T. Wiley Graphics, 1967-1979," 1980 (catalogue).

Museum of Contemporary Art, Chicago, "Vito Acconci: A Retrospective: 1969 to 1980," 1980.

109. William T. Wiley, *Ecnud*, 1975, lithograph, printed in color, 23 X 29 (58.4 X 73.7)

The David and Alfred Smart Gallery, University of Chicago, "Master Prints from Landfall Press," March 13-April 27, 1980 (brochure).

Walker Art Center, Minneapolis, "Artist and Printer," December 7, 1980-January 18, 1981. Traveled to: Sarah Campbell Blaffer Gallery, University of Houston, February 22-April 5, 1981.

Malinda Wyatt Gallery, Venice, California, "Works from Landfall Press," December 1980-January 1981.

1981
Trisolini Gallery of Ohio University, Athens, "Contemporary Prints from Landfall Press," January 13-February 7, 1981. Traveled to: Stone Press Gallery, Seattle, March-April 1981 (brochure).

United States International Communications Agency (organizer), "The Landfall Press, 1970-1980." Traveled to: Bhirasri Institute of Modern Art, Bangkok, Thailand, March 3-17, 1981; Binational Center (AUA), Bangkok, Thailand, March 17-April 1, 1981; Osaka, Japan, April 6-19, 1981; Fukuoka City Museum of Art, Fukuoka, Japan, April 24-May 7, 1981; Hokkaido Museum of Art, Sapporo, Japan, May 11-24, 1981; Fukui Prefectural Museum, Fukui, Japan, May 29-June 12, 1981; Tottori Prefectural Museum, Tottori, Japan, June 15-29, 1981; Tokyo American Center, July 6-21, 1981; Singapore National Museum of Art Gallery, September 25-October 12, 1981; Thomas Jefferson Cultural Center, Manila, October 17-December 15, 1981; Jakarta, Indonesia, January 15-May 1982; Seoul, South Korea, September-November, 1982; Australia, January-February 1983 (catalogue).

Fox Graphics Gallery, Boston, "Selected Prints Published by Landfall Press," March-April 1981.

1982
George Schelling, Signet Fine Arts, St. Louis, Missouri, "William T. Wiley Prints," February 1982.

Landfall Press Gallery, Chicago, "Woodcuts '82," September 10-25, 1982.

Landfall Press Gallery, Chicago, "Stanley Singleton: Recent Paintings," October 1-November 13, 1982.

Landfall Press Gallery, Chicago, "Jim Dine: Prints," December 1-January 8, 1983 (catalogue).

110. Robert Arneson, *Squint*, 1981, lithograph, printed in color, 40 1/4 X 30 (102.2 X 76.2)

1983

Landfall Press Gallery, Chicago, "Robert Arneson: Masks and Portraits," 1983 (catalogue).

Quay Gallery, San Francisco, "Jack Lemon and the Landfall Press: An Exhibition of Prints by Ten Contemporary Artists," January 4-29, 1983. Traveled to: Mackenzie Art Gallery, University of Regina, Saskatchewan, February 11-March 6, 1983; Moody Gallery, Houston, March 25-April 16, 1983; Tower Park Gallery, Peoria Heights, Illinois, July 9-September 4, 1983.

Theodore Lyman Wright Art Center, Beloit College, Beloit, Wisconsin, "Robert Arneson: Lithographs and Sculptures," August 10-October 10, 1983. Traveled to: Saginaw Art Museum, Michigan, December 18, 1983-January 15, 1984.

1984

Springfield Art Museum, Springfield, Missouri, "Robert Arneson: Masks and Portraits, 1983-1984," February 5-March 14, 1984. Traveled to: Arts Signature in the Performing Arts Center Gallery, Tulsa, March 16-April 16, 1984; Gallery Karl Oskar, Shawnee Mission, Kansas, April 17-May 28, 1984; The Snite Museum of Art, University of Notre Dame, South Bend, Indiana, September 28-October 26, 1984; Ball State University Museum of Art, Muncie, Indiana, November 11-December 16, 1984 (catalogue).

1985

Goshen College Art Gallery, Goshen, Indiana, "Landfall Press Publications," 1985.

University Art Museum, University of New Mexico, Albuquerque, "Fifty Artists/Fifty Painters," February 2-March 24, 1985 (catalogue).

Swan Parson Gallery, Northern Illinois University, DeKalb, Illinois,"The Atelier in America: A Collaboration Between Printer and Artist," November 17-December 15, 1985 (catalogue).

1986

Landfall Press Gallery, Chicago, "Jeanette Pasin Sloan, Graphics 1977-1986," 1986 (catalogue).

The Art Institute of Chicago, "Landfall Press Publications," July 16, 1986-January 1987.

Trisolini Gallery of Ohio University, Athens, Ohio, "Works on Paper," September 15-October 11, 1986 (brochure).

Springfield Art Museum, Springfield, Missouri, "Robert Cottingham: A Print Retrospective, 1972-1986," September 28-October 29, 1986. Traveled to: Hunter Museum of Art, Chattanooga, Tennessee, November 30, 1986-February 1, 1987; The Nelson-Atkins Museum of Art, Kansas City, Missouri, March 1-April 12, 1987; Spiva Art Center, Joplin, Missouri, June 7-July 6, 1987; Museum of Art, University of Oklahoma, Norman, August 23-September 27, 1987; Cedar Rapids Museum of Art, Iowa, October 25-December 31, 1987 (catalogue).

1987

Landfall Press Gallery, New York, "Group Exhibition," 1987.

David Winton Bell Gallery, Brown University, Providence, Rhode Island, "Pulled and Pressed: Contemporary Prints and Multiples," September 12-October 25, 1987 (catalogue).

The David and Alfred Smart Gallery, University of Chicago, "The Chicago Imagist Print: Ten Artists' Works, 1958-1987," October 6-December 6, 1987 (catalogue).

111. Robert Cottingham, *Barrera-Rosa's*, 1986, linocut, printed in color, 22 1/2 X 46 (57.2 X 116.8)

1988

The Museum of Modern Art, New York, "Committed to Print: Social and Political Themes in Recent American Printed Art," January 31-April 19, 1988 (catalogue).

Musée d'Art et d'Histoire, Geneva, "Pat Steir," June 30-September 18, 1988. Traveled to: The Tate Gallery, London, November 14, 1988-February 12, 1989 (catalogue).

Landfall Press Gallery, Chicago and New York, "Christo: Prints 1971-1988 from Landfall Press," September 25-November 12, 1988.

Landfall Press Gallery, Chicago and New York, "Words in Print," December 2, 1988-January 28, 1989 (brochure).

1989

San Antonio Art Institute, "Prints from Landfall Press," January-February 1989.

Landfall Press Gallery, Chicago and New York, "Prints by Sculptors," February 17-April 28, 1989.

Landfall Press Gallery, Chicago and New York, "Perspectives in Realism," April 28-May 26, 1989.

Walker Art Center, Minneapolis, "First Impressions: Early Prints by Forty-Six Contemporary Artists," June 4-September 10, 1989. Traveled to: Laguna Gloria Art Museum, Austin, Texas, December 2, 1989-January 21, 1990; The Baltimore Museum of Art, February 25-April 22, 1990; Neuberger Museum of Art, State University of New York at Purchase, June 21-September 16, 1990 (catalogue).

The Butler Institute of American Art, Youngstown, Ohio, "Chuck Close Editions," September 17-November 26, 1989 (catalogue).

Landfall Press Gallery, Chicago and New York, "William T. Wiley: A Decade of Prints, Lithographs, Etchings, Woodcuts and Monoprints," October 13-December 1, 1989.

Landfall Press Gallery, Chicago, "Chicago Painters in Print," December 1, 1989-January 19, 1990.

Landfall Press Gallery, New York, "Vernon Fisher, Navigating by the Stars," December 1, 1989-January 19, 1990 (brochure).

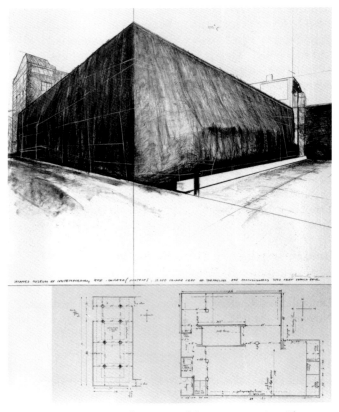

112. Christo, *Wrapped Museum of Contemporary Art, Chicago (Project)*, 1972, lithograph, printed in color, 41 7/8 X 32 (106.4 X 81.3)

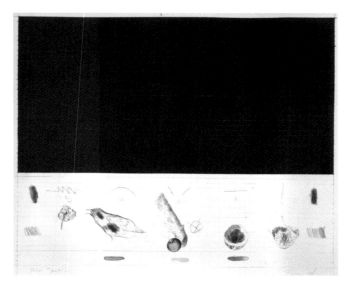

113. Pat Steir, *Between the Lines*, 1974, lithograph, printed in color, 27 1/4 X 32 (69.2 X 81.3). This print was included in the traveling exhibition "First Impressions," 1989.

1990

Landfall Press Gallery, Chicago, "Chicago Painters in Print," 1990.

The Tyler Museum of Art, Texas, "Prints by William T. Wiley," January-April 8, 1990.

Independent Curators Incorporated, New York (organizer), "Contemporary Illustrated Books: Word and Image, 1967-1988." Traveled to: Franklin Furnace Archive, Inc., New York, January 12-February 28, 1990; The Nelson-Atkins Museum of Art, Kansas City, Missouri, April 5-June 3, 1990; The University of Iowa Museum of Art, Iowa City, February 8-April 7, 1991 (catalogue).

Landfall Press Gallery, New York, "Vito Acconci: Graphic Retrospective, 1970-1990," January 26-March 6, 1990.

Landfall Press Gallery, Chicago, "Politics in Print," January 26-March 6, 1990.

Landfall Press Gallery, Chicago and New York, "Twenty Years of Landfall Press," September 7-October 31, 1990.

Landfall Press Gallery, Chicago, "Paschke Prints: 1971-1990," November 2, 1990-January 5, 1991.

Landfall Press Gallery, New York, "Realism Re-Examined," November 15, 1990-January 5, 1991.

1991

Landfall Press Gallery, New York, "Dennis Oppenheim in Print: A Retrospective of Early Graphic Works and New Editions," January 19-March 30, 1991.

Landfall Press Gallery, Chicago, "Group Show: Beckman, Brown, Buck, Bulatov, Christo, Dwyer, Lostutter, Oppenheim, Pasin Sloan, Ruppersberg, Twaddle, Venet," January 19-February 15, 1991.

Landfall Press Gallery, New York, "New Editions," April 26-May 31, 1991.

Landfall Press Gallery, Chicago, "Two Texans: Vernon Fisher and Randy Twaddle," April 26-May 31, 1991.

The Federal Reserve Bank of Chicago, "Landfall Press: A Survey of the First Twenty Years," May 1-June 12, 1991.

Landfall Press Gallery, New York, "Christo Graphics: 1971-1991," opened October 8, 1991.

1992

Landfall Press Gallery, New York, "Tony Fitzpatrick and 'Angry up the Blood': An Illustrated Book of Poetry and Selected Etchings," March 14-April 30, 1992.

Lorenzo Rodriguez Gallery, Chicago, in conjunction with Landfall Press, "New Etchings, Tony Fitzpatrick," April 10-May 9, 1992.

Landfall Press Gallery, New York, "Five Artists," Winter 1992.

114. Eric Bulatov, *New York*, 1989, lithograph, printed in color, 30 X 22 (76.2 X 55.9)

115. Tony Fitzpatrick, *Crow House*, 1992, hard-ground etching, soft-ground etching, and aquatint, with chine collé, 7 7/8 X 7 7/8 (20 X 20), 14 X 14 (35.6 X 35.6)

1993

The Fine Arts Museums of San Francisco, "John Buck: Woodblock Prints," October 16, 1993-February 27, 1994 (catalogue).

1994

Kansas City Gallery of Art, University of Missouri, Kansas City, "Vito Acconci: A Graphic Retrospective," February 4-March 11, 1994.

1995

Mary and Leigh Block Gallery, Northwestern University, Evanston, Illinois, "Printmaking in America: Collaborative Prints and Presses, 1960- 1990," September 22-December 3, 1995. Traveled to: The Jane Voorhees Zimmerli Art Museum, Rutgers University, New Brunswick, New Jersey, April 23-June 18, 1995; The Museum of Fine Arts, Houston, January 23-April 2, 1996; National Museum of American Art, Smithsonian Institution, Washington, D.C., May 10-August 4, 1996.

The Art Institute of Chicago, "Landfall Press 25th Anniversary Exhibition," November 29, 1995-March 5, 1996.

1996

The Museum of Modern Art, New York, "Thinking Prints: Books to Billboards, 1980-95," June 20-September 10, 1996 (catalogue).

PLATES

All the works reproduced in the color plate section will be exhibited at the Milwaukee Art Museum. There will be a slight variation in the exhibited works at the other venues.

Captions for the plates appear in short form; full data is given in the listing of exhibited works, beginning on page 204. The works are arranged alphabetically by artist, then chronologically within the sequence for the artist.

1. Vito Acconci

Stones for a Wall, 1977,
lithographs

Top row, left to right: *Approved—Now the Stones Will Stand One More Day*; *Approved—Sometimes You Can Get Blood from a Stone (When There's a Dream of Radicalism)*; *Approved—There's Always Another Secret Behind the Wall*;
Approved—You Know Where You Are, You Sucker; *Approved—We Try to Go Deeper (They Told us to Shape)*;
Bottom row, left to right: *Approved—After All, They Told Us to Form*; *Approved—But Don't Be Fooled, This Is a Message from the American Lover*; *Approved—They Told Us to Build (And We Hit Rock Bottom)*; *Approved—Finally, It's Blowing Up in My Hands*;
Approved—Let the Grass Go Over, Let the Sky Come Through

105

2. William G. Allan

Tamales, from the *Landfall Press Etching Portfolio,* 1975,
etching and aquatint

106

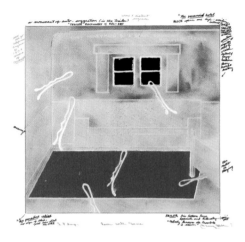

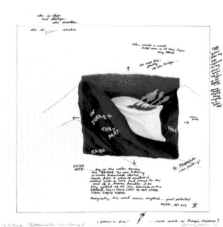

3. Terry Allen
Juarez Suite, 1976,
lithographs
Top row, left to right: *Pillow in the Mountains*; *Room with Horns*; *Bed with Heart*;
Bottom row, left to right: *Bed with Ditch*; *Ditch with Heart*; *Pillow in the Mountains II*

107

4. Robert Arneson
Cherry Pie, 1975,
lithograph

108

PLATES

5. Robert Arneson
Brick, from the *Brick Suite*, 1976,
terracotta

109

PP 2   ARNESON...

6. Robert Arneson
Up Against It, 1980,
lithograph

110

7. Robert Arneson
The Colonel's At It Again, 1987,
lithograph

111

PLATES

8. Don Baum
Domus, 1992,
lithograph

9. Phyllis Bramson

The Eroticism of Seeing and *A Flash of Spiritual Meaning* (diptych), 1981,
lithograph

113

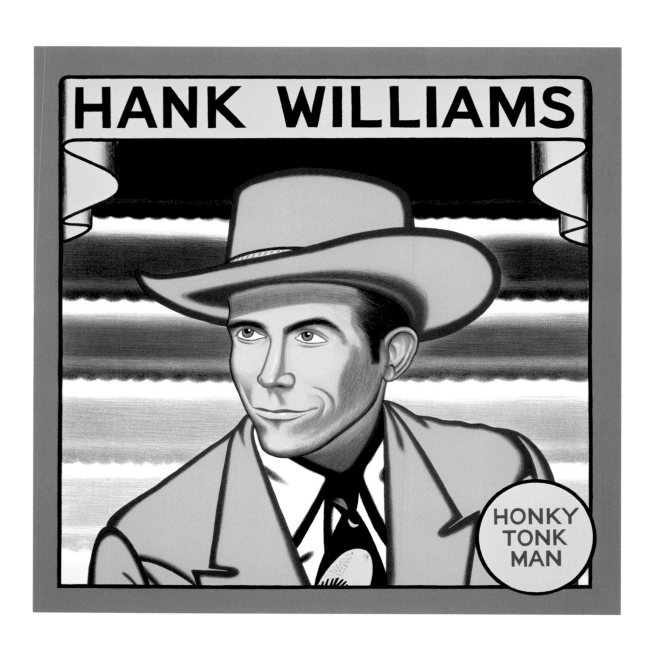

10. Roger Brown

Hank Williams, Honky Tonk Man, 1991,
lithograph

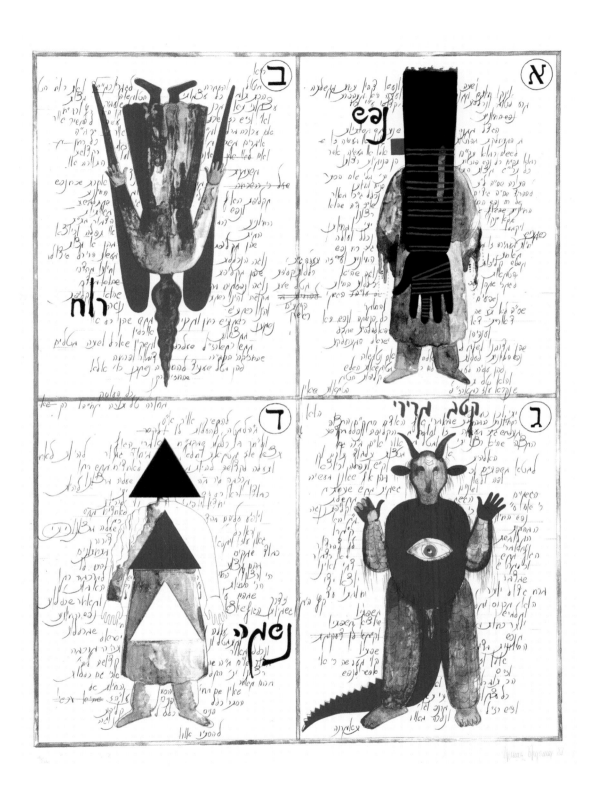

11. Grisha Bruskin

Untitled, 1988,
lithograph

115

PLATES

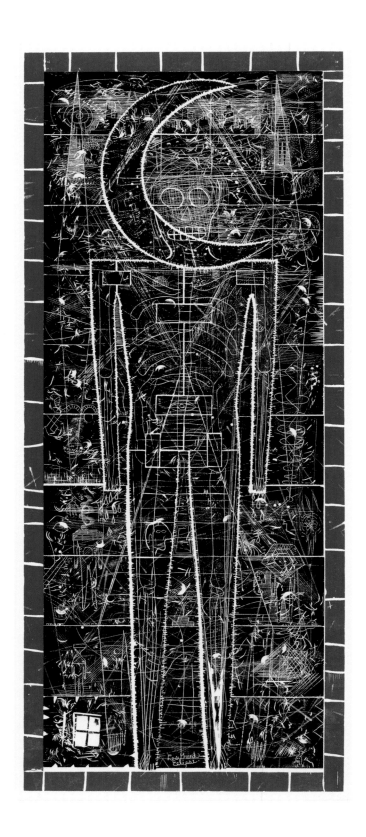

12. John Buck
Untitled (La Grand Eclipse), 1982,
woodcut

116

PLATES

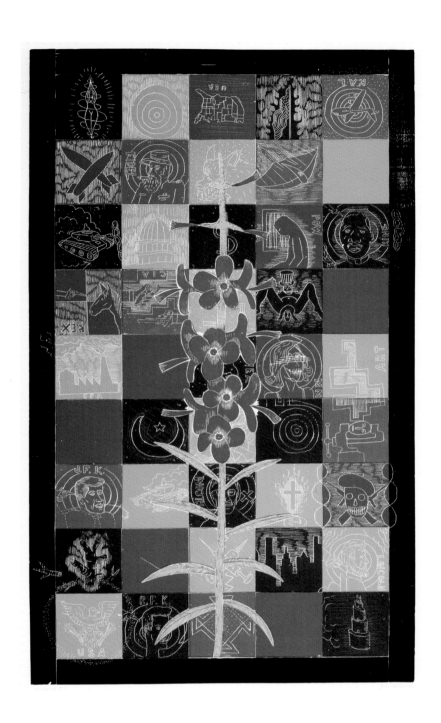

13. John Buck
Fireweed, 1991,
woodcut

117

PLATES

14. Dan Christensen
Untitled, 1972,
lithograph

118

PLATES

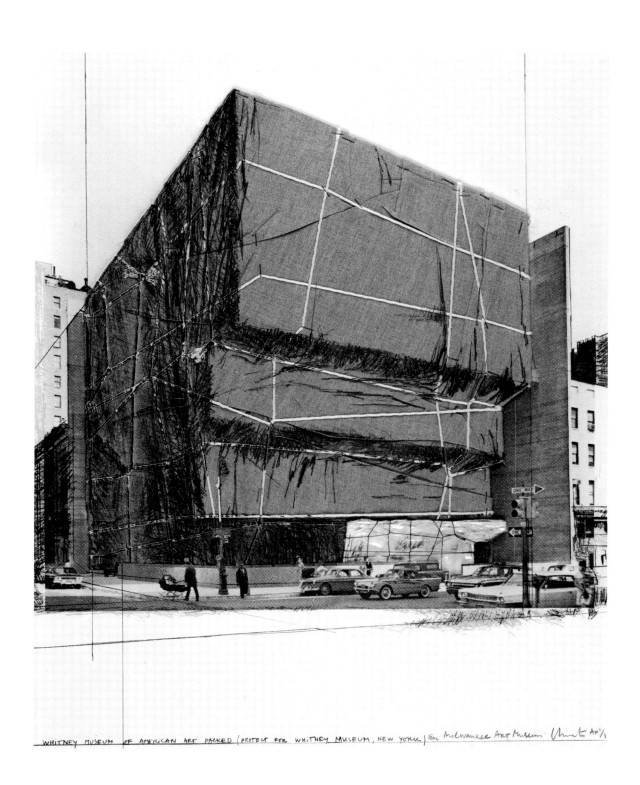

WHITNEY MUSEUM OF AMERICAN ART PACKED (PRITECT FOR WHITNEY MUSEUM, NEW YORK) FOR Milwaukee Art Museum Christo Ap'1

15. Christo
The Whitney Museum, New York, Packed, from the portfolio *(Some) Not Realized Projects,* 1971, lithograph, with collage

119

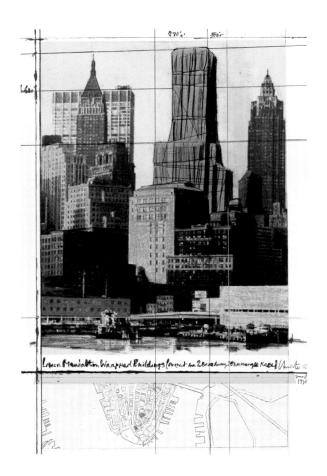

16, 17. Christo
Left: *Wrapped Venus, Villa Borghese, 1963,* from the *Landfall Press Etching Portfolio,* 1975,
etching, with collage
Right: *Lower Manhattan Wrapped Buildings, Project for 2 Broadway, 20 Exchange Place,* 1990,
lithograph, with collage

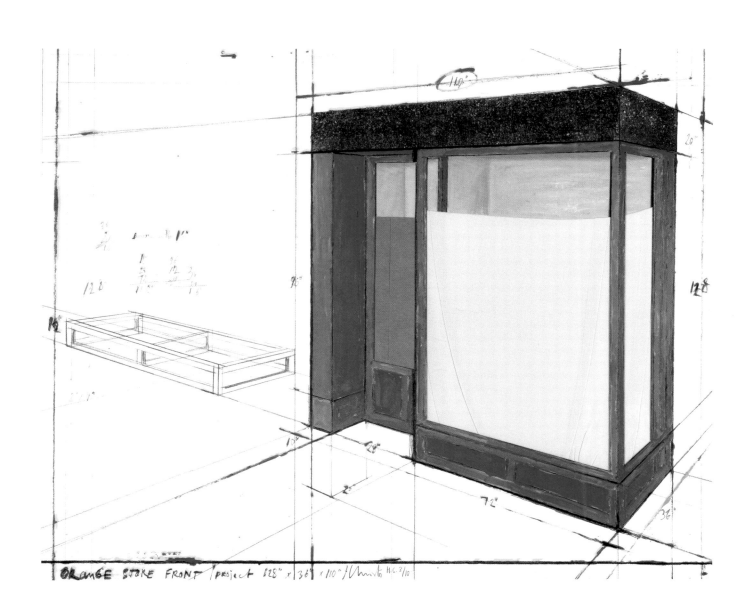

ORANGE STORE FRONT / Project 128" x 36" x 110" / Christo H.C. 2/10

18. Christo
Orange Store Front, Project, 1991,
lithograph, with collage

121

19. Robert Cottingham
Fox, 1973,
lithograph

122

20. Robert Cottingham
Art, 1992,
lithograph

21. Jack Cowin
Future Considerations, 1986,
lithograph

22. Peter Dean
Hear No Evil, 1984,
lithograph

125

PLATES

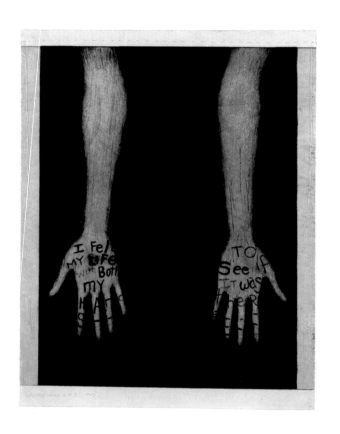

23. Lesley Dill
A Word Made Flesh, 1995,
lithograph and etching
Left: *Arms;*
Right: *Back*

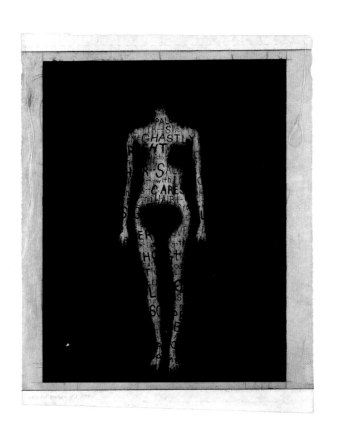 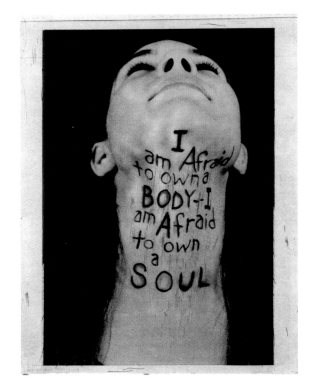

24. Lesley Dill
A Word Made Flesh, 1995,
lithograph and etching
Left: *Front;*
Right: *Throat*

25. Jim Dine
The Red Bandana, 1974,
lithograph

128

26. Jim Dine
The Yellow Robe, 1980,
lithograph

129

27. Nancy Dwyer
Mayhem, 1991,
lithograph

28. Nancy Dwyer
Out of My Mind, 1991,
lithograph

29. Martha Erlebacher
Still Life #2, 1978,
lithograph

132

PLATES

30. Vernon Fisher

Composition in Red, White, and Blue, 1985,
lithograph

133

31. Vernon Fisher
Perdido en el mar, 1989,
lithograph

134

32. Vernon Fisher
Rules for Bending Circles, 1993,
lithograph

135

33. Charles Gaines
Color Regression #2, 1980,
lithograph

136

PLATES

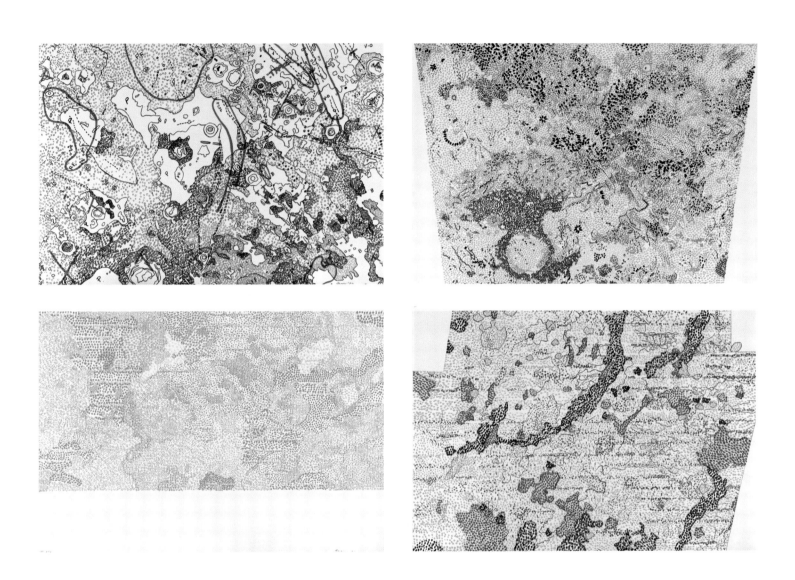

34. Nancy Graves
Lunar Maps, 1972,
lithographs
Top row, left to right: *IV ("Julius Caesar Quadrangle of the Moon")*; *V ("Montes Appenninus Region of the Moon")*;
Bottom row, left to right: *VI ("Maskelyne DA Region of the Moon")*; *VII ("Sabine D Region of the Moon,*
Lunar Orbiter Site IIP-6 Southwest Mare Tranquilitatis")

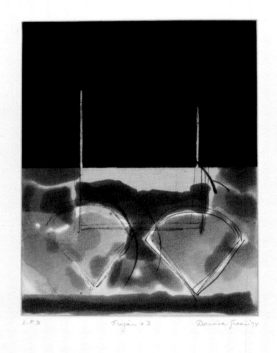

35, 37. Denise Green
1994
etching and aquatint, with chine collé
Top: *Trojan #1*;
Bottom: *Trojan #3*

138

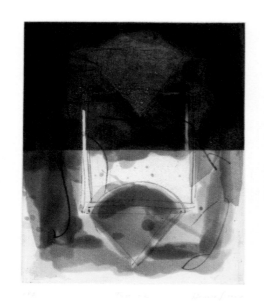

36, 38. Denise Green
1994,
etching and aquatint, with chine collé
Top: *Trojan #2*;
Bottom: *Trojan #4*

139

39. Richard Hull
Change, 1986,
lithograph

140

PLATES

40. Luis Jiménez

Bronco (Horse) and *Bronco (Cowboy)* (diptych), 1978,
lithograph

141

41. Luis Jiménez
Honky Tonk, 1981,
lithograph, with gold glitter

42, 43. Ronald Jones

1990, woodcuts

Left: *Untitled (This "collapse board"…was designed for a male body…)*;
Right: *Untitled (This "collapse board"…was designed for a female body…)*

44. Roberto Juarez
March Law, 1994,
etching and aquatint, with chine collé

45. Peter Julian
Untitled (diptych), 1982,
lithograph

145

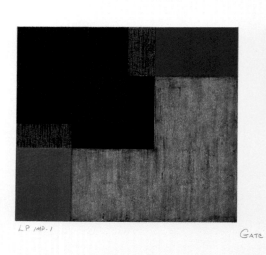

LP IMP-1   Gate

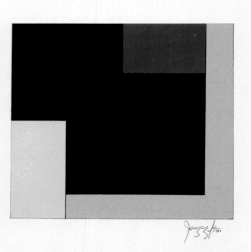

46. James Juszczyk
Gate, 1980,
lithograph

146

PLATES

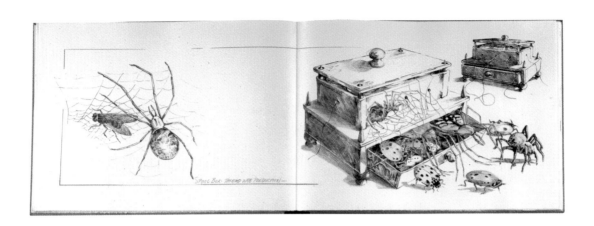

47. Ellen Lanyon
Wonder Book, 1971,
book of lithographs, with colored pencil and hand lettering

48. Sol LeWitt
Lines of One Inch, Four Directions, Four Colors (Set of 16), 1971,
lithographs

148

PLATES

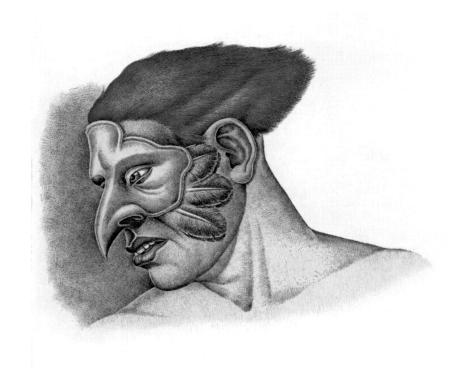

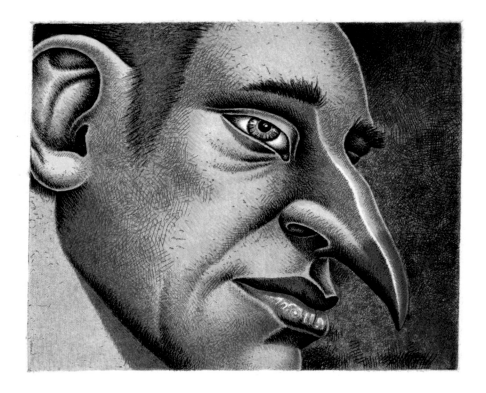

49, 50. Robert Lostutter
Top: *Ross' Turaco Looking Back*, 1988,
etching
Bottom: *Green Oropendola*, 1989,
etching

149

PLATES

51, 52. Marilyn Minter
1989, serigraphs
Top: *Hands Dumping*;
Bottom: *Hands Folding*

53. Marilyn Minter
Hands Washing, 1989,
serigraph

151

PLATES

54. Greg Murdock
State of Grace, 1993,
etching and aquatint, with chine collé

152

55. Don Nice

Double Sneaker, 1975,
lithograph

153

PLATES

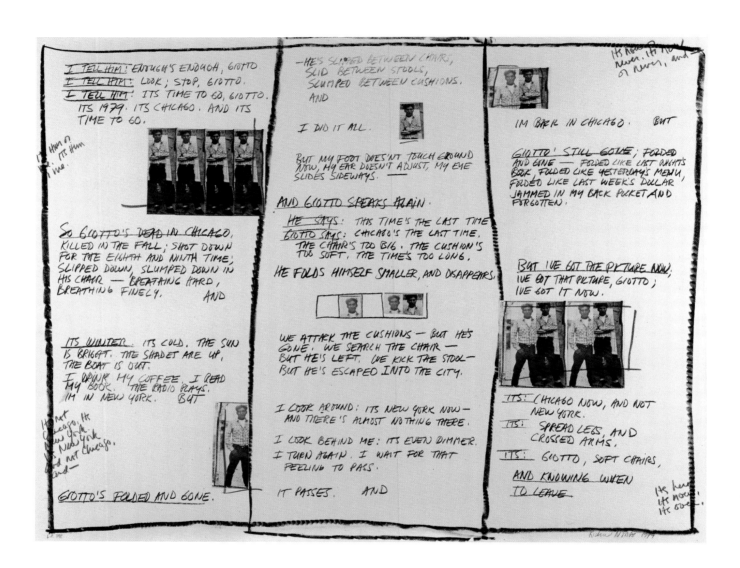

56. Richard Nonas
Giotto, 1980,
lithograph, with china marker and collage

154

PLATES

57. Claes Oldenburg
Store Window: Bow, Hats, Heart, Shirt, 29¢, 1973,
lithograph

155

58. Claes Oldenburg
Picasso Cufflink, 1974,
lithograph

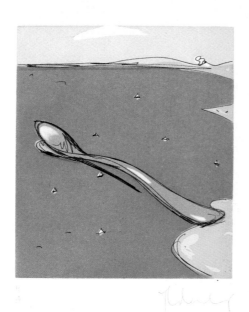

59. Claes Oldenburg
Spoon Pier, from the *Landfall Press Etching Portfolio*, 1975,
soft-ground etching, aquatint, and sugar-lift etching

60. Ed Paschke

Hairy Shoes, 1971,
lithograph

158

PLATES

61, 62. Ed Paschke
Top: *Fem-Verde*, 1987,
lithograph
Bottom: *Poderosa*, 1991,
lithograph

159

63. Philip Pearlstein

Figure Lying on Rug, from the portfolio *Six Lithographs Drawn from Life,* 1970,
lithograph

64. Philip Pearlstein

Girl on Orange and Black Mexican Rug, 1973,
lithograph

161

PLATES

65. Philip Pearlstein

Nude on Iron Bench, from the *Landfall Press Etching Portfolio,* 1975,
lift-ground etching and aquatint

66. Philip Pearlstein
Two Nudes on Blue Coverlet, 1977,
lithograph

67. Joseph Piccillo
Edge Event III, 1982,
lithograph

164

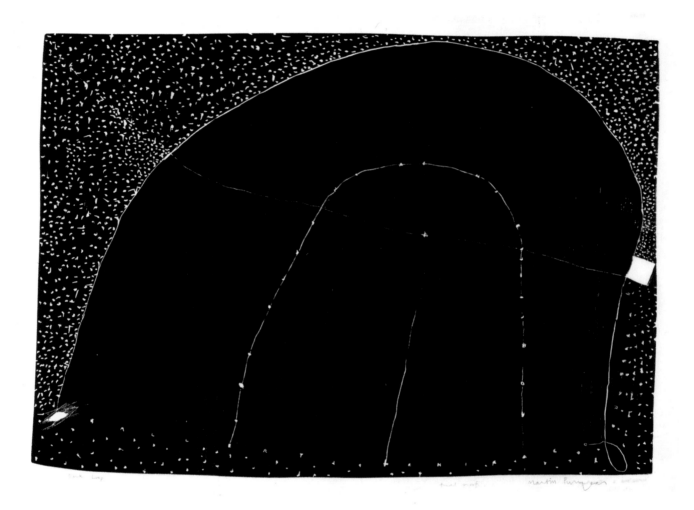

68. Martin Puryear
Dark Loop, 1982,
woodcut

165

PLATES

69. Allen Ruppersberg
Preview Suite, 1988,
lithographs
Top row, left to right: *It's Not Art (That Counts Now); Are You Crying?; What Should I Do?; Nostalgia 24 Hours a Day; Good Luck!;*
Bottom row, left to right: *Nothing-Nobody; Everything Is Over; Adults Only Please; No I've Got Something in My Eye; Who's Afraid of the New Now?*

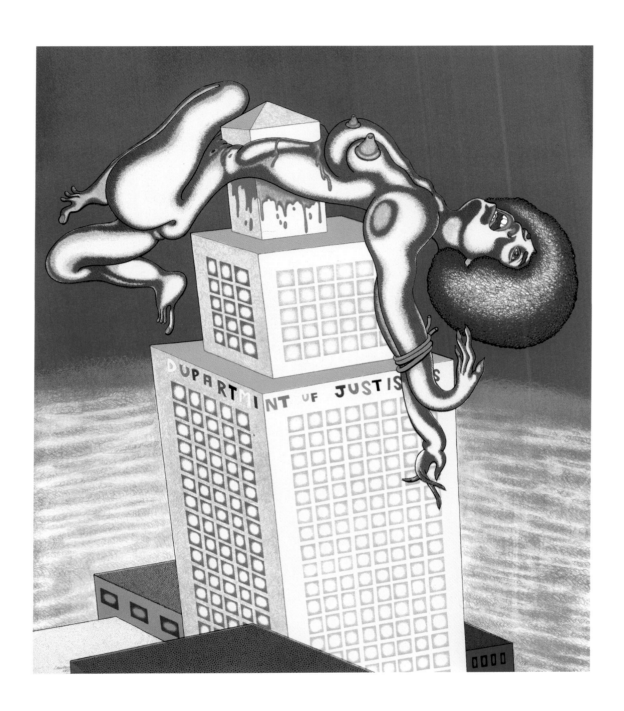

70. Peter Saul
Angela Davis, 1972,
lithograph

167

PLATES

71. Peter Saul
Politics, 1985,
lithograph

168

PLATES

72. Kenneth Showell
Terni, 1970,
lithograph

73. Jeanette Pasin Sloan
Jeanette Pasin Sloan, 1986,
Top row, left to right: *Binary*, hard-ground etching and aquatint; *Boston Red*, woodcut;
Bottom row, left to right: *Sergeant First Class*, lithograph; *Sergeant First Class—State I*, lithograph

170

74. T.L. Solien
Bad Blood, 1984,
lithograph and woodcut

171

75. Pat Steir
Roll Me a Rainbow, 1974,
lithograph

172

76. Randy Twaddle
Extended Orbits (diptych), 1989,
lithograph

173

PLATES

77. Jack Tworkov
*L-SF-ES #1,*1978,
hard-ground etching and aquatint

174

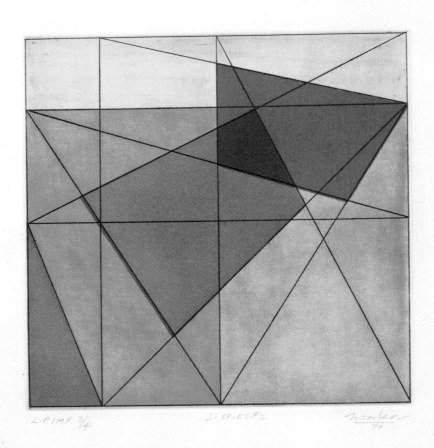

L.P.IMP. 3/4   L-SF-ES#2   tworkov
                                              78

78. Jack Tworkov
L-SF-ES #2, 1978,
hard-ground etching and aquatint

175

79. Jack Tworkov
*L-SF-ES #3,*1978,
hard-ground etching and aquatint

176

PLATES

80. Tom Uttech
Kasakogwog, 1990,
lithograph

177

PLATES

81. Bernar Venet

Two Undetermined Lines, 1990,
lithograph

178

PLATES

82. H.C. Westermann

An Affair in the Islands, 1972,
lithograph

179

83. H.C. Westermann
Death Ship in a Port, 1972,
lithograph

Landfall Press Imp.   H.C. Westermann

84. H.C. Westermann
Holiday Inn, 1972,
lithograph

181

PLATES

85. William T. Wiley
Thank You Hide, 1972,
lithograph

86. William T. Wiley

Seasonall Gate, from the *Landfall Press Etching Portfolio*, 1975,
lithograph and hard-ground etching

183

PLATES

87. William T. Wiley
Mr. Unatural, 1976,
lithograph

88, 89. William T. Wiley
1977,
soft-ground etching and aquatint
Top: *Green Shoes—State I*;
Bottom: *Green Shoes—State II*

185

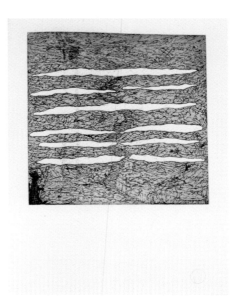

90. William T. Wiley
Suite of Daze, 1977,
book of 14 etchings

186

PLATES

91. William T. Wiley

Once Upon a Time When All Is Flawless, 1982,
lithograph

187

PLATES

92. Karl Wirsum
Skull Daze, 1971,
lithograph

93. Karl Wirsum

Blue Burger Quartet à la Carte…(pie in the sky not included), 1994,
lithograph

189

ARTISTS' BIOGRAPHIES

Following are brief biographies of the artists included in the Landfall Press exhibition. Whenever possible, photographs of them working at Landfall, or examples of their prints, have been included.

116. Deborah Ripley, director of the New York branch of the Landfall Press Gallery, discussing a sheet from *Wav(er)ing Flag* with Vito Acconci during his Landfall exhibition, 1990.

VITO ACCONCI
Born in 1940 in the Bronx, New York, Acconci earned a BA from Holy Cross College, Worcester, Massachusetts, and an MFA from the University of Iowa. His first solo exhibition was held at the Rhode Island School of Design in 1969.

Acconci investigates the psychological and political aspects of Western culture. A renowned Conceptual and Performance artist, he works in a variety of media, including photography, video, and printmaking. He created two sets of lithographs at Landfall Press, the first in 1977 and the second in 1990.

WILLIAM G. ALLAN
Born in Everett, Washington, in 1936, Allan received a BFA from the San Francisco Art Institute, where he subsequently taught from 1967 to 1969. Solo exhibitions of his work were held at the San Francisco Art Institute in 1970 and the Whitney Museum of American Art in 1974.

Allan worked at Landfall Press in 1973 and 1975, where he created several prints notable for their meticulous drawing and realism.

TERRY ALLEN
Born in Wichita, Kansas, in 1943, Allen received a BFA from the Chouinard Art Institute in Los Angeles. He has worked since 1960 in a wide variety of media, including painting, sculpture, film and video, theater, poetry, and music.

Allen has also been interested in the graphic arts, and has worked at Landfall Press on several occasions since 1972. These works, such as the *Juarez Suite* (1976), which consists of six lithographs and a sound recording, treats several of Allen's recurring themes: politics, subculture, and gender.

ROBERT ARNESON

Born in Benicia, California, in 1930, Arneson earned a BFA from the College of Arts and Crafts, and an MFA from Mills College, both in Oakland. His first solo exhibition was held in 1960 at The Oakland Art Museum. He worked primarily in California until his death in 1992.

Arneson's first publication with Landfall Press was the lithograph *Cherry Pie* (1975), followed by *Brick*, a ceramic multiple produced in his Benicia studio in 1976. From 1975 to 1987, he created a number of lithographs and etchings with Jack Lemon.

117. Robert Arneson, *Son of Sam*, 1981, lithograph, printed in color, 38 1/4 X 28 (97.2 X 71.1)

DON BAUM

Born in Escanaba, Michigan, in 1922, Baum attended Michigan State College; the School of The Art Institute of Chicago; the School of Design, Chicago; and the University of Chicago. He mounted his first solo exhibition in 1957. He currently lives, works, and teaches in Chicago.

Baum created a three-dimensional multiple, entitled *Domus*, at Landfall Press in 1992. Similar to his unique sculptures, this work addresses several of his favorite themes: religion, ritual, and memory.

WILLIAM BECKMAN

Born on a Minnesota farm in 1942, Beckman earned an MFA from the University of Iowa.

Beckman's self-portrait lithographs executed at Landfall Press in 1988 typify his straightforward sensibility. Stripped of incidental detail, these works are confrontational and address the issues of gender, role playing, and control.

PHYLLIS BRAMSON

Born in Madison, Wisconsin, in 1941, Bramson attended a summer session at Yale University on a Yale/Norfolk Art Scholarship in 1962, earned a BA from the University of Illinois, an MA from the University of Wisconsin, and an MFA from the School of The Art Institute of Chicago. She was included in the 1990 Landfall Press exhibition "Chicago Painters in Print," and currently teaches at the University of Illinois, Chicago.

Bramson's theatrical paintings and prints, including lithographs and woodcuts produced at Landfall in 1981 and 1984, explore the themes of desire and seduction.

ROGER BROWN

Born in Hamilton, Alabama, in 1941, Brown attended the American Academy of Art, Chicago, and later received a BFA and an MFA from the School of The Art Institute of Chicago. He had a major solo exhibition at the Hirshhorn Museum and Sculpture Garden, Washington, D.C., in 1987.

Brown's whimsical, yet unsettling Chicago Imagist paintings and prints comment on politics and popular culture. Prints are an important part of Brown's oeuvre. He has worked in a variety of media, including intaglio, lithography, and serigraphy, and has produced several prints at Landfall Press periodically from the 1970s to the 1990s.

118. Roger Brown, *Family Tree Mourning Print*, 1987, woodcut, printed in color, 10 13/16 X 13 13/16 (27.5 X 35.1)

119. Grisha Bruskin working on his lithograph *Untitled*, 1989, in the West 18th Street shop.

GRISHA BRUSKIN

Russian artist Grisha Bruskin was born in Moscow in 1942, and trained at the Art Department of the Moscow Textile Institute. His first solo show in the West was in 1990 at Marlborough Gallery, New York. Bruskin currently lives and works in New York.

Primarily a painter, Bruskin has produced one lithograph at Landfall Press. His work deals with human social systems and the ways in which they structure people's lives.

JOHN BUCK

Born in Ames, Iowa, in 1946, Buck attended the Kansas City Art Institute, the Skowhegan School of Painting and Sculpture in Maine, and earned an MFA from the University of California, Davis. He currently teaches sculpture at Montana State University.

Buck regularly began making prints in the early 1980s after a trip to central China, where he saw craftsmen making immense rubbings from stone tablets. His initial professional venture into printmaking occurred at Landfall Press in 1982, and he has returned from time to time to make large-scale woodcuts.

120. John Buck, *Green River*, 1984, woodcut, printed in color, 43 1/4 X 60 (109.9 X 152.4)

DAN CHRISTENSEN

Born in Nebraska in 1942, Christensen earned a BFA from the Kansas City Art Institute. He received a Guggenheim Fellowship in 1969.

Christensen was an early collaborator at Landfall Press. He returned in 1980 to produce several monotypes, and again two years later to work in lithography.

CHRISTO

Christo Javacheff was born in Gabrovo, Bulgaria, in 1935. He attended the Fine Arts Academy, Sofia, from 1951 to 1956, followed by training in theater design in Prague and a semester of study at the Fine Arts Academy, Vienna.

Christo funds his major, public installations through the sale of graphic editions, many of which have been printed by Landfall Press. The collaged prints produced by Landfall depict projects for wrapping objects and buildings throughout Europe and the United States.

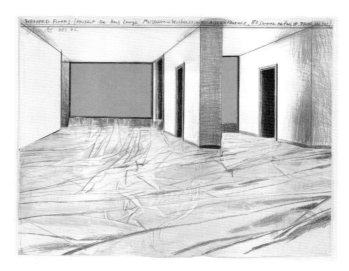

121. Christo, *Wrapped Floors/Project for the Hans Lange Museum*, 1983, lithograph, printed in color, with collage, 22 1/4 X 27 7/8 (56.5 X 70.8)

CHUCK CLOSE

Born in Monroe, Washington, in 1940, Close was educated at the University of Washington and Yale University. He currently lives and works in New York.

Close is a methodical artist interested in stretching the technical limits of traditional printmaking processes. He made his first print, a mezzotint, at Crown Point Press in 1972, and produced several lithographs at Landfall Press in 1975.

ROBERT COTTINGHAM

Born in Brooklyn, New York, in 1935, Cottingham was educated at Brooklyn's Pratt Institute from 1959 to 1963. He mounted his first solo exhibition in 1968 at Molly Barnes Gallery, Los Angeles.

In 1972, Cottingham was invited to contribute a lithograph (his first print) to a portfolio published by Shorewood Press. That same year, Jack Lemon brought him to Landfall Press, where he has continued to work periodically to the present.

123. Peter Dean, *Summer Interior*, 1984, lithograph, printed in color, 24 1/4 X 38 1/8 (61.6 X 96.8)

PETER DEAN

Dean was born in Berlin in 1934. His family fled Nazi Germany and immigrated to the United States in 1938. Dean studied at Cornell University and the University of Wisconsin, where he received his BS in geology. He turned to painting by the mid-1960s when his expressionist, figurative canvases began to attract attention. Dean died of Lou Gehrig's disease in 1993.

Although Dean initially felt that his thickly painted imagery did not translate well into print, Jack Lemon encouraged him to successfully make lithographs at Landfall Press in 1984.

LESLEY DILL

Born in Bronxville, New York, in 1950, Dill attended Skidmore College and Trinity College, Hartford, and earned a BA in English. Subsequently, she earned an MA in art education from Smith College and an MFA from the Maryland Institute, Baltimore. Her first solo exhibition was in 1983.

Dill is a figurative artist who uses sculpture and printmaking to explore the human experience. She first began to work at Landfall Press in 1992 and continues to make collaged editions there that draw on her interests in the poetry of Emily Dickinson as well as clothing and the body as metaphors of cloaking and revealing.

122. Robert Cottingham catching up on his reading in the West Ontario Street shop, 1974.

JACK COWIN

Born in Indianapolis in 1947, Cowin earned a BFA in printmaking from Indiana University and an MFA in printmaking and painting from the University of Illinois. He currently teaches at the University of Regina, Saskatchewan.

Cowin first began to work at Landfall Press in 1983. He notes that Jack Lemon encouraged him to work in a larger scale and credits Lemon with stimulating his career as a printmaker.

JIM DINE

Born in Cincinnati in 1935, Dine earned a BFA from Ohio University. His first solo exhibition was held at the Reuben Gallery, New York, in 1960, and his first retrospective was presented at the Whitney Museum of American Art in 1970.

After moving to New York in 1958, Dine came into contact with a number of innovators, such as performance artist Alan Kaprow and sculptor Claes Oldenburg. In the 1960s, Dine began to work extensively in printmaking, and has since worked with master printers throughout Europe and the United States, including Jack Lemon. Landfall Press printed several of Dine's editions, which were published by Pace Editions and Petersburg Press.

NANCY DWYER

Born in New York in 1954, Dwyer received her BFA from the State University of New York, Buffalo. She has been the recipient of many awards including the National Endowment for the Arts Fellowship in 1982.

Dwyer uses words and images derived from television, advertising, and electronic media in her paintings, sculptures, and graphics. In 1991, she created two prints at Landfall Press based on earlier paintings.

MARTHA ERLEBACHER

Born in New Jersey in 1937, Erlebacher received her MFA from Pratt Institute, Brooklyn, New York. Although first trained in Abstract Expressionism, she subsequently turned to the art of the Italian Renaissance for inspiration for her carefully delineated nudes and still lifes.

Although Erlebacher has a much wider reputation as a painter, she also works in lithography, and has worked at Landfall Press on several occasions in the 1970s and 1980s.

VERNON FISHER

Born in Fort Worth, Texas, in 1958, Fisher was educated at Hardin-Simmons University, Abilene, Texas, and the University of Illinois. He currently teaches at North Texas State University in Denton.

Fisher combines drawing, painting, photography, sculpture, and text to create non-sequential narratives inspired by Pop art and Southern literary traditions. Landfall Press has published a collection of Fisher's short stories, *Navigating by the Stars*, as well as a number of his lithographs from 1983 to the present.

124. Vernon Fisher, *Dark Night Full of Stars*, 1985, lithograph, printed in color, 30 X 33 5/8 (76.2 X 85.4)

TONY FITZPATRICK

Born in Chicago in 1958, Fitzpatrick is a former prizefighter, poet, occasional movie actor, and self-taught artist. From 1990 to 1994, he operated the World Tattoo Gallery in Chicago, and co-founded Big Cat Press in the same city in 1992.

Fitzpatrick's bleak and iconic drawings, prints, and paintings on slate are influenced by Haitian artistic sources and reveal the darker aspects of American culture. Landfall has published some two dozen of his etchings.

125. Tony Fitzpatrick, *My Snakebit Heart*, 1993, hard-ground etching, soft-ground etching, spit-bite etching, aquatint, printed in color, with chine collé, 10 7/8 X 8 1/2 (27.6 X 21.6), 17 3/8 X 14 7/8 (44.1 X 37.8)

CHARLES GAINES

Born in 1944, Gaines earned an MFA from the Rochester Institute of Technology, and currently lives and works in California.

He employed a mathematical process he had outlined in his 1978 book, *Regression Series Drawing*, to create a series of three lithographs at Landfall Press in 1980.

NANCY GRAVES

Born in Pittsfield, Massachusetts, in 1940, Graves received a BA from Vassar College, and a BFA and MFA from Yale University. Her first solo exhibition was in 1964. The Fort Worth Art Museum organized a retrospective of her work in 1987. She died in 1995.

Although primarily a sculptor, Graves was engaged in painting, printmaking, film, and stage design. In 1972, when she had momentarily turned from sculpture to two-dimensional media, Jack Lemon invited her to work at Landfall Press. This was her first experience with lithography since her days at Yale, as well as her first venture working with a fine-arts press.

126. Denise Green, *Circle Invaded by a Square*, 1982, lithograph, printed in color, 36 X 36 1/8 (91.4 X 91.8)

DENISE GREEN

Born in Melbourne, Australia, in 1946, Green studied at the École des Beaux-Arts, Paris, and Hunter College in New York. Through the work of Mark Rothko and Robert Motherwell, she was inspired to express emotion and spirituality through abstraction. Green currently lives and works in New York.

Green first went to Landfall Press in 1981. Although she has subsequently worked at several university printshops, Landfall Press continues to serve as her primary printmaking venue.

RICHARD HULL

Born in Oklahoma City in 1955, Hull studied at the Kansas City Art Institute, Skowhegan School of Painting and Sculpture, Maine, and the School of The Art Institute of Chicago. His first solo exhibition was held in 1979.

Hull's etchings, lithographs, and monoprints, produced at Landfall Press from 1986 to 1993, are noted for their vigorous, gestural marks similar in nature to those found in the prints of California artist William T. Wiley, another frequent collaborator at Landfall Press.

127. Richard Hunt in the West Ontario Street shop drawing on a lithographic stone for his 1971 *Ravinia Print*.

RICHARD HUNT

Born in Chicago in 1935, Hunt earned a BAE from the School of The Art Institute of Chicago and was awarded a Guggenheim Fellowship in 1962-63. Hunt lives, works, and teaches in Chicago. He has received numerous public sculpture commissions throughout the country.

Primarily a sculptor, Hunt has made several lithographs at Landfall Press. These dynamic organic compositions closely resemble his work in three dimensions.

128. Luis Jiménez, *Rodeo Queen*, 1981, lithograph, printed in color, with glitter, 42 3/4 X 29 (108.6 X 73.7).

LUIS JIMÉNEZ

Born in El Paso in 1940, Jiménez attended the University of Texas at El Paso and the University of Texas at Austin. After three months in Mexico City, he moved to New York, where he had his first solo exhibition in 1969. He currently lives and works in New Mexico.

Jiménez makes drawings and prints to develop ideas for monumental sculpture. Jack Lemon has invited him to Landfall Press on several occasions, beginning in 1978. The combination of Jiménez's vigorous draftsmanship and Landfall's rich printing have resulted in many notable lithographs.

RONALD JONES

Born in Falls Church, Virginia, in 1952, Jones earned a BFA from Huntington College, Alabama; an MFA from the University of South Carolina; and a PhD from Ohio University. A resident of New York, he is an artist, educator, and writer.

Jones works primarily in sculpture, but uses such diverse media as computers and opera to express his social and political ideas. He created his first print, a facsimile of an international identity card, in 1987. Three years later, he made two woodcuts at Landfall Press. These seemingly straightforward abstract compositions take on a strongly disquieting nature when one realizes that their compositions were derived from "collapse boards" used to restrain prisoners during execution.

129. Ronald Jones signing the edition of one of his 1990 woodcuts in the curating room in the West 18th Street shop (see Pls. 42, 43).

ROBERTO JUAREZ

Born in Chicago in 1952, Juarez received a BFA from the San Francisco Art Institute. He has had solo exhibitions at the André Emmerich Gallery, Zurich, the San Francisco Art Institute, the Robert Miller Gallery, New York, among other venues.

Juarez is primarily a painter, but has made one intaglio and several monoprints at Landfall Press.

PETER JULIAN

Born in 1952, Julian received a BFA from Southern Methodist University, Dallas, and currently lives and works in New York.

Julian is primarily a painter, but has made a lithographic diptych at Landfall Press. The intense color and bold brushwork of these images are characteristic of his Neo-Expressionist canvases.

JAMES JUSZCZYK

Born in Chicago in 1943, Juszczyk was educated at the University of Illinois, the Cleveland Institute of Art, and the University of Pennsylvania. His first solo exhibition was held in 1970.

Juszczyk produced three prints at Landfall Press in 1980. These works, like his paintings, explore variations on simple geometric, spatial, and chromatic relationships.

LEONARD KOSCIANSKI

Born in Cleveland, Ohio in 1952, Koscianski received his BFA from the Cleveland Institute of Art in 1977. He received his MFA in 1979 from the University of California, Davis.

Koscianski is now an adjunct member of the faculty of Towson State University, Baltimore. He has completed four lithographs and several monoprints at Landfall Press. His prints focus on the basic animal forces found in nature, presenting them in beautiful yet violent aspects.

ELLEN LANYON

Born in 1926, Lanyon was educated at the School of The Art Institute of Chicago and the University of Iowa. She began exhibiting in 1945.

Due to an allergy to turpentine, Lanyon stopped oil painting in the late 1960s and turned for a time almost exclusively to drawing and printmaking. She worked on several occasions at Landfall Press from 1971 to 1985. In these prints and other work, Lanyon explored several themes: transformation, magic, dreams and myths, and collective memory.

131. Alfred Leslie (right) watching Jack Lemon roll out a flat spread of ink on a lithograph stone in the West Ontario Street shop, 1974.

ALFRED LESLIE

Born in the Bronx, New York, in 1927, Leslie studied at New York University, Pratt Institute, and the Art Students League. His first exhibition was held at the Tibor de Nagy Gallery, New York, in 1951. He currently lives and works in New York.

Leslie created two series of lithographs at Landfall Press in the mid-1970s. The three male portraits, including one of himself, which he executed in 1974 are typical of his confrontational, full-face paintings of the period. The second group, depicting his wife, Connie, nursing, are more intimate, yet retain much of the expressive intensity of the earlier works.

130. Ellen Lanyon working on her *Wonder Book*, published 1971, in the West Ontario Street Shop. In the background, Jack Lemon confers with James McGarrell (right), on a print from McGarrell's portfolio, *The Quincy Inventions*, published 1970.

132. Sol LeWitt (left) and Jack Lemon conferring in the second floor curating room in the West Ontario Street shop, 1971 (see Pl. 48).

SOL LeWITT

Born in Hartford, Connecticut, in 1928, LeWitt earned a BFA from Syracuse University. His first solo exhibition was held at the Daniels Gallery in New York in 1965. He currently lives and works in Connecticut.

A pioneer in the Conceptual art movement, LeWitt has created prints in a variety of media, at a number of printshops, including two large series of lithographs at Landfall Press in 1971.

DAVID LIGARE

Born in Oak Park, Illinois, in 1945, Ligare was educated at the Art Center College of Design in Los Angeles. His first solo exhibition was held in 1970.

Since he visited Greece at the age of eighteen, classical art and mythology have had a major impact on Ligare's painting and printmaking. He works in a highly realistic style and is especially interested in the effects of brilliant sunlight.

ROBERT LOSTUTTER

Born in Kansas in 1939, Lostutter studied at the School of The Art Institute of Chicago. He currently lives and works in Chicago.

Lostutter has made prints at Landfall Press on several occasions since 1974. Described as "emotional realism," these works are fantastic bird-man portraits with an underlying eroticism and ambiguity.

MARILYN MINTER

Born in Shreveport, Louisiana, in 1948, Minter was educated at the University of Florida and Syracuse University. Her first solo exhibition was in 1975.

A painter in the tradition of Pop art, Minter treats popular culture with a distinctively feminist twist. Her imagery, culled from advertising and mass media, calls into question social issues, such as the perceived roles of men and women in society. Minter explored this theme in three serigraphs Landfall Press published in 1989. These works were printed commercially in Chicago on metal plates and constitute one of the three print series Minter has produced.

GREG MURDOCK

Born in Saskatoon, Saskatchewan, in 1954, Murdock earned a BFA from the University of Saskatchewan in 1977, attended the Instituto Allende, San Miguel de Allende, Mexico, in 1977-78, and graduated with honors from Emily Carr College of Art and Design, Vancouver, in 1981. He has had solo exhibitions of his drawings and sculptures at the Littlejohn-Smith Gallery, New York, and the Equinox Gallery, Vancouver.

In 1993, Jack Lemon invited Murdock to work at Landfall Press to make two intaglio prints.

DON NICE

Born in California in 1932, Nice received his MFA from Yale University. He was dean of the School of Visual Arts, New York, from 1964 to 1966. He has designed posters for several festivals held at Lincoln Center for the Performing Arts, New York, and created a mural for the 1980 Olympic games in Moscow.

Nice has worked at Landfall Press on several occasions, beginning in 1975, when he made *Double Sneaker*, a playful lithographic image characteristic of his Pop-inspired paintings.

RICHARD NONAS

Born in New York in 1936, Nonas studied literature and cultural anthropology at Columbia University, the University of North Carolina, and the University of Michigan. After working as an anthropologist for ten years, Nonas turned to sculpture.

Nonas produced one print with Jack Lemon in 1979. This work, entitled *Giotto*, combines photographic imagery with poetry and brings together his artistic and academic interests.

133. Claes Oldenburg in the artist's work room in the West Ontario Street shop drawing on a lithographic stone for *Coffee Cup*, 1973.

134. Dennis Oppenheim working on his lithograph *Study for Revolving Kissing Racks* in the West 18th Street shop, 1991.

CLAES OLDENBURG

Born in Stockholm in 1929, Oldenburg moved to the United States as an infant. He attended Yale University and the School of The Art Institute of Chicago. His first solo exhibition was held in 1959 at the Cooper Union Museum Library, New York.

Oldenburg is famous for his playful, monumental sculptures of such common objects as typewriter erasers, electrical plugs, and lipstick tubes. Many of his proposed projects, however, have been realized only in drawings and prints.

A consummate draftsman, Oldenburg produced several lithographs at Landfall Press from 1972 to 1976. Two, *Picasso Cufflink* (1974) and *Bat Spinning* (1975), refer to two of Chicago's most prominent public sculptures, Picasso's giant head in the Daley Center plaza and Oldenburg's own sculpture for the Social Security Administration building.

DENNIS OPPENHEIM

Born in Electric City, Washington, in 1938, Oppenheim earned a BFA at the School of Arts and Crafts, Oakland, and an MFA at Stanford University. His first retrospective was held at the Museum Boymans-van Beuningen, Rotterdam, in 1976.

Many of Oppenheim's conceptually based works are ephemeral performances and temporary installations. To give permanence to his ideas, Oppenheim has turned to printmaking, and has worked with Jack Lemon on several occasions from 1968 to 1992.

ED PASCHKE

Born in Chicago in 1938, Paschke earned a BFA and MFA from the School of The Art Institute of Chicago. His first solo exhibition was held at the Richard deMarco Gallery in Edinburgh, in 1973. Paschke currently teaches at Northwestern University, Evanston, Illinois.

A noted Chicago Imagist painter and printmaker, Paschke has created many prints at Landfall Press since 1971. Derived from imagery on television and advertising, these works use symbols, masks, and personae to comment, often cynically, on American politics, business, and culture.

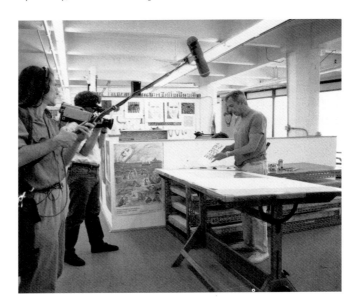

135. Ed Paschke in the West 18th Street shop discussing his technique for a film crew, c. 1989.

136. Philip Pearlstein signing the edition of his lithograph *Girl on Iron Bench*, 1974, with Landfall Curator Carol Plummer assisting, in the West Ontario Street shop.

PHILIP PEARLSTEIN

Born in Pittsburgh in 1924, Pearlstein earned a BFA from the Carnegie Institute of Technology and an MA from the Institute of Fine Arts, New York University, in 1955. In 1972, he became a full professor of art at Brooklyn College.

Pearlstein refers to himself as a "Post-Abstract Realist." He worked extensively at Landfall Press from 1970 to 1982. These lithographic nude studies are complex, patterned compositions of figure and setting.

JOSEPH PICCILLO

Born in Buffalo, New York, in 1941, Piccillo earned an MA in art education from State University College, New Paltz, New York, and has received several SUNY research fellowships.

Piccillo is a painter noted for his powerful images of galloping horses. He created several lithographs of this subject at Landfall Press in 1982 and 1993.

MARTIN PURYEAR

Born in Washington, D.C., in 1941, Puryear studied biology and art at the Catholic University of America, Washington, D.C. He then went to Sierra Leone with the Peace Corps, where he was introduced to traditional African woodworking techniques. His interest in woodworking was furthered at the Swedish Royal Academy of Art, Stockholm, where he studied printmaking and sculpture. He earned an MFA in sculpture at Yale University in 1971 and had his first one-person exhibition the following year.

Puryear has made one print, *Dark Loop*, 1982, with Jack Lemon. This woodcut is suggestive of Puryear's organic, abstract sculptures fabricated from wood, rope, animal skins, and other natural materials.

BARBARA ROSSI

Born in Chicago in 1940, Rossi joined a convent for a time after graduating from high school. She subsequently earned a BFA from St. Xavier College and an MFA from the School of The Art Institute of Chicago in 1970, where she currently teaches.

Rossi, who gained recognition as a Chicago Imagist in the 1960s, is an accomplished printmaker. She pulls her own intaglios (a medium at which she excels), but made use of Landfall Press in the early 1970s for the production of lithographs.

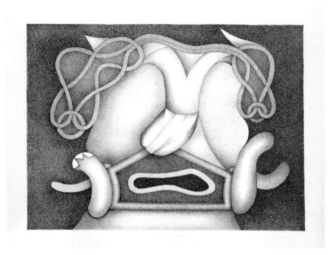

137. Barbara Rossi, *Footprint Picture*, 1975, lithograph, 18 1/8 X 24 (46 X 61)

ALLEN RUPPERSBERG

Born in Cleveland in 1944, Ruppersberg earned a BFA from the Chouinard Institute, Los Angeles. His first solo exhibition was held at the Eugenia Butler Gallery, Los Angeles, in 1969. He currently lives and works in New York and Los Angeles.

Ruppersberg is a Conceptual artist who juxtaposes familiar images, such as snapshots and postcards, and narrative texts, either of his own invention or appropriated from literature, to point out their complex and often ambiguous meanings. In 1988, Jack Lemon invited Ruppersberg to create a suite of ten lithographs based on an earlier installation piece.

PETER SAUL

Born in San Francisco in 1934, Saul attended Washington University, St. Louis; the California School of Fine Arts, San Francisco; and Stanford University. Saul's first retrospective was held at the Madison Art Center, Wisconsin, in 1980-81. He currently lives in Austin, Texas.

Saul's savage satires of American politics and culture have lampooned subjects ranging from to Ronald Reagan to Davy Crockett. He produced several lithographs at Landfall Press in 1972 and 1985.

KENNETH SHOWELL

Born in Huron, South Dakota, in 1939, Showell earned a BFA from the Kansas City Art Institute and an MFA from Indiana University. He currently lives and works in New York.

A Color Field painter, Showell created two lithographs at Landfall Press in 1970.

JEANNETTE PASIN SLOAN

Born in Chicago in 1946, Pasin Sloan began her academic career as an art history major at Marymount College, Tarrytown, New York. While a mother at home, she became interested in painting and subsequently decided to study art at the University of Chicago, where she graduated with an MFA in graphic arts. Her first solo exhibition was held at Northeastern Illinois University in 1975. Pasin Sloan currently lives in River Forest, Illinois.

In 1978, Pasin Sloan made her first lithographs with Jack Lemon and has worked at Landfall Press extensively to the present.

T.L. SOLIEN

Born in Fargo, North Dakota, in 1949, Solien, earned a BA from Moorhead State University, Moorhead, Minnesota, in 1973, and an MFA from the University of Nebraska in 1977.

Solien first worked at Landfall Press in 1984 and returned in 1990.

PAT STEIR

Born in Newark, New Jersey, in 1940, Steir studied at Pratt Institute, Brooklyn, New York, and Boston University. She was art director for Harper & Row, New York, from 1966 to 1969. She has taught at several colleges and traveled extensively in the United States, Europe, and Japan. A painter, printmaker, and poet, Steir currently lives and works in New York and Amsterdam.

Jack Lemon invited Steir to make lithographs at Landfall Press in 1971 after seeing her paintings in New York, although her only prior printmaking experience had been as a student at Pratt. She returned five years later to work in Landfall's new intaglio department. Steir credits these early projects with developing her interest in the serious pursuit of printmaking.

138. Pat Steir in the West Ontario Street shop drawing on a lithographic stone for *Wish #1*, 1974 (see Fig. 99).

RANDY TWADDLE

Born in Elmo, Missouri, in 1957, Twaddle studied at Northwest Missouri State University, Maryville, and the University of Missouri, Columbus. His first solo exhibition was in 1985. Twaddle currently lives and works in Houston.

Twaddle is known for his serial paintings and large-format drawings that disturbingly juxtapose graphic silhouettes of everyday objects, such as a gun, knife, and surveillance camera. Between 1985 and 1991, he created several editions at Landfall Press that utilize the diptych and triptych formats of his unique pieces.

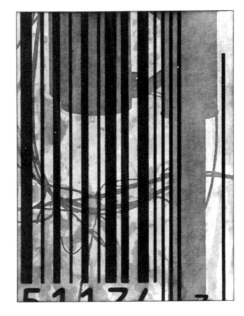

139. Randy Twaddle, *UPC Print*, 1992, aquatint, soft-ground etching, and spit-bite etching, 32 3/4 X 23 3/4 (83.2 X 60.3), 40 X 29 7/8 (101.6 X 75.9)

JACK TWORKOV

Born Jacob Tworkovsky in Biala, Poland, in 1900, Tworkov immigrated to the United States in 1913. He attended Columbia University as an English major, the National Academy of Design, New York, and the Art Students League, New York, and earned an MFA from Yale University. His first solo exhibition was held at the ACA Gallery, New York, in 1940, and his first retrospective was held at the Whitney Museum of American Art in 1974. Tworkov died in 1982.

Noted for his gestural, Abstract Expressionist-inspired paintings, Tworkov made a number of etchings and lithographs at Landfall Press on several occasions between 1975 and 1980.

140. Bernar Venet working on a drawing for his 1990 lithograph, *Two Undetermined Lines*, (see Pl. 81)

BERNAR VENET

Venet was born in Château-Arnoux-Saint-Auban, France, in 1941. He exhibited an exceptional aptitude for drawing and painting at a very early age, and was invited to exhibit in the Salon de Peinture Pechiney, Paris, when he was eleven years old. Venet lived in Nice from 1957 to 1966 and then moved to New York, where he continues to reside. Venet was awarded the Paris Grand Prix des Arts in 1989.

A renowned Conceptual artist, Venet combines painting, drawing, text, and found objects to make installation pieces that address the issues of perception and comprehension of knowledge. Jack Lemon invited Venet to work at Landfall Press in 1981 and 1990.

KARA WALKER

Born in Stockton, California, in 1969, Walker earned a BFA from Atlanta College of Art in 1991 and an MFA from the Rhode Island School of Design in 1994. She currently lives in Providence.

Walker is a young painter and printmaker who has recently attracted attention for her disarming, yet caustic narratives of nineteenth-century slavery and African-American history. Her recent series of etchings published by Landfall Press adopts the silhouette format typical of her paintings and drawings. She depicts a slave-master drama in which the themes of power and exploitation continue to have deep meaning for black Americans today.

H.C. WESTERMANN

Born in Los Angeles in 1922, Westermann joined the Marine Corps in 1942 and served as a gunner on a carrier in the Pacific during World War II. After the military, Westermann attended the School of The Art Institute of Chicago, was an acrobat for a while, and worked as a handyman to support himself. He had his first solo exhibition in 1958 and until 1961 lived in Chicago, where he was an important influence on the emerging Chicago Imagist school. The Whitney Museum of American Art organized a major survey of his work in 1978. Westermann died in 1981 of a heart attack.

Something of a loner, Westermann drew on intuition and personal experience to create sculptures and drawings of houses, ships, and personages loaded with irony, absurdity, and paradox. The eight lithographs he created at Landfall Press in 1972 suggest the many illustrated letters and comic drawings he sent to friends over the years.

141. H.C. Westermann in the West Ontario Street shop, with three of his lithographs from 1972 tacked to the wall, *A Crash in the Jungle, Death Ship in a Port*, and *Oomu*.

WILLIAM T. WILEY

Born in Bedford, Indiana, in 1937, Wiley earned a BFA from the San Francisco Art Institute in 1960, the same year he had his first solo exhibition. In 1962 he earned an MFA from the same school and began teaching at the University of California, Davis, where he remained until 1973. In 1968, he collaborated with composer Steve Reich on a theater event at the Hansen-Fuller Gallery, San Francisco, and at Sacramento State College. The Walker Art Center, Minneapolis, organized a retrospective of Wiley's work in 1979.

A painter, sculptor, and printmaker, Wiley was an important member of the 1960s California Funk movement. He often presents himself in his art as a self-deprecating jester who takes good-natured, yet sharp jabs at American culture and politics. Wiley worked extensively at Landfall Press from 1972 to 1989, creating more than forty etchings and lithographs that demonstrate his superb draftsmanship and insightful humor.

KARL WIRSUM

Born in Chicago in 1939, Wirsum earned a BA from the School of The Art Institute of Chicago and began to exhibit with the city's "Hairy Who" artists in 1966.

Inspired as a child by his father's cartoons and later by the bright colors and bold patterning of Mexican folk art, Wirsum is an inventive artist who works freely with a variety of printmaking media. Executed in rubberstamp, linoleum cut, rubbing, serigraph, etching, or lithography, the conceptual range of his prints goes from the traditional single-sheet format to puppets, articles of clothing, tickets, stationery, balloons, and other types of objects. Although many are either unique impressions or mass-produced posters, Wirsum has produced several editioned works, including three lithographs at Landfall Press.

ROBERT YARBER

Born in Dallas, in 1948, Yarber was educated at Cooper Union College, New York, and Louisiana State University, Baton Rouge. He currently lives and works in New York.

Yarber is known for his paintings of middle-class life on the threshold of impending doom. In 1989, Jack Lemon, who knew Yarber through mutual friends, invited the artist to Landfall Press to make his first print. The lithograph, entitled *The Corruption of Ecstasy*, was closely based on a previous painting.

142. William T. Wiley (left) and Brenda Richardson looking at his lithograph *Checking It All Out*, 1972, in the West Ontario Street shop.

DUANE ZALOUDEK

Born in Enid, Oklahoma, in 1931, Zaloudek was educated at the Portland Museum Art School, Oregon. His first solo exhibition was held at Adeles Gallery, Portland, in 1955. From 1962 to 1965, he was artist-in-residence at Portland University, Oregon, and in 1970-73, he was a visiting artist at the University of California, Davis.

A Color Field painter and watercolorist, Zaloudek produced three etchings at Landfall Press in 1991.

WORKS IN THE EXHIBITION

The works listed here are those exhibited at the Milwaukee Art Museum. There will be slight variations in the exhibited works at the other venues.

The prints are arranged alphabetically by artist, then chronologically within the listings for the artist.

The data in each entry is organized as follows: title of print; title of portfolio or suite, if applicable; date; medium and support; edition information, followed by the Landfall Press inventory number; dimensions; printer(s); publisher(s); Milwaukee Art Museum accession number, with credit line in special circumstances.

If the date of the print is the same as the date of its portfolio or suite, the date is given after the title of the portfolio. If the dates are different, the date of the print is given after the print, the date of the portfolio after the portfolio.

If a print is color, it is noted as "printed in color"; otherwise the print is black-and-white. The make of paper is given whenever known, based on the print document sheets in the Landfall Press Archive. Edition information, which also comes from these document sheets, is provided as follows: regular edition, artist's proof (A.P.), printer's proof (P.P.), Landfall Press Impressions (L.P.I.), subscribers' proofs (S.P.), copyright proofs (C.P.). Special editions, such as sales examples or roman numeral editions, are added whenever necessary. Working proofs are noted as such, without indication of paper type. The edition information is followed by the inventory number assigned to the print by the Press.

Dimensions are in inches, followed by centimeters; height precedes width precedes depth. Plate and sheet size are given only for intaglios; all other dimensions are sheet size.

The printers are listed in the order that they appear on the document sheets; assistants are indicated by the word "with" preceding their names. As master printer, Jack Lemon supervised all editions, even those on which he did not physically work. Although Landfall served as publisher in most instances, there are some works for which Landfall only served as printer; hence the publisher is always noted.

All the works in the exhibition, except for the three Dennis Oppenheim lithographs loaned by The Museum of Modern Art, New York, and some recent editions loaned by Landfall Press, are in the collection of the Milwaukee Art Museum. The credit lines for accession numbers with the following prefixes are: LP1992, Gift of Jack Lemon and Sue and Dick Pieper; LP1993, LP1994, Gift of Jack Lemon. Pieces from other sources are listed with their credit lines.

All the final editions in this checklist are reproduced in the catalogue (except for the two white-on-white etchings by Duane Zaloudek, which are not reproduced at the artist's request). Most of the prints are in the color plate section, arranged alphabetically by artist. Those reproduced as black-and-white figures elsewhere in the catalogue are indicated by a figure number citation at the end of the entry.

VITO ACCONCI
Approved—Now the Stones Will Stand One More Day, from the portfolio *Stones for a Wall*, 1977
Lithograph, printed in color, on white HMP paper
Edition: 10, 1 A.P., 2 P.P., 2 L.P.I., 2 C.P. (VA-77-649)
30 1/8 X 24 (76.5 X 61)
Printed by Jack Lemon, with Milan Milojevic
Published by Landfall Press
LP1992.1.1

Approved—Sometimes You Can Get Blood from a Stone (When There's a Dream of Radicalism), from the portfolio *Stones for a Wall*, 1977
Lithograph, printed in color, on white HMP paper
Edition: 10, 1 A.P., 2 P.P., 2 L.P.I., 2 C.P. (VA-77-650)
30 1/4 X 23 7/8 (76.8 X 60.6)
Printed by Jack Lemon, with Milan Milojevic
Published by Landfall Press
LP1992.1.2

Approved—There's Always Another Secret Behind the Wall, from the portfolio *Stones for a Wall*, 1977
Lithograph, printed in color, on white HMP paper
Edition: 10, 1 A.P., 2 P.P., 2 L.P.I., 2 C.P. (VA-77-651)
30 1/4 X 23 7/8 (76.8 X 60.6)
Printed by Jack Lemon, with Milan Milojevic
Published by Landfall Press
LP1992.1.3

Approved—You Know Where You Are, You Sucker, from the portfolio *Stones for a Wall*, 1977
Lithograph, printed in color, on white HMP paper
Edition: 10, 1 A.P., 2 P.P., 2 L.P.I., 2 C.P. (VA-77-652)
30 1/4 X 23 7/8 (76.8 X 60.6)
Printed by Jack Lemon, with Milan Milojevic
Published by Landfall Press
LP1992.1.4

Approved—We Try to Go Deeper (They Told Us to Shape), from the portfolio *Stones for a Wall*, 1977
Lithograph, printed in color, on white HMP paper
Edition: 10, 1 A.P., 2 P.P., 2 L.P.I., 2 C.P. (VA-77-653)
30 X 24 (76.2 X 61)
Printed by Jack Lemon, with Milan Milojevic
Published by Landfall Press
LP1992.1.5

Approved—After All, They Told Us to Form, from the portfolio *Stones for a Wall*, 1977
Lithograph, printed in color, on white HMP paper
Edition: 10, 1 A.P., 2 P.P., 2 L.P.I., 2 C.P. (VA-77-654)
30 X 23 3/4 (76.2 X 60.3)
Printed by Jack Lemon, with Milan Milojevic
Published by Landfall Press
LP1992.1.6

Approved—But Don't Be Fooled, This Is a Message from the American Lover, from the portfolio *Stones for a Wall*, 1977
Lithograph, printed in color, on white HMP paper
Edition: 10, 1 A.P., 2 P.P., 2 L.P.I., 2 C.P. (VA-77-655)
30 1/4 X 24 (76.8 X 61)
Printed by Jack Lemon, with Milan Milojevic
Published by Landfall Press
LP1992.1.7

Approved—They Told Us to Build (And We Hit Rock Bottom), from the portfolio *Stones for a Wall*, 1977
Lithograph, printed in color, on white HMP paper
Edition: 10, 1 A.P., 2 P.P., 2 L.P.I., 2 C.P. (VA-77-656)
30 X 23 5/8 (76.2 X 60)
Printed by Jack Lemon, with Milan Milojevic
Published by Landfall Press
LP1992.1.8

Approved—Finally, It's Blowing Up in My Hands, from the portfolio *Stones for a Wall*, 1977
Lithograph, printed in color, on white HMP paper
Edition: 10, 1 A.P., 2 P.P., 2 L.P.I., 2 C.P. (VA-77-657)
30 1/8 X 24 (76.5 X 61)
Printed by Jack Lemon, with Milan Milojevic
Published by Landfall Press
LP1992.1.9

Approved—Let the Grass Go Over, Let the Sky Come Through, from the portfolio *Stones for a Wall*, 1977
Lithograph, printed in color, on white HMP paper
Edition: 10, 1 A.P., 2 P.P., 2 L.P.I., 2 C.P. (VA-77-658)
30 1/2 X 24 (77.5 X 61)
Printed by Jack Lemon, with Milan Milojevic
Published by Landfall Press
LP1992.1.10

WILLIAM G. ALLAN
Tamales, from the *Landfall Press Etching Portfolio*, 1975
Aquatint, printed in color, on hand-made Twinrocker Mill paper
Edition: 50, 12 A.P., 2 P.P., 5 L.P.I., 5 S.P., 1 C.P., 25 roman numeral edition (WA-74-008E)
8 X 10 (20.3 X 25.4)
28 X 22 (71.1 X 55.9)
Printed by Timothy F. Berry
Published by Landfall Press
LP1992.6.1

TERRY ALLEN
Bed with Ditch, from the *Juarez Suite*, 1976
Lithograph, printed in color, on Special Rives BFK paper
Edition: 50, 10 A.P., 2 P.P., 4 L.P.I., 5 S.P., 2 C.P. (TA-75-557)
12 5/8 X 12 5/8 (32.1 X 32.1)
Printed by Jack Lemon, with Ted Stanuga and Robert Rashkow
Published by Landfall Press
LP1992.15.11

Bed with Heart, from the *Juarez Suite*,
1976
Lithograph, printed in color, on
Special Rives BFK paper
Edition: 50, 10 A.P., 2 P.P., 4 L.P.I.,
5 S.P., 2 C.P. (TA-75-556)
12 5/8 X 12 5/8 (32.1 X 32.1)
Printed by Jack Lemon, with
Ted Stanuga and Robert Rashkow
Published by Landfall Press
LP1992.15.10

Ditch with Heart, from the *Juarez Suite*,
1976
Lithograph, printed in color, on
Special Rives BFK paper
Edition: 50, 10 A.P., 2 P.P., 4 L.P.I.,
5 S.P., 2 C.P. (TA-75-558)
12 5/8 X 12 5/8 (32.1 X 32.1)
Printed by Jack Lemon, with
Ted Stanuga and Robert Rashkow
Published by Landfall Press
LP1992.15.12

Pillow in the Mountains, from the
Juarez Suite, 1976
Lithograph, printed in color, on
Special Rives BFK paper
Edition: 50, 10 A.P., 2 P.P., 4 L.P.I.,
5 S.P., 2 C.P. (TA-75-554)
12 5/8 X 12 5/8 (32.1 X 32.1)
Printed by Jack Lemon, with
Ted Stanuga and Robert Rashkow
Published by Landfall Press
LP1992.15.8

Pillow in the Mountains II, from the
Juarez Suite, 1976
Lithograph, printed in color, on
Special Rives BFK paper
Edition: 50, 10 A.P., 2 P.P., 4 L.P.I.,
5 S.P., 2 C.P. (TA-75-559)
12 5/8 X 12 5/8 (32.1 X 32.1)
Printed by Jack Lemon, with
Ted Stanuga and Robert Rashkow
Published by Landfall Press
LP1992.15.13

Room with Horns, from the *Juarez
Suite*, 1976
Lithograph, printed in color, on
Special Rives BFK paper
Edition: 50, 10 A.P., 2 P.P., 4 L.P.I.,
5 S.P., 2 C.P. (TA-75-555)
12 5/8 X 12 5/8 (32.1 X 32.1)
Printed by Jack Lemon, with
Ted Stanuga and Robert Rashkow
Published by Landfall Press
LP1992.15.9

ROBERT ARNESON
Cherry Pie, 1975
Lithograph, printed in color, on
Arches Cover White paper
Edition: 38, 5 A.P., 2 P.P., 5 L.P.I.,
5 S.P., 2 C.P. (RA-74-502)
22 3/8 X 30 1/8 (56.8 X 76.5)
Printed by David Keister, with
Ron Wyffels
Published by Landfall Press
LP1994.14.01

Brick, from the *Brick Suite*, 1976
Terracotta
Edition: 50
4 1/2 X 8 1/2 X 2 5/8
(11.4 X 21.6 X 6.7)
Manufactured by the artist at his stu-
dio, Benicia, California
Published by Landfall Press
LP1992.28.1

California Brick, from the *Brick Suite*,
1976
Spit-bite etching, soft-ground etching, and aquatint, with hand burnishing on Arches Cover White paper
Edition: 50, 5 A.P., 1 P.P., 4 L.P.I.,
5 S.P., 2 C.P. (RA-75-024E)
9 1/4 X 9 7/8 (23.5 X 25)
16 X 16 1/2 (40.6 X 41.9)
Printed by Timothy F. Berry
Published by Landfall Press
LP1992.24.1
Figure 50

Up Against It, 1977
Conté crayon and wash on wove
paper
40 1/2 X 29 1/2 (102.9 X 74.9)
M1990.146 Gift of Allen and
Vicki Sampson

Up Against It, 1980
Lithograph, printed in color, on
Arches Cover White paper
Edition: 35, 10 A.P., 2 P.P., 5 L.P.I.,
10 S.P., 2 C.P. (RA-79-758)
40 1/4 X 30 (102.2 X 76.2)
Printed by Mary McDonald, with
Barbara Spies
Published by Landfall Press
LP1992.38.1

The Colonel's At It Again, 1987
Lithograph, printed in color, with
hand coloring, on black German
Etching paper
Edition: 26, 10 A.P., 2 P.P., 5 L.P.I.,
10 S.P., 2 C.P. (RA-85-924)
38 1/8 X 28 (96.8 X 71.1)
Printed by Jack Lemon and
Barbara Spies, with Heidijo Lemon
Published by Landfall Press
LP1992.29.18

DON BAUM
Domus, 1992
Lithograph, printed in color, on blue-
white Navajo Smooth Cover paper,
mounted on museum board
Edition: 100, 15 A.P., 4 P.P., 5 L.P.I.,
10 S.P. (DB-92-41)
16 1/2 X 9 X 13 1/2
(41.9 X 22.9 X 34.3)
Printed by Rohner Printing Company
and die-cut by Knight Steel Rule
Published by Landfall Press
LP1993.1.1

WILLIAM BECKMAN
Self-Portrait with Black Shirt, 1988
Lithograph on Heavy Arches paper
Edition: 5, 3 A.P. (WB-88-1001)
42 1/4 X 34 (107.3 X 86.4)
Printed by Barbara Spies, with
David Jones
Published by Landfall Press
LP1994.54.01
Figure 48

PHYLLIS BRAMSON
The Eroticism of Seeing, 1981
Lithograph, printed in color, with
collage, acrylic, and glitter, on Arches
Cover White paper
Edition: 30, 10 A.P., 2 P.P., 4 L.P.I.,
10 S.P., 2 C.P. (PB-81-794)
41 7/8 X 26 (106.4 X 66)
Printed by Jack Lemon, with Barbara
Spies and Scott Russell
Published by Landfall Press
LP1992.50.1

A Flash of Spiritual Meaning, 1981
Lithograph, printed in color, with
collage, acrylic, and glitter, on Arches
Cover White paper
Edition: 30, 10 A.P., 2 P.P., 4 L.P.I.,
10 S.P., 2 C.P. (PB-81-793)
41 7/8 X 26 (106.4 X 66)
Printed by Jack Lemon, with
Barbara Spies and Scott Russell
Published by Landfall Press
LP1992.51.1

ROGER BROWN
Fear No Evil, 1991
Lithograph on Arches paper
Edition: 50, 10 A.P., 4 P.P., 5 L.P.I.,
10 S.P., 2 C.P., 5 H.C., 2 sales exam-
ples (RB-90-62)
36 1/4 X 35 7/8 (92.1 X 91.1)
Printed by Barbara Spies Labus, with
Betsy Haude and David Stricker
Published by Landfall Press
LP1992.56.1
Figure 70

Hank Williams, Honky Tonk Man,
1991
Lithograph, printed in color, on
Arches paper
Edition: 75, 10 A.P., 4 P.P., 5 L.P.I.,
5 S.P., 2 C.P., 5 H.C., 2 sales exam-
ples (RB-90-64)
40 1/4 X 40 (102.2 X 101.6)
Printed by Barb Spies Labus, with
Betsy Haude and David Stricker
Published by Landfall Press
LP1992.57.1

GRISHA BRUSKIN
Untitled, 1988
Lithograph, printed in color, on
Arches Cover White paper
Edition: 100, 10 A.P., 3 P.P., 10 L.P.I,
20 S.P. (GB-88-993)
40 1/4 X 30 (102.2 X 76.2)
Printed by Barbara Spies Labus, with
David Jones and Fred Baehr
Published by Landfall Press
M1989.79 Gift of George and
Jane Kaiser

JOHN BUCK
Untitled (La Grande Eclipse), 1982
Woodcut, printed in color, on
Japanese Suzu paper
Edition: 20, 6 A.P., 1 P.P., 3 L.P.I.
(JB-82-842)
76 1/2 X 31 5/8 (194.3 X 80.3)
Printed by David Holzman, with
Barbara Spies
Published by Landfall Press
M1983.186 Gift of the Members
of the Milwaukee Art Museum
Print Forum

Untitled (La Grande Eclipse), 1982
Woodcut, printed in color
Trial Proof
77 1/2 X 33 1/2 (196.9 X 85.1)
LP1992.66.1

Fireweed, 1991
Woodcut, printed in color, on Rives
BFK paper
Edition: 25, 10 A.P, 2 P.P., 3 L.P.I,
5 S.P., 2 C.P. (JB-91-74)
66 3/4 X 40 (169.6 X 101.6)
Printed by Steve Campbell and
Barbara Spies Labus, with
Betsy Haude
Published by Landfall Press
LP1993.3.1

DAN CHRISTENSEN
Untitled, 1972
Lithograph, printed in color, on
Special Arjomari paper
Edition: 75, 10 A.P., 2 P.P., 4 L.P.I., 5
S.P., 2 C.P. (DC-71-233)
48 3/8 X 26 (122.9 X 66)
Printed by Jack Lemon and Jerry
Raidiger, with William Coons and
Arthur Kleinman
Published by Landfall Press
LP1992.74.1

CHRISTO
*The Whitney Museum, New York,
Packed*, from the portfolio *(Some) Not
Realized Projects*, 1971
Lithograph, printed in color, with
collage, on Special Arjomari paper,
mounted on museum board
Edition: 100, 10 A.P., 2 P.P., 4 L.P.I.,
10 S.P. (CJ-71-191)
27 3/4 X 21 7/8 (70.5 X 55.6)
Printed by Jack Lemon and
Jerry Raidiger, with Donald Holman
and Arthur Kleinman
Published by Landfall Press
LP1992.302.1

Wrapped Venus, Villa Borghese, 1963,
from the *Landfall Press Etching
Portfolio*, 1975
Hard-ground etching, soft-ground
etching, and lithograph, with collage,
on handmade Twinrocker Mill paper
Edition: 50, 12 A.P., 2 P.P., 5 L.P.I.,
5 S.P., 1 C.P., 25 roman numeral edition (CJ-74-011E)
24 X 18 (61 X 45.7)
28 X 22 (71.1 X 55.9)
Printed by Timothy F. Berry
Published by Landfall Press
LP1992.93.1

*Lower Manhattan Wrapped Buildings,
for 2 Broadway, 20 Exchange Place*,
1990
Lithograph, printed in color, with
collage, on Arches Cover White
paper, mounted on museum board
Edition: 125, 30 A.P., 20 L.P.I, 2 C.P.
(CJ-90-45)
40 1/8 X 26 (101.9 X 66)
Printed by Jack Lemon and Barbara
Spies, with Steve Klepac, David
Jones, and Carolann Fischer
Published by J. Rosenthal Fine Arts,
Chicago
LP1992.77.1

Orange Store Front, Project, 1991
Lithograph, printed in color, with
collage, on Arches White paper,
mounted on museum board
Edition: 100, 35 A.P., 20 L.P.I, 10
S.P., 2 C.P., 10 H.C. (CJ-90-68)
27 X 31 5/8 (68.6 X 80.3)
Printed by Barbara Spies Labus, with
Steve Campbell and Betsy Haude
Published by Lief Holmer Gallery,
Nassjo, Sweden, and Claes Distner
Gallery, Karlshamm, Sweden
LP1992.79.1

CHUCK CLOSE
Keith/Four Times, 1975
Lithograph, printed in color, on
Arches Satine paper
Edition: 50, 10 A.P., 2 P.P., 2 L.P.I.
(CC-74-457)
30 X 88 (76.2 X 223.5)
Printed by Jack Lemon and David
Keister, with Ron Wyffels and Tom
Cvikota
Published by Parasol Press, New York
LP1992.97.1
Figure 41

ROBERT COTTINGHAM
Fox, 1973
Lithograph, printed in color, on
Special Arjomari paper
Edition: 100, 10 A.P., 2 P.P., 4 L.P.I,
5 S.P., 2 C.P. (RC-73-361)
22 7/8 X 23 (58.1 X 58.4)
Printed by David Keister and Tom
Minkler, with David Panosh, Laura
Holland, and Tom Cvikota
Published by Landfall Press
LP1992.305.1

F.W., from the *Landfall Press Etching
Portfolio*, 1975
Etching and aquatint, with chine
collé, on Japanese Gasen paper on
handmade Twinrocker Mill paper
Edition: 50, 12 A.P., 2 P.P., 5 L.P.I.,
5 S.P., 1 C.P., 25 roman numeral edi-
tion (RC-74-012E)
10 1/2 X 10 1/2 (26.7 X 26.7)
28 X 22 (71.1 X 55.9)
Printed by Timothy F. Berry, with
Carol Plummer
Published by Landfall Press
LP1992.105.2
Figure 53

Art, 1992
Lithograph, printed in color, on Rives
BFK paper
Edition: 60, 15 A.P., 4 P.P., 5 L.P.I.,
10 S.P., 2 C.P. (RC-91-88)
46 X 45 3/4 (116.8 X 116.2)
Printed by Barbara Spies Labus, with
Betsy Haude, John Klein, Robert
Brinker, and Steve Campbell
Published by Landfall Press
LP1993.4.2

JACK COWIN
Future Considerations, 1986
Lithograph, printed in color, on Rives
BFK Gray paper
Edition: 75, 10 A.P., 2 P.P., 5 L.P.I.,
5 S.P. (JC-86-927)
18 X 24 (45.7 X 61)
Printed by Jack Lemon, with
Barbara Spies and Heidijo Lemon
Published by Landfall Press
LP1994.52.01

PETER DEAN
Hear No Evil, 1984
Lithograph, printed in color, on
Arches Cover White paper
Edition: 25, 10 A.P., 2 P.P., 5 L.P.I.,
10 S.P., 2 C.P. (PD-83-868)
26 X 34 (66 X 86.4)
Printed by Jack Lemon, with
Barbara Spies
Published by Landfall Press
LP1992.121.1

LESLEY DILL
*Poem Dress "The Soul Selects Her Own
Society,"* 1993
Lithograph, with thread, on deacidi-
fied Indian newspaper
Edition: 50, 10 A.P., 3 P.P., 5 L.P.I., 5
S.P., 1 C.P. (LD-93-58)
10 X 7 X 3 1/2 (25.4 X 17.8 X 8.9)
Printed by Barbara Spies Labus and
Steve Campbell, with Carl Johnson
and Jennifer Luk; cut, assembled, and
sewn by Jennifer Luk
Published by Landfall Press
LP1994.04.01
Figure 84

Arms, from the suite *A Word Made
Flesh*, 1994
Lithograph and etching, printed in
color, on mulberry paper tea-stained
by immersion, hand-sewn on Arches
Buff paper
Edition: 25, 10 A.P., 2 P.P., 3 L.P.I.,
5 S.P., 1 C.P. (LD-94-08)
25 3/4 X 21 5/8 (65.4 X 54.9)
29 1/2 X 22 (74.9 X 55.9)
Printed by Steve Campbell and
Barbara Spies Labus, with C. Tyler
Johnson; assembled and sewn by
Jennifer Luk
Published by Landfall Press
Courtesy Landfall Press

Back, from the suite *A Word Made
Flesh*, 1994
Lithograph, etching, and aquatint,
printed in color, on mulberry paper
tea-stained by immersion, hand-sewn
on Arches Buff paper
Edition: 25, 10 A.P., 2 P.P., 3 L.P.I.,
5 S.P., 1 C.P. (LD-94-07)
25 7/8 X 21 1/2 (65.7 X 54.6)
29 1/2 X 22 (74.9 X 55.9)
Printed by Steve Campbell and
Barbara Spies Labus, with C. Tyler
Johnson; assembled and sewn by
Jennifer Luk
Published by Landfall Press
Courtesy Landfall Press

Front, from the suite *A Word Made
Flesh*, 1994
Lithograph, etching, and aquatint,
on mulberry paper tea-stained by
immersion, hand-sewn on Arches
Buff paper
Edition: 25, 10 A.P., 2 P.P., 3 L.P.I,
5 S.P., 1 C.P. (LD-94-02)
25 7/8 X 21 1/2 (65.7 X 54.6)
30 X 22 (76.2 X 55.9)
Printed by Steve Campbell and
Barbara Spies Labus, with C. Tyler
Johnson; assembled and sewn by
Jennifer Luk
Published by Landfall Press
Courtesy Landfall Press

Throat, from the suite *A Word Made Flesh*, 1994
Lithograph, etching, and aquatint, printed in color, on mulberry paper tea-stained by immersion, hand-sewn on Arches Buff paper
Edition: 25, 10 A.P., 2 P.P., 3 L.P.I., 5 S.P., 1 C.P. (LD-94-06)
28 7/8 X 21 7/8 (73.3 X 55.6)
29 1/2 X 22 (74.9 X 55.9)
Printed by Steve Campbell and Barbara Spies Labus, with C. Tyler Johnson; assembled and sewn by Jennifer Luk
Published by Landfall Press
Courtesy Landfall Press

JIM DINE
The Red Bandana, 1974
Lithograph, printed in color, on handmade Twinrocker Mill paper
Edition: 50, 15 A.P. 2 P.P., 2 L.P.I. (JD-73-401)
47 7/8 X 35 1/8 (121.6 X 89.2)
Printed by Jack Lemon, with Tom Minkler
Published by Pace Editions, New York
M1994.397 Gift of the artist

The Yellow Robe, 1980
Lithograph, printed in color, on Arches Aquarelle rolled paper
Edition: 50, 10 A P., 1 P.P., 2 L.P.I. (JD-80-771)
49 X 35 1/4 (124.5 X 89.5)
Printed by Jack Lemon, with Tom Blackman and Mary McDonald
Published by Pace Editions, New York
LP1992.143.1

The Yellow Robe, 1980
Lithograph, printed in color
Trial Proof
49 X 35 1/4 (124.5 X 89.6)
LP1992.143.2

NANCY DWYER
Mayhem, 1991
Lithograph, printed in color, and die-cut on Arches paper on Rives paper
Edition: 25, 10 A.P., 2 P.P., 4 L.P.I., 10 S.P., 2 C.P. (ND-90-55)
20 3/8 X 18 (51.8 X 45.7)
Printed by Jack Lemon and David Jones, with Barbara Spies Labus and Steve Campbell
Published by Landfall Press
LP1992.144.1

Out of My Mind, 1991
Lithograph, printed in color, on white wove paper
Edition: 25, 10 A.P., 2 P.P., 5 L.P.I., 10 S.P., 2 C.P.
17 7/8 X 17 7/8 (45.4 X 45.4)
Printed by Jack Lemon and Steve Campbell, with Betsy Haude and David Stricker
Published by Landfall Press
LP1992.145.1

MARTHA ERLEBACHER
Still Life #2, 1978
Lithograph, printed in color, on Arches Cover White paper
Edition: 60, 4 A.P., 2 P.P., 2 L.P.I. (ME-76-612)
26 X 34 3/4 (66 X 88.3)
Printed by Jack Lemon and Fred Gude, with Milan Milojevic and Ted Carter
Published by Landfall Press and G.W. Einstein Co., New York
LP1994.65.01

VERNON FISHER
Composition in Red, White, and Blue, 1985
Lithograph, printed in color, on Arches Cover White paper
Edition: 20, 10 A.P., 2 P.P., 5 L.P.I., 10 S.P., 2 C.P. (VF-85-912)
30 1/8 X 42 3/8 (76.5 X 107.6)
Printed by Jack Lemon and Barbara Spies, with Heidijo Lemon
Published by Landfall Press
LP1994.17.01

Perdido en el mar, 1989
Lithograph, printed in color, on Rives BFK paper
Edition: 50, 10 A.P., 2 P.P., 5 L.P.I., 10 S.P., 2 C.P. (VF-89-03)
30 X 34 1/4 (76.2 X 87)
Printed by David Jones, with Kevin Finegan
Published by Landfall Press
LP1992.159.1

Rules for Bending Circles, 1993
Lithograph, printed in color, on Rives BFK paper
Edition: 30, 10 A.P., 4 P.P., 5 L.P.I., 10 S.P., 2 C.P. (VF-92-25)
36 X 41 (91.4 X 104.1)
Printed by Barbara Spies Labus, with C. Tyler Johnson
Published by Landfall Press
LP1994.05.01

TONY FITZPATRICK
Black-Eyed Fight Dog, 1991
Hard-ground etching, soft-ground etching, spit-bite etching, with chine collé, on HMP paper
Edition: 20, 8 A.P., 2 P.P., 5 L.P.I., 5 S.P., 1 C.P. (TF-91-83)
11 3/4 X 9 3/4 (29.8 X 24.8)
24 X 23 (61 X 58.4)
Printed by Steve Campbell
Published by Landfall Press
LP1993.9.1
Figure 83

CHARLES GAINES
Color Regression #2, 1980
Lithograph, printed in color, on Rives BFK paper
Edition: 30, 10 A.P., 2 P.P., 5 L.P.I., 10 S.P., 2 C.P. (CG-78-740)
28 X 31 5/8 (71.1 X 80.3)
Printed by Mary McDonald, with Barbara Spies
Published by Landfall Press
M1982.208B Gift of Dr. and Mrs. Christopher Graf

NANCY GRAVES
IV ("Julius Caesar Quadrangle of the Moon"), from the portfolio *Lunar Maps*, 1972
Lithograph, printed in color, on Arches Cover paper and mylar laminate
Edition: 100, 6 A.P., 2 P.P., 2 L.P.I. (NG-72-328)
22 1/2 X 30 (57.2 X 76.2)
Printed by Jerry Raidiger, with Arthur Kleinman
Published by Carl Solway Gallery, Cincinnati
LP1992.171.2

*V ("Montes Appenninus Region of the
Moon"), from the portfolio Lunar
Maps*, 1972
Lithograph, printed in color, on
Arches Cover paper
Edition: 100, 6 A.P., 2 P.P., 2 L.P.I.
(NG-72-320)
22 1/2 X 30 (57.2 X 76.2)
Printed by David Keister, with
Arthur Kleinman
Published by Carl Solway Gallery,
Cincinnati
LP1992.172.2

*VI ("Maskelyne DA Region of the
Moon"), from the portfolio Lunar
Maps*, 1972
Lithograph, printed in color, on
Arches Cover paper and amime net
Edition: 100, 6 A.P., 2 P.P., 2 L.P.I.
(NG-72-315)
22 1/2 X 30 (57.2 X 76.2)
Printed by David Keister, with
David Panosh
Published by Carl Solway Gallery,
Cincinnati
LP1992.173.2

*VII ("Sabine D Region of the Moon,
Lunar Orbiter Site IIP-6 Southwest
Mare Tranquilitatis"), from the portfo-
lio Lunar Maps*, 1972
Lithograph, printed in color, on
Arches Cover paper
Edition: 100, 6 A.P., 2 P.P., 2 L.P.I.
(NG-72-329)
22 1/2 X 30 (57.2 X 76.2)
Printed by David Keister, with
David Panosh
Published by Carl Solway Gallery,
Cincinnati
LP1992.174.2

DENISE GREEN

Trojan #1, 1994
Etching and aquatint, printed in
color, with chine collé, on Rives
BFK paper
Edition: 25, 5 A.P., 2 P.P., 4 L.P.I.,
5 S.P., 2 C.P. (DG-94-13)
11 X 9 (27.9 X 22.9)
16 X 14 (40.6 X 35.6)
Printed by Steve Campbell
Published by Landfall Press
Courtesy Landfall Press

Trojan #2, 1994
Etching and aquatint, printed in
color, with chine collé, on Rives
BFK paper
Edition: 25, 5 A.P., 2 P.P., 4 L.P.I.,
5 S.P., 2 C.P. (DG-94-16)
11 X 9 (27.9 X 22.9)
16 X 14 (40.6 X 35.6)
Printed by Steve Campbell
Published by Landfall Press
Courtesy Landfall Press

Trojan #3, 1994
Etching and aquatint, printed in
color, with chine collé, on Rives
BFK paper
Edition: 25, 5 A.P., 2 P.P., 4 L.P.I.,
5 S.P., 2 C.P. (DG-94-15)
11 X 9 (27.9 X 22.9)
16 X 14 (40.6 X 35.6)
Printed by Steve Campbell
Published by Landfall Press
Courtesy Landfall Press

Trojan #4, 1994
Etching and aquatint, printed in
color, with chine collé, on Rives
BFK paper
Edition: 25, 5 A.P., 2 P.P., 4 L.P.I.,
5 S.P., 2 C.P. (DG-94-14)
11 X 9 (27.9 X 22.9)
16 X 14 (40.6 X 35.6)
Printed by Steve Campbell
Published by Landfall Press
Courtesy Landfall Press

RICHARD HULL

Change, 1986
Lithograph, printed in color, on
Arches Cover White paper
Edition: 65, 10 A.P., 2 P.P., 2 L.P.I.,
10 S.P., 2 C.P. (RH-85-918)
40 1/4 X 30 (102.2 X 76.2)
Printed by Barbara Spies, with
Heidijo Lemon
Published by Phyllis Kind Gallery,
New York and Chicago, and
Landfall Press
M1987.124 Gift of Dr. William
Wagner and Dr. Jean Schott-Wagner

RICHARD HUNT

Untitled, 1971
Lithograph on wove paper
Edition: no information available
(RH-71-150)
30 X 21 7/8 (76.2 X 55.6)
Printed by Jerry Raidiger
Published by Landfall Press
LP1992.309.1
Figure 65

LUIS JIMÉNEZ

Bronco (Cowboy), 1978
Lithograph, printed in color, on
Arches Cover White paper
Edition: 35, 10 A.P., 2 P.P., 4 L.P.I.,
7 S.P., 2 C.P. (LJ-78-704)
39 1/2 X 28 1/8 (100.3 X 71.4)
Printed by Jack Lemon, with
Milan Milojevic and Ted Carter
Published by Landfall Press
LP1992.224.1B

Bronco (Horse), 1978
Lithograph, printed in color, on
Arches Cover White paper
Edition: 35, 10 A.P., 2 P.P., 4 L.P.I.,
7 S.P., 2 C.P. (LJ-78-703)
39 1/2 X 28 1/8 (100.3 X 71.4)
Printed by Jack Lemon, with
Milan Milojevic and Ted Carter
Published by Landfall Press
LP1992.224.1A

Honky Tonk, 1981
Lithograph, printed in color, with
gold glitter, on Arches Cover White
paper
Edition: 50, 10 A.P., 2 P.P., 5 L.P.I.,
10 S.P., 2 C.P. (LJ-81-788)
35 X 50 (88.9 X 127)
Printed by Jack Lemon, with
Barbara Spies and Scott Russell
Published by Landfall Press
LP1992.226.1

RONALD JONES

Untitled (This "collapse board" was used during executions at the Walla Walla Prison, Washington. This version was designed for a male body. A prisoner condemned to death by hanging may be strapped to one of these boards as a method of restraint during the execution. According to one prison official, the "collapse board" exists "for individuals who don't have the courage to stand," or "intestinal fortitude."), 1990
Woodcut, printed in color, on Japanese paper
Edition: 10, 5 L.P.I. (RJ-90-54)
63 7/8 X 26 1/8 (162.2 X 66.4)
Printed by Steve Klepac
Published by Landfall Press
LP1992.233.1A

Untitled (This "collapse board" was used during executions at the Walla Walla Prison, Washington. This version was designed for a female body. A prisoner condemned to death by hanging may be strapped to one of these boards as a method of restraint during the execution. According to one prison official, the "collapse board" exists "for individuals who don't have the courage to stand," or "intestinal fortitude."), 1990
Woodcut, printed in color, on Japanese paper
Edition: 10, 5 L.P.I. (RJ-90-57)
63 7/8 X 26 1/8 (162.2 X 66.4)
Printed by Steve Klepac
Published by Landfall Press
LP1992.233.1B

ROBERTO JUAREZ

March Law, 1994
Etching and aquatint, printed in color, with chine collé, on newspaper on Rives BFK paper
Edition: 25, 6 A.P., 2 P.P., 5 L.P.I., 2 C.P. (RJ-94-04)
22 X 32 7/8 (55.9 X 83.5) sheet trimmed to plate
Printed by Steve Campbell
Published by Landfall Press and Diane Villani Editions, New York
Courtesy Landfall Press

PETER JULIAN

Untitled, 1982
Lithograph, printed in color, on Rives BFK paper
Edition: 30, 10 A.P., 2 P.P., 5 L.P.I., 10 S.P., 2 C.P. (PJ-82-836-837)
Diptych, 36 1/4 X 28 (92.1 X 71.1) each
Printed by Jack Lemon, with Barbara Spies, James Renier, and Warren Nisley
Published by Landfall Press
LP1992.314.1-.315.1

JAMES JUSZCZYK

Gate, 1980
Lithograph, printed in color, on Rives BFK paper
Edition: 35, 10 A.P., 2 P.P., 5 L.P.I., 10 S.P., 2 C.P. (JJ-79-766)
20 X 34 (50.8 X 86.4)
Printed by Mary McDonald, with Barbara Spies
Published by Landfall Press
LP1992.238.1

Gate, 1980
Mixed media and adhesive tape on paper
14 X 29 7/8 (35.6 X 75.9)
LP1992.238.2

LEONARD KOSCIANSKI

Fire-Eaters, 1991
Lithograph, printed in color, on Arches paper
Edition: 35, 10 A.P., 4 P.P., 5 L.P.I., 10 S.P., 2 C.P. (LK-90-63)
30 3/8 X 23 5/8 (77.2 X 60)
Printed by Barbara Spies Labus, with Betsy Haude and David Stricker
Published by Landfall Press
LP1992.250.1
Figure 81

ELLEN LANYON

Wonder Book, 1971
Book: lithographs, printed in color, with colored pencil and hand lettering, on Special Arjomari paper
Edition: 25
15 3/8 X 20 1/4 (39.1 X 51.4) each
Printed by Jack Lemon and Jerry Raidiger and bound by George Baer
Published by the artist and Landfall Press
LP1992.256.1

ALFRED LESLIE

Alfred Leslie, 1974
Lithograph on Arches Cover White paper
Edition: 50, 10 A.P., 2 P.P., 5 L.P.I., 5 S.P., 1 C.P. (AL-74-477)
40 1/4 X 30 (102.2 X 76.2)
Printed by David Keister, with Tom Hayduk
Published by Landfall Press
LP1992.280.1
Figure 46

Connie with Baby, 1976
Lithograph on Arches Cover Creme paper
Edition: 20, 1 L.P.I. (AL-74-480)
40 3/8 X 30 (102.6 X 76.2)
Printed by Jack Lemon, with Kent Lovelace
Published by Landfall Press
LP1992.281.1
Figure 47

SOL LEWITT

Lines of One Inch, Four Directions, Four Colors (Set of 16), 1971
Lithograph, printed in color, on Magnani (Italia) paper
Edition: 50, 10 A.P., 2 P.P., 4 L.P.I., 10 S.P. (SL-70-115-130)
16 sheets, 23 X 23 (58.4 X 58.4) each
Printed by Jerry Raidiger, Robert Hicks, and D.R. Holman
Published by Landfall Press
LP1992.581.1-.16

DAVID LIGARE

Sand Drawing #23, from the suite *Sand Drawings*, 1973
Lithograph, printed in color, on J. Barcham Green paper
Edition: 75, 10 A.P., 2 P.P., 4 L.P.I., 5 S.P., 2 C.P. (DL-72-346)
30 X 25 (76.2 X 63.5)
Printed by David Keister, with Laura Holland
Published by Landfall Press
LP1992.295.1
Figure 43

ROBERT LOSTUTTER

Ross' Turaco Looking Back, 1988
Etching, hand-colored
Trial Proof
6 3/4 X 7 5/8 (17.1 X 19.4)
16 X 16 1/2 (40.6 X 41.9)
LP1992.540.5

Green Oropendola, 1989
Etching, hand-colored, on Arches
paper
Edition: 10, 5 A.P., 1 P.P., 2 L.P.I.
(Rl-89-40)
2 7/8 X 3 1/2 (7.3 X 8.9)
14 X 11 (35.6 X 27.9)
Printed by Steve Campbell
Published by Landfall Press
LP1994.69.01

MARILYN MINTER

Hands Dumping, 1989
Serigraph, printed in color, on
anodized aluminum, mounted on
aluminum frame
Edition: 35, 5 A.P., 1 P.P., 5 L.P.I., 10
S.P. (MM-89-19)
23 5/8 X 29 3/4 (60 X 75.6)
Printed by Proto Productions, with
Marilyn Minter and Jack Lemon
Published by Landfall Press
LP1992.319.1

Hands Folding, 1989
Serigraph, printed in color, on
anodized aluminum, mounted on
aluminum frame
Edition: 35, 5 A.P., 2 P.P., 5 L.P.I., 10
S.P., 2 H.C. (MM-89-20)
23 5/8 X 29 3/4 (60 X 75.6)
Printed by Proto Productions, with
Marilyn Minter and Jack Lemon
Published by Landfall Press
LP1992.320.1

Hands Washing, 1989
Serigraph, printed in color, on
anodized aluminum, mounted on
aluminum frame
Edition: 35, 5 A.P., 1 P.P., 5 L.P.I., 10
S.P. (MM-89-21)
29 3/4 X 23 5/8 (75.6 X 60)
Printed by Proto Productions, with
Marilyn Minter and Jack Lemon
Published by Landfall Press
LP1992.321.1

GREG MURDOCK

State of Grace, 1993
Etching and aquatint, printed in
color, with chine collé, on Arches
Cover White paper
Edition: 30, 6 A.P., 2 P.P., 5 L.P.I.
(GM-92-45)
35 X 29 3/4 (88.9 X 75.6)
Printed by Steve Campbell
Published by Equinox Gallery,
Vancouver, and Landfall Press
LP1993.33.1

DON NICE

Double Sneaker, 1975
Lithograph, printed in color, on
handmade Twinrocker Mill paper
Edition: 50, 15 A.P., 2 P.P., 5 L.P.I.,
1 C.P. (DN-74-500)
35 X 47 5/8 (88.9 X 121)
Printed by David Keister, with
Ron Wyffels and Tom Hayduk
Published by Landfall Press
LP1992.331.1

RICHARD NONAS

Giotto, 1979
Lithograph and red china marker,
with collage, on Arches Cover White
paper
Edition: 25, 5 A.P., 2 P.P., 2 L.P.I.
(RN-79-747)
35 1/8 X 45 (89.2 X 114.3)
Printed by Fred Gude, with
Thomas Blackman
Published Landfall Press and
Donald Young Gallery, Chicago
LP1994.48.01

CLAES OLDENBURG

*Store Window: Bow, Hats, Heart,
Shirt, 29¢*, 1973
Lithograph, printed in color, on
J. Barcham Green paper
Edition: 75, 10 A.P., 2 P.P., 4 L.P.I.,
5 S.P., 2 C.P. (CO-72-333)
22 3/4 X 26 7/8 (57.8 X 68.3)
Printed by David Keister, with Laura
Holland
Published by Landfall Press
M1981.71 Gift of Mrs. Jacob Kainen,
Chevy Chase, Maryland

Picasso Cufflink, 1974
Lithograph, printed in color, on
Arches Cover White paper
Edition: 90, 15 A.P., 2 P.P., 4 L.P.I.,
30 S.P., 2 C.P., 30 roman numeral
edition, 15 E.A.(?), 15 H.C., 15 P.P.
(not printer's proofs), 4 L.P. (not
Landfall Press Impression)
(CO-73-423)
36 X 26 7/8 (91.4 X 68.3)
Printed by David Keister and
David Panosh, with Ron Wyffels,
Thomas Minkler, and Gregory
Grenon
Published by Landfall Press,
Petersburg Press, London, and
Propyläen Verlag, Berlin
LP1992.343.1

Picasso Cufflink, 1974
Lithograph, printed in color
Working Proof
36 X 26 7/8 (91.4 X 68.3)
LP1992.343.4

Picasso Cufflink, 1974
Lithograph, printed in color
Working Proof
36 X 26 7/8 (91.4 X 68.3)
LP1992.343.8

Picasso Cufflink, 1974
Lithograph, printed in color
Working Proof
36 X 26 7/8 (91.4 X 68.3)
LP1992.343.10

Picasso Cufflink, 1974
Lithograph, printed in color
Working Proof
36 X 26 7/8 (91.4 X 68.3)
LP1992.343.11

Spoon Pier, from the *Landfall Press
Etching Portfolio*, 1975
Soft-ground etching, aquatint, and
sugar-lift etching, printed in color, on
handmade Twinrocker Mill paper
Edition: 50, 12 A.P., 2 P.P., 5 L.P.I.,
5 S.P., 1 C.P., 25 roman numeral edition (CO-74-004E)
12 1/2 X 10 3/8 (31.8 X 26.4)
28 3/8 X 22 7/8 (72.1 X 58.1)
Printed by Timothy F. Berry
Published by Landfall Press
LP1992.347.1

Geometric Mouse Pyramid Doubled,
1976
Lithograph, printed in color, on
Arches Cover White paper
Edition: 50, 25 A.P., 2 P.P., 7 L.P.I.,
25 S.P., 2 C.P. (CO-76-594)
35 X 26 (88.9 X 66)
Printed by Jack Lemon, with Thomas
Cvikota
Published by Landfall Press and
Multiples, Inc., New York
LP1994.74.01
Figure 7

DENNIS OPPENHEIM
Annual Rings, from the portfolio
Projects, 1973
Lithograph, printed in color, on
Arches Cover White paper
Edition: 81, 5 A.P., 2 P.P., 2 L.P.I.
(DO-73-377)
30 1/16 X 22 3/8 (76.3 X 56.8)
Printed by David Keister, with
Ellen Ferar
Published by John Gibson and
Multiples, Inc., in collaboration with
Sonnabend Gallery, New York
Courtesy The Museum of Modern
Art, New York; The Associates Fund,
266.91.2
Figure 14

Ground Mutations, from the portfolio
Projects, 1973
Lithograph, printed in color, on
Arches Cover White paper
Edition: 81, 5 A.P., 2 P.P., 2 L.P.I.
(DO-73-379)
29 7/8 X 19 3/8 (75.7 X 49.2)
Printed by David Keister, with
Jack Lemon and Tom Cvikota
Published by John Gibson and
Multiples, Inc., in collaboration with
Sonnabend Gallery, New York
Courtesy The Museum of Modern
Art, New York; The Associates Fund,
266.91.4
Figure 15

2000 Foot Shadow Projection, from the
portfolio *Projects*, 1973
Lithograph, printed in color, on
Arches Cover White paper
Edition: 81, 5 A.P., 2 P.P., 2 L.P.I.
(DO-73-383)
22 1/2 X 30 5/16 (57.2 X 77)
Printed by Tom Minkler, with
Jay Orbeck (bears chopmark of
David Keister)
Published by John Gibson and
Multiples, Inc., in collaboration with
Sonnabend Gallery, New York
Courtesy The Museum of Modern
Art, New York; The Associates Fund,
266.91.9
Figure 16

ED PASCHKE
Hairy Shoes, 1971
Lithograph, printed in color, on Rives
BFK paper
Edition: 30, 2 P.P., 2 L.P.I.
(EP-71-218)
17 7/8 X 23 7/8 (45.4 X 60.6)
Printed by Jerry Raidiger and
Mike Rottman
Published by Landfall Press
LP1994.23.01

Fem-Verde, 1987
Lithograph, printed in color, on
Arches Cover White paper
Edition: 50, 10 A.P., 2 P.P., 2 L.P.I.,
23 S.P. (EP-87-935A)
28 X 36 (71.1 X 91.4)
Printed by Barbara Spies, with
Heidijo Lemon and Derek Moore
Published by Landfall Press
LP1992.351.1

Poderosa, 1991
Lithograph, printed in color, on
Arches Cover White paper
Edition: 60, 15 A.P., 3 P.P., 5 L.P.I.,
10 S.P., 2 C.P. (EP-90-60)
30 X 40 (76.2 X 101.6)
Printed by Jack Lemon, with
Barbara Spies Labus
Published by Landfall Press
LP1994.75.01

PHILIP PEARLSTEIN
Figure Lying on Rug, from the portfolio
Six Lithographs Drawn from Life, 1970
Lithograph, printed in color, on
Arches paper
Edition: 50, 2 A.P., 2 P.P., 4 L.P.I.,
4 Nova Scotia College of Art and
Design Impressions, (PP-70-000;
NSCAD no. 121)
30 X 22 (76.2 X 55.9)
Printed by Robert Rogers and
Jerry Raidiger
Published by Landfall Press
LP1994.79.01

Girl on Orange and Black Mexican Rug,
1973
Lithograph, printed in color, on
Arches Cover Creme paper
Edition: 100, 10 A.P., 2 P.P., 4 L.P.I.,
5 S.P., 2 C.P. (PP-73-342)
24 1/2 X 34 (62.2 X 86.4)
Printed by David Keister, with
Glenn Brill
Published by Landfall Press
M1992.286.1 Gift of Jeanette
Pasin Sloan

Nude on Iron Bench, from the *Landfall
Press Etching Portfolio*, 1975
Lift-ground etching and aquatint, on
handmade Twinrocker Mill paper
Edition: 50, 12 A.P., 2 P.P., 5 L.P.I.,
5 S.P., 1 C.P., 25 roman numeral
edition (PP-74-003E)
17 7/8 X 23 5/8 (45.4 X 60)
22 1/4 X 28 (56.5 X 71.1)
Printed by Timothy F. Berry
Published by Landfall Press
LP1992.377.1

Two Nudes on Blue Coverlet, 1977
Lithograph, printed in color, on
handmade wove paper
Edition: 65, 10 A.P., 2 P.P., 4 L.P.I.,
7 S.P., 2 C.P., 2 presentation proofs
(PP-77-616)
27 1/4 X 39 5/8 (69.2 X 100.6)
Printed by Jack Lemon, with Milan
Milojevic
Published by Landfall Press
LP1992.384.1

JOSEPH PICCILLO
Edge Event III, 1982
Lithograph on Arches Cover White
paper
Edition: 16, 9 A.P., 1 P.P., 2 L.P.I.,
2 C.P. (JP-81-824)
38 1/2 X 31 1/8 (97.8 X 79.1)
Printed by Jack Lemon, with
Barbara Spies and James Renier
Published by Landfall Press
LP1992.391.1

MARTIN PURYEAR
Dark Loop, 1982
Woodcut on Kozo paper
Edition: 35, 10 A.P., 2 P.P., 5 L.P.I.,
15 S.P. (MP-82-848)
22 5/8 X 30 1/4 (57.5 X 76.8)
Printed by Barbara Spies, with
Heidijo Lemon
Published by N.A.M.E. Gallery,
Chicago, and Landfall Press
M1989.90 Gift of J. Thomas Maher
III with National Endowment for the
Arts Matching Funds

BARBARA ROSSI
Eye Deal, 1973
Lithograph, printed in color, with
chine collé, on Suminagashi paper on
Rives BFK paper
Edition: 40, 2 P.P., 2 L.P.I.
(BR-73-414)
24 X 18 (61 X 45.7)
Printed by Thomas Minkler, with
Gregory Grenon
Published by the artist and
Landfall Press
LP1992.395.1
Figure 22

ALLEN RUPPERSBERG
Adults Only Please, from the portfolio
Preview Suite, 1988
Lithograph, printed in color, on
Arches Cover White paper
Edition: 30, 5 A.P., 2 P.P., 5 L.P.I.,
1 C.P. (AR-88-974)
22 1/8 X 13 3/4 (56.2 X 34.9)
Printed by David Jones and Barbara
Spies Labus, with Fred Baehr
Published by Landfall Press
LP1992.399.1

Are You Crying?, from the portfolio
Preview Suite, 1988
Lithograph, printed in color, on
Arches Cover White paper
Edition: 30, 5 A.P., 2 P.P., 5 L.P.I.,
1 C.P. (AR-88-968)
22 1/8 X 13 3/4 (56.2 X 34.9)
Printed by David Jones and
Barbara Spies Labus, with Fred Baehr
Published by Landfall Press
LP1992.400.1

Everything Is Over, from the portfolio
Preview Suite, 1988
Lithograph, printed in color, on
Arches Cover White paper
Edition: 30, 5 A.P., 2 P.P., 5 L.P.I.,
1 C.P. (AR-88-973)
22 1/8 X 13 3/4 (56.2 X 34.9)
Printed by David Jones and Barbara
Spies Labus, with Fred Baehr
Published by Landfall Press
LP1992.401.1

Good Luck!, from the portfolio
Preview Suite, 1988
Lithograph, printed in color, on
Arches Cover White paper
Edition: 30, 5 A.P., 2 P.P., 5 L.P.I.,
1 C.P. (AR-88-971)
22 X 13 7/8 (55.9 X 35.2)
Printed by David Jones and Barbara
Spies Labus, with Fred Baehr
Published by Landfall Press
LP1992.402.1

It's Not Art (That Counts Now), from
the portfolio *Preview Suite*, 1988
Lithograph, printed in color, on
Arches Cover White paper
Edition: 30, 5 A.P., 2 P.P., 5 L.P.I.,
1 C.P. (AR-88-967)
22 1/8 X 13 7/8 (56.2 X 35.2)
Printed by David Jones and Barbara
Spies Labus, with Fred Baehr
Published by Landfall Press
LP1992.403.1

No I've Got Something in My Eye,
from the portfolio *Preview Suite*, 1988
Lithograph, printed in color, on
Arches Cover White paper
Edition: 30, 5 A.P., 2 P.P., 5 L.P.I.,
1 C.P. (AR-88-975)
22 1/8 X 13 3/4 (56.2 X 34.9)
Printed by David Jones and Barbara
Spies Labus, with Fred Baehr
Published by Landfall Press
LP1992.404.1

Nostalgia 24 Hours A Day, from the
portfolio *Preview Suite*, 1988
Lithograph, printed in color, on
Arches Cover White paper
Edition: 30, 5 A.P., 2 P.P., 5 L.P.I.,
1 C.P. (AR-88-970)
22 1/8 X 13 3/4 (56.2 X 34.9)
Printed by David Jones and
Barbara Spies Labus, with Fred Baehr
Published by Landfall Press
LP1992.405.1

Nothing-Nobody, from the portfolio
Preview Suite, 1988
Lithograph, printed in color, on
Arches Cover White paper
Edition: 30, 5 A.P., 2 P.P., 5 L.P.I.,
1 C.P. (AR-88-972)
22 1/8 X 13 3/4 (56.2 X 34.9)
Printed by David Jones and
Barbara Spies Labus, with Fred Baehr
Published by Landfall Press
LP1992.406.1

What Should I Do?, from the portfolio
Preview Suite, 1988
Lithograph, printed in color, on
Arches Cover White paper
Edition: 30, 5 A.P., 2 P.P., 5 L.P.I.,
1 C.P. (AR-88-969)
22 1/8 X 13 3/4 (56.2 X 34.9)
Printed by David Jones and
Barbara Spies Labus, with Fred Baehr
Published by Landfall Press
LP1992.407.1

Who's Afraid of the New Now?, from
the portfolio *Preview Suite*, 1988
Lithograph, printed in color, on
Arches Cover White paper
Edition: 30, 5 A.P., 2 P.P., 5 L.P.I.,
1 C.P. (AR-88-976)
22 1/8 X 13 3/4 (56.2 X 34.9)
Printed by David Jones and
Barbara Spies Labus, with Fred Baehr
Published by Landfall Press
LP1992.408.1

PETER SAUL

Angela Davis, 1972
Lithograph, printed in color, on
Special Arjomari paper
Edition: 100, 5 A.P., 2 P.P., 2 L.P.I.
(PS-72-308)
34 7/8 X 30 (88.6 X 76.2)
Printed by David Keister and
Arthur Kleinman
Published by Dorthea Speyer Gallery,
Paris
LP1992.411.1

Politics, 1985
Lithograph, printed in color, on Rives
BFK Gray paper
Edition: 25, 10 A.P., 2 P.P., 5 L.P.I.,
10 S.P., 2 C.P. (PA-84-897)
32 3/4 X 23 1/2 (83.2 X 59.7)
Printed by Jack Lemon, with
Michael Riley and Barbara Spies
Published by Landfall Press
LP1992.413.1

KENNETH SHOWELL

Terni, 1970
Lithograph, printed in color, on
German Etching paper
Edition: 50, 10 A.P., 2 P.P., 4 L.P.I.,
10 S.P., C.P., 1 presentation proof
(KS-70-101)
30 1/8 X 22 (76.5 X 55.9)
Printed by Jerry Raidiger
Published by Landfall Press
LP1992.416.1

JEANETTE PASIN SLOAN

Binary, from the portfolio *Jeanette
Pasin Sloan*, 1986
Hard-ground etching and aquatint,
on J. Barcham Green paper
Edition: 20, 10 A.P., 2 P.P., 5 L.P.I.,
10 S.P., 2 C.P., 25 portfolio proofs
(JPS-86-926E)
13 3/4 X 14 5/8 (34.9 X 37.1)
24 1/8 X 22 (61.3 X 55.9)
Printed by Jack Lemon
Published by Landfall Press
LP1992.419.1

Boston Red, from the portfolio *Jeanette
Pasin Sloan*, 1986
Woodcut, printed in color, on Kizuki
Hanga paper
Edition: 20, 10 A.P., 2 P.P., 5 L.P.I.,
10 S.P., 2 C.P., 25 portfolio proofs
(JPS-86-921W)
24 1/8 X 22 1/8 (61.3 X 56.2)
Printed by Michael Berdan
Published by Landfall Press
LP1992.420.8

Sergeant First Class, from the portfolio
Jeanette Pasin Sloan, 1986
Lithograph, printed in color, on Rives
BFK paper
Edition: 40, 10 A.P., 2 P.P., 5 L.P.I.,
10 S.P., 2 C.P., 25 portfolio proofs
(JPS-86-917A inscribed on reverse of
print; JPS-85-917A on print docu-
mentation)
24 1/4 X 22 (61.6 X 55.9)
Printed by Barbara Spies and
Jack Lemon, with Heidijo Lemon
Published by Landfall Press
LP1992.433.1

Sergeant First Class—State I, from the
portfolio *Jeanette Pasin Sloan*, 1986
Lithograph, printed in color, on Rives
BFK paper
Edition: 5 A.P., 4 L.P.I., 25 portfolio
proofs (JPS-85-917A inscribed on
reverse of print; JPS-85-917B on print
documentation)
24 1/4 X 22 (61.6 X 55.9)
Printed by Barbara Spies and
Jack Lemon, with Heidijo Lemon
Published by Landfall Press
LP1992.434.1

T.L. SOLIEN

Bad Blood, 1984
Lithograph and woodcut, printed in
color, on handmade HMP paper
Edition: 51, 10 A.P., 2 P.P., 2 L.P.I., 2
C.P. (TLS-84-901)
31 1/2 X 41 1/4 (80 X 104.8)
Printed by Jack Lemon, with
Barbara Spies
Published by The New Van Straaten
Gallery, Chicago, and Landfall Press
LP1992.440.1

PAT STEIR

Roll Me a Rainbow, 1974
Lithograph, printed in color, on
Arches Cover White paper
Edition: 35, 10 A.P., 2 P.P., 4 L.P.I., 5
S.P., 2 C.P. (IPS-73-425)
21 7/8 X 29 1/2 (55.6 X 59.7)
Printed by David Panosh and
Thomas Minkler, with Richard Finch
and Gregory Page
Published by Landfall Press
Courtesy Landfall Press

Being, from the *Burial Mound Series*,
1976
Drypoint on handmade HMP paper
Edition: 35, 5 A.P., 1 P.P., 4 L.P.I.,
2 C.P., 1 Teaberry Impression
(PS-76-040E)
10 X 10 (25.4 X 25.4) sheet trimmed
to plate
Printed by Timothy F. Berry
Published by Landfall Press
LP1992.455.5.1
Figure 28

Identity, from the *Burial Mound Series*,
1976
Drypoint on handmade HMP paper
Edition: 35, 5 A.P., 1 P.P., 4 L.P.I.,
2 C.P., 1 Teaberry Impression
(PS-76-039E)
10 X 10 (25.4 X 25.4) sheet trimmed
to plate
Printed by Timothy F. Berry
Published by Landfall Press
LP1992.455.4.1
Figure 29

I Don't Know, from the *Burial Mound
Series*, 1976
Drypoint on handmade HMP paper
Edition: 35, 5 A.P., 1 P.P., 4 L.P.I.,
2 C.P., 1 Teaberry Impression
(PS-76-041E)
10 X 10 (25.4 X 25.4) sheet trimmed
to plate
Printed by Timothy F. Berry
Published by Landfall Press
LP1992.455.6.1
Figure 25

Introduction, from the *Burial Mound Series*, 1976
Drypoint, soft-ground etching, and spit-bite etching, on handmade HMP paper
Edition: 35, 5 A.P., 1 P.P., 4 L.P.I., 2 C.P., 1 Teaberry Impression (PS-76-042E)
10 X 10 (25.4 X 25.4) sheet trimmed to plate
Printed by Timothy F. Berry
Published by Landfall Press
LP1992.455.7.1
Figure 23

Little Line, from the *Burial Mound Series*, 1976
Drypoint on handmade HMP paper
Edition: 35, 5 A.P., 1 P.P., 4 L.P.I., 2 C.P., 1 Teaberry Impression (PS-76-036E)
10 X 10 (25.4 X 25.4) sheet trimmed to plate
Printed by Timothy F. Berry
Published by Landfall Press
LP1992.455.1.1
Figure 27

Meaning, from the *Burial Mound Series*, 1976
Drypoint on handmade HMP paper
Edition: 35, 5 A.P., 1 P.P., 4 L.P.I., 2 C.P., 1 Teaberry Impression (PS-76-038E)
10 X 10 (25.4 X 25.4) sheet trimmed to plate
Printed by Timothy F. Berry
Published by Landfall Press
LP1992.455.3.1
Figure 24

Space, from the *Burial Mound Series*, 1976
Drypoint on handmade HMP paper
Edition: 35, 5 A.P., 1 P.P., 4 L.P.I., 2 C.P., 1 Teaberry Impression (PS-76-037E)
10 X 10 (25.4 X 25.4) sheet trimmed to plate
Printed by Timothy F. Berry
Published by Landfall Press
LP1992.455.2.1
Figure 26

RANDY TWADDLE
Extended Orbits, 1989
Lithograph on Rives BFK paper
Edition: 20, 5 A.P., 2 P.P., 5 L.P.I. (RT-89-01-02)
Diptych, 30 1/8 X 30 (76.5 X 76.2) each
Printed by Jack Lemon
Published by Landfall Press
LP1992.478.1-.479.1

Untitled, 1991
Aquatint, soft-ground etching, and spit-bite etching, on Rives BFK paper
Edition: 20, 6 A.P., 2 P.P., 5 L.P.I., 5 S.P., 2 C.P., 4 H.C. (RT-90-69)
33 5/8 X 23 3/4 (85.4 X 60.3)
40 X 29 7/8 (101.6 X 75.9)
Printed by Steve Campbell, with Jack Lemon
Published by Landfall Press
LP1992.481.1
Figure 79

JACK TWORKOV
L-SF-ES-#1, 1978
Hard-ground etching and aquatint, with hand burnishing, printed in color, on Rives BFK paper
Edition: 25, 10 A.P., 2 P.P., 4 L.P.I., 10 S.P., 2 C.P. (JT-78-072E)
9 3/4 X 9 3/4 (24.8 X 24.8)
16 1/4 X 16 (41.3 X 40.6)
Printed by Timothy F. Berry
Published by Landfall Press
LP1992.553.2

L-SF-ES-#2, 1978
Hard-ground etching and aquatint, with hand burnishing, printed in color, on Rives BFK paper
Edition: 25, 10 A.P., 2 P.P., 4 L.P.I., 10 S.P., 2 C.P. (JT-78-073E)
9 7/8 X 9 3/4 (25.1 X 24.8)
16 1/4 X 15 7/8 (41.3 X 40.6)
Printed by Timothy F. Berry
Published by Landfall Press
LP1992.535.2

L-SF-ES-#3, 1978
Hard-ground etching and aquatint, with hand burnishing, printed in color, on Rives BFK paper
Edition: 25, 10 A.P., 2 P.P., 4 L.P.I., 10 S.P., 2 C.P. (JT-78-074E)
9 7/8 X 9 3/4 (25.1 X 24.8)
16 1/4 X 16 (41.3 X 40.6)
Printed by Timothy F. Berry
Published by Landfall Press
LP1992.536.2

TOM UTTECH
Kasakogwog, 1990
Lithograph, printed in color, on Rives BFK paper
Edition: 25, 10 A.P., 1 P.P., 5 L.P.I., 10 S.P., 2 C.P. (TU-89-41)
35 7/8 X 40 7/8 (91.1 X 103.8)
Printed by Jack Lemon and Barbara Spies Labus, with Betsy Haude and Steve Campbell
Published by Landfall Press
LP1992.492.1

BERNAR VENET
Two Undetermined Lines, 1990
Lithograph, printed in color, on Somerset paper
Edition: 30, 10 A.P., 4 P.P., 10 L.P.I., 1 C.P. (BV-89-26)
45 1/2 X 39 1/8 (115.6 X 99.4)
Printed by Barbara Spies Labus, with Jack Lemon
Published by Landfall Press
LP1992.496.1

KARA WALKER
The Means to an End...A Shadow Drama in Five Acts, 1995
Hard-ground etching and aquatint, on Somerset Satin paper
Edition: 20, 5 A.P., 2 P.P., 2 L.P.I., 5 S.P., 1 C.P. (KW-95-06-10)
5 sheets, 25 1/4 X 33 (64.1 X 83.8) each, sheet trimmed to plate
Printed by Steve Campbell
Published by Landfall Press
Courtesy Landfall Press
Figure 85

H.C. WESTERMANN

An Affair in the Islands, 1972
Lithograph, printed in color, on Rives
BFK paper
Edition: 60, 10 A.P., 2 P.P., 2 L.P.I.
(HCW-72-323)
25 1/4 X 33 (64.1 X 83.8)
Printed by Jerry Raidiger, with
David Panosh
Published by Allan Frumkin Gallery,
New York, and Landfall Press
LP1992.497.1

Death Ship in a Port, 1972
Lithograph, printed in color, on Rives
BFK paper
Edition: 60, 10 A.P., 2 P.P., 2 L.P.I.
(HCW-72-253)
25 X 33 (63.5 X 83.8)
Printed by Jerry Raidiger, with
Arthur Kleinman
Published by Allan Frumkin Gallery,
New York, and Landfall Press
LP1992.499.1

Holiday Inn, 1972
Lithograph, printed in color, on Rives
BFK paper
Edition: 60, 10 A.P., 2 P.P., 2 L.P.I.
(HCW-72-324)
25 X 33 (63.5 X 83.8)
Printed by Jerry Raidiger, with
Arthur Kleinman
Published by Allan Frumkin Gallery,
New York, and Landfall Press
LP1992.501.1

WILLIAM T. WILEY

Thank You Hide, 1972
Lithograph, printed in color, on
Special Arjomari paper
Edition: 65, 10 A.P., 2 P.P., 4 L.P.I.,
10 S.P., 2 C.P. (WTW-72-265)
35 X 48 1/8 (88.9 X 122.2)
Printed by Jerry Raidiger and Arthur
Kleinman
Published by Landfall Press
LP1994.43.01

Seasonall Gate, from the *Landfall Press
Etching Portfolio*, 1975
Lithograph and hard-ground etching,
printed in color, on handmade
Twinrocker Mill paper
Edition: 50, 12 A.P., 2 P.P., 2 L.P.I.,
5 S.P., 1 C.P., 25 roman numeral edi-
tion (WTW-74-002E)
23 3/4 X 17 3/4 (60.3 X 45.1)
28 X 22 (71.1 X 55.9)
Printed by Timothy F. Berry
Published by Landfall Press
LP1992.531.1

Mr. Unatural—State II, 1976
Lithograph, printed in color, on
Arches Cover Creme paper
Edition: 65, 10 A.P., 1 P.P., 5 L.P.I.,
5 S.P., 2 C.P.(WTW-75-566)
36 1/8 X 25 (91.8 X 63.5)
Printed by Jack Lemon, with Ted
Stanuga and Thomas Cvikota
Published by Landfall Press
LP1992.566.1

Green Shoes—State I, 1977
Soft-ground etching and aquatint,
printed in color, on Arches Cover
Creme paper
Edition: 18, 2 A.P., 1 P.P., 2 L.P.I.,
5 S.P. (WTW-76-052E-State I)
17 3/4 X 23 1/2 (45.1 X 59.7)
22 X 30 (55.9 X 76.2)
Printed by Timothy F. Berry
Published by Landfall Press
LP1994.55.01

Green Shoes, 1977
Pencil on vellum
22 X 30 (55.9 X 76.2)
LP1992.515.2

Green Shoes, 1977
Etching and aquatint
Working Proof
17 3/4 X 23 1/2 (45.1 X 59.7)
22 3/8 X 30 (56.8 X 76.2)
LP1992.515.6

Green Shoes, 1977
Etching and aquatint
Working Proof
17 3/4 X 23 1/2 (45.1 X 59.7)
22 1/4 X 29 7/8 (56.5 X 75.9)
LP1992.515.9

Green Shoes, 1977
Etching and aquatint
Working Proof
17 3/4 X 23 1/2 (45.1 X 59.7)
22 1/4 X 29 7/8 (56.5 X 75.9)
LP1992.515.15

Green Shoes, 1977
Copper plate
18 X 24 (45.7 X 61)
LP1992.515.17

Green Shoes, 1977
Copper plate
18 X 24 (45.7 X 61)
LP1992.515.18

Green Shoes—State II, 1977
Soft-ground etching and aquatint,
printed in color, on Arches Cover
Creme paper
Edition: 25, 2 A.P., 1 P.P., 2 L.P.I.,
5 S.P., 2 C.P.
(WTW-77-052E)
17 3/4 X 23 1/2 (45.1 X 59.7)
22 X 30 (55.9 X 76.2)
Printed by Timothy F. Berry
Published by Landfall Press
LP1992.515.1

Suite of Daze, 1977
Book: 14 etchings, on Arches Creme
or Arches Cover White paper, and
the text from the *I-Ching*, or *Book of
Changes* (the Richard Wilhelm translation rendered into English by Cary
R. Baynes), bound in leather and
chamois
Edition: 50, 5 A.P. (WTW-76-017#)
16 7/8 X 13 (42.9 X 33) sheet, plates
variable
Printed by Timothy F. Berry; text set
and printed by Holbrook Teler,
Spring Creek Typesetting Service;
bound by A & H Bindery
Published by Landfall Press
LP1992.534.1

*Once Upon a Time When All Is
Flawless*, 1982
Lithograph, printed in color, on four
scarves (one linen, three nylon), in a
wooden case
Edition: 15, 5 A.P., 1 P.P., 3 L.P.I.,
5 S.P., C.P. (WTW-80-773)
28 X 26 (71.1 X 66)
Printed by Jack Lemon, with Barbara
Spies
Published by Landfall Press
LP1994.45.01

KARL WIRSUM

Skull Daze, 1971
Lithograph, printed in color, on
German Etching paper
Edition: 50, 4 A.P., 2 P.P., 2 L.P.I.
(KW-71-217)
24 X 34 (61 X 86.4)
Printed by Jerry Raidiger and
Michael Rottman
Published by Landfall Press
LP1992.21.1

*Blue Burger Quartet à la Carte…(pie in
the sky not included)*, 1994
Lithograph, printed in color, on Rives
BFK paper, hand cut and assembled
with hot glue
Edition: 25, 6 A.P., 2 P.P., 2 L.P.I.,
5 S.P., 1 C.P. (KW-94-01)
12 X 12 1/2 X 3 1/2
(30.5 X 31.8 X 8.9)
Printed by Barbara Spies Labus, with
C. Tyler Johnson; assembled by
Jennifer Luk
Published by Landfall Press
Courtesy Landfall Press

ROBERT YARBER

The Corruption of Ecstasy, 1989
Lithograph, printed in color, on black
Arches paper
Edition: 25, 6 A.P., 2 P.P., 5 L.P.I.,
6 S.P., 2 C.P. (BY-88-998)
30 X 44 (76.2 X 111.8)
Printed by Jack Lemon and
David Jones, with Fred Baehr, Steve
Campbell, and Kevin Finegan
Published by Landfall Press
LP1992.558.1
Figure 76

DUANE ZALOUDEK

Untitled, 1991
Etching, printed in color, on ivory
wove paper
Edition: 20, 10 A.P., 2 P.P., 5 L.P.I.,
2 C.P., 2 sales examples (DZ-91-79)
19 3/4 X 18 (50.2 X 45.7)
29 7/8 X 27 7/8 (75.9 X 70.8)
Printed by Steve Campbell
Published by Landfall Press
LP1993.42.1

Untitled, 1991
Etching, printed in color, with chine
collé, on Seiko Sen paper on
Arches paper
Edition: 20, 10 A.P., 2 P.P., 5 L.P.I., 2
C.P., 2 sales examples (DZ-91-81)
19 3/4 X 18 (50.2 X 45.7)
29 7/8 X 27 7/8 (75.9 X 70.8)
Printed by Steve Campbell
Published by Landfall Press
LP1993.43.1

143. Jack Lemon, c. 1976-78

Tyler Graphics
The Extended Image

Walker Art Center
Minneapolis

Abbeville Press   Publishers
New York

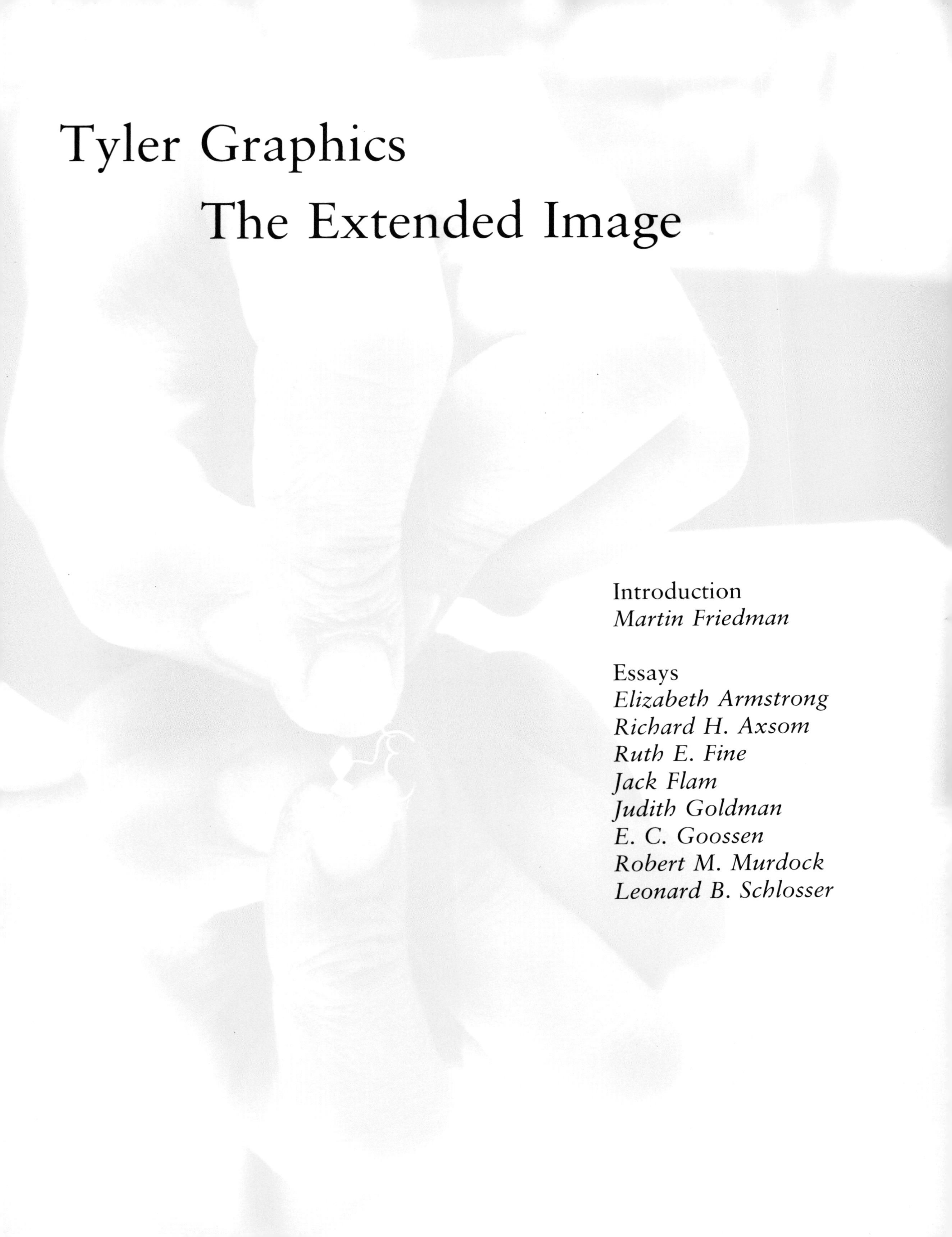

Tyler Graphics

The Extended Image

Introduction
Martin Friedman

Essays
Elizabeth Armstrong
Richard H. Axsom
Ruth E. Fine
Jack Flam
Judith Goldman
E. C. Goossen
Robert M. Murdock
Leonard B. Schlosser

This publication was supported by generous grants from the Luce Fund for Scholarship in American Art, a program of The Henry Luce Foundation, Inc., and from the National Endowment for the Humanities.

Library of Congress Cataloging in Publication Data

Tyler Graphics, the extended image.

  Bibliography: p. 242
  Includes index.
  Contents: Kenneth Tyler: the artisan as artist/Judith Goldman—Robert Motherwell's graphics/Jack Flam—Spontaneity and the print/ E. C. Goossen—[etc.]
  1. Tyler Graphics Ltd.
  2. Tyler, Kenneth E.
  3. Prints, American—Themes, motives.
  4. Prints—20th century—United States—Themes, motives.
   I. Armstrong, Elizabeth.
   II. Walker Art Center.
NE508.T96   1987
769.9747'245   87-1298
ISBN 0-89659-750-4 (Abbeville Press)
ISBN 0-89659-772-5 (pbk.)

First edition

Publication director: Elizabeth Armstrong
Editors: Andrea P. A. Belloli and Karen Jacobson
Designer: Lorraine Ferguson
Production manager: Dana Cole

Unless otherwise indicated, paper is white. Only support papers are identified; the various papers used in collages, which differ from the support papers in almost every case, are identified in *Tyler Graphics: Catalogue Raisonné, 1974–1985*. For works comprising more than one sheet, the number of sheets is noted and the overall dimensions are provided. Dimensions are in inches; height precedes width. Works that also appear in the catalogue raisonné are identified by a Tyler catalogue raisonné number, which appears in parentheses at the end of each caption.

Throughout this publication the titles of individual works and books are given in italics, and titles for series and portfolios are given in roman type.

(front cover)
David Hockney
Piscine à minuit, Paper Pool 19   1978
colored, pressed paper pulp
six sheets: 72 x 85½
Collection Walker Art Center, Minneapolis
Gift of Mr. and Mrs. Kenneth E. Tyler
(Tyler 243:DH19)

(back cover, top)
David Hockney spooning colored pulp onto top right panel of *Piscine avec trois bleus*, Paper Pool 6, 1978, Tyler Graphics Ltd.

(back cover, bottom)
David Hockney applying colored pulp using a turkey baster to a panel of *A Large Diver*, Paper Pool 27, 1978, Tyler Graphics Ltd.

(title page)
Line being inscribed into copper plate with a square burin, Tyler Graphics Ltd.

Contents

Introduction

Martin Friedman

By the time Kenneth Tyler established Tyler Graphics Ltd. in Bedford Village, New York, he had accumulated considerable experience in collaborating with some of this country's most gifted artists. Tyler had joined the Tamarind Lithography Workshop in Los Angeles as a printer-trainee in 1963, became technical director in 1964, and remained until 1965, when he established his own workshop, Gemini Ltd. In 1966 that company was absorbed into a new entity, Gemini G.E.L. (Graphics Editions Limited), founded by Tyler, Sidney B. Felsen, and Stanley Grinstein. In February 1974, seeking new challenges, Tyler shifted his base of operations to the East Coast, where, among other considerations, his printmaking facilities would be more accessible to many of the artists with whom he wanted to work.

At Gemini G.E.L., Tyler had persuaded a number of prominent young painters and sculptors, including Frank Stella, Claes Oldenburg, and Roy Lichtenstein, to extend their imagery to printmaking, and once lured into the print workshop, they reveled in the profusion of new materials and processes he provided. With the establishment of such independent print studios, American printmaking took on a vivid new character as important talents from the world of painting and sculpture were attracted to its expressive possibilities. Under Tyler's aegis, printing techniques were freely combined, images grew to heroic scale, and prints occasionally developed into three-dimensional constructions that crossed the border into sculpture. With his enthusiastic assistance, these young artists revolutionized the public's perception of printmaking, heretofore considered more an arcane craft than a medium for innovative expression.

Within a few years of its founding in New York, Tyler Graphics was justifiably regarded as one of this country's leading print shops. The roster of artists working there grew to reflect a diversity of stylistic approaches. Among the new arrivals in 1976 were Helen Frankenthaler, Richard Hamilton, and Michael Heizer; a year later Nancy Graves came aboard; in 1978 Kenneth Noland and Alan Shields tried out the

Roy Lichtenstein
American Indian Theme VI 1980
woodcut on Suzuki paper
37½ x 50¼
Collection Walker Art Center, Minneapolis
Tyler Graphics Archive
(Tyler 351:RL19)

papermaking facilities at Bedford Village. These artists and many others found themselves working in a highly supportive atmosphere where first-rate technicians and equipment were readily available to help translate their ideas into the printmaking media.

But even as Tyler was expanding the production of the Bedford Village studio and developing these new artistic relationships, he began to think about the fate of his life's efforts. He was concerned about the ultimate disposition of the rapidly growing archive that documented not only every print produced at Bedford Village but also the evolution of Tyler Graphics itself. While there was no lack of collectors, private and institutional, for Tyler Graphics's production, he wanted to place this important material in a single institution where it would not only be stored under ideal conditions but would also be made available to artists, scholars, and public alike. Tyler's objective had been realized in part, although not in a systematic or complete fashion, by the Australian National Gallery in Canberra. That museum has a collection of all prints produced by Tyler from 1965 to 1973, including images made at Tamarind, Gemini Ltd., and Gemini G.E.L., and has also acquired a number of prints issued by Tyler Graphics, but its collection is far from a complete representation.

There were precedents for Tyler's desire to find a permanent home for his archive and collection. The directors of two of America's most distinguished print studios had recently grappled with a similar issue and resolved it successfully. In 1981 the archive prints of Universal Limited Art Editions (ULAE), the highly esteemed Long Island–based studio founded by Tatyana Grosman in 1957, were acquired by the Art Institute of Chicago. And in 1982 Felsen and Grinstein arranged for Gemini G.E.L.'s archival materials to be housed permanently in the National Gallery of Art, Washington, D.C. Among the museums whose staffs met with Tyler during the early stages of his investigations was the Walker Art Center. As it happened, the Walker was able to respond to him quickly and positively for several reasons. First, the museum had been collecting prints for many years, with particular emphasis on the work of artists who, since the mid-1960s, had utilized this medium seriously. Since many of these artists were already represented in the Walker's collection by paintings and sculptures, having examples of their printmaking would enable it to show a wider spectrum of their production.

Then there was the matter of timing. The Walker was about to embark on a major construction project that would result in substantial additional exhibition and program space. Fortunately, the availability of the Tyler Graphics Archive coincided with the design phase of this addition. A generous contribution from The McKnight Foundation to the museum's capital campaign made possible the construction of such space as part of the new addition to the building.

Thanks to this fortuitous combination of circumstances, the Walker Art Center was able, through gift and purchase, to proceed with the

Richard Smith
Cartouche IV-4 1980
colored, pressed paper
pulp; fabric; grom-
mets; string;
aluminum tubes
three panels:
60 x 60
Collection Walker Art
Center, Minneapolis
Gift of Dr. Maclyn E.
Wade, 1983
(Tyler 803:RS42)

acquisition of the Tyler Graphics Archive. The museum's agreement
with Tyler provided that it would receive the archive print of each
editioned image already produced. Also, Tyler agreed to provide the
Walker with archive prints from all future editions issued by Tyler
Graphics. At the time the agreement was signed in 1983, the museum
received some twelve hundred proofs, prints, and working sketches as
well as a number of unique images, such as David Hockney's large-scale
Piscine à minuit, Robert Zakanitch's *Straightback Swans II,* and a
Richard Smith Cartouche. A substantial number of recent prints have
since been added. Notable among these are Stella's Swan Engravings,
1982–85, Robert Motherwell's America–La France Variations, 1984,
and Hockney's *An Image of Celia,* 1986.

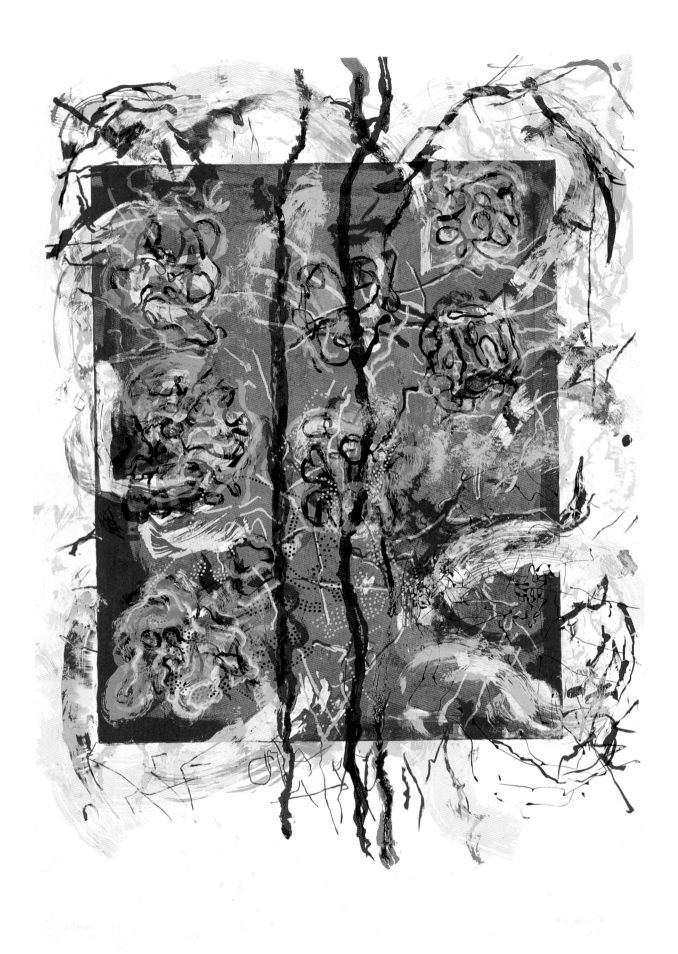

To commemorate its acquisition of the Tyler Graphics Archive and focus public attention on this significant collection of images by leading contemporary American and European artists, the Walker Art Center, in collaboration with Abbeville Press, is issuing this volume and a catalogue raisonné of Tyler Graphics's production from 1974 to 1985. The organization of these volumes was the responsibility of Elizabeth Armstrong, associate curator, Walker Art Center, whose involvement with the Tyler Graphics Archive dates from its arrival at the museum in 1983. In addition to working on this publication, she has organized several exhibitions at the Walker that have utilized material from the archive, including, in 1984, *Prints from Tyler Graphics* and, in 1985, *Paperworks from Tyler Graphics* and *Robert Motherwell: The Collaged Image.*

This volume, *Tyler Graphics: The Extended Image*, features interpretive essays by distinguished specialists on the work of artists represented in the archive. The initial essay, by Judith Goldman, traces Tyler's biography and the evolution of his prolific career from his days at Tamarind to the present. Following this is a series of pieces by Jack Flam, E. C. Goossen, Robert M. Murdock, Elizabeth Armstrong, and Richard H. Axsom on artists associated with the Tyler Graphics print workshop. In several instances these articles deal with the production of Tyler's distinguished visitors within the contexts of major stylistic currents. Jack Flam discusses the emblematic forms in Motherwell's prints in terms of the Abstract Expressionist ethos. Elizabeth Armstrong writes about the print imagery of Lichtenstein, Oldenburg, Hockney, Hamilton, and Malcolm Morley in terms of Pop Art manifestations in the United States and England.

Two chapters discuss Tyler's emphasis on handmade paper as a primary artistic as well as material ingredient of printmaking. Leonard B. Schlosser draws upon his considerable knowledge of the history and chemistry of paper to discuss Tyler's innovative use of that medium, while Ruth E. Fine surveys the paperworks produced at the workshop.

For all his visible accomplishments, Tyler shows few signs of settling down to a predictable routine. Young as well as established artists are attracted to his studio, where they are encouraged to pursue ambitious projects, virtually all of which seem to run well beyond their allotted time frames. Largely because of the creative interactions that prevail in Tyler's workshop, the boundaries of printmaking continue to expand well beyond the broad limits he himself helped establish some twenty years ago.

Nancy Graves
Approaches the Limit of II 1981
lithograph, etching on Arches Cover paper
48 x 31⅝
Collection Walker Art Center, Minneapolis
Tyler Graphics Archive
(Tyler 209: NG8)

Gemini II   The Master printer of Los Angeles   David Hockney 73

Kenneth Tyler
The Artisan as Artist

Judith Goldman

Everything about him is considered: the moustache; the hair, designed to fit the head like a helmet; and the sunglasses, which are the kind worn by the hero in 1960s movies when he confronts the southern sheriff. The Kenneth Tyler in David Hockney's 1973 portrait (p. 12) has a cool countenance. He is a man who believes in appearances, not a man to turn a casual face to the world. Tyler once wore chamois jackets and drove a white Mercedes, a 280SL. Hockney catches the vanity and sets down the dude and another aspect as well: a man in an industrial apron, with a diffident slouch and large hands. Those hands rivet our attention. They tell the story of Tyler the worker, of the printer and technological Houdini who made the dude possible.

The portrait illuminates more than Tyler. *The Master Printer of Los Angeles* also tells something of the relationship between artisan and artist, specifically between Tyler and Hockney. Kenneth Tyler, after all, is not any master printer; he is David Hockney's. Despite its look of objectivity, the portrait offers a personal view, a wry, mocking, firsthand rendering of a story so complex it might as aptly have been titled "A Print within a Print."

Tyler, shown seated with one of his products—a print—looks like a sportsman showing off a prize fish. He is proud, and with reason, for hanging behind him on the wall is his catch of the day: a lithograph, the 1973 *Rain,* by David Hockney, or, rather, a replica of *Rain,* rendered pint-size by Hockney and printed by Tyler. Compared to the tiny lithograph, the master printer looms large. Giving Tyler pride of place, Hockney, in his blunt, ironic fashion, queries who is the artist—the painter or printer? By evoking the master printer's complex psychology, Hockney hints at the illusions that can afflict his subject: the false modesty, the grandiose imaginings. Note Tyler's bearing: the touch of smugness in his slouch; the soft curve of his shoulder, which reveals an obedient mien and untold passivity. The portrait is double-edged, at once chastising and flattering. It shows the master printer as vain, but subservient and that in the end it is the artisan who serves the artist.

David Hockney
The Master Printer of Los Angeles 1973
lithograph, screenprint on Arches Cover paper
47½ x 31⅝
Collection Walker Art Center, Minneapolis
Gift of Kenneth E. Tyler, 1985

Kenneth Tyler no longer lives in Los Angeles or drives a Mercedes, and little about him suggests the dude. He dresses now in nondescript clothes, in flannel shirts, corduroys, and practical shoes. His black hair has gone gray. In 1973, the same year Hockney drew *The Master Printer of Los Angeles,* Tyler left Los Angeles and Gemini G.E.L., the print-publishing firm he had helped found. He was forty-two years old. Having printed more than three hundred editions and published more than six hundred, he was not only one of the country's preeminent craftsmen, he was a major publisher who, along with June Wayne and the late Tatyana Grosman, was largely responsible for changing the course of the American print.

Tyler came east with a considerable reputation and a controversial one. Hyperactive and aggressive, he is a man of boundless and obsessive energy who is as ambitious as the artists he chooses to publish. As the founding partner and driving force of Gemini G.E.L., he had transformed the publishing of artists' lithographs into what appeared (at least to outsiders) to be a glamorous business. Tyler operated the lithography workshop the way old movie bosses had run the studios. Or so it seemed. Making a lithograph at Gemini came to mean living well: swimming in blue pools, driving big cars. Extravagant extras attended working there—parties, grand living quarters—but in retrospect the luxuries Gemini accorded its visiting artists only reflected the party atmosphere that characterized the 1960s. "After a while," Tyler recently admitted, "I found I was in the entertainment business."[1] It was the Hollywood style that set tongues wagging, particularly in the East, where, a decade earlier, Abstract Expressionist painters had established angst, sacrifice, and nothing less than a quest for the sublime as prerequisites for making art. Gemini's rise brought the predictable reaction of outrage in what was, for perhaps its last moment, a small, staid art world. This happened partly because of the firm's Southern California location and partly because in 1965 printmaking was considered a poor relation to painting and sculpture and, as such, was relegated to the ancillary world of academic artists, to illustrators and pipe-smoking Sunday hobbyists. To traditional graphic artists who printed their own work and looked to the old masters, to Albrecht Dürer and Rembrandt van Rijn, for inspiration, Gemini's razzle-dazzle technics were an affront to craftsmanship, an insult to their media. To painting and sculpture collectors, the attention being accorded these multiple images from the Hollywood Hills seemed unfathomable.

Tyler, as if compensating for the prints' ambiguous status, was constantly attempting to expand the boundaries of editioned art. At Gemini under his auspices, artists created objects out of vinyl, polyurethane, leather, and lead, and Tyler soon earned the reputation of being willing to try anything to produce a print. He hired scientists, industrial designers, metal embossers, papermakers, foundries, commercial printers. He commissioned presses designed to his specifications and developed and patented a rigid, honeycomb-structured paper that he named Tycore, after himself. When necessary, Tyler employed a cast of thousands. Although the phenomenon of the workshop print involving an assembly line of engravers, printers, and colorists was actually not new, Tyler brought the production number to contemporary printmaking. Updating the media, he gave the print a late twentieth-century twist by marrying graphics to the technology of its time.

Tyler's innovations were not only technological. His entrepreneurial talents introduced a new era in which every publication represented a sales effort. Gemini prints entered the world with considerable fanfare. Elegant promotional brochures preceded editions. These contained essays by prominent critics illustrated with close-up photographs of sensitive-looking artists leaning over the porous surfaces of lithographic stones. The prints themselves came with documentation sheets that revealed more than anyone might want or need to know about how a print was made, including the number of times it had passed through the press, the number and names of its colors, the names of all participants, the signature of the artists, and the flourishing signature of Kenneth Tyler. The documentation sheets, reminiscent of the warranties that accompany household appliances, guaranteed authenticity.

Gemini prints had a look: pristine and perfectly registered, they had sleek, smooth surfaces, which Tyler has described as having "spit and polish." A sharp precision marked Gemini printing, an evenness that could be seen in the straight, hard, clean edges of lithographs by Josef Albers, Ellsworth Kelly, and Frank Stella. What most characterized the Gemini imprint was Tyler's penchant for the mechanical, his industrial aesthetic, and his insatiable taste for the technological possibility. Gemini prints were bigger and more complex than prints had been before and relied on technologies that, until then, had been the domain of science and industry.

Many prints, like Roy Lichtenstein's *Haystack,* 1969, and Robert Rauschenberg's *Booster,* 1967 (p. 16), have become so closely associated with the art of that time, so recognizable as icons of the 1960s, that it is difficult to realize how innovative and radical they once appeared. For centuries the art of the print had been a draftsman's art in which the hand told all. The hand drew on copper and on stone; the hand wiped; the hand printed. Gemini prints, in contrast, appeared untouched by human hands. Their sleek, industrial look reflected the then-reigning aesthetics of Pop and Minimalist art, but that fact did not temper critical opinion. To print connoisseurs, cleanliness was not next to godliness. Gemini prints were deemed antiseptic. Furthermore, detractors found the rainbow-colored roll in Jasper Johns's 1969 Color Numeral Series (see p. 16) garish, they thought the layer of Mylar covering the surface of Ronald Davis's Cube Series common enough for a dime-store table mat, and there were those who simply dismissed the elaborate three-dimensional objects Tyler helped create as products—whether a bronze plaque by Lichtenstein or a model of a vintage automobile molded out of polyurethane by Claes Oldenburg.

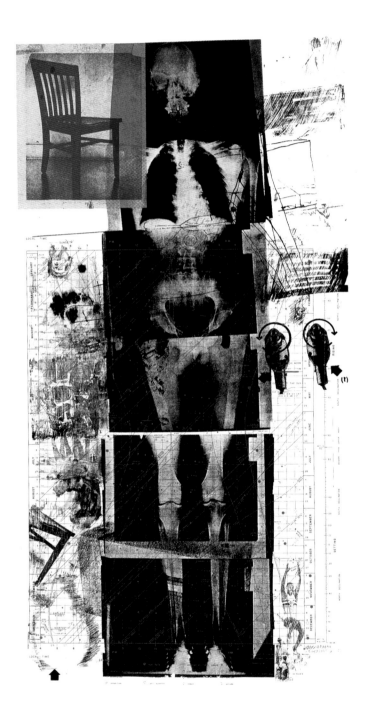

16

Gemini under Tyler attracted its share of criticism, but Gemini under Tyler also changed the ground rules of print publishing. In 1960, when June Wayne founded the Tamarind Lithography Workshop in Los Angeles, creating an educational system to train artisans as lithographers, she started a graphics revolution that Tyler would continue. Not only did he modernize and merchandise the graphic arts, Tyler Americanized the print. At Gemini, big was better. And the prints Tyler published were not only big; they were bright, shiny as new cars, and light-years away from the small-format, black-and-white images that had dominated printmaking. Mirroring every technological advance, these were prints in touch with their times, with an age in which a man would walk on the moon.

Tyler's years in Los Angeles constitute the first phase of his career. The second began in 1974, the year he moved east to open Tyler Graphics Ltd. in Bedford Village, New York. Given the success and visibility of Gemini and the fact that the workshop's aesthetic was considered a reflection of Tyler's own, many people expected that his new studio would be an eastern version, a re-creation of the L.A. workshop. But from its location to its publications, the new studio had little in common with its predecessor besides its master printer's zealous energy. In the heart of Los Angeles, Gemini occupies an industrial building on Melrose Avenue; in contrast, Tyler housed the new studio in a nineteenth-century white clapboard carriage house off a winding country road. Instead of noise, he opted for silence; instead of smog, he chose clean air and a view across an apple orchard. The man in the chamois jacket who drove the white Mercedes had changed.

The publications from the new studio reflected this transformation. The respect and emphasis Tyler had once reserved for the machine-made and chrome-plated he now gave to the handmade and hand-articulated. He did not abandon his taste for the technological; Lichtenstein, for example, worked with industrial techniques to create his very ambitious Entablature series (see pp. 129–30). But soon after Tyler moved east, he began to promote one-of-a-kind works: monoprints, hand-painted prints, works made of paper pulp. By 1976 the same artists who had once been beneficiaries of Tyler's state-of-the-art industrial aesthetic were making images that relied on old-fashioned techniques. The hand was evident everywhere: in paper-pulp works by Ellsworth Kelly, Kenneth Noland, and Frank Stella; in monoprints by Nancy Graves; in intaglio prints on hand-colored papers by Ronald Davis. The individual and the autographic had replaced the hard surface of the machine-printed image and the glossy sheen of manufactured objects.

Tyler says he moved east because he needed to get back in touch with real values. He claims he had burnt himself out in Los Angeles; he had also had an irreparable falling out with his two Gemini partners, Sidney B. Felsen and Stanley Grinstein. But Tyler's old-fashioned turn also dovetailed with a general change in the aesthetic climate. "Ken has a completely uncanny sense of timing," says art dealer Irving Blum, who

(left)
Robert Rauschenberg
Booster 1967
lithograph, screenprint
on Curtis Rag paper
71⅞ x 35¹⁄₁₆
Collection Walker Art
Center, Minneapolis
Gift of Kenneth E.
Tyler, 1985

Jasper Johns
Figure 0 1969
lithograph on
Copperplate Deluxe
paper
37 x 30
Collection Walker Art
Center, Minneapolis
Gift of Kenneth E.
Tyler, 1985

has known him since his Los Angeles days and whose now-defunct Ferus Gallery showed many of the artists Gemini first published. "He began Gemini at exactly the right moment. One year later and it wouldn't have worked. And he did the same thing with Tyler Graphics. He's been incredibly lucky."[2] Tyler has had more than luck; he has what every publisher needs: a nose, a highly developed sense of what is in, or about to be in, the air.

To discover what is in artistic favor, Tyler watches, listens, and asks endless questions of the people he respects, a group that includes painters, critics, and the occasional curator. By inclination he is a listener, not a talker, unless he is selling, and then an entirely different personality takes charge, that of the man who studied Dale Carnegie's *How to Win Friends and Influence People*. Tyler knew a reaction to the cool look of 1960s art was inevitable. In the early 1970s he had watched artists create work that was difficult to sell (minimal art) and work that could not be consumed or transported (earthworks). When he encouraged artists to try old-fashioned methods, Tyler was advocating an antidote to an aesthetic he had once avidly promoted. Detractors found his chameleonlike about-face opportunistic, but in fact, he was only acting as a publisher must, as a calibrator of his time. He was also following his own very compulsive need to create new graphic options. In his obsession to surpass himself, Tyler is quite like an artist.

A major change occurred when he moved east. He stopped thinking of himself solely as a master printer (a designation he now cannot abide) and began regarding himself as a collaborator. His new role had far-reaching effects. It modified his view of process and altered his self-image. Tyler ceased to regard himself as just an artisan who assisted artists by etching, proofing, and printing their stones. Rather he thought of himself as a consultant on every aspect of a print: on techniques, on colors, on directions the artist might consider taking. Although there were many people who thought it impossible, the fact is that Tyler had grown more ambitious.

The collaborations initiated at Tyler's Bedford studio grew increasingly elaborate; requiring more money and time, they reflected his new preference for lengthy, open-ended projects that were not predetermined. In 1978 David Hockney spent about six weeks there creating his extraordinary series of paper-pulp pools. From 1981 through 1985 Frank Stella's majestic Swan Engravings and Circuits Series kept Tyler's presses busy, as one image led to the next. In recent years Tyler's taste for the technological possibility has grown more recondite and become a taste for the complex. He coaxes artists into combining media, into layering and grafting one graphic technique on top of another. In his Circuits prints Stella combined etching, woodcut, relief printing, and dyed, handmade paper, merging them so successfully that they appear indivisible, and it is impossible and, finally, beside the point to differentiate between them.

Tyler has remained as generous a host in the East as he was in the West, except that his style has changed from laid-back L.A. to country. Artists no longer get grand hotel suites; they stay in a homey apartment over the studio. But Tyler still goes to any length to make an artist comfortable. Late in 1984, before Celia Birtwell, David Hockney's longtime model and friend, came to pose for her portrait, he and Tyler went driving around Westchester County, scouting for props and objects that would make the English-born Birtwell feel at home. Hockney finally found a blue chintz-covered couch and chair that had a cozy English look. For *An Image of Celia* (p. 158), his Cubist-inspired portrait of 1984–86, Hockney posed Birtwell in the chair, which still sits at one end of the otherwise bare artist's studio.

The time that can be spent creating a mise-en-scène or editioning complex prints causes some publications to be very expensive, with prices that begin at five figures. Tyler has been criticized for being less a print publisher than a creator and purveyor of intentionally very limited, expensive art. His success and ambition have in fact brought him his share of critics, who have called him everything from a bully to an artist manqué. He has also been described by his detractors, who consist mainly of art dealers and other artisans, as competitive and technologically obsessive.

The criticism most often directed at Tyler is that he interferes and can become too involved with the artistic process. In the trade one occasionally hears someone refer to a print by Frank Stella or Ellsworth Kelly or David Hockney as really being by Ken Tyler. "Sometimes he pushes you in a bit of a mad way," Hockney has said. "He doesn't always know how long it takes you to work out an idea in your head but that's hardly a fault. All Ken's interested in is working with artists. He was wise enough to know he couldn't be one. So he became a great artisan and found interesting artists who enjoy his skills and wanted to use them. There's no comparison between Ken and any other publisher. Ken gets his hands dirty. He rolls up his sleeves and actually collaborates with you. He's the chief collaborator, not just the publisher and not just the printer."[3]

Tyler the publisher puts Tyler the artist manqué to good use. He lets the man who likes to get his hands dirty invent techniques and procedures that help create art that is not his own. He is not the publisher for every artist. The insecure had best stay away. He is at his best with strong artists. "I think," Hockney has explained, "that Ken likes the challenge of working with me."[4] "I know the printers I've worked with are the best," Stella said recently. "I know Ken thinks he's great and he is. He loves the challenge. He likes to be artistic, so there are things I can do to keep him busy."[5] Collaborating with Tyler is an unrelenting process, a balancing act. For artists who know how to keep him busy, who can channel his ambition, imagination, and technological wizardry, the printed results have been staggering: they include some of the most important and innovative graphics of the twentieth century.

Tyler's taste for the technological is a legacy from his childhood. He was born in 1931 in East Chicago, Indiana, an industrial town twenty miles southeast of Chicago. The home of Inland Steel, East Chicago is a town of refineries, steel mills, and neighborhoods of two-family, two-story, plain wood-frame bungalows with mom-and-pop taverns on every corner. Industry dominates the area. The plants of U.S. Steel and Standard Oil crowd the land along the lake, smells from the neighboring soap factories fill the air, and at night the glow of fires from the mills looks like the midnight sun against the lake's desolate and suffocating blackness.

Tyler's father, Paul Tyria (he changed the family name to Tyler), was three years old when he came to America in 1906 from Sagomar, Hungary. He apprenticed as a stonemason and at fourteen took a job at U.S. Steel as a water boy (he led the mule that carried the water), and aside from an unsuccessful attempt at running a lunchroom in 1931 and a short stint that same year slaughtering lambs, for the rest of his life Tyria worked in the mills. In 1922 he met Elizabeth Szilagy, who had been born in a neighboring Hungarian town, and two years later they married.

The Tylers had three children, Dorothy, Raymond, and Kenneth Eugene. With the birth of each child they moved, going from a two- to a three- to a four-room apartment. Sometimes they moved in with relatives; sometimes they found their own place. They seemed to be in constant flux until 1934, when they settled in a modest house in an Eastern European section of East Chicago. Tyler had a Hungarian childhood. Hungarian was the first language spoken at home, where he and his family lived with both his Hungarian grandmothers.

As a child, Tyler saw little of his father, who often worked the night shift and slept during the day. Tyria was a hardworking, hot-tempered, solitary man. He spoke only adequate English but was good with his hands and had a natural gift for carving stone. He was so expert at cutting rope and floral designs that a friend offered him a job as a stonemason. But as much as he loved working with stone, he turned the job down because the friend's drinking habits worried his wife.

Tyler regards his father as a frustrated sculptor. "He tinkered with stone all his life," Tyler has recalled. "He would carve tombstones for friends, and he was always having me move his damn rocks from one part of the property to the next. My love of stones, of the physicality of work comes from him. He made everything himself. He forged and ground his own chisels. Reading was hard for him, but he was always teaching himself. He'd write away for government reports, and he'd go to the library and bring home books on how to build arches. To figure out how arches were made I remember him making a compass out of a piece of wood and string and drawing with it on brown butcher's paper that he'd roll out on the floor of the barn.

"My earliest recollections are not of someone reading a book or listening to music or talking to you but of someone quietly working with their hands, not jabbering or yakking. I like big collaborative efforts. I like it when the shop is bustling and fifteen people are running around doing all sorts of things, when the artist is cooking and the printers are cooking and things get done. But if there's something I long for it's the solitude of the painter, of the craftsman."

Tyler's strongest bond with his father was work. Before he left for the mills, Tyria gave his son chores. He would ask him to remove nails from old boards or to sort nails by size or to straighten nails with an anvil and hammer. He was a hard taskmaster; if his son did the job improperly, he'd explode. Tyler admired his father's mechanical abilities but feared his temper. "I liked my father when he was working," Tyler once said, "but I didn't like him beyond that because I didn't know him beyond that."

In 1945, when the family moved from East Chicago to a farm on Ridge Road, outside Gary, Tyler developed his abiding taste for the outdoors and country life. Rising early before leaving for school, he'd feed the pigs and milk the cows. He also operated a roadside flower stand that had an ideal location across the street from three cemeteries.

To this day, work remains extremely important to Tyler. "I was never exposed to idleness," he has explained. "Everyone around me worked. It was just what you did. Once you've been working for a long time, it's in you; it's programmed. So when someone throws a lot of stuff on the floor and says, 'Sort it out'—it's not a problem. You don't say, 'Oh, my God, I've got to do that?' You just do it. And if it takes four hours, it takes four hours. You don't have any preconceived ideas. You just have the assignment. Then you discover that all these things help you, that they make you a bit more adaptable, a bit quicker than the next guy. I realized this at Tamarind, the first day I got there. The other guys didn't like cleaning up; they didn't want to get their hands dirty and it didn't bother me because I'd washed off cows and shoveled manure."

In grammar school and junior high, Tyler drew all the time. "It was just something I did," he has said. "It was private." His first love, however, was music, and it was his music teacher, Victor Barberi, who first encouraged him to pursue an art career. Barberi was Tyler's pied piper. He was dark, sophisticated, drove a Packard, lived in Chicago, and had three jobs. That he held down three jobs dazzled Tyler. Aside from teaching, Barberi worked for the Wurlitzer Music Company and, as its representative, encouraged students to take music lessons. As a free-lance sideline, he leased the same students instruments. "He was a real operator," Tyler has recalled with an admiring smile. "He was getting it both ways. Wurlitzer paid him and so did my parents."

His teacher's eye for the angles caught Tyler's fancy, and Barberi, equally taken by the twelve-year-old's energy, took Tyler on as his student assistant. Tyler painted walls, ran errands, and helped construct sets for school musicals. In return, Barberi gave him a saxophone, pen nibs, poster paints; took him for rides in the Packard; brought him home for Italian meals; and not only advised Tyler to attend Saturday classes at the Art Institute of Chicago but paid his tuition.

Tyler's classes at the Art Institute left him wanting to be an artist. But what moved him even more in that direction was the importance art and music had for the people he most admired, people whom Tyler has described as being "better and different, and smarter than anyone else." One of these people was Larry Shrago, who was four years older than Tyler and who attended the American Academy of Design, a commercial art school in Chicago. Shrago had great technical skills and a gift for verisimilitude. "It was 1948 and 1949 and there he was painting like the guys in the museum," Tyler has recalled, "making portraits like Frans Hals." To Tyler, Shrago's talent seemed awesome, and he began to listen to him the way he had once listened to Barberi. Tyler read every book his friend mentioned. He studied reproductions of paintings and would sometimes copy them and bring them to Shrago to critique.

In 1950, when he completed high school, Tyler entered the Art Institute of Chicago, but the outbreak of the Korean War interrupted his studies. Because art schools were not draft-exempt, he transferred to the University of Indiana. He was a terrible student, he has said, because he went girl-crazy, and after a semester, having run out of money, he returned home to the farm on Ridge Road, found a job in the steel mills, and attended school at night. The first thing he did was look up his old friend Shrago, who was about to leave for Paris to study painting. Tyler decided to join him. He applied for and received a scholarship to the Sorbonne, but his application for a passport did not get him to Paris; it got him drafted.

In Fort Belvoir, Virginia, at the Corps of Engineers officers' training school, Tyler was a model soldier. He learned how to operate heavy earth-moving equipment—cranes and bulldozers—and still had time to continue his art education. As the regiment's staff artist, he edited and printed the company newspaper; drew its cartoons; designed announcements, cards, and booklets; and painted a series of historical murals. In return he received art supplies, a studio, and ample encouragement. "Your most impressive quality, one I believe is characteristic of a true artist rather than a technician, is the perfection which you seek in your work," read a letter of commendation from a commanding officer. "This has been manifested repeatedly by your refusal to submit low quality work. You have set very high standards for yourself in your field and through your determination and singlemindedness, you will, I am confident, attain your goal."

In 1954 Tyler returned to the Art Institute of Chicago on the GI bill. It was an exciting time to be in Chicago. The Bauhaus was in residence at the Institute of Design, where Walter Gropius taught classes in texture by darkening rooms and having students touch Brillo pads and pieces of rubber. Tyler met Gropius's students at the University of Chicago, where art students took their required academic courses. He heard Frank Lloyd Wright lecture at Orchestra Hall and saw Josef

Albers's paintings for the first time at the Fairweather-Hardin Gallery. The most intellectual and pragmatic of cities, Chicago is a place that values ideas over emotions and prefers the solution to the struggle. Tyler, brimming with confidence gained in the army and filled with purpose, thrived in that atmosphere.

On the South Side, Tyler found a room in a boarding house. The other occupants were Episcopal seminary students, and Tyler's three-year infatuation with the church began. Within no time he was listening to organ music, attending services, and thinking about becoming a priest: "I had little education. I had gotten away, but I was convinced that I was not suited to business and not suited to art and that I might be suited to the church. I was certainly going in that direction. I attended church regularly—except I wasn't very religious. I was a borderline case."

Tyler's real satisfaction came from church decoration. While a student, he usually held down a full-time job, and one of them was designing liturgical art. At the Daprato Studio, Tyler fashioned crosses out of silver and modeled holy families out of plaster. He liked the work and could envision someday directing a workshop that produced church art: stained glass, bronzes, mosaics, and ceramics. Tyler's jobs have had a major influence on his development. His sense of theater, for example, which is evident in everything he does, from the layout of his workshops to the scale of his projects, was informed by his job at Acme, Carsens, Pausbeck Scenic Studios from 1954 to 1958. There he designed, painted, and constructed stage sets, working on everything from large, three-story-high opera sets to tiny ones for cabarets, including a set with palm trees and large peacocks that he painted for Sally Rand's burlesque show.

At the Art Institute, Tyler worked as a monitor in an evening painting class, where he met Kay Kolman, a day student who modeled for the class. A year later the two married. Kay was Jewish. Marrying outside his faith posed no problems for Tyler, although both his family and Kay's had objections. Despite religious differences, the two shared ambitions and backgrounds. Both planned to be artists and to support themselves by teaching. Both had grown up in Hungarian households. In every other respect they were opposites. Kay was practical, organized, down-to-earth, good at stretching money and food. Ken, in contrast, was impetuous, a nonstop worker, always throwing himself headfirst into projects, never thinking about the consequences.

In the years following his marriage, Tyler held a series of jobs, all of which he excelled at and not one of which satisfied him. At Evanston Township High School, he taught art and designed the scenic studio for the school's new theater. In those years a teacher's salary was approximately thirty-two hundred dollars a year, and he supplemented that income by selling the one-foot-high plaster madonnas that he and Kay cast in their bathtub. When they still could not make ends meet, Tyler stopped teaching, and he and Kay found work at Duffy's Majestic Garage, Kay as the bookkeeper and Ken as the general manager. At

Duffy's, Tyler's workaholic nature began to show itself. He did everything; he priced jobs, bought inventory, was responsible for sales and sales promotion. Although his salary was twice what he had earned teaching, he regarded the Duffy's job as a filler until a better one came along. When he took his next job, as a traveling salesman for Thompson Wire and Steel Company, a medium-sized manufacturer of strip metal, he had just turned twenty-nine and had pretty much given up plans to be an artist.

At Thompson, Tyler developed skills that would serve the future print publisher well. He was a natural salesman, and the job allowed him to perfect the talent. To this day, mention Thompson Steel to Tyler, and he starts selling. Without missing a beat, he conjures up the snake-oil man. "Thompson," he tells you, "had better manufacturing facilities, better research teams. We were small enough to make any product, any specialty item. You were better off working with us than with U.S. Steel." Tyler did so well that his boss enrolled him in Dale Carnegie's course "How to Win Friends and Influence People," where he learned how to make presentations, how to speak in public, how to close a deal, and how to win. Upon completion of the course, Tyler received the Dale Carnegie Regional Championship Award. Tyler honed another skill at Thompson: his talent for research and development. He was a born problem solver who could quickly identify a client's needs and as quickly satisfy them. Years later he would transfer these skills to his master printer's repertoire, matching an artist's aesthetic with a graphic technique and discovering industrial methods to solve artistic problems.

Despite the money Tyler earned, the Thompson job took its toll. When he entertained clients (which he did every day), he drank too much. Three-martini lunches became a habit. He regularly overate and, after two years on the road, weighed nearly two hundred pounds. He had taken the job to benefit his family, whom he now rarely saw, since he spent most of his time traveling from client to client. On one of his trips he suffered what he thought was an attack of ptomaine poisoning, arriving at the hospital just in time for an emergency appendectomy. Tyler was very sick and came to regard his recovery as a miracle. Because he believed he had been given a second chance, he decided to quit his job. He wanted to be an artist, not a salesman.

In 1962 Tyler returned to school, where he took an interest in printmaking. At the Art Institute of Chicago he had had only the briefest exposure to lithography, having wandered in and out of the classes taught by Max Kahn, who, at the time, was Chicago's resident printmaker. But Tyler had never learned how to keep an image on a stone and had found the medium frustrating. That he ended up in 1962 at the Herron School of Art in Indianapolis proved to be a lucky coincidence with far-reaching effects. At the time, Garo Antreasian headed Herron's art department. A well-known printmaker and painter, Antreasian had just returned from the Tamarind Lithography Workshop, where he had spent a year as its first technical director. Nowhere could

Tyler have found a teacher with interests more sympathetic to his own. Devoted to lithography, Antreasian had two main concerns: to modernize and update the medium and to discover ways to convert industrial products to artistic uses.

Tyler's timing was impeccable. In the early 1960s the graphic arts were undergoing major changes. For decades American printmaking had been ignored or, when noticed at all, treated as a minor art form, its activities relegated to universities and regional print exhibitions. (The Brooklyn Museum Annual was the only major museum exhibition devoted to graphics.) A complicated, long-standing set of prejudices had prevented America from fostering a continuous graphic arts tradition. Ironically, the fact that prints were multiples tainted them for American painters, who came to regard them as a low, not a high, art. That the print's roots were common rather than elitist triggered a peculiarly American bias against the print as craft, for the American painter equated craft with work, not art. Abstract Expressionists scorned printmaking because its fragmented methods precluded the immediate gesture. Art dealers considered prints a nonprofit venture. More often than not, the graphic arts were treated as a cause or political tool, not an art form. Regularly funded by foundations, print exhibitions were sent traveling to underdeveloped countries as emissaries of political good will.

For all of these reasons, American printmaking had flourished in fits and starts. In the 1830s a golden age of lithography occurred when commercial firms such as Currier and Ives developed to satisfy the needs of a new middle class. In the 1900s, under the influence of James McNeill Whistler and of Americans returning from grand tours laden with prints of Chartres and Venetian lagoons, an etching revival took hold. America's strongest indigenous graphic style was the narrative one seen in the urban landscapes, seamy sites, and slice-of-life scenes etched by Reginald Marsh, Edward Hopper, and John Sloan. The discontinuity that marked the history of the American print was inevitable, however, because there was no artisan-craftsman tradition and no master printers. It followed that until the second half of the twentieth century no American painters used the graphic arts the way their European counterparts did.

This began to change in 1960 due largely to the efforts of two women: Tatyana Grosman and June Wayne. In 1957 Grosman founded Universal Limited Art Editions (ULAE), combining a Russian mystic's love of stones with an Oriental's taste for paper and a European's sensibility for printing to set the standard for quality in printed art. Printmaker June Wayne's achievement was of a different order. When Wayne did not make her prints with Lynton Kistler, the only lithography printer working with artists in Los Angeles, she traveled to Paris to work with a French master printer, Marcel Durassier. In 1959, acting on her concern that lithography was a dying art in America, Wayne founded Tamarind with the aid of a grant from the Ford Foundation. One of Tamarind's goals was to resurrect the fading art of lithography by training master printers and introducing mature artists to the medium. It was hard going at first. In 1960 even finding applicants for the printer's program was difficult. But by the early 1970s Tamarind had succeeded beyond anyone's wildest imagination. Most major American cities had a lithography studio, and chances were good that these studios had Tamarind-trained printers. By far the most successful printer ever to pass through Tamarind's program was Kenneth Tyler.

In 1962, when he entered Garo Antreasian's class at the Herron School of Art, Tyler was clearly a man in the right place at the right time. He was "skinny, feisty and extremely motivated. He'd been out in the world and he knew he didn't want to be a salesman or to live in that world. He wanted to get on with it," Antreasian has recalled.[6] Tyler had only marginal talent as an artist, but he was a quick study who understood modern technology and was extremely good with his hands.

Because he wanted to learn as much as quickly as possible, Tyler assisted his teacher whenever he could. Working with Antreasian printing large lithographic editions, Tyler picked up efficient tricks. He learned the easiest way to register color, the best way to roll out inks. But it was his work with Antreasian developing an experimental press with a mechanical, hydraulic cylinder that had the most telling effect. Antreasian wanted to build a small press to print large lithographs. This posed problems. In a traditional lithographic press, the scraper bar, which creates the pressure that is necessary to transfer an image off the stone, remains stationary, while the press bed moves, like a swing, beneath it. This means that the printing of a six-foot-long lithograph requires twelve feet of space. Antreasian envisioned a press that required only half that room because it had a stationary bed and a movable scraper bar. Antreasian knew his principle was sound but had no notion of how to build the press. Needing to develop a prototype, he began visiting machine shops. Tyler accompanied him.

Tyler's work on the experimental press signaled the direction his career would take, and to this day he acknowledges his enormous debt to Antreasian. The experience taught him how to apply his considerable talent for research and development to lithography. It also gave him a taste for big prints that he would later satisfy. Meanwhile, his nimble grasp of technology, his enterprise, and his drive so impressed Antreasian that he suggested Tyler accept a three-month fellowship sponsored by Tamarind.

Tamarind was above all an educational institution, and one of its main goals was to create a work force of master printers. Its staff accomplished this by systematically researching every aspect of lithography, performing studies on the durability of paper, on the colorfastness of inks, on the reproductive qualities of metal plates. Paying equal attention to economics, the workshop published reports on how to price a lithograph and how to maintain a graphics inventory.

Although Tyler shared Tamarind's interest in technology and economics, he had mixed feelings about the workshop's program, which he found too regimented. "When you read a recipe," he commented recently, "you're not reading it for four or five tablespoons of this or a pinch of salt; you're reading it for the gist of it, for its uniqueness. The problem with Tamarind was also probably its strength—that it was essentially educational. There was a mythical rule book and that for me was the block that was difficult to get over. If you're programmed to believe that printmaking can be done only one way, that it has to go on a certain kind of paper and has to have a certain ritual that goes into making it, then you couldn't be farther away from the concept of making art. So the whole concept of someone coming and intuitively doing something and using a little bit of this and a little bit of that would not be acceptable in the Tamarind classroom. Tamarind paid homage to the fact that the artist was in complete control, but every time you turned around, there was another rule to conform to."

Despite his cavils with the program, Tyler thrived at Tamarind. He worked hard both as a fellow printer and as a researcher. Soon he was research director, and by August of 1964 he had succeeded Irwin Hollander as studio manager. He was not, however, cut out for a workshop environment, unless he directed the workshop. He had twice as much energy, focus, and drive as anyone else. He also had, according to one observer, a tendency to take over and to play favorites.

Tyler's time at Tamarind was a pivotal experience, for he met his two most important role models there: the printer Marcel Durassier and the painter Josef Albers. Durassier, who knew Pablo Picasso and had printed for Joan Miró, brought romance to the profession of printing. Although he spent only two weeks at Tamarind, it was time enough to convince Tyler to become a master printer. From Durassier he learned a rub-up technique that, he has said, was as much a philosophy as a procedure. It was, according to Tyler, "about not knowing too much, about battling the old goat of lithography." But Durassier's rub-up technique was more than a philosophy. It was a way to etch a stone, and had Tyler not known it, he never would have been able to etch the delicate washes that were so crucial to the success of Jasper Johns's Color Numeral Series. But the most important lesson Tyler learned from Durassier was that once an artist completed his work on a stone, the stone became the printer's responsibility.

If Durassier offered Tyler a vision of the master printer, Albers gave him permission to pursue that vision. At Tamarind, Tyler collaborated with Albers on two lithographic suites, Day and Night and Midnight and Noon. They were both difficult projects that involved overlapping inks to create tones of black. The demanding prints tested Tyler's talent. Albers, at seventy-three, was highly opinionated and could be cantankerous, but he and Tyler got on famously. A former teacher at the Bauhaus, a believer in the "Temple of Socialism," Albers regarded the arts and crafts as equal and did not consider the handmade to be, by definition, of a higher order than the machine-crafted. He gave Tyler reading assignments: articles from Bauhaus and Yale journals, Gropius's early writings, and his own books on color. Albers became Tyler's mentor of mentors.

Tyler's conversations with Albers led him to a conclusion: "I decided I didn't want to become another educator who was a frustrated painter or another printmaker who was a frustrated painter. If I was going to become a printmaker I wanted to devote all my energies to it and I wanted to become the best. Mid-life was just around the corner, and I felt I'd spent a great deal of time in school and a great deal of time working. I wanted to get into a profession where I could spend the rest of my life and derive a great deal of satisfaction. I desperately needed a sense of accomplishment, and I needed it in an area that I chose. I arrived at this decision clearly and reasonably. I had not been painting for a long time, and I didn't feel I was going to start competing as a painter and win support. I had already shown a tremendous talent for printmaking and I knew I was better than the other printers, if for no other reason than none of them worked hard enough to amount to anything. So I thought, just concentrate on printmaking and see if you can make a go of it. Run a workshop."

In 1965, soon after leaving Tamarind, Tyler borrowed five hundred dollars from his mother-in-law and settled into free studio space he'd been given in the back of his friend Jerry Solomon's frame shop. Gemini Ltd., a custom lithography studio, began with one commission, a Nicholas Krushenik poster for the Los Angeles County Museum of Art, and enough money to last a month. The new studio immediately attracted attention. Subscriptions to publications at five hundred and a thousand dollars sold easily. Tyler and his wife printed more than fifty editions, including a series by David Hockney, A Hollywood Collection (see p. 147), commissioned by an English publisher, and the portfolio About Women, a collaboration between the painter John Altoon and the poet Robert Creeley. Expenses, however, regularly exceeded profits, and after twelve months Stanley Grinstein, one of Gemini's original subscribers, and his friend Sidney B. Felsen became the Tylers' silent backers. A few months later, Felsen, Grinstein, and the Tylers publicly joined forces, and Gemini Ltd., the custom print shop, became Gemini G.E.L., the publishing workshop, giving Tyler the financial support that allowed him to bring the nineteenth-century craft of lithography into the twentieth century.

Gemini also had a patron, Josef Albers. The new studio's first publication was Albers's White Line Squares, and the artist agreed to donate four-fifths of its profits to the fledgling workshop. When they worked together at Tamarind, Albers had given Tyler a diagrammatic drawing of *Homage to the Square* and had authorized him to transfer it to lithographic plates. That drawing became the basis for White Line Squares. Following Albers's specifications, Tyler drew most of the plates;

his wife, Kay, drew others. Tyler mixed the colors, matching them to the samples Albers sent from Connecticut. The portfolio consisted of sixteen images of colored squares within squares, each a didactic demonstration of the relativity of color. It was a difficult project, made even more so when Tyler ruptured a disk in his lower back. For the more than nine months the project took, Tyler was in pain, but no one in the workshop knew how severe it was or that Tyler was wearing a steel corset. The project proceeded smoothly except that having an absentee artist made the printers feel alienated. To counteract this, Tyler began to tape his conversations with Albers. When the printers heard the artist's voice, Tyler explained in an interview with English art historian Pat Gilmour, it helped boost morale. "They heard great joy from Albers when he saw a beautiful proof or a beautiful color. I think [hearing him] made a profound difference in the attitude of our little workshop."[7] White Line Squares represented the perfect Bauhaus balance between artist and craftsman, and in its execution it became a symbol of the grand collaborations to come.

Soon after the publication of Albers's White Line Squares, Robert Rauschenberg and Jasper Johns went to work at Gemini. The two jewels in the crown of Tatyana Grosman, the then-reigning print publisher, Johns and Rauschenberg were both natural printmakers; they were also the two most influential artists of the day, and there were many who felt their presence assured Gemini's success. The prints they made there reflect the influence of place, for they are different from those made at Grosman's Long Island studio, ULAE. Far larger, Rauschenberg's prints incorporate X-rays, while Johns's lithographs of numbers, with their smooth surfaces and color-blended rolls, have a buoyant swagger and appear less poetic than their ULAE counterparts. But the credit for Gemini's fast success belongs as much to Tyler as to the artists. "He was this very idealistic hick," art historian Barbara Rose has recalled. "He talked a lot about the great printmaking tradition and he had this megalomaniacal belief that he could change that tradition through technology. He was pushy and he pushed artists to their limits."[8]

Tyler's inordinate stubbornness also contributed to his success. Once he fastens onto an idea, nothing dissuades him. For example, in 1967 he decided he wanted to work with Frank Stella, who was then living in nearby Corona del Mar. Tyler telephoned Stella, who was emphatic: he hated printmaking. Refusing to accept Stella's no, Tyler kept calling until, according to Barbara Rose (who was married to Stella at the time), he became a pest. Stella, hoping finally to get rid of him, told Tyler that he didn't like to draw and that on the rare occasions he did so, he drew only with Magic Markers. Someone else might have taken Stella's refusal as discouraging news; to Tyler it was an opportunity and a challenge. He went to work immediately and within days arrived at Stella's house carrying Magic Markers filled with lithographic tusche. Stella, impressed as much by Tyler's relentless drive as by his inventiveness, began his career in printmaking.

Six years after its founding, Gemini had published 285 editions, many of which extended the traditional definition of the print. It was an extraordinary achievement, which the Museum of Modern Art in New York recognized with its 1971 retrospective *Technics and Creativity* and the publication of a catalogue raisonné documenting Gemini's publications. But while the venerable Modern acknowledged the new workshop, the New York critics panned the show. Calling it thin and characterizing the prints as slick, manufactured, and commercial, critics dismissed Gemini as a tinsel-town studio and dubbed it the MGM of printmaking workshops. Tyler wore his chamois jacket to the opening. He was nervous. He says he knew it was all over even before the reviews came out. "The problem was," Tyler has explained, "Gemini had become an entertainment center. You'd get this artist, then you'd get that artist, then you'd get this collector. Then bam, bam, bam. All of a sudden you can't see the forest for the trees because all you have is a production schedule. Then you'd do a multiple that didn't work and you'd have to redo it. Then instead of making four prints—you would make a dozen. Then it becomes like the movie industry. You've had all the top stars and you're sitting around thinking, 'now what am I going to do for the next one?' And you panic. And you get into a terrible depression and you say, 'I can't do that again,' and you do it anyway. Then you suddenly run out of steam. So in 1973, when my brother died of a heart attack at forty-nine and I went back to the Midwest for the funeral, I thought, 'I've got to stop. I've got to change.'"

"From the middle 1960s through the early seventies Ken had this enormous energy and enthusiasm," his friend the writer Michael Crichton has commented. "He could keep himself entertained. He was always trying to find new technologies, new ways to do things. He developed a whole Gemini procedure, a way Gemini worked, and after a while, it worked as smoothly as a clock. At some point, I think Ken was confronted with the kind of success that is its own trap—when you become so successful you don't know yourself anymore. You lose your sense of definition. It seems natural that he had to change, to move east."[9]

Another factor brought about change. The same year his brother died, 1973, Tyler fell out with his Gemini partners. It is an event he refuses to discuss except to say that it was a divorce, and, like most divorces, it was acrimonious, a shattering experience. Nevertheless, with typical vigor Tyler packed up his family and moved east, planning to start all over again. He wanted to change how he lived and where he worked. Gemini had become the unofficial clubhouse for the L.A. art world, the visitors' bureau that everyone checked out upon arriving in town. As Gemini's director, Tyler had begun to feel like a hotelier.

Tyler wanted a studio in the country. He had heard about the simple gardener's cottage on eastern Long Island in which Tatyana Grosman housed her workshop, and the advantages of a quiet workplace held great appeal for him. When he had returned to Indiana for his brother's funeral, he had also felt nostalgia for the flat farmland of his childhood. He had thought about being young and, as people do when they reminisce, about the first time he had left the Midwest. This had occurred in the summer of 1952, when he and his English teacher from the University of Indiana, Ray Warden, drove east to Cape Cod. Tyler never forgot that trip because it was the first time he saw the ocean and because Warden—who was an intellectual, an Episcopalian (Warden was responsible for Tyler's initial interest in the Episcopal church), and a T. S. Eliot buff—was one of Tyler's early role models. Years later, as he was deciding where to establish his new studio, what Tyler remembered about Warden was the farm he had outside Indianapolis, where he raised Black Angus cattle.

As much as he wanted to be close to nature, Tyler also felt it essential to be near the artists with whom he worked. This ruled out true farmland, leaving him a choice between New York City and its suburban environs. He bought land in Southampton because Roy Lichtenstein lived there, and almost settled there, but after spending a week with Robert Motherwell in Connecticut, he changed his mind, deciding that the Hamptons would be too social, too similar to the life he'd left behind. Although Motherwell helped convince Tyler to settle in Bedford, it was nothing he said that brought Tyler to the conclusion, but rather the way he lived, the emphasis he placed on simplicity, privacy, and time. Making art was Motherwell's main priority, and watching him convinced Tyler that life on the fast track did not have staying power.

Tyler opened his new studio in 1974. Once again he worked in tandem with his wife, Kay (from whom he was divorced in 1979), and once again Josef Albers was the first artist with whom they worked. Following his now-usual procedure, Albers did not touch the plate or mix the colors. He designated colors with descriptions—"spring green" or "honey yellow"—meant to evoke the shade he wanted. Then Tyler and printers Charles Hanley and Kim Halliday came up with the correct color. It was a game of verbal charades, but it was easier now that Albers was Tyler's neighbor. Often their conversations took place in person. For Tyler, having Albers close by was important, for he was starting over, and it was from Albers that he had taken his original inspiration.

For Tyler, the Bedford studio represented a change. He thought of it as a radical break with his past and, even now, more than a dozen years later, still does. But Tyler Graphics did not represent the sharp severing Tyler believes it did; in fact, his career as a print publisher represents an amazing continuum. "What has made Tyler's career so remarkable," according to William S. Lieberman, curator of twentieth-century art at the Metropolitan Museum of Art, "is that he has not only continued what was extraordinary to begin with, but he has continued with such a sense of adventure."[10]

Whether he is in the East or in the West, Tyler is Tyler. He still has a taste for bigness. He remains, for example, publisher of the largest print created to date, only the print is no longer Rauschenberg's *Booster* but Stella's 1984 *Pergusa Three Double* (p. 33). And although prints from Tyler Graphics represent diverse, ever-changing aesthetics, they do have a look, one that is revelatory of Tyler's sensibility. That look, found in their scale and ambitiousness, is particularly evident in editions utilizing handmade papers. Unlike most handmade papers, that produced at Bedford is not fragile or delicate; it is thick, appears sturdy, and has a tough surface—an industrial moxie—that is pure Tyler.

Although Tyler's career represents a continuum, he has also shown a remarkable capacity for change. While he cautiously builds on what he knows, he daringly takes risks, forging ahead into entirely unknown areas. What sustains him is his extraordinary energy, ambition, and considerable success. But what truly motivates him is his love of artists. It is what artists do that interests him, and it is what he can do for artists that fascinates and drives him.

Most publishers coax, cajole, and flatter. Tyler does this and more. He participates, collaborates, and solves problems. He does more, because aside from the publisher, the salesman, the printer, and the research and development man, there is the fan; there is Tyler the hero-worshiper, who is abject in his devotion to artists—and who injures easily if his affection goes unreciprocated. Artists are Tyler's lifeline. He wanted to be an artist, and even now he sometimes appears uneasy about his roles as printer, publisher, and mechanical genius, troubled as to whether what he does is as important as what an artist does. Whatever reassurance he needs Tyler finds by becoming an extension of an artist, by devising new techniques that suit that artist alone.

Tyler does not simply show artists how to do things. He does them. He builds the maquette, blows up the collage, and creates work in the style of. Involving himself in the printmaking process in a way no other publisher does, Tyler matches an artist to a medium and, if necessary, invents techniques. For Stella's Circuits Series, Tyler transformed the indented lines left by laser beams on wood backing sheets into patterns for metal relief plates.

Artists work differently with Tyler because of what he brings to the process. For example, Motherwell is a master at collage who knows how to place paper and charge it with meaning. He first included collage in a print in *Gauloises bleues*, 1968. After that, Motherwell simulated the effect of collage by replicating labels and wrappers in aquatint and lithography. Labels appeared frequently and always actual size until 1975, when the artist completed *Bastos* (p. 54) at Tyler's. Working in his usual fashion, Motherwell collaged a Bastos cigarette wrapper over a drawing. He liked the image, although the illegibility of the cigarette label's type troubled him. Tyler had an idea, which he tried out after Motherwell left the studio. When Motherwell next saw *Bastos*, the small label had been enlarged and transformed into a field of blue. While Tyler takes pride in contributions like this one, he never insists that his way is better, and he never wants credit (it is often difficult to know Tyler's part in a print unless the artist tells you). "He's very gentle with

Frank Stella
Pergusa Three Double 1984
relief, screenprint, woodcut, engraving on hand-colored TGL handmade paper
two sheets: 102 x 66
Collection Walker Art Center, Minneapolis
Tyler Graphics Archive
(Tyler 605:FS64)

33

me," commented Motherwell,[11] who used the enlarged Bastos label in his print.

By the time Helen Frankenthaler arrived at Tyler's studio, she was already an experienced printmaker who had worked in every graphic medium. With her 1973 and 1975 woodcuts *East and Beyond* and *Savage Breeze,* she had already made singular contributions to the medium by creating the illusion of deep perspective and simultaneously merging color and paper on a flat surface. Connoisseurs and curators, heralding these prints, compared them to ukiyo-e masterpieces. As the proofs for *Savage Breeze* reflect, however, the final version did not come easily. In one proof the surface is boringly flat; in another an ungainly white line separates colors; in a third Frankenthaler attempted to create deep space, affixing crayoned paper to a corner. Every proof attempted a solution. Frankenthaler had so much trouble making the image that she considered abandoning it. In contrast, *Essence Mulberry* (p. 62), the first woodcut she made at Tyler's, was an altogether different experience. *Essence Mulberry*'s proofs reflect the same order of involvement as those for *Savage Breeze*, but they show Frankenthaler enjoying the possibilities instead of struggling.

Setting forth possibilities is one of Tyler's talents. According to Frankenthaler, "Ken makes artists feel they can't fail at the project they're about to undertake. He makes himself, his enormous energy and inventiveness, and all the tools of his workshop available. This means that if an artist has something in mind, there's a real exchange as the art develops. The alternative could be to find oneself in an abyss, not knowing the mechanics available to make a poetic statement. I think Ken and I have come a long way since we began working together. I give him more room to make suggestions and he understands my rhythm better. I used to feel that Ken was insinuating himself too much but after ten years I've figured out how to work with him, and he's figured out how to work with me. When I didn't know how to achieve what *Essence Mulberry* needed I turned to him and said how do you get the color of a mulberry when it bleeds. He sensed what I meant and got it. Ken presents me with all the possibilities that are in my vocabulary. I might transcend them and knock them out, but he's given me the possibilities."[12]

Techniques are not only possibilities to Tyler; techniques are his art form, and he becomes as obsessive about them as artists do about their imagery. In 1975 he was so taken with the possibilities of handmade paper-pulp images that he convinced both Frank Stella and Ellsworth Kelly to work with him at John Koller's studio in Woodstock, Connecticut. In 1978, still fascinated with this medium, Tyler built a paper studio in his Bedford workshop. Kenneth Noland came and made a series of delicate chevrons and circles out of paper pulp in pastel shades (see p. 217). But the medium's potential wasn't realized until later that year, when David Hockney came to Bedford and produced his extraordinary Paper Pools (see pp. 220–21, 240), which, with their simple, limpid colors and their immense scale and dauntingly direct compositions, represent the best work yet created out of paper pulp.

Tyler has the patience of a stubborn man. He believes in waiting, and when he has his heart set on a project he will wait forever. For years he had wanted to travel with Hockney and publish a diary-sketchbook of the journey, but one event or another had interfered. Once Hockney and Tyler did manage to travel together as far as the Grand Canyon; a blizzard, however, arrived at the same time they did, covering the mountains Hockney planned to draw. In the intervening years Tyler devised a technique, suited to sketching on the spot, that allowed Hockney to draw on clear Mylar sheets, which, once back in the studio, could be transferred to lithographic plates. Then Tyler waited; he waited for Hockney to finish stage sets, and he waited for him to travel to China with poet Stephen Spender, and he waited for him to collaborate with Spender on a book documenting the trip. Finally, in October 1984 Hockney and Tyler traveled to Mexico. A year and a half after that trip, twenty-four lithographs had been completed, and the project remained unfinished.

These intense, lengthy collaborations characterize Tyler Graphics. Tyler sets no limits, particularly when he joins forces with Hockney or Stella. Of all the artists he has worked with, Hockney and Stella might be said to be paradigmatic of his career. Tyler has grown up and kept up with them. The differences between a traditional portrait by Hockney and one of his paper-pulp pools reflect something of the distance Tyler has traveled. But his astounding progress, the degree to which he has changed, particularly technically, can perhaps best be seen by comparing the modest simplicity of a small 1967 Black Series I lithograph by Frank Stella (see p. 163) with a majestic 1982 Swan Engraving (see p. 175). With the achievement of the Swan Engravings, many publishers and artists might rest on their laurels, at least for a while, but not Tyler or Stella. For the last two years Stella has been working with computers to create three-dimensional images—and that project is nowhere near completion. "Ken always wanted to try things," Stella recently commented. "In the beginning I would punish him by saying no to every idea. Now I gratify him by saying yes. Now no process is too outrageous or too expensive."[13]

One aspect of Tyler's personality that still suggests the Los Angeles dude is that whenever he finishes an ambitious project, he worries about what to do next. Growing anxious, he sometimes turns petulant and childishly decides that there are no more artists in the world good enough for him to publish. At heart, however, he is an incurable optimist whose presses will never stop. Recently he purchased a twelve-thousand-square-foot industrial building on the highest point in Mount Kisco, New York. It is there that he plans to install a new studio.

"Some of David Hockney's Best Work has been made by Ken Tyler," ran the advertisement for the Australian National Gallery's 1985 exhibition of Tyler publications. Hockney agrees. In fact, the man in

Trial. proof I   David Hockney 1989

Hockney's most recent portrait of Tyler (p. 36) bears only the slightest resemblance to the one shown in *The Master Printer of Los Angeles*. The passive, obedient manner is gone. In the recent portrait Tyler is shown in shifting, multiple perspective. His eyes go one way, his ears go another. His moustache is lopsided. He appears to be eating the phone. In a state of perpetual motion, in flux, working, developing ideas, devising increasingly advanced techniques to create multiple art, waiting, Tyler still serves the artist. But he has evolved and extended himself, past that old goat lithography. Trusted enough to assume the guise of the artist, Tyler has mastered Helen Frankenthaler's feel for color, Robert Motherwell's talent for automatic gesture, David Hockney's sense of line, and Frank Stella's insatiable passion for adventure. He participates and collaborates. Active, not passive, Kenneth Tyler now has no time for grandiose imaginings.

David Hockney
An Image of Ken
1987
lithograph on Moulin
du Verger paper
30 x 22
Courtesy Tyler
Graphics Ltd.

Notes

1. Unless otherwise noted, all quotes from Kenneth Tyler are from interviews and conversations with the author that occurred during 1985 and 1986.
2. Irving Blum, conversation with author, June 1985.
3. David Hockney, conversation with author, May 1985.
4. Ibid.
5. Frank Stella, in Judith Goldman, *Frank Stella: Fourteen Prints with Drawings, Collages, and Working Proofs*, exh. cat. (Princeton, N.J.: Art Museum, Princeton University, 1983), p. 13.
6. Garo Antreasian, conversation with author, October 1985.
7. Kenneth Tyler, in Pat Gilmour, *Ken Tyler, Master Printer, and the American Print Renaissance* (New York: Hudson Hills Press in association with the Australian National Gallery, 1986), p. 40.
8. Barbara Rose, conversation with author, January 1986.
9. Michael Crichton, conversation with author, March 1986.
10. William S. Lieberman, conversation with author, March 1986.
11. Robert Motherwell, conversation with author, March 1986.
12. Helen Frankenthaler, conversation with author, March 1986.
13. Frank Stella, conversation with author, March 1986.

38

Robert Motherwell's Graphics

Jack Flam

Robert Motherwell has made graphic works longer than any other major artist of his generation.[1] His first prints were done in 1943, and since 1965 he has produced a considerable body of graphic works, which have a broad stylistic range very similar to that of his paintings and drawings. In addition to its high artistic quality, Motherwell's graphic oeuvre is of particular interest because it coincides with the American print renaissance of the 1960s and early 1970s and because it is an excellent reflection of that revolution in the aesthetics and economics of printmaking.

Most of the Abstract Expressionist artists had little or no interest in graphic works, and Motherwell himself made only a few prints before 1965. In many ways, Abstract Expressionist painting seemed to be antithetical to the whole enterprise of traditional printmaking. The reasons for this were both aesthetic and economic. Abstract Expressionist painting stressed fluid manipulation of paint, expressively nuanced individual touch, and discovery of forms through process and accident. These are characteristics that were difficult, if not impossible, to obtain with traditional graphic techniques, which tended to be linear, to require complex technical procedures and careful planning, and to avoid rather than invite accidental effects. Historically, the graphic media were closely related to illustration and to books and were essentially logogenic. Indeed, the word *graphics,* which comes from the Greek *graphikos,* ultimately derives from *graphein,* "to write." In English the primary definitions of the word have to do with "clear and lively description" and with that which is "sharply outlined or delineated."[2] The graphic, in other words, was traditionally associated with values that were something like the opposite of those of Abstract Expressionism.

Furthermore, for the Abstract Expressionist painters, the act of creation was conceived of as heroic and private. During the 1940s, especially, the very notion of artistic collaboration must have seemed foreign to them. Moreover, there was at that time no particular *need* to make prints, since there was virtually no audience for their work. As

Robert Motherwell
Lament for Lorca
1982
lithograph on TGL
handmade paper
44 x 61
Collection Walker Art
Center, Minneapolis
Tyler Graphics Archive
(Tyler 413:RM32)

has been remarked time and again, most of the abstract artists who were later drawn to printmaking did not come to it out of a deep inner need but were brought to it by the print workshops that began to develop a large market for multiple images during the 1960s.[3] Unlike painting, printmaking entailed costly machinery, elaborate technical procedures, collaborative work effort, and sophisticated marketing. There was little reason to bother with the complex procedures necessitated by making more than one example of an image unless there was a market for it.[4]

Motherwell's first graphic works were intaglio prints done in 1943: three or four copperplate etchings and at least one burin engraving (see p. 41).[5] Although their mood appears to have been created in part by textural effects (such as those produced by foul biting) that are unique to the medium, their imagery—like that in much of Motherwell's early work—is largely linear. These first prints are, in a sense, line drawings that were given their special voice, but not necessarily their specific form, by the intaglio medium. After he finished them, almost twenty years were to elapse before Motherwell worked in a graphic medium again.

In the 1940s printmaking appears not to have particularly interested Motherwell for precisely the same reasons that it did not interest the other Abstract Expressionists. There was also, I believe, another important reason, which had to do with what might be called the self-protective instinct that is an important asset for any ambitious young artist. The place where Motherwell made his first prints was Stanley William Hayter's Atelier 17, the Parisian workshop that was temporarily located in New York City from 1940 to 1950 and that was an important forerunner of the American print renaissance. Hayter was an early and influential experimenter with new printmaking techniques and a specifically modernist printmaker who was very much interested in creating varied linear and textural effects that could accommodate abstract imagery better than traditional methods could.[6] During World War II, his Atelier 17 was a meeting place for European artists in exile, a fact that Motherwell evidently found both stimulating and daunting. According to his own later account, "Hayter repeatedly urged me to come down to his studio, which I did, reluctantly. As a neophyte, a self-taught artist, working publicly in a shop with André Masson, Max Ernst, Matta, Seligmann, and two dozen other well-known artists . . . embarrassed me. Though Hayter did tell me several times I was a born printmaker, I, from my acute shyness made more so by working alongside professional artists, quit making prints there and only resumed years later."[7] Years later, others would also remark upon Motherwell's shyness when he was working outside his own studio.

When Motherwell did begin to make prints in a serious fashion, not only had he reached his artistic maturity, thereby becoming more or less immune to involvement in technique for its own sake, but the nature of print production had also changed. New techniques had been

Robert Motherwell
Personnage 1943–44
etching
13³⁄₁₆ x 9¹⁵⁄₁₆
Collection
Metropolitan Museum
of Art, New York

Robert Motherwell
Poet II 1961–62
lithograph on German
Copperplate paper
29⁷⁄₈ x 21¹⁄₈
Collection Walker Art
Center, Minneapolis
Gift of the artist, 1984

developed that made it possible to capture in prints some of the spontaneity, fluidity, and expressive nuances of abstract painting. Moreover, this could now be done without an artist's having to become deeply involved in the craft of printmaking, since the expansion of the print market had also created changes in the working relationship between artists and printers. The major catalyst for these changes was the founding and development of the workshops that produced and published artists' prints: Universal Limited Art Editions, Tamarind Lithography Workshop, and Gemini G.E.L.

When Motherwell began to do graphics again, it was at Universal Limited Art Editions (ULAE), at the invitation of Tatyana Grosman. Motherwell had been one of the first artists Grosman had contacted to do work for ULAE in 1957, but at the time he had not been sufficiently interested. In 1959, ever persistent, she sent some lithographic stones to his New York studio for him to work on, and although he did not do so then, in 1961–62 he produced his first editioned lithographs, *Poet I* and *Poet II* (p. 41), at ULAE's workshop in West Islip, New York. Although the imagery of these two compositions is quite modest (based on the letter "P," reversed in printing), it embodies a characteristic that would persist throughout Motherwell's graphic oeuvre: the composition makes little concession to the medium itself but forces the print medium to accommodate *it*.

An understanding of what might be called Motherwell's passive domination of the various graphic media is essential to an understanding of his printmaking. Motherwell has on several occasions said that he knows very little about printing and that he has no clear mental image of how he makes prints.[8] These remarks have been verified by the printers with whom he has worked.[9] But, as they have also pointed out, Motherwell always seems to have a very clear idea of what it is that he wants, is able to describe this with remarkable precision, and is able to recognize it when he sees it. In his printmaking he creates the imagery and then directs (rather than executes) the actual physical printing. Thus, although his prints are clearly related to his paintings and drawings, this difference in procedure clearly differentiates his graphics, both technically and visually, from his other work.

In his prints Motherwell transcribes the imagery of his drawings and paintings into another medium and then subtly orchestrates the resulting interaction so that his imagery and the medium can accommodate each other. What seems to be of primary importance to him is that the image be *right*, independent of the medium in which it is going to be realized. As a result, he seems quite willfully to have avoided learning too much about the technical subtleties of the medium—since for someone like himself they could only get in the way of the ideas and feelings he wants to express.

To put it another way, one might say that each graphic medium has its own set of inherent qualities, and an artist who works in a given medium has a kind of choice as to how far he wants to give himself over to exploring the possibilities of the medium per se. Artists like Hayter, Lee Chesney, or Gabor Peterdi—that is, artists who were involved in exploring the qualities inherent in the intaglio medium—pulled their imagery out of the medium itself, so to speak. For them, it was necessary to master all the procedures that the medium entailed, from the preparation of plates and grounds to the mastery of the complex manipulations involved in printing. An artist like Motherwell, in contrast, proceeds in an almost diametrically opposite way, and indeed might be said to *avoid* knowing too much about the craft involved, as if to preserve a kind of necessary innocence. As he himself remarked after he had been seriously involved with printmaking for about a decade, "there is still a kind of cold war between the old guard, constantly talking about how you technically do or complicate works in any way possible, and artists who simply have a statement they want to make as clearly and forcibly as they can, within the nature of this particular medium."[10] Motherwell, then, has virtually ignored the technical complexities of plate or stone preparation and of printing. He has relied upon the printers with whom he has worked to cover the technical side, while he has given his attention to what was possible for *him* to do at that particular time with that particular printer in that particular medium. Thus, the development of his understanding of printmaking has involved a growing awareness of how to deal with these factors rather than a steady accumulation of technical knowledge.

Painting and drawing (and collage making) have always been Motherwell's main activities. And it is with these activities, in the privacy of his own studio, working with his own hands directly on the picture surface, that he is in complete control of all relevant technical aspects. It is here that the bulk of his pictorial ideas develop. It is here that he allows himself the greatest freedom to improvise, to revise, and—if necessary—to destroy. And it is here that he has defined the parameters of the imagery he brings to his prints. One of the major tensions behind his whole printmaking enterprise has been created by his desire to push the various print media to accept the full range of his imagery.

This was so from the very beginning of his earnest involvement in printmaking. In one of his earliest ventures, the calligraphic lithographs he did with Irwin Hollander in 1965–66, for example, he translated the imagery of his then-recent Beside the Sea and Lyric Suite series into another medium by recontextualizing the already familiar procedure of painting with a brush.[11] This adaptation had to do with several factors that Motherwell would come to know intimately over the years: the nature and choice of materials, the effect of the reversal of the mark when it was printed, and the new range of touch and of textures that the print media were capable of producing. The translation of his imagery into lithographs could not have been done by anyone other than Motherwell, but at the same time, he could not have made the lithographs without expert collaboration, which in this case was provided by Hollander.

This collaboration is particularly instructive. At the beginning of the project, Hollander's role was that of a guide to the possibilities available to the artist. He gave Motherwell the choice of a number of different tusche consistencies (American, French, and German) and of a number of different surfaces on which to work (stone, aluminum, and zinc), each of which would take the medium differently. After Motherwell had worked awhile with each and had acquainted himself with their various qualities, such as touch, flow, and surface (which are so essential to his imagery), he decided to work on zinc. When he sat down to paint on the plate, he first "played" a bit with the brush in order to achieve a rapport with the viscosity of the tusche he had chosen. Then, having familiarized himself with these new extensions of his mind and hand, his whole bearing changed as he began to work, moving rapidly and decisively, "like a Japanese killer with the brush!"[12]

After the painting had been done, the plate went back into Hollander's hands, and the mechanics of the printing process once again came into direct play in order to translate the tusche drawings on the plate into printed images. Papers were chosen, proofs were made, revisions were done, and eventually the edition was printed, by Hollander, but with Motherwell constantly telling Hollander what he wanted. The result was not a drawing and not a painting, but, as Hollander has described it, "an *original with a different surface* . . . in fifty copies!"[13]

Hollander's description of Motherwell's print as an original with a different surface in fifty copies points to an essential difference between Motherwell's prints and his paintings and drawings. The original aspect of Motherwell's prints comes, I think, from the fact that the translation of his imagery into the various print media is rarely mechanical in any sense. Despite the similarities in their imagery, the prints are different from the paintings and drawings because the process is different, and the different process results in a different surface, texture, and feel. In a print like *Automatism A,* 1965–66 (p. 45), we understand the gestures of the brush to be spontaneous, but we also understand that we are looking at an indirect, rather than a direct, record of those gestures, that identical examples of those exact same gestures exist, that what we are looking at is a replicated image of a series of unique gestures. Thus, when Motherwell creates an image like this, there are several intangible but very important factors that have to be considered, having to do with directness and scale.

One of Motherwell's great gifts as a printmaker is his sensitivity to the scale and surface of prints. Traditionally, prints have had a certain range of physical size. The largest were generally smaller than small paintings, and the size of the paper they were printed on was usually around the size of a book or, at most, a folio. The modern print, by contrast, tends to be larger, sometimes almost mural-sized. But although Motherwell's paintings are often quite large, his prints are not. And yet, even when working quite small, he often manages to create an effect of

Robert Motherwell
Automatism A
1965–66
lithograph on Rives
BFK paper
28⅛ x 21³⁄₁₆
Collection Walker Art
Center, Minneapolis
Gift of the artist, 1984

large scale. This, I think, is because he is able to "frame" his graphic imagery within the physical and psychological confines of the print medium. As a result, his prints almost never have the look of imitation paintings or drawings but speak in another language. The analogy that comes to mind is that of literary translation in its most rigorous form. Even in a translation in which the syntax has been transformed into impeccable English, you are nonetheless somehow aware of the fact that you are reading a translation. And if it is a good one, this knowledge in a curious way adds to your enjoyment of what you are reading. *Why* you know it is a translation is often difficult to ascertain. This knowledge is based on a combination of several elements, including the foreign quality of the setting, of the sentiments involved, or of the thought patterns or behavior of the characters. And if the translation is of a particularly good book, you feel that reading it has given you a kind of *privilege,* that you have been intimately exposed to something to which you otherwise would not have had access.

This sense of seeing something from a privileged vantage point is, for me, one of the most appealing aspects of Motherwell's prints. They give one the privilege of being able to have intimate contact with images that might otherwise be difficult to make intimate contact with. I am not talking here about the fact that they are more easily affordable than his paintings or drawings. What I am speaking of is their quality of intimacy. And this is produced in some measure not only by their size but also by the extremely sensitive use that is made of the paper on which they are printed. This sensitivity is a kind of equivalent to the fine sense of paint surface that Motherwell's paintings have, but it is also different. For it is often produced by the opposite of "touch"— indeed, it is often produced by restraint from touch.

This might best be seen in the prints in which the actual drawing is the most reduced, those related to the format of the Open paintings. In these paintings the surface and brushwork of the colored ground that surrounds the rectangular lines play an enormous role in the overall expression, in both plastic and metaphorical terms. As a result, one might expect that the Open images would be almost impossible to translate into prints or that if Motherwell did so, it would be with a heavily brushed or textured ground (such as he sometimes uses in his aquatints). But in fact, the prints that Motherwell has done in the Open format employ a nearly flat color ground. Its expressive nuancing is not carried by varied brushwork or texture but by the way the paper takes the flat, dense rectangle of ink. In a sense Motherwell makes the *paper* do the "brushwork" for him, and in doing so he effects an extraordinary and unexpected translation from painted to printed image.

In other words, it is the process of printing that translates part of the process of painting into something else. If we look at a print like *Untitled,* 1968 (p. 47), done shortly after the first Open paintings, we understand that it is a translation, and part of its interest lies in how well it works in its new language. Indeed, it is impossible to look at any of the Open prints without thinking of the Open paintings. Yet at the same time, the translation of painted into printed imagery involves such a strong plastic transformation that the Open prints become independent images.[14] (Sometimes, as in the "Stone" images Motherwell did in 1970 and 1971 [see p. 47], the lithographic stone actually determined the shape and texture of the open field, transforming the composition into a uniquely lithographic image and, indeed, into a kind of commentary on the process of printmaking.)[15]

This kind of transformation can be seen in virtually all the major kinds of images that Motherwell works with. It is as true of the Elegies (see pp. 38, 50–51) and of the calligraphic images as it is of the Open

compositions. And in recent years Motherwell has even managed to achieve a surprisingly effective translation of his collages into prints (see pp. 57, 61). In each case his understanding of the nuances of scale and of the particular qualities of papers and inks—of how certain plastic possibilities can be *embodied* in printmaking—have guided the translations of his formal vocabulary into images in which he paints and draws, but in which the final products are different from paintings and drawings. They are, quintessentially, prints—originals with a different scale and surface, in multiple copies.

Motherwell's lifelong involvement with and love for the printed word have also had an effect on his printmaking. In fact, two of his major printmaking projects have been illustrated books: the twenty-one etchings and aquatints he did for a selection of poems from Rafael Alberti's *A la pintura,* published in 1972 (see p. 48), and the nineteen lithographs he did to accompany the same poet's "El Negro Motherwell," published in book form as *El Negro* in 1983 (see pp. 50–51, 58).[16] It is interesting to note that both of these books contain texts translated from the Spanish. In part, this is because the Alberti texts

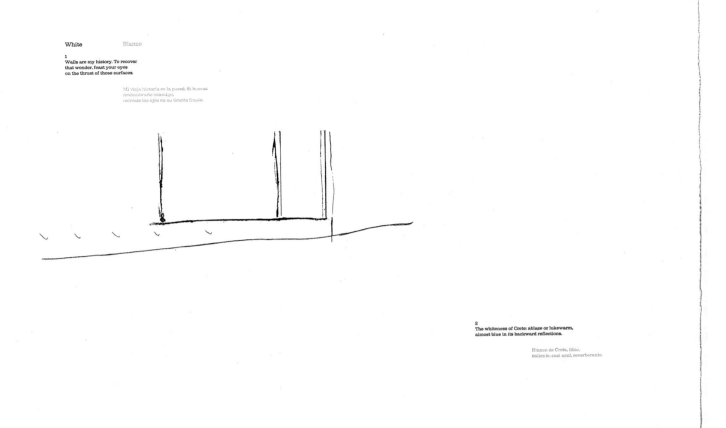

White   Blanco

1
Walls are my history. To recover
that wonder, feast your eyes
on the thrust of those surfaces.

Mi vieja historia es la pared. Si buscas
deslumbrarte conmigo,
recréate los ojos en su tirante frente.

2
The whiteness of Crete: ablaze or lukewarm,
almost blue in its backward reflections.

Blanco de Creta, tibio,
caliente, casi azul, reverberante.

that Motherwell chose are directly about painting. But the Alberti texts were probably chosen also because they required a kind of emotional translation on Motherwell's part, and this sort of emotional translation is one that he has been making throughout his creative life. The emotional range as well as the subject matter of the two Alberti poems are somewhat foreign to both English and American poetry. And it is precisely that emotional range, which might be described as Catholic and Mediterranean, that has so appealed to Motherwell. Several of his most important early works have Spanish or Hispanic titles (*The Little Spanish Prison; Pancho Villa, Dead and Alive*), and his most famous series of paintings is known as Elegies to the Spanish Republic. It is particularly interesting that the "seed" idea for the Elegy format was developed from the illustration of a poem[17] and that the first picture done in the developed Elegy format was *At Five in the Afternoon*, which took its title from the refrain in the first section of Federico García Lorca's *Llanto por Ignacio Sánchez Mejías*, 1935—an "elegy" for a bullfighter who was killed in the ring. This foreign, specifically Spanish, connection in Motherwell's work has had a very specific function: it has allowed the artist to explore a broad range of sensual and emotional experiences—such as stark contrasts, vivid colors, an obsession with death, and high

Robert Motherwell
White 1-2 1971,
from *A la pintura*
1968–72
etching, aquatint,
letterpress on J. B.
Green paper
25½ x 38
Collection Art
Institute of Chicago

tragedy—that lie outside the range of generally accepted experience or behavior in English-speaking cultures.

Furthermore, French and Spanish poetry—the works of poets such as Charles Baudelaire, Arthur Rimbaud, Stéphane Mallarmé, García Lorca, Octavio Paz, and Alberti—have provided Motherwell with a notion of what he has wanted his painting to accomplish; they have given him a kind of standard by which to measure his own work, as well as specific points of reference for the metaphorical content of his pictures. They have made permissible, perhaps even possible, a number of things that might otherwise not have been so. In a sense they have constituted a necessary fiction.

This aspect of Motherwell's work is frequently misunderstood, and it has repeatedly been remarked—often pejoratively—that Motherwell is in certain ways a "European" artist. In fact, his collages apart, Motherwell's art is no more "European" than that of any other American artist of his generation; perhaps less so, since there is something quintessentially "American" about the straightforward clarity of so much of his imagery. What is "European" about Motherwell's whole endeavor as an artist, though, is his sense of belonging to an international modernist culture, and this is reflected in his constant references to the literature of that culture. It is there that he most clearly stands at a certain distance from the English-speaking world to which, in another sense, he so inextricably belongs. He has, to paraphrase Dore Ashton, chosen "his poets" from other languages and other cultures,[18] while continuing to speak very much in his native tongue. (In fact, one is tempted to compare Motherwell's resistance to mastering foreign languages with his resistance to knowing too much about the technical intricacies of printmaking; in each case he seems to be motivated by the necessity of retaining his own voice.)

The tension between these two poles of culture and sensibility, Northern and Mediterranean, is reflected throughout his work, in his titles (*The Homely Protestant* versus *Jour la maison, nuit la rue*) as well as in his imagery, which alternates between the organic and the geometric, the spontaneous and the highly calculated, and which runs a gamut of expression ranging from the lyrical to the violent to the austerely serene. This range of imagery is also present in his prints. And it is one of the great triumphs of Motherwell's career as a graphic artist that he has been able to translate so much of the expressive range of his paintings into graphic works.

A la pintura was not only Motherwell's first illustrated book, it was also his first extended etching project, and it marked a kind of turning point in his printmaking career. After he finished it, his production in all the graphic media increased considerably, and the year after it was published, he bought his own etching press and engaged Catherine Mousley as his personal intaglio printer. Since then he has continued to do most of his etchings in his own printing studio, while the bulk of his lithographs have been done at outside workshops.[19]

Robert Motherwell
*Black with No Way
Out,* from *El Negro*
1983
lithograph on TGL
handmade paper

15 x 37¾
Collection Walker Art
Center, Minneapolis
Tyler Graphics Archive
(Tyler 434:RM53)

His etchings and his lithographs, then, represent not only two different techniques but also two different working contexts. And, given Motherwell's personality and working procedures, the different contexts are in their own way nearly as important as the different techniques. The act of creation remains essentially solitary and intimate for Motherwell; he prefers to work in his own studio and is generally uneasy about working in the presence of others. Moreover, he pays great attention to his working environment. This not only entails making his surroundings conducive to thought and work but also involves surrounding himself with his own best pictures. Thus, when he makes prints, he likes to have his own paintings and collages around him, as well as his earlier prints. These serve as points of reference by which he can judge the work at hand, and I daresay that his insistence on seeing his prints within this larger context is an important factor in the high level of quality that he has maintained in them.

At the same time that Motherwell is so attached to his solitude and his own working environment, he also seems to have a strong desire to get away from the confines of his own studio and to work with others. It is no accident that he started making prints seriously at a time of crisis in his professional life, when he felt a strong need to escape the solitude of his studio, and that he began *A la pintura* at a time when he was going through a deep personal crisis.

Motherwell's continuous production of prints began shortly after his 1965 retrospective exhibition at the Museum of Modern Art, New York, at a time when he was depressed and, by his own account, "overcome by an almost metaphysical loneliness."[20] It was then that he met Irwin Hollander. "This coincided with my desire to get out of the torment of my private studio," Motherwell has said. "So the printer and I struck up an agreement which was as much to my advantage psychologically as it was to his economically. The psychological advantage lay in cooperation and the sociability of working with a craftsman, choosing the size of paper or of a stone, conversing, discussing and having a working relationship with another human being. And though my approach was in many ways primitive, it was then that I began to get deeply interested in printmaking. I had always loved working on paper, but it was the camaraderie of the artist-printer relationship that tilted the scale definitively, a phenomenon that I think often happens when artists grow older and more isolated."[21]

A la pintura, Motherwell's first extended etching project, which he worked on over a period of four years, coincided with the gradual breakup of his marriage to Helen Frankenthaler. Once again, the prospect of relief from the crushing solitude of his own studio appealed to him, and he began to travel to West Islip to work at Tatyana Grosman's Universal Limited Art Editions.[22] At the time, Motherwell wanted "a more painterly quality" than he had found in lithography and "more intense color" than he had seen in engraving, so ULAE master printer Donn Steward introduced him to aquatint.[23] Although

Steward later estimated that Motherwell spent only about forty days at ULAE during the four years that they worked on the book,[24] Motherwell's experience there provided a thread of continuity during a very tumultuous period in his life, when he divorced and remarried, changed dealers, and moved from New York City to Connecticut.

Although the camaraderie and human exchange that Motherwell finds in print studios are very appealing to him, it should also be noted that when he is concentrating on the creation of a work, he can withdraw to a state of isolated inner concentration even in a busy studio. Steward has remarked on this sort of concentration and on Motherwell's ability to reach a kind of symbiotic accord with a printer. "He would be sitting there looking at something," Steward has recalled, "and I would reach out and put a pencil in his hand, and he would start marking. He had not yet known he was going to mark, and hadn't asked for the pencil, but obviously that was what he wanted. *He wasn't even aware that I had done it.* . . . He must have just thought he had picked the pencil up."[25]

For an artist like Motherwell, this sort of symbiotic relationship with a printer is of the utmost importance. And it is this human sympathy, as much as a certain artistic accord, that underlies his relationship with Kenneth Tyler. Motherwell first worked with Tyler in 1973, while the latter was still at Gemini G.E.L. in Los Angeles. During that year Motherwell spent a total of four weeks at Gemini, producing eighteen editions.[26] Shortly afterward, Tyler left Gemini and established his New York workshop just a few miles from Motherwell's home in Greenwich, Connecticut. Since 1974 Motherwell has printed most of his lithographs at Tyler's workshop, and in 1983 Tyler became Motherwell's print dealer and distributor. During the time that the two men's professional collaboration developed, they also became good friends. Especially because they are also neighbors, Motherwell has been able to work more closely with Tyler than with any other printer outside his own studio.

Tyler has also provided Motherwell with another necessary quality: his extreme sensitivity to and mastery of printmaking techniques. As was remarked earlier, for Motherwell, the printers he works with become extensions of his own will; they help give tangible form to the ideas and images he has in his head. Tyler, because of his extraordinary technical virtuosity, is not only able to realize what Motherwell wants but is also able to extend the parameters of what it is possible to get. For example, in one of the early Tyler workshop prints, *Bastos, 1975* (p. 54), it was possible to increase the size of the collagelike image by photographically enlarging the Bastos cigarette wrapper and transferring it to aluminum plates—a process that was further elaborated in prints like *St. Michael III, 1979* (p. 55). In *Samurai II, 1980* (p. 56), the congruence of Motherwell's and Tyler's love of paper is apparent in the sensitivity with which the collage was done. And in collage prints such as *Redness of Red, 1985* (p. 57), Tyler's virtuosity is apparent in the vivid way in which the translation of collage to print has been effected.

54

(opposite)
Robert Motherwell
Bastos 1975
lithograph on
Arjomari paper
62⅜ x 40
Collection Walker Art
Center, Minneapolis
Tyler Graphics Archive
(Tyler 383:RM2)

Robert Motherwell
St. Michael III 1979
lithograph, screenprint
on gray HMP
handmade paper
41½ x 31½
Collection Walker Art
Center, Minneapolis
Tyler Graphics Archive
(Tyler 398:RM17)

Robert Motherwell
Samurai II   1980
lithograph, collage on
natural Sekishu
handmade paper
laminated to two
joined sheets of natural
Nepal handmade paper
57 x 24½
Collection Walker Art
Center, Minneapolis
Tyler Graphics Archive
(Tyler 401:RM20)

Robert Motherwell
Redness of Red   1985
lithograph, screen-
print, collage on
Arches Cover paper
24 x 16
Collection Walker Art
Center, Minneapolis
Tyler Graphics Archive
(Tyler 458:RM77)

In *El Negro,* 1983 (see pp. 50–51, 58), which is the product of what is probably the most ambitious printmaking collaboration that Motherwell and Tyler have undertaken to date, the technical complexity is less apparent. Here the desired effect was one of relative simplicity, and only those who saw the book evolve are aware of the complex decisions that were involved at every stage of its production.[27] This is because the expressive language of *El Negro* is relatively simple—quite close, indeed, to that of drawing. For all the breadth and strength of its imagery, it is essentially an intimate work. This collaboration was also an excellent example of the way in which Motherwell and Tyler have been able to pace themselves for long projects. Because Tyler's workshop is so busy during the week, he and Motherwell did much of the work on *El Negro* over weekends, and while they worked on it the Tyler workshop became a kind of home away from home for the artist.

One of Tyler's strengths as a printer and publisher is his passion for having things come out right, regardless of financial expense or expenditure of time. This is a characteristic and a commitment that he and Motherwell share. Part of Tyler's patience, which by his own account was in good measure learned from Motherwell,[28] consists in understanding just how demanding an artist like Motherwell is of himself—and, by extension, of those with whom he works. The basis of this exigency is the primacy of the image, regardless of technical limitation—

Robert Motherwell
Airless Black, from
El Negro 1983
lithograph on TGL
handmade paper
15 x 25 ¾
Collection Walker Art
Center, Minneapolis
Tyler Graphics Archive
(Tyler 428:RM47)

or of technical temptations. Tyler himself is aware of this and has remarked: "You're really involved with what Bob has to say *as a painter.* The technique and all the 'cooking' that one does in the print studio doesn't matter to him. Whether he picks up a brush and does a black outline drawing, whether it's on a stone or metal plate, and how it's going to look as a print 'goes'—as the technique of printing 'goes'— doesn't seem to come into the conversation. It's really more about . . . *what's on his mind,* where his image is going, what he's trying to create in that print he's working on now. There isn't the foggiest idea of how it's going to be technically. . . . That's exciting because *it's printmaking without any kind of program.*"[29]

Tyler's description of the creation of *Bastos* is an interesting case in point. When Motherwell made the drawing for the image, Tyler had the feeling that it was just what the artist wanted. The problem—given the complexities of translation—was whether it could be made into a print edition. The technical solution came from Tyler, and it worked. "Those are the nice moments of collaboration," Tyler later remarked, "where the printer really makes a contribution right from the very beginning, without a terrific amount of struggle." And then, with a penetrating insight into one of the problems of collaboration, he continued, "*Because sometimes the contribution you're making is putting an added burden on the artist.* You're taking him one step further than he really wants to go."[30]

The "contribution," of course, is what an artist like Motherwell wants; the "one step further" is what he dreads. The dividing line between these two extremes is actually very subtle, and the balance between them is crucial. One might even say that it is in this balance— fraught as it is with questions of personality, ego, will, and taste—that the real crux of artistic collaboration lies. The collaboration between Robert Motherwell and Kenneth Tyler has been remarkably productive precisely because of their mutual awareness of all the things that might go wrong and their mutual commitment to having them come out right.

Notes

1. Motherwell's prints are reproduced in Stephanie Terenzio and Dorothy C. Belknap, *The Prints of Robert Motherwell: A Catalogue Raisonné, 1943–1984* (New York: Hudson Hills Press, 1984). The first part of this publication, by Terenzio, consists of an introduction and interviews with twelve printers who have worked with Motherwell; there are also numerous quotes from the artist. Belknap compiled the catalogue raisonné and selected bibliography.

2. *Webster's Third International Dictionary* (Springfield, Mass.: G. and C. Merriam Co., 1971), p. 990.

3. See, for example, the remarks by Ben Berns, Tatyana Grosman, and Tony Towle in Terenzio and Belknap, *Catalogue Raisonné,* pp. 41, 56, 67.

4. Motherwell's first prints (see ibid., nos. 1, 1A) were not printed in editions. The only two known actual prints were marked "proof" and "1/1," respectively.
5. Only one actual print survives: *Personnage*, 1943–44 (see ibid., no. 1A). Of another print (see ibid., no. 1), only a photograph is known. Motherwell remembers "three or four" others.
6. Hayter published his ideas shortly after the war in *New Ways of Gravure* (New York: Pantheon, 1949).
7. "A Special Genius: Works on Paper," *Bulletin of the Rhode Island School of Design* (Winter 1977): 20–34, cited in Terenzio and Belknap, *Catalogue Raisonné*, p. 28.
8. Robert Motherwell, conversations with author, 1984–85.
9. This is a recurrent theme in Terenzio's interviews. See Terenzio and Belknap, *Catalogue Raisonné*, pp. 23–152.
10. "A Special Genius," cited ibid., p. 38.
11. Motherwell had made a number of lithographs related to Beside the Sea in 1962–63, but they were not printed in editions. See ibid., pp. 274–75.
12. Irwin Hollander, ibid., p. 26.
13. Ibid., p. 32.
14. See, for example, ibid., nos. 34, 35, 60–69.
15. The three related "Stone" images are reproduced ibid., p. 180, nos. 72–74.
16. See ibid., nos. 82–102, 268–91.
17. The text that Motherwell incorporated into the first Elegy-like image was the second stanza of Harold Rosenberg's unpublished "The Bird for Every Bird." Motherwell later said, however, that he was inspired less by this poem than by the work of García Lorca, in which he was deeply immersed at the time. See Robert C. Hobbs, "Motherwell's Concern with Death in Painting: An Investigation of His Elegies to the Spanish Republic, Including an Examination of His Philosophical and Methodological Considerations" (Ph.D. diss., University of North Carolina, Chapel Hill, 1975), p. 4.
18. Dore Ashton, "Robert Motherwell: The Painter and His Poets," in H. H. Arnason, *Robert Motherwell*, 2d ed. (New York: Harry N. Abrams, 1982), pp. 8–14.
19. From 1976 to 1978 Motherwell's lithographs were printed in his own studio.
20. "A Special Genius," cited in Terenzio and Belknap, *Catalogue Raisonné*, p. 32.
21. Ibid., p. 98. Compare Motherwell's statement to Heidi Colsman-Freyberger: "Well, apart from my feeling for paper, for plates and stones, which are sine qua nons for making prints, the aspect that I love after a lifetime in the solitude of my studio is the collaboration, the working with other people, the camaraderie, the extraordinary selflessness and sensitivity of very good publishers . . . and printers. . . . In making prints, one's full depth of appreciation for the marvelousness of craftsmanship is enormously reinforced. And I like first-rate craftsmen as human beings as well as any group of people I know" (Terenzio and Belknap, *Catalogue Raisonné*, p. 98).
22. Tony Towle has characterized ULAE at that time as "a sort of refuge for him" (Terenzio and Belknap, *Catalogue Raisonné*, p. 73).
23. Robert Motherwell, "The Book's Beginnings," in *Robert Motherwell's A la pintura: The Genesis of a Book*, exh. cat. (New York: Metropolitan Museum of Art, 1972), n.p.
24. Donn Steward, in Terenzio and Belknap, *Catalogue Raisonné*, p. 61.
25. Ibid., p. 64.
26. See ibid., nos. 112–29.
27. I say this on the basis of my own experiences while the book was being worked on. An astonishing number of changes of all kinds—in imagery, color, paper, binding, typeface, even the translation of the text—were constantly being made, even after the actual printing had started.
28. See Terenzio and Belknap, *Catalogue Raisonné*, pp. 90–92.
29. Ibid., pp. 81–84.
30. Motherwell has also commented on this tension in the artist-printer relationship: "The problem of working with craftsmen is their general tendency to exaggerate nuances. It is almost impossible to get a certain kind of obsessed craftsman not to overemphasize what should be subtle. . . . But several times in my life I have worked with printers who, in effect, become alter egos. They intuitively sensed what I was after, and in many cases the work became better" ("A Special Genius," cited ibid., p. 136).

Robert Motherwell
America-La France Variations IV 1984
lithograph, collage on TGL handmade paper
46½ x 32⅛
Collection Walker Art Center, Minneapolis
Tyler Graphics Archive
(Tyler 446:RM65)

papeteries arjomari·prioux

Archives   Helen Frankenthaler '77

Spontaneity and the Print

E. C. Goossen

Helen Frankenthaler is primarily a painter and will always be known for her contributions as such to the history of twentieth-century art. However, she has often turned her talents to other means of expression, including designs for the ballet, ceramics, sculpture, and prints. While she has never concentrated on any one of these other modes as she has on painting, she has, for example, made nearly ninety prints. Two-thirds of these were done before she first worked with Kenneth Tyler in 1976 at his Bedford Village press, where she created several of her finest prints. In at least one instance, *Essence Mulberry* (p. 62), she appears to have achieved the same degree of historical and personal triumph as she did with her famous 1952 painting, *Mountains and Sea* (p. 64).

Throughout her career as a painter, Frankenthaler has developed what might be called a continuously emergent style, a kind of progressive flow from one stage to the next without abrupt transitions. There have been moments, though, when one could point to a particular picture and see how it had brought together her immediate and more remote past and set the tone for the next phase. Until *Essence Mulberry*, the progress of her work in graphics had not produced such an important benchmark, probably because the character of her work in that medium clearly derived from her preoccupations in painting. In the 1960s and early 1970s her prints confirmed the validity of her approach to art and the transmutability of her characteristic spontaneity into the rigidities of the segmented time-world of printmaking. Having said that, however, it is important to note that Frankenthaler's prints can clearly stand on their own merits. She has had more than routine success in avoiding the Scylla and Charybdis of painters who only occasionally make prints, that is, the tendency merely to reproduce their paintings.

Ultimately, and ironically, Frankenthaler has found ways to make the negative aspects of printmaking work positively for her. In printmaking there are inevitable interruptions of the creative time frame between one mechanical stage and the next. For an artist who finds her subject and her means in the process of making a work of art, any hiatus

Helen Frankenthaler
Essence Mulberry
1977
woodcut on buff
Maniai handmade
paper
39½ x 18½
Collection Walker Art
Center, Minneapolis
Tyler Graphics Archive
(Tyler 180:HF4)

between inception and conclusion can be a disaster. Her ability to sense that an idea is slipping away before it is entirely lost has been crucial to Frankenthaler's success. At certain points, according to Tyler and others who have worked alongside her, Frankenthaler has called a halt in the course of making a print. The proofs of its current state, the plates, and the earlier proofs have been taken back to her own studio, where the energy and the idea could be retrieved and reinstituted and the urge to proceed recaptured. That there is a certain silence needed

for Frankenthaler to develop an idea is apparent, and the evanescence of that idea, even as she is realizing it, is both its charm and its meaning.

At the outset of her printmaking career it was obviously easier for Frankenthaler to produce directly in the lithograph an equivalent of her liquid brush stroke and her spilled color. The greasy crayon on the stone has its unique quality of immediacy and is particularly susceptible to bold handling, while etching, aquatint, and drypoint used individually or together almost instantly immerse the artist in subtleties and possibilities that may well swamp the best of intentions. In these complex processes one can arrive at a *look* of instantaneousness that is immediately denied by one's visual sense that a given work is an *illustration* of a moment—not the moment itself. This may seem like nit-picking, but there is a major qualitative difference between the two experiences: in the first instance the viewer receives the painting or print *passively* and treats it as a record of a prior event, while in the second instance he is drawn into active participation with the event before him, one that is continuously in process.

Helen Frankenthaler
*Mountains and
Sea* 1952
oil on canvas
86⅜ x 117¼
National Gallery of
Art, Washington, D.C.
Collection of the artist,
loan

This creation of an image that seems to be in a state of suspension between becoming visibly stable and passing away into nullity has been a consistent characteristic of Frankenthaler's work since about 1951. A rigorous training in the principles of Cubist painting had taught her the value of structure, but it was not until she came into contact with Jackson Pollock's huge drip pictures that she became aware of Cubism's shortcomings, especially its tendency to illustrate rather than to present the simultaneous views of the world for which it was acclaimed. Pollock's paintings apparently gave Frankenthaler the confidence and the clue as to how to step away from the descriptive and the historical toward the immediate and the present. She was able to fulfill this desire in her painting through the development of her soak-stain technique and, as noted, in lithographs through manipulation of the crayon in the manner of a smearing brush. In each case she evoked the genies of the materials and the methods, making them serve her ends rather than vice versa.

In a series of screenprints and pochoirs, Frankenthaler further explored the possibility of transferring her kind of image and sensibility, indeed her aesthetic philosophy, to the multiples that printmaking offered. Both of these methods, like lithography, were more or less susceptible to her particular signature, since their forte is looseness and immediacy of statement. Etching, which she approached more tentatively, has a range of feeling and means superior to all other graphic media, but it is jealous of the other arts and protective of its tradition. So much skill is required just to do a mundane job in etching that only the most zealous of artists (among them Albrecht Dürer, Rembrandt van Rijn, James McNeill Whistler, and Edgar Degas) have had the patience to bend the craft away from its practical prejudices and to make it answer to the requirements of high art. There are so many stages in the etching process that at each point control must be wrested away from accidental and mechanical results and redirected toward an acceptable end. While Frankenthaler has indicated that she is "not interested in the techniques of printmaking" or in "the patience it requires,"[1] her work in these media belies either her statements or the value of the knowledge and patience printmaking presumably demands. She quite obviously has a command of all that is necessary to the production of major prints, understands the processes and the potentials, and can recognize a possible addition to her repertory when it appears.

One of the prime characteristics of Frankenthaler's work over the years has been her use of liquidity in combination with color, which is, of course, a key to the immediacy and energy in her painting. She has cultivated this quality with the greatest of discretion in both her drawing and her palette. In 1972 Donn Steward, with whom she was then working, apparently rediscovered the technique Degas had used in a single print, the 1879 *Buste de femme*. This technique involved a way of combining "spirits of wine" (i.e., brandy) with rosin in suspension to increase the sense of liquidity in an aquatint. Frankenthaler's 1972–74 edition entitled *Message from Degas* employs the French artist's experimental process. Thus, Frankenthaler was able to achieve a smoky, misty field similar in nature to certain canvases she was working on at that time, yet entirely geared and scaled, here, to the world of prints.

One would think that the etching-aquatint process, so thoroughly one of liquids (acids and inks), ought easily to lend its support to an artist seeking the essence of liquidity. The opposite seems normally to be the case, since the acid-bitten plates tend to give back their dry, metallic hardness rather than the fluidity that gave them the images to print. Nevertheless, in two of three aquatints Frankenthaler made in Rome during 1973 (*Pranzo Italiano* and *Ponti*), she managed to make the images appear true to their origins and to display the flowed areas in full depth. How she achieved this is not entirely clear, though her intention is documented by the fact that she accepted the plates for printing. One critic misread the treatment of these areas as showing "a marked interest in texture," a quality he likes to find in prints and a view that may have developed out of his wish that Frankenthaler become a traditional printmaker with an accordingly reoriented aesthetic.[2]

By the time she began work on the woodcut *Essence Mulberry* in 1977, Frankenthaler had already produced three lithographs and a poster at Tyler Graphics. It is notable that while the facilities at Tyler's workshop allow for extraordinarily large prints, as had 2RC Editrice, the printing studio in Rome, Frankenthaler's sense of scale for this form of expression has remained more or less traditional despite the fact that hugeness has been highly popular in recent years. She seems to feel that graphic work is a specific métier and should not attempt to compete in size, or in other ways, with painting. In any event the largest dimension of a work in this medium that she has made so far has been about forty inches inclusive of margins, or, as in the case of *Essence Mulberry*, the meaningful emptiness below the edge-to-edge image above.[3]

The story of the genesis of *Essence Mulberry* fast became an art legend: how the mulberries were ripe in Tyler's backyard and a pail of the crimson juice found its way to the studio, where Frankenthaler dripped some on paper, thus producing an image that had the look not only of her own works on canvas but also of the delicate, faded colors she had recently admired in a show of medieval woodcuts at the Metropolitan Museum of Art in New York. Experimentation with the juicy color led to its duplication in ink and then to the creation of a woodcut.

While her fascination with faded medieval prints may have aroused the artist's taste for a particular kind of color, *Essence Mulberry* would seem closer to Japanese painting and prints as aesthetic precedents. But what was taken or learned from either source was so prepared for in her own work prior to this occasion that one cannot talk of influences but must speak of recognitions. For example, the faded color of the medieval prints probably attracted her because of its close relationship to her own low-density colors applied transparently like watercolor and used as a foil for her saturated, opaque hues. Her range, then—from pellucid to opaque, from watery to saturated—combined with the capacity for the transparent medium to reveal the canvas's weave, the paper's body, the wood's grain, gives her an enviable vocabulary of forms and potential meanings. The manipulation of all these variables, particularly within the world of printmaking, has presented a formidable challenge.

Virtually all of Frankenthaler's developed vocabulary appears in the woodcut *Essence Mulberry,* much of it in new combinations, as well as her superb color sense, drawing, and placement. When one realizes that this work is the result of six separate blocks (two rejected for the final edition), each itself the result of laborious cutting away and continuous modification by the artist, it is clear that *Essence Mulberry* is a major tour de force of visual unity. That Frankenthaler should have found here an equivalent for the spontaneity of her major paintings is, oddly enough, a tribute to her perseverance, indicating that said spontaneity is a *principle* of her work, not a recorded physical gesture. In *Essence Mulberry* she achieves the feeling that the image is just now coming to life as we look at it through the same means she has employed elsewhere: the liquidity of the drawing, the spatial gradients established between opacity and various levels of transparency, and the revelations of materiality in the wood grains and the matrix of the Japanese papermaking frame. *Essence Mulberry* does not immediately look like a Frankenthaler, yet no one else could have made it. On closer inspection it is *quintessential* Frankenthaler. The reason one is put off the track for a moment is that she has added something to the contemporary abstract print that was not there before, and that is to interweave the making and the means so totally that, to quote William Butler Yeats, it is impossible to "know the dancer from the dance." It is amazing in a way to consider that the final version of *Essence Mulberry* was an inversion of the original orientation of the image itself, a revelation of how Frankenthaler seems to keep some works alive by refusing to give up until all options and possibilities have been explored.

The artist's willingness to record her circuitous route to a satisfactory solution is demonstrated in the series of Experimental Impressions (see p. 68) related to *Earth Slice* (p. 69), done at Tyler's workshop over a period of several months in 1977–78. The difference between these and the classic retained "proofs" of old and new masters (like the revised galleys of Marcel Proust) lies in the fact that each of the nine was a version that might have been accepted and was a variant combination of *some* of the seven plates produced, though only a select four were used in the end. On the one hand, what we have here seems like playing cards dealt out randomly in what might have been the longest game in town. On the other hand, each of the "experiments" must have represented a limit to a particular direction, which, though satisfactory in itself, did not fulfill the same set of requirements as the last choice did, and *that* was not an "experiment" but a goal. Even that goal constituted an offering to the gods of printmaking, however.

Helen Frankenthaler
*Experimental
Impression I* 1978
monoprint on Dutch
Etching paper
12¾ x 24½
Courtesy Tyler
Graphics Ltd.
(Tyler 183:HF7)

Helen Frankenthaler
*Experimental
Impression IV* 1978
monoprint on Dutch
Etching paper
18 x 29
Private collection
(Tyler 186:HF10)

Helen Frankenthaler
*Experimental
Impression V* 1978
monoprint on Dutch
Etching paper
20 x 31
Courtesy Tyler
Graphics Ltd.
(Tyler 187:HF11)

Helen Frankenthaler
Earth Slice 1978
etching, aquatint on
mauve HMP
handmade paper
15½ x 26
Collection Walker Art
Center, Minneapolis
Tyler Graphics Archive
(Tyler 182:HF6)

Helen Frankenthaler
Ganymede 1978
etching, aquatint on
Arches Cover paper
22½ x 16½
Collection Walker Art
Center, Minneapolis
Tyler Graphics Archive
(Tyler 192:HF16)

Ganymede (p. 69) is a selected segment of about one quarter of *Earth Slice*, cut down from the latter's four steel-faced copper plates, oriented anew, and—with its reds and yellows—quite distinct from the browns and greens of its source.

Color has always been Frankenthaler's main access to mood and meaning, while her drawing has given them definition and a place to happen. *Sure Violet* (pp. 72–73), an ambiguous land-, sea-, or skyscape, is a case in point. It is also a case for some of the advantages of printmaking. If the proofs tell the correct story, this relatively simple and subtle aquatint went through a series of graduated color modifications without any major changes in the basic structure of the drawing. This chronology is a disclosure of the kind of search for the perfect answer that Frankenthaler undertakes. The successive proofs allow her to pursue her ultimate solution without having to discard each possible permutation of the original idea (as she would have to do with a thinly painted watercolor or oil). It is also of note that the progression is *linear* rather than *bracketed* (as in an artilleryman's search for his target); in *Sure Violet* the color goes, in nine steps, from intense and dark to lighter and less assertive. Each of the inks used, twelve in all, seems to have been readjusted every step of the way until the overall version was finely tuned.

Frankenthaler's 1980 woodcut *Cameo* (p. 71) had a series of trial proofs that, under inspection, show drastic reductions of the original idea at each new stage. *Cameo* gets successively stronger as it gets more evanescent. This steady search for the essence is remarkable because it goes against the usual tendency to add more and more visual "interest" when the first proofs are unsatisfactory. But the reduction of the elements of this image did not mean a reduction of the number of colors used in the final stage. Though one's first impression of *Cameo* is that it comprises only two or three colors, in fact, there were eight colors and five runs of the five blocks involved. *Cameo* is a prime example of Frankenthaler's subtle manipulation of color and space, of her capacity to maintain a quality of delicacy and nuance over a long period of corrections, and, finally, of her sure sense of when to stop.

Perhaps the real triumph of Frankenthaler's printmaking ventures is the increasing seriousness with which she has addressed the print's possibilities. Unlike many artists who have diverted themselves with the medium—often, it would seem, primarily to produce more widely marketable versions of their signature—she seems willing to go to great lengths to generate new experiences for herself and her audience. Since her last works done at Tyler Graphics, for example, she has traveled to Japan for a three-week work period just to make one print with the craftsmen of Kyoto. The striking result bodes well for the future of her personal investigation of printmaking.

The four groups of prints that Joan Mitchell has made with Tyler Graphics were done in early 1981, in one intense period when she was on a sojourn in the United States from the tiny town of Vétheuil, located

Helen Frankenthaler
Cameo 1980
woodcut on gray-pink
TGL handmade paper
42 x 32
Collection Walker Art
Center, Minneapolis
Tyler Graphics Archive
(Tyler 195:HF19)

Helen Frankenthaler
Sure Violet, color trial
proof 3/16   1979
etching, aquatint,
drypoint on TGL
handmade paper
31¼ x 43⅜
Collection Walker Art
Center, Minneapolis
Tyler Graphics Archive

Helen Frankenthaler
Sure Violet, color trial
proof 6/16   1979
etching, aquatint,
drypoint on TGL
handmade paper
31¼ x 43⅜
Collection Walker Art
Center, Minneapolis
Tyler Graphics Archive

Helen Frankenthaler
Sure Violet, color trial
proof 9/16   1979
etching, aquatint,
drypoint on TGL
handmade paper
31¼ x 43⅜
Collection Walker Art
Center, Minneapolis
Tyler Graphics Archive

Helen Frankenthaler
Sure Violet 1979
etching, aquatint,
drypoint on TGL
handmade paper
31 x 43
Collection Walker Art
Center, Minneapolis
Tyler Graphics Archive
(Tyler 194:HF18)

in the Seine valley about forty-five miles northwest of Paris. The Bedford, Sides of a River, Flower, and Brush prints, multicolored lithographs from aluminum plates that share the same dimensions, are all part of the Bedford Series.

Mitchell has taken a very direct approach to printmaking. There is little evidence, at least in the final prints, that she has had to compromise the medium or herself. This is in spite of the fact that in making her kind of expressionistic art she might expect to face some difficulties in the time lapses between proofing plates, sometimes as many as ten, and the final amalgamation into a single image. It becomes clear as one studies these prints and compares them with her paintings

Joan Mitchell
Flower I 1981
lithograph on
Arches 88 paper
42½ x 32½
Collection Walker Art
Center, Minneapolis
Tyler Graphics Archive
(Tyler 369:JM7)

(see p. 75), however, that this is hardly a mind or a hand that works without a goal, as purely mental as it sometimes may be, and that as the image gathers force, its pieces fit together like a precut jigsaw puzzle. *Precut* may be too strong a term for what actually takes place, yet there is a certain inevitability about each gestural mark or brush stroke that suggests a strong element of planning.

Mitchell's way of thinking about and making pictures has not

Joan Mitchell
Flying Dutchman
1961–62
oil on canvas
78¾ x 78¾
Courtesy Xavier
Fourcade, Inc.

changed essentially since the early 1950s, when she established her point of view very clearly. Since then she has proven its workability; what *has* changed, perhaps, is her sense of color and the way she wants it to read. The Abstract Expressionist generation out of which she came was forever searching for abstract subject matter with transcendent implications, even though it professed to believe that art was its own message. Mitchell had, it might seem, one foot in each camp. An inheritor of the early moderns' faith in Paul Cézanne and in that sense a pre-Cubist, she builds a picture with strokes of color. Her technique tends to be more turgid and less pure than Cézanne's, and since it is farther from its source in nature, it is more dependent on the nature of the stroke

(left)
Joan Mitchell
Sides of a River I
1981
lithograph on
Arches 88 paper
42½ x 32½
Collection Walker Art
Center, Minneapolis
Tyler Graphics Archive
(Tyler 366:JM4)

(top, right)
Joan Mitchell
Sides of a River II
1981
lithograph on
Arches 88 paper
42½ x 32½
Collection Walker Art
Center, Minneapolis
Tyler Graphics Archive
(Tyler 367:JM5)

Joan Mitchell
Sides of a River III
1981
lithograph on
Arches 88 paper
42½ x 32½
Collection Walker Art
Center, Minneapolis
Tyler Graphics Archive
(Tyler 368:JM6)

itself. And if Cézanne, in his progress toward greater abstraction, blurred the difference between the subject matter and its treatment, Mitchell's generation converted the treatment into subject matter. But unlike those contemporary painters who "discover" the subject in the process of painting, Mitchell works from an idea and builds on it as Cézanne did with his views of Mont Sainte-Victoire, his bathers, and his oranges. That Claude Monet, Henri Matisse, and Pollock have also played a part in the development of Mitchell's painting does not erase the effect of her initial inventive leap back to Cézanne, which enabled her to bypass the standard routes through Cubism and the subsequent history of twentieth-century art and gave her a method for producing pictures acceptable to the taste of a period some fifty years later.

In the 1950s and early 1960s Mitchell's palette tended toward the darker ranges, browns and blacks, offset by middle-range oranges and greens, a kind of "serious" painting in the Western tradition that credits rich and umbrageous color with profound content. The fatness of her paint allowed the color to break away from its strict association with the brush stroke as it bled downward, opening new spaces and veiling others. This intentional dripping of color has continued into her work of the 1980s, as in the Grande Vallée series, and its equivalent can be found in some of the lithographs made at Tyler's workshop in the same period.

While the 1981 lithographs are most distinctly prints and not paintings or "works on paper," they do reflect the problems and solutions of Mitchell's work over the years. They also represent some outlets for her art that have been unavailable to her in painting and thus have clearly expanded her oeuvre as a whole. One of those outlets is an apparent sense of release from the burden of painting. To one so deeply immersed in the meaningfulness of each act and each response of the *matière,* the very lightness of the crayon and the possibility of testing colors beforehand so that they will not invade others without permission seems to have been inspirational. Though the mood of her last decade's painting has grown lighter, surer, more floral than eventful, the lithographs have gone even further in gaiety and affection for the result.

If there is any problem that Mitchell has had with the litho print, it must have been in getting into sync with wrist and arm motions quite different from those comfortable to her in painting. Scale, of course, might also have presented some difficulties, but since her prints are three and a half feet high and nearly three feet wide, the sweeping stroke is still possible and the spatial expanse sufficient to allow her to play off sizable concentrations of colored squiggles against gracefully looping reaches of crayoned color (*Sides of a River II;* p. 76) or clotted calligraphic forms against a grassy field of orange pink (*Flower I;* p. 74). These are works that would not read well at a larger scale; nor would they be adequately served by a smaller one. Their marks are not precise enough to be miniaturized or grand enough to supply large ideas. They are, in other words, just right and well within a classical idea of the print. But all this apparent ease of plan and execution is shown to be the result of extraordinary care in preparation of the individual plates, which can number as many as ten and never fewer than two. How carefully the imprints were layered is not evident in the perusal of any one version of, say, Sides of a River (p. 76) until all three are inspected, visually disassembled, and compared. And while one feels that in the looseness of the design the register could have been fudged, it clearly was not; indeed, the artist must of necessity have transferred stages of the basic drawings to subsequent plates as the images were developed. Each plate carried a different color, but it was the resonance between the colors rather than their distinguishable areas that was the goal; the overlay, the scumbling effect had to be built up through a combination of predication and trial and error.

In studying the three final versions of the Sides of a River and Flower images, it appears that in one of each of the groups, in the first instance, number III, and in the second, number II (pp. 76, 79), there are the bare bones of the enterprise as a whole. These lithographs are composed of only two plates and two colors. With such a minimum number of interacting images, we are given an essence (not necessarily *the* essence) of the structural framework that informs the other versions and establishes the underlying dialogue. The efflorescence of these paired drawings in subsequent combinations reveals almost as much about Mitchell's painting as it does about her prints. It indicates that her creative process begins with an idea either sketched on the canvas or held securely in the mind and then enlarged upon at will. However, as noted previously, the print process allows for different choices evolving from the same essential structure, while in painting, a repetition of even a part would be impossible with any exactitude.

Another variation on Mitchell's approach to the print occurs with the group *Bedford I, Bedford II,* and *Bedford III* (pp. 80–81), in which the plates that make up the three lithographs have been so shuffled in both color and image that there is only the generalized presence of blue and pink plus the common title to connect them at all. Each of the Bedford group is composed of many aluminum plates—seven, eight, or ten to be exact—so that there is a density of color and field that is less evident in the other Bedford Series prints. Moreover, at least one plate slid over from *Sides of a River II* and *Sides of a River III,* and though it is hard to determine from what appears to be the final amalgamation in *Bedford II,* some of the eight plates involved may have been ones that found no place in any of the other groupings. More power to the artist who can delve into her own identity and find new ways to put it together and to use it. This is not so far removed from the way in which painters often leave "unfinishable" canvases to another day when the old inspiration or a new light may come to their rescue. In *Bedford II* a mélange becomes an assertion and builds to colored space that approximates the color-field painting in which Mitchell's usual drawn elements are camouflaged but not lost.

Joan Mitchell
Flower II 1981
lithograph on
Arches 88 paper
42½ x 32½
Collection Walker Art
Center, Minneapolis
Tyler Graphics Archive
(Tyler 370:JM8)

Mitchell also produced two lithographs entitled *Brush* and *Brush, State I* at Tyler Graphics in 1981. These seem, however, like exercises in calligraphic skill, well within the conventions of lithography, albeit with Mitchell's personal touch. In other words, they seem to *use* the artist's known capacities rather than extend them as do the other works in this print group. Perhaps the most successful of these, both as demonstrations of the artist's power and as gestures that move beyond the level of automatic attraction, are the three Sides of a River, in which theme and execution are indistinguishable. They stand with Mitchell's best paintings.

Joan Mitchell
Bedford I 1981
lithograph on
Arches 88 paper
42½ x 32½
Collection Walker Art
Center, Minneapolis
Tyler Graphics Archive
(Tyler 363:JM1)

Joan Mitchell
Bedford III 1981
lithograph on
Arches 88 paper
42½ x 32½
Collection Walker Art
Center, Minneapolis
Tyler Graphics Archive
(Tyler 365: JM3)

(opposite)
Joan Mitchell
Bedford II 1981
lithograph on
Arches 88 paper
42½ x 32½
Collection Walker Art
Center, Minneapolis
Tyler Graphics Archive
(Tyler 364:JM2)

When, in the late 1960s, Nancy Graves came on the scene with her life-size replicas of camels, it was hardly foreseeable that she would become best known for highly colored openwork sculpture more closely related to Pablo Picasso, Julio González, and David Smith than to paleontological reconstructions. Her work has remained figurative, not

only in sculpture but in painting and printmaking, though in the latter two forms of expression the figural references are often so obscured as to be barely visible. Graves seems to enjoy contradictions: abstraction versus representation, two versus three dimensions, naturalistic versus pure color, and so on. In her painting and sculpture thus far, she has capitalized on the conflicts between abstraction and representation and has shown that she is a confirmed anti-Hegelian in her refusal to accept his clear-cut and canonical divisions of art into precise areas of

Nancy Graves
Extend-Expand
1983
bronze with
polychromed patiná
85 x 51 x 33⅝
Collection Museum
of Modern Art,
New York
Gift of Mr. and Mrs.
Sid R. Bass

competence. Yet even though she is attracted to the license offered by mixed media and the formal eclecticism of Postmodernism, one senses a traditionalist under the glitter and paint of her more recent work.

According to Nancy Spector, Graves has said that she has found "the problems of two- and three-dimensionality contradictory,"[4] which of course they are and have been since the beginning of art. This truism nevertheless seems to have escaped many of Graves's contemporaries, and it is her recognition of it that gives her an edge on many of them. But contradictions do haunt her work at times, as in the sculpture *Extend-Expand*, 1983 (p. 82), for example, in which both drawing and painting seem to be her preoccupations, while the third dimension, though real, often appears illusory. Similarly, in paintings of the same year from the Shadow series, the intermixture of sculptural aluminum or fiberglass projections, which, like the painted portions, lie on a monochrome surface, indicates a wish to turn the painting into a three-dimensional object. In light of Graves's confrontation with perhaps irreconcilable desires, it is worthwhile to take a careful look at her work in printmaking to see how she deals with these problems in a more resolutely two-dimensional medium.

Graves has worked at Tyler Graphics twice to date: in 1977 and again in 1981. The more recent sojourn there produced a group of thirty-one monoprints and three edition prints. The monoprints were made using varying combinations of three etched plates. Twenty-six of the combinations are single-sheet prints, four are composed of two sheets joined into diptychs, and one is a triptych. The largest subgroup that features an identifiable, continuing format includes a handprint, nine dribble-drawn lines from one edge, a squarish flowerlike form, and a music staff reaching from one side toward the center. This format is that of one of the three magnesium plates, since it appears in about one-half of the "edition." The other two plates are more ambiguously marked on the whole, though one of them is definitely composed of linear sexual inferences in the manner of Arshile Gorky and Picasso, while the other presents broad, calligraphic swaths in expressionistic swirls. The specific relationships between these images become less and less clear as one reviews the various combinations that were attempted.

It is this trial-and-error method that makes the monoprint as an expressive means somewhat chancy. Graves's esoteric "subject matter" does not allow the viewer any clues as to what the color shifts mean seriatim. Thus, one judges these prints as separate entities that either please or displease on what turns out to be a formalistic basis. One begins to note that the best ones, such as *Owad* (p. 84) and *Gardli*, are the result of close-valued colors, which, in the overlays, knit the drawings together in one integral space. Other prints that gratify one's desire for wholeness and clarity are *Tate*, *Confo*, and *Chala* (p. 85), each remarkable for its distance from its origin in monoprint.

One work from this series, *Creant* (p. 85), exhibits Graves's secret passion and strength most clearly while at the same time compromising

Nancy Graves
Owad 1981
monoprint on blue
TGL handmade paper
31¾ x 43¾
Collection Walker Art
Center, Minneapolis
Tyler Graphics Archive
(Tyler 213:NG23)

Nancy Graves
Chala 1981
monoprint on TGL
handmade paper
30½ x 39¾
Collection of the artist

Nancy Graves
Creant 1981
monoprint on TGL
handmade paper
30 x 40
Private collection

itself to a degree as a print. *Creant* is really a drawing, white chalk on a black ground, of a scene of high sexuality, derived in idea possibly from *Myrrhina and Kinesias* or a similar Picasso etching from the 1930s. It is this matrix drawing that is part of *Cegena* and other Graves monoprints, though it is far more camouflaged there. One wonders why such an articulate drawing should turn up as part of a palimpsest of relatively more abstract imagery and exercises in color variations.

Having noted Graves's predilection for figuration, it might be appropriate to mention again that most of her sculpture has been executed in that twentieth-century mode known as "drawing in space." Hers is a kind of loaded linearity as opposed to the clean-line approach of so many of her predecessors in this manner of spatialized sculpture. Her lines are twisted into curlicues and webs, become clusters of cells, change into seaweed and bones, and proceed through color after color created by the patination of her bronze surfaces. It is this affection for drawn color and graphic line that accounts for the success of a group of prints done in 1977. In contrast to the monoprints, these prints use color judiciously and render their spaces open and light (see pp. 86–87). Here the lines may tremble or scribble and remain abstract even when they hint at submerged subject matter. The colors retain their characters as reds, blues, greens, ochers, and so on, since they are free from overt associations with anything else. The connection between these prints

Nancy Graves
Toch 1977
etching, aquatint, drypoint, engraving, hand-colored on Arches Cover paper
31½ x 35½
Collection Walker Art Center, Minneapolis
Tyler Graphics Archive
(Tyler 204:NG3)

and the process by which they evolved may indeed be a clue to both their uniqueness and their success. Essentially they are etchings with an aquatint dimension; sometimes they include drypoint and engraving. But in all of them *hand-coloring* was accepted as a method to arrive at the final proof. This bow in the direction of the singularity of each unit of the edition broke with the idea of a pure print but lent the freshness of pastel colors to the operation as a whole. The method had a certain rigor in that the two or three lines laid down in pastel by the artist were regularized by being drawn in the channel of a plastic stencil. While this may have been arduous work, the effort demonstrates once more Graves's dissatisfaction with the limitations of each of the forms of art she has explored and her continuing direct confrontation of the contradictions posed by all of them.

Nancy Graves
Ngetal 1977
etching, aquatint,
engraving, drypoint,
hand-colored on
Arches Cover paper
31½ x 35½
Collection Walker Art
Center, Minneapolis
Tyler Graphics Archive
(Tyler 206:NG5)

Notes

1. Helen Frankenthaler, "The Romance of Learning a New Medium for an Artist," *Print Collector's Newsletter* 8 (July–August 1977): 67.
2. Thomas Krens, *Helen Frankenthaler Prints: 1961–1979*, exh. cat. (New York: Harper & Row, 1980), p. 45.
3. One exception in regard to size must be noted. *Lot's Wife,* a print made at Universal Limited Art Editions in 1971, was a triptych composed of plates measuring about 40 by 30 inches, which, when assembled, measured 130 by 36¼ inches.
4. Nancy Spector, in *Six in Bronze,* ed. Phyllis Tuchman, exh. cat. (Williamstown, Mass.: Williams College Museum of Art, 1983), n.p.

Variations on Geometry

Robert M. Murdock

A number of the artists who have worked with Kenneth Tyler at Tyler Graphics Ltd. have been distinguished by their use of geometric form in painting and sculpture; several of them (Josef Albers, Ellsworth Kelly, Frank Stella, Ronald Davis) also produced prints with Tyler at Gemini G.E.L. While there may be various reasons for this, the crucial one, it seems, is that geometric or emblematic imagery lends itself particularly well to the pristine quality and technical perfection in color, registration, and printing that characterize Tyler editions. The artists represented in this chapter work with geometry and color to varying degrees, from Albers's screen-printed squares—containers for color interaction that surpass the subtlety and nuance in his painting—to Michael Heizer's mixed-media prints, in which color is secondary to form—segmented circles and schematic diagrams that relate directly to his sculpture. In their collaborations with Tyler, Kelly and Kenneth Noland have also repeated characteristic forms from their other work. All of these artists have used printmaking as an extension of their usual medium; in some cases they have utilized the technical range available at the Tyler Graphics workshop to explore new areas or approaches.

Since the inception of Constructivist and Suprematist art in prerevolutionary Russia around 1915 and the formation of De Stijl in the Netherlands in 1917, nonobjective art or geometric abstraction has remained a persistent modern tendency. Even when partially eclipsed by expressionist currents, it has continued in the work of individual artists, taken on new forms, and found young practitioners. The circle, square, and triangle exert definitive, universal, and inexorable power as emblems of modernism.

Among the artists considered in this chapter, Josef Albers provides the bridge with early twentieth-century geometric abstraction and the Bauhaus, just as Robert Motherwell is linked to Surrealism, Abstract Expressionism, and the modernist tradition of collage. Universally acknowledged as masters of modern painting, these two artists were the first to work extensively with Tyler at his Bedford Village workshop.

Josef Albers
Never Before d 1976
screenprint on
Arches 88 paper
19 x 19
Collection Walker Art
Center, Minneapolis
Tyler Graphics Archive
(Tyler 61:JA43)

As mentioned earlier in this book (see "Kenneth Tyler: The Artisan as Artist"), Albers's collaboration with Tyler began during the printer's years at Tamarind Lithography Workshop. At Tyler Graphics they collaborated on four portfolios of screenprints: Gray Instrumentation I, Gray Instrumentation II, Mitered Squares, and Albers's last work with Tyler, Never Before (see pp. 88, 91–93). All have an extreme subtlety and range of color that reflect Albers's theory concerning optics and make these portfolios technical tours de force. Some of the color relationships are more refined variations on the juxtapositions found in Albers's *Interaction of Color,* published by Yale University Press in 1963. While that publication is a sophisticated textbook of graphic, visual demonstrations for the student of color (widely used by artists and art students then and now), the Tyler prints make some of the same points in a more refined manner. The elements of Albers's color theory presented in these portfolios include the differing appearance of a single color when placed in relation to other colors, the circumstances under which different colors appear the same, and the intensification of one color by another. At Tyler Graphics individual color areas were printed separately, with precise registration and minimal overlapping that created a uniformity in inking and tone and a richness in the velvety mat surface. The Tyler documentation notes that Albers "directed the mixing of each mat opaque color, which in the printing sequence was fitted side by side. This registration technique achieves a very flat ink surface on the paper."[1] The simplicity of the preceding description fails to convey the technical difficulty of achieving such precision.

In viewing a series of twelve Albers images, one consciously or unconsciously attempts to determine the artist's system or sequence from one image to the next and overall, whereas his Homage to the Square paintings function more as discrete objects, even though they may be shown as a group. Each Gray Instrumentation portfolio contains many nuances of color, shape (number and size of nesting squares), space, light, and atmosphere. Gray Instrumentation I is literally what its title denotes: a series of variations on value and intensity of the color gray. From an initial blue gray, the colors range to a dense almost-black through gray brown, medium gray brown, medium gray green, pearl gray, and pale gray green. The twelfth print returns to blue gray, and the innermost square is surrounded by a white line square, probably an allusion to the earlier Gemini portfolio of that name as well as a concluding statement for this one. In the manner of a musical structure or mathematical progression, the number of squares in each plate varies as follows: 4, 3, 4, 3; 3, 4, 3, 3; 3, 4, 4, 4.

Gray Instrumentation II is a tone poem about the relative intensity of the palest possible colors. It begins with four pale green squares, similar in hue and intensity to the next to the last plate of the preceding portfolio; it ends quietly with a pearl gray. The ten intervening images range from light gray green and blue gray to light tan. The strongest color after the initial green is ocher, which, though assertive in this

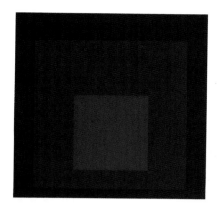

(top)
Josef Albers
Gray Instrumentation
Ig 1974
screenprint on
Arches 88 paper
19 x 19
Collection Walker Art
Center, Minneapolis
Tyler Graphics Archive
(Tyler 25:JA7)

Josef Albers
Gray Instrumentation
If 1974
screenprint on
Arches 88 paper
19 x 19
Collection Walker Art
Center, Minneapolis
Tyler Graphics Archive
(Tyler 24:JA6)

(top)
Josef Albers
Gray Instrumentation
Ib 1974
screenprint on
Arches 88 paper
19 x 19
Collection Walker Art
Center, Minneapolis
Tyler Graphics Archive
(Tyler 20:JA2)

Josef Albers
Gray Instrumentation
Ik 1974
screenprint on
Arches 88 paper
19 x 19
Collection Walker Art
Center, Minneapolis
Tyler Graphics Archive
(Tyler 29:JA11)

context, would undoubtedly appear very pale if compared with even the lightest color in one of Albers's oils.

Both Gray Instrumentation I and Gray Instrumentation II and the next portfolio, Mitered Squares, have accompanying sheets of text by the artist, which were intended to be interspersed and exhibited with the prints. A paragraph from Mitered Squares exemplifies the nature of the Albers texts as well as of his lifelong quest:

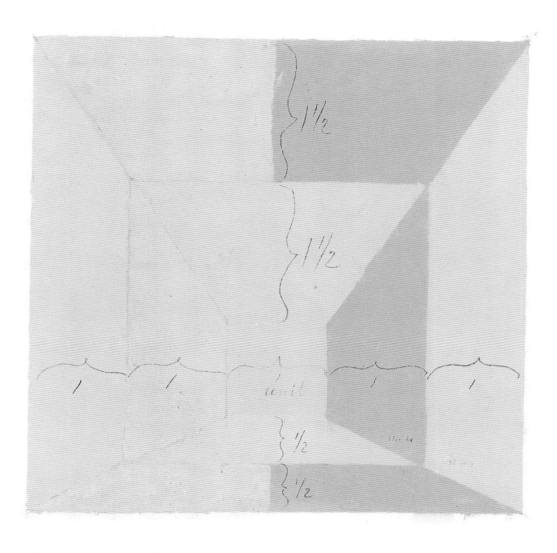

Josef Albers
gouache study for
Mitered Squares
1976
gouache on paper
13⅞ x 11⅞
Collection Walker Art
Center, Minneapolis
Tyler Graphics
Archive, 1987

(opposite)
Josef Albers
Mitered Squares f
1976
screenprint on
Arches 88 paper
19 x 19
Collection Walker Art
Center, Minneapolis
Tyler Graphics Archive
(Tyler 50:JA32)

In my own work
I am content to compete
with myself
and to search with simple palette
and with simple color
for manifold instrumentation

This portfolio continues the range of pale color variation in some plates, but in others, stronger hues of blue, brown, and red appear. Because of the more dynamic graphic configuration, suggesting either a tunnellike recess or a convex, three-dimensional structure, the central square becomes a focal element, more important optically than the mitered shapes surrounding it. In the Gray Instrumentation portfolios the outer squares are more balanced with, if not equal in importance to, the central ones. In a gouache study for Mitered Squares (p. 93), notations in Albers's hand reveal the division of space for the series and show that the central square is the basic module. In width the image comprises five units, each equal to the central square, with two on either side of center; the asymmetrical vertical division consists of two units above, each one and a half times the size of the square, and two below, each half its size. This ambiguous geometric structure is a recurrent theme in Albers's paintings and prints, as well as in his well-known image *Steps*, 1931, which shifts visually as one views it; multiple readings of its configuration are possible.

In his print suite Never Before, 1976, Albers returned to a complex form that he had first used in a 1949 painting, *Indicating Solids;* in 1971 he painted a larger oil in the same configuration, also using the title *Never Before.* Albers developed this series of twelve screenprint variations from more than a hundred collages; in each he began with the central color, then chose the color surrounding it. In this final portfolio, completed just before his death in 1976, the shifting orthogonal movement and bright color seem exuberant, showing Albers, as one author has noted, "at his most youthfully spirited and vital."[2]

It should be remembered that Albers was already fully developed as a graphic artist before he began working in oil and that he had made prints beginning with his earliest linocuts around 1917.[3] Even when color interaction became his consuming interest, he continued to develop linear black-and-white compositions, and the graphic scheme of the paintings and colored prints remained essential to his aesthetic. The editions with Tyler integrate the painterly and graphic strains in Albers's work to the ultimate degree, and the rich, uniformly inked screen printing is analogous in effect to the regular brush strokes in his oils.

Tyler recalls that when Josef and Anni Albers visited the workshop (they came almost every week), they would arrive in time for luncheon, during which there would be lively discussion, and that Josef Albers would often choose some object, such as a leaf or flower that he had picked up, to illustrate a particular color relationship as the lesson for the day.[4] Albers's role as teacher remained as strong as those of painter and graphic artist. Albers the humanist also came out at these meetings, and his choice of descriptive words for colors such as "spring green" and "honey yellow" reveals his ingrained affinity for nature and humanity. His texts and lectures are characterized by this same humanistic vocabulary, which often seems at odds with the mathematical, even scientific appearance of his work.

Anni Albers's prints done at Tyler Graphics are an outgrowth of her previous work as a weaver and printmaker. Her Triangulated Intaglios (see p. 95) are tightly articulated optical patterns of interlocking shapes that may be read as overlapping triangles or as eccentric "woven" shapes on a grid. In this series she used etching and aquatint for the first time, with a special "soft-hard" ground to retain the character of her related ink drawings while adding texture to the printed image.[5]

Albers's work as a weaver dates back to 1922, when she was a student at the Bauhaus; her first prints were made at the Tamarind

Anni Albers
Triangulated Intaglio II 1976
etching, aquatint on Arches Cover paper
24 x 20
Collection Walker Art Center, Minneapolis
Tyler Graphics Archive (Tyler 2:AA2)

workshop in Los Angeles when she accompanied her husband there in 1963. She was invited by the director, June Wayne, to try a lithograph, which resulted in *Enmeshed I* (p. 96), an open, curvilinear, ropelike pattern on a painterly ground.[6] The complex interweaving of line, which curves in, through, around, and back on itself, recalls the artist's 1940s drawings and gouaches of knot forms as well as her 1959 drawings for a rug.[7] The linear configuration also refers literally to weaving and knotting.

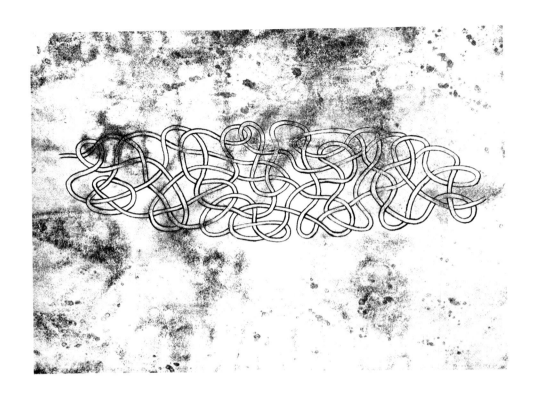

Anni Albers
Enmeshed I   1963
lithograph
20 x 27
Collection the
University Art
Museum,
University of New
Mexico, Albuquerque

Anni Albers
Mountainous II
1978
embossing on TGL
handmade paper
22½ x 21
Collection Walker Art
Center, Minneapolis
Tyler Graphics Archive
(Tyler 8:AA8)

A portfolio of Albers's lithographs was published in 1964, and she was invited back to Tamarind the following year. After 1963 she worked almost exclusively in printmaking, and because she had no access to a lithography workshop after leaving Tamarind, she began making screenprints, which became her principal medium. In 1969, during the early days of Gemini, she made three prints, including another lithograph whose design anticipates the Triangulated Intaglios.[8] Albers has referred to the graphic media as "mysteries" and has credited Tyler for his help and expertise in producing the intaglio prints. She also has noted that her prints were not reproductions of work in other media but were "developed entirely out of the chosen technique."[9] This statement is illustrated by Mountainous (see p. 96), a series of six white embossed prints on handmade paper. While akin to Josef Albers's better-known white embossings produced at Gemini, they reveal Anni's individual sensibility. As in the Triangulated Intaglios and her Second Movement series, the complex forms are tightly articulated in each plate but also function as opposing rhythmic pairs when viewed in sequence. The suite represents Tyler's collaboration at its purest and most restrained.

Jack Tworkov, like Josef Albers, is identified with Yale University, where he chaired the art department during the 1960s just as Albers

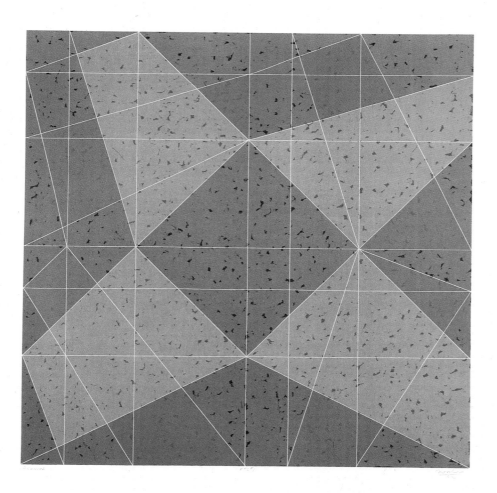

Jack Tworkov
KTL #1   1982
lithograph on Arches
Cover paper
27½ x 27½
Collection Walker Art
Center, Minneapolis
Tyler Graphics Archive
(Tyler 611:JT1)

had headed the department of design during the previous decade. It was during the mid-1960s that Tworkov's work evolved from a gestural abstract expressionist style to more geometric paintings characterized by a pale palette and measured brush strokes over a grid structure. Though of the same generation as the Abstract Expressionists and associated with them, Tworkov shifted away from painterly abstraction to a cooler geometric and minimalist direction that also characterized the work of numerous younger artists during the mid to late 1960s. In his four-color lithograph *KTL #1* (p. 97), produced by Tyler Graphics, Tworkov employed his characteristic vertical, horizontal, and diagonal grid lines to divide the space and describe a central diamond and several irregular four-sided shapes. The colors are muted blue gray, reddish tan, light brown, and dark brown.[10]

Unlike Tworkov, who used grids in a nonobjective context, Ronald Davis has employed the grid as an illusionistic spatial device. Davis's paintings and prints consist of geometric structures rendered in dramatic perspective and in an indeterminate abstract space. The folded planes of color and the illusionistic forms they create recall the shaped fiberglass pieces for which he became known in the 1960s (see p. 98). In 1972 Davis discontinued the use of resin and fiberglass for aesthetic and health reasons and returned to painting on canvas in a rectangular format. The grid, perspective lines, and staining of the canvas around the image in *Frame and Beam* (p. 99) unify the composition and enliven the areas of void. In addition to suggesting depth and recession into space through three-point perspective, Davis has added cast shadows to heighten the illusion of three-dimensional forms in space. The placement of the architectural images and the open space they inhabit evoke Renaissance compositions as well as the forced perspective and vast, empty squares in the paintings of Giorgio de Chirico. In Davis's canvases, however, the vantage point is not frontal but usually above and slightly to the viewer's left, so that no horizon line is visible and recession into space is from the viewer's lower left to the upper right.

Ronald Davis
Single Sawtooth
1971
polyester resin and fiberglass
52¼ x 94⅝
Collection Mr. and Mrs. Harry W. Anderson

Ronald Davis
Frame and Beam
1975
acrylic and dry pigment
114³⁄₁₆ x 186½
Collection Seattle Art
Museum
Purchased with the aid
of funds from the
National Endowment
for the Arts; Merrill
Foundation

In his lithograph-screenprints on multicolored paper of 1979, Davis simulated painterly effects by using strong planes of color and perspectival lines over a watery, atmospheric field. As in many Tyler editions, including his own earlier work done at Gemini, the technical processes were various and complex. *Invert Span* (p. 100), for example, involved five aluminum lithography plates, one stone, two hand-drawn photo screens (each used in eight runs), and thirty-four colors, both printed and created from paper pulps and dyes. Davis simulated the uneven quality of a carpenter's "snap line" on the plates for the grid in these prints. Of the four works from 1979, *Invert Span* is the most literal in terms of illusion—the structure seems to be anchored on the ground in "real" space. In *Arc Arch* (p. 101) and the other two prints, the forms appear to float on water or in atmosphere, and the allusions to painterly gesture on their surfaces seem more tangible and physical than the delicate folded shapes. The technical significance of these works is the marriage of papermaking and printing and the luminosity achieved by using the paper pulp as atmospheric ground or substrate.

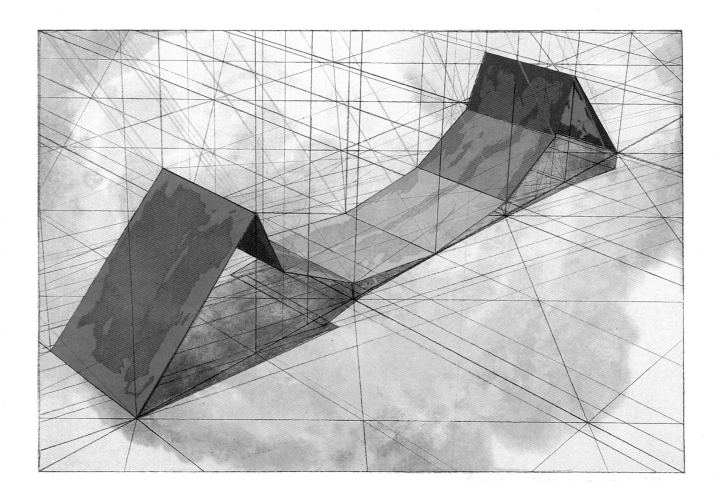

Ronald Davis
Invert Span   1979
screenprint, lithograph
on hand-colored TGL
handmade paper
32 x 42
Collection Walker Art
Center, Minneapolis
Tyler Graphics Archive
(Tyler 167:RD6)

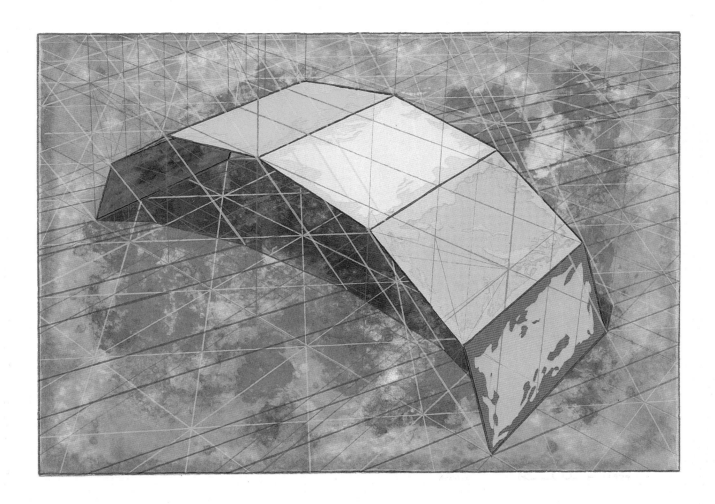

Ronald Davis
Arc Arch 1979
screenprint, lithograph
on hand-colored TGL
handmade paper
32 x 42
Collection Walker Art
Center, Minneapolis
Tyler Graphics Archive
(Tyler 168:RD7)

Kenneth Noland's collaboration with Tyler Graphics has consisted primarily of paper-pulp works, which are discussed elsewhere in this volume (see "Paperworks at Tyler Graphics"). In 1978, however, he produced two exceptional prints in more traditional graphic media: *Blush,* a color lithograph, and *Echo,* an aquatint with embossing (pp.

102–3). Each repeats a characteristic motif—the "target," or concentric circles, and the chevron—from his paintings of the late 1950s and 1960s. *Blush,* a thirteen-color lithograph printed from as many aluminum plates, translates the effect of the artist's earlier stain paintings into lithography. The core circle is a rich blood red offset by lavender and yellow rings; the outermost circle is luminous orange pink. Its color and soft-edged contours create a glow around the image and suggest motion. Somewhat uncharacteristically, Noland added a gray band with a thin red stripe along the bottom edge of the print. The other important 1978 work, *Echo,* consists of red, green, light blue, and yellow V shapes on an eggshell ground color. Embossing was used to pull the chevron form into relief. While these graphic processes enabled Noland to bring color and form to the surface more than in his paintings of the 1960s (in which pure color was absorbed into unprimed canvas), the prints nevertheless reaffirm the artist's underlying concept of geometric shapes and pure color as autonomous elements. In their translation from painting to graphic, Noland's prints with Tyler might be compared with those of Josef Albers, with whom Noland studied at Black Mountain

Kenneth Noland
Echo 1978
aquatint, embossing
on Arches Cover paper
20 x 24
Collection Walker Art
Center, Minneapolis
Tyler Graphics Archive
(Tyler 463:KN2)

(opposite)
Kenneth Noland
Blush 1978
lithograph on Rives
BFK paper
36 x 30
Collection Walker Art
Center, Minneapolis
Tyler Graphics Archive
(Tyler 462:KN1)

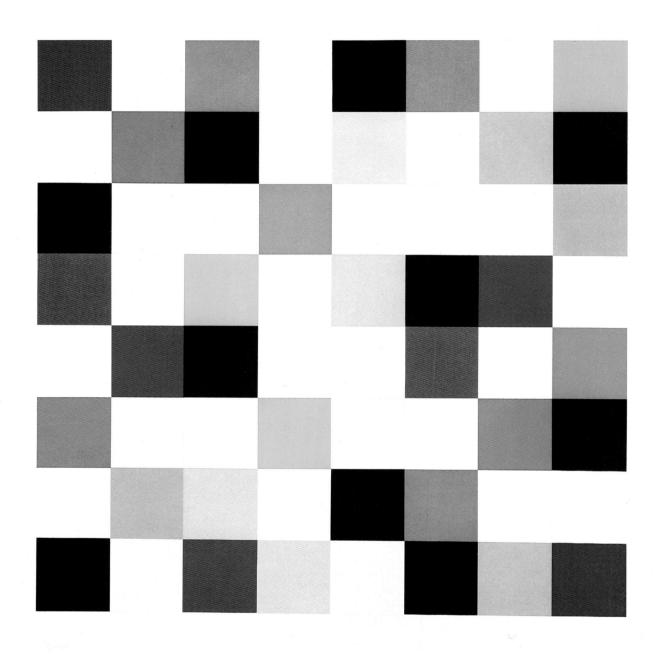

College in 1946–48. Both artists utilized the technical resources at the Tyler workshop to add greater richness and nuance to their characteristic images in painting.

Ellsworth Kelly's work captures the essence of pure form, color, and structure; it is intuitive, often inspired by nature, objects, or environment rather than by mathematical or geometric systems. His mature aesthetic evolved in part out of European geometric abstraction—including the work of Piet Mondrian, Theo van Doesburg, Georges Vantongerloo, Jean Arp, and Sophie Taeuber-Arp—but he also admired the work of Pablo Picasso, Constantin Brancusi, and Paul Klee. Kelly's relative isolation in Paris during the late 1940s and early 1950s solidified his individual approach to the work of art as object as well as his concern with abstract shape and literal space. His work is based on purity of material as well as of color and form—the smoothness of painted steel, the mat surface of paintings and prints, the pure or creamy white of the paper stock on which the images are printed.

Kelly's extensive involvement with print publishing dates back to 1964–66, with a series of twenty-seven color lithographs of his abstract images as well as a suite of plant lithographs, both published by Maeght in Paris. His collaboration with Gemini in Los Angeles began in 1970, when Tyler was still there, and has continued in the 1980s. Kelly's prints with Gemini tended toward color shapes in the early 1970s and toward black, white, and gray images in the mid-1970s, with a return to color in the early 1980s, as in "*18 Colors (Cincinnati)*."[11] His work with Tyler Graphics has allowed him to expand upon forms used previously—simple black shapes or plant images, for example—and to explore some new areas, such as colored squares and paper-pulp pieces, which are also discussed elsewhere in this volume (see "Paperworks at Tyler Graphics"). Tyler has noted, "Without my work with Albers, Kelly's geometric prints would have been less successful."[12] Indeed, as with those by Albers, Kelly's images demanded precision in registration and printing as well as extreme accuracy and uniformity of hue. The saturated color and velvety surface produced by screen printing proved as appropriate for Kelly's colored squares as for Albers's series.

Screenprints such as *Colors on a Grid, Screenprint 1976*, 1976 (p. 104), and *Nine Squares*, 1977, originated in paintings and collages Kelly made in France in the early 1950s. The number of squares, the size of the collage or canvas, and the sequence of colors may vary, but the basic format and system—alternating squares of color and white space—remain the same. Kelly developed the original colored squares as collages from paper stock purchased in art supply stores; he then matched the colors in oil for the finished paintings.[13] He created *Colors on a Grid, Screenprint 1976* after his painting *Colors for a Large Wall*, 1951. The sequence, hue, and intensity of colors in the print are very close to those of the original painting, and the flawless printing and registration of the colored squares approximate the effect of the physical separation of squares into modular units in the paintings. In the color

Ellsworth Kelly
*Colors on a Grid,
Screenprint 1976*
1976
screenprint, lithograph
on Arches 88 paper
48¼ x 48¼
Collection Walker Art
Center, Minneapolis
Tyler Graphics Archive
(Tyler 294:EK1)

(opposite)
Ellsworth Kelly
Daffodil 1980
lithograph on Arches
Cover paper
39¼ x 28¼
Collection Walker Art
Center, Minneapolis
Tyler Graphics Archive
(Tyler 329:EK36)

Ellsworth Kelly
Wild Grape
Leaf 1980
lithograph on Arches
Cover paper
27½ x 24¾
Collection Walker Art
Center, Minneapolis
Tyler Graphics Archive
(Tyler 332:EK39)

study for the original work, one of the largest Kelly made in France (it consists of sixty-four panels, each eight by eight feet), the sequence of colors was arbitrary and intuitive; that sequence was followed exactly in the finished painting.[14] Similarly, *Nine Squares* was inspired by a 1953 collage, *Nine Colors on White*.[15] Kelly also made a smaller paper-pulp piece, *Nine Colors* (p. 211), in 1977, with the same color sequence, though with less intensity due to the difference of medium. He made several trial proofs with subtle color variations for these prints. Kelly's screenprints are closer in pictorial effect to the original collages and reinforce his belief in the concrete reality of individual colors.

Since 1949, drawings of plants have been a leitmotiv in Kelly's work, with the largest number created after 1959. Rather than being a sidelight, however, plant imagery is integral to the forms of his painting and sculpture. Despite their specificity of image, they are quite abstract, reconstituting the essential shape of the plant with exceptional delicacy and economy of line. Plant lithographs by Kelly were published by Maeght in the mid-1960s and by Gemini in the 1970s. The most complex of those published by Tyler Graphics is *Daffodil,* 1980 (p. 106), with a nervous line delineating the edges of the flower and its outer structure.

Collage has remained an essential element in Kelly's work, a part of his overall creative process as well as a medium in itself. While the colored squares represent a literal translation of collage into painting, he has also used collage in a more informal way: in chance configurations, as conceptual studies, or to create almost sculptural contrasts of color, material, and shape. *Saint Martin Landscape,* 1979 (p. 109), which appears at first to be an anomaly in Kelly's work, does in fact have a precedent in his postcard collages from the 1950s through the 1970s (see p. 109), but in the print, postcard and collage have been enlarged several times in a dramatic shift of scale. While some of the earlier collages were visionary proposals for large-scale sculpture, the voluptuous female figure against the lush Caribbean landscape in the lithograph-screenprint-collage seems like a wry comment on Kelly's own geometric work and its full, rounded shapes; the composition might also be read as a tongue-in-cheek allusion to "figure-ground" or to Henri Matisse's *Luxe, calme et volupté.* Kelly has noted that at the time, he was interested in the idea of fragmented elements and that he had made similar collages around 1974. This image also relates to his early figure drawings and collages, some of which were biomorphic in form.[16] Kelly made eight color trial proofs for *Saint Martin Landscape* in which the flesh tones range from magenta to orange and sky and landscape were printed in different color intensities.

Wall, 1979, is a print of exceptional power and density, a hand-drawn aquatint, the image a parallelogram within a rectangle. Kelly had used the same configuration in a 1956 painting, *Wall Study,*[17] and the abstract shape in the print also seems related to his photographs of architecture. As in many of Kelly's works, the negative areas are critical—in this case the slivers of white between the edges of the black shape

Ellsworth Kelly
*Saint Martin
Landscape* 1979
lithograph,
screenprint, collage on
Arches 88 paper
26⅞ x 33½
Collection Walker Art
Center, Minneapolis
Tyler Graphics Archive
(Tyler 324:EK31)

Ellsworth Kelly
*Four Blacks and
Whites: Upper
Manhattan* 1957
collage on postcard
3½ x 5½
Collection of the artist

and those of the plate, and the band of white along the bottom edge. The line of the impression has also become an important visual element, defining the outer rectangle. Both the composition and the medium of aquatint anticipate Kelly's Concorde series, printed at Gemini in 1982.[18]

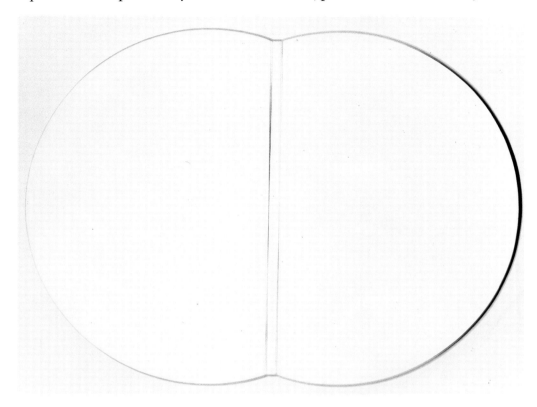

Ellsworth Kelly
White Plaque: Bridge Arch and Reflection
1955
oil on wood, two panels separated by a wood strip
64 x 68
Collection Peter Palumbo, Ascot, England

(opposite)
Ellsworth Kelly
Untitled Relief 1978
white lacquer finish on welded aluminum shell with honeycomb aluminum core and aluminum tubes;
artist's proof
72 x 54 x 7
Collection Walker Art Center, Minneapolis
Tyler Graphics Archive
(Tyler 321:EK28)

Severe geometry, monochrome, and monolithic form have characterized Kelly's recent work in painting and sculpture. In 1978 he created *Untitled Relief* (p. 110), a relief sculpture in an edition of four. As in his 1968 folded sculptures, the illusion of the shape and planes, and the effects of light and shadow they create, are as important as the iconic nature of the form itself. The depth between the larger and smaller segments, combined with the fact that the piece is mounted three and a half inches out from the wall, create a floating effect. The folded shape in relief had appeared earlier in *Blue on Blue*, 1963,[19] but *Untitled Relief* seems closer in spirit to *White Plaque: Bridge Arch and Reflection*, 1955 (p. 111), begun in Paris (the arch was inspired by that of the Pont de la Tournelle) and completed in his first year in New York. Uniting these early and late works are Kelly's use of white, associated with light; the fullness of the curves; the translation of negative shadow space into relief form; and the purity of the surface.

Sculptor Michael Heizer's printmaking has afforded him the opportunity to explore the forms that interest him in graphic media and to reinterpret themes from earlier work. His first prints with Tyler in 1977 illustrate his ongoing interest in the analysis of the circle. The segmented circle or cylinder has appeared before and since in numerous Heizer paintings, sculptures, prints, and drawings, including a 1970

Archiv

Heizg 77

Archiv

Heizg 77

Archiv

Heizg 77

earthwork in Nevada, *Circular Surface Planar Displacement Drawing* (p. 114); the major 1976–80 commission in Lansing, Michigan, *This Equals That;* and wood sculptures using this form, such as *Circle I,* 1976, and *Ghana,* 1977. The prints *Circle I, Circle II,* and *Circle III* (p. 112), etchings with aquatint, reveal the same basic divisions of the circle used in the 1976 sculpture and retain the hard-edged purity of the individual shapes. *Circle I* was printed in brown ink on gray stock, with gestural, deeply etched markings in each section; *Circle II* is the same image in black on gray with the addition of a dark gestural incident in the upper right; *Circle III* is the image reversed, with the sections breaking apart. Each of these editions was preceded by trial proofs with subtle variations in inking and paper stock. *Circle IV* (p. 112), a color lithograph in warm yellow, orange, and red brown, is very different from the preceding three; it is free and painterly, only roughly observing the confines of the circle. Related to it are twenty-four untitled collages— unique works that incorporate fragments of lithographs and monotype screenprints and hand-painting. Strong verticals and a sense of centrifugal energy break up the images, and dark strokes of umber and blue black anchor the individual sections. Other colors used include yellow, lavender, magenta, and red brown (see p. 115).

Heizer's sculpture since the late 1960s has often involved colossal scale and massive earth moving and engineering, as in *Double Negative, Dragged Mass,* and *Complex One.* Displacement and replacement have been key elements in these and other herculean projects. The materials themselves—earth, granite, steel, concrete—have been chosen for their inherent characteristics of weight, mass, color, or surface, and Heizer's straightforward use of them, frequently with no additions by his hand, is an outstanding characteristic of his work. Geometric structure underlies all of his pieces, from the eccentrically shaped canvases he made in the 1960s to works of the 1980s such as *Levitated Mass* and *45°, 90°, 180°/Geometric Extraction.*

Heizer often restates earlier concepts at a different scale or in a different medium or context, translating an idea from granite or earth to bronze or steel and reducing its original dimensions to those that a gallery space can accommodate. The resulting works, because of the loss of size, weight, and mass, often appear schematic, shell-like, though they still function as sculpture. The same kind of process occurs with Heizer's prints: while clearly of a different medium and size, they retain direct references to his sculpture. In 1983, at the Tyler workshop, he created prints related to *Dragged Mass, Levitated Mass,* and *45°, 90°, 180°,* all a combination of lithography, etching, and screen printing (see pp. 117–18). These prints resemble working drawings, with diagrammatic, sketchy rendering and notations on the print that provide clues to process, structure, and perspective points. The central images were deeply etched into magnesium plates and printed as reliefs, and Heizer enhanced the surfaces with seemingly arbitrary areas of sprayed color— blue green, red, and yellow.

Dragged Mass, constructed in 1971 for his exhibition at the Detroit Institute of Arts and now destroyed, remains a signal work for Heizer, both as a sculptural concept and as a social gesture. It created public controversy at the time for what was seen as a violent, destructive act and, by some, as a metaphor for the slaughter of the Vietnam War. A thirty-ton block was dragged back and forth by two Caterpillar tractors across the greensward in front of the museum until Heizer was satisfied with the amount of dirt that had piled up in the path of the block. In the print, rather than the usual photographic view from above or from the side, we see the piece from below the ground—as Heizer notes on the face of the print, it is a "visualization looking up through earth/

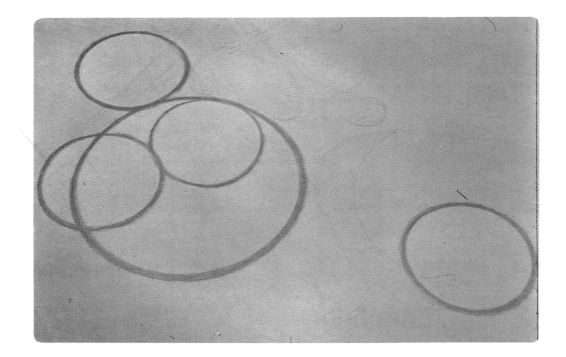

transparent earth." In an exhibition at the Whitney Museum of American Art, New York, in 1985, Heizer created a geometric version of *Dragged Mass,* constructed out of corrugated board over a wood and aluminum framework, which filled the largest gallery in the museum. On the surface of the board were screen-printed patterns derived from photographic images of rock formations.[20]

Levitated Mass, Heizer has stated, is a concept developed in 1969, at the same time as *Dragged Mass* and *Displaced/Replaced Mass* (p. 116), commissioned by Robert Scull and located in Silver Springs, Nevada.[21] All three of these works have to do with pure mass as weight. The sculpture *Levitated Mass* was commissioned by IBM for its regional headquarters in New York in 1982, to be placed outside the building designed by Edward Larrabee Barnes. The scored slab of granite appears to levitate in a stainless-steel enclosure that corresponds to the shape of the block; water circulates beneath the stone, creating a fountainlike

Michael Heizer
*Circular Surface
Planar Displacement
Drawing* 1970
earthwork
Jean Dry Lake, Nevada

Michael Heizer
#11 Untitled 1979
hand-colored
monotype, collage on
Rives BFK paper
mounted on four-ply

rag board
30 x 30
Collection Walker Art
Center, Minneapolis
Gift of Dr. Maclyn E.
Wade, 1984

structure in the urban setting. In the print the piece is seen in cross section, thereby revealing the secret of the illusion of "levitation" and providing more information about the work than would a photograph or the sculpture itself.

Heizer has created several versions and sizes of $45°$, $90°$, $180°$ since 1980. $45°$, $90°$, $180°$/Geometric Extraction was commissioned for a special exhibition at the Museum of Contemporary Art, Los Angeles, in 1984. A permanent version from the same year exists at Rice University, Houston, in granite and concrete, and four smaller-scale variations were made in 1982. The concept of the three angles is obvious, but the placement of the elements provides the critical variable. In the MOCA piece their arrangement was very formal and architectural, with the elements in an enclosure; the Houston installation is open and spacious, the slabs supported by arms of concrete. A notation on the

print gives a clue to Heizer's intent that the elements relate as if in "a megalithic dialogue." The same inscription appears on the print of *Levitated Mass*.

Heizer's collaboration with Tyler has exemplified the technical range available at the Tyler Graphics workshop by accomplishing the artist's objectives and reinterpreting sculpture and drawing in graphic media. For Heizer as well as for the other artists discussed here, a combination of various print media has often been required in order to achieve the desired image. Reviewing the Tyler production of these disparate artists, it becomes clear that collaboration is the key to the quality and unique character of the editions.

Michael Heizer
Displaced/Replaced Mass 1969
granite
Silver Springs, Nevada

(opposite, top)
Michael Heizer
Dragged Mass 1983
lithograph,
screenprint, etching on TGL handmade paper
32 x 46½
Collection Walker Art Center, Minneapolis
Tyler Graphics Archive
(Tyler 235:MH84)

(opposite, bottom)
Michael Heizer
Levitated Mass 1983
lithograph,
screenprint, etching on TGL handmade paper
32 x 46½
Collection Walker Art Center, Minneapolis
Tyler Graphics Archive
(Tyler 234:MH83)

material accumulates
consecutive pulls

pushes up

Cable
to point

X object

looking
from start

end of cut

cable hitch
pt.

path

base of cut

visualization
looking up thru
earth / transparent earth

Archive Heizer 83

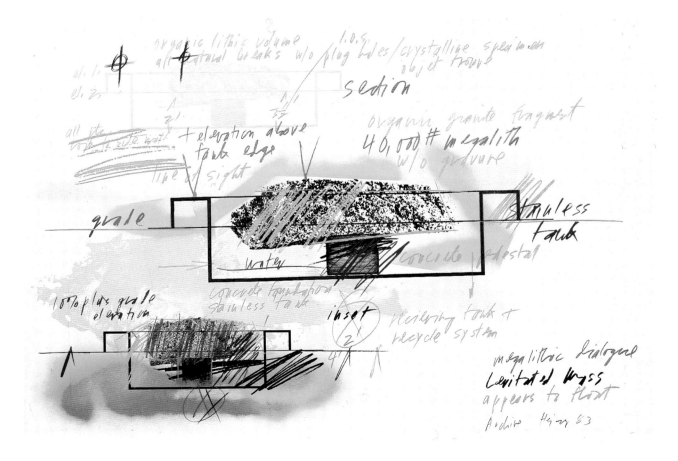

organic lithic volume
all natural breaks w/o plug holes

i.o.s.
crystalline specimen
object trouve

section

el. 1'
el. 2'

1'
2'

1'
2'

organic granite fragment
40,000# megalith
w/o gravure

all the
work to scale with

elevation above
tank edge

line of sight

grade

Stainless
Tank

water

concrete pedestal

concrete foundation
stainless tank

18% plus grade
elevation

inset
2

recieving tank +
recycle system

4'

megalithic dialogue
Levitated Mass
appears to float

Archive Heizer 83

117

Michael Heizer
45°, 90°, 180° 1983
lithograph,
screenprint, etching,
stamping on TGL
handmade paper
32 x 46½
Collection Walker Art
Center, Minneapolis
Tyler Graphics Archive
(Tyler 233:MH82)

Notes

1. Print documentation sheet, Tyler Graphics Ltd., Bedford Village; signed by Josef Albers and Kenneth Tyler; dated January 10, 1975. Unless otherwise noted, other technical descriptions used in this essay have been drawn from the Tyler documentation sheets.

2. Nicholas Fox Weber, *Josef Albers: Never Before,* publisher's brochure (Bedford Village, N.Y.: Tyler Graphics, 1976), n.p.

3. Mary Laura Gibbs, "Printmaking," in *Josef Albers: Paintings and Graphics, 1917–1970,* exh. cat. (Princeton, N.J.: Art Museum, Princeton University, 1971), p. 21.

4. Kenneth Tyler, conversation with author, May 21, 1985.

5. Nicholas Fox Weber, in Gene Baro, *Anni Albers,* exh. cat. (Brooklyn: Brooklyn Museum, 1977), p. 13.

6. Gene Baro, "A Conversation," ibid., p. 7. See also Richard S. Field, "Anni Albers: Prints and Drawings," in *The Woven and Graphic Art of Anni Albers,* exh. cat. (Washington, D.C.: Smithsonian Institution Press, 1985), p. 108.

7. These have been reproduced in both Baro, *Anni Albers,* and *The Woven and Graphic Art of Anni Albers.*

8. Ruth E. Fine, *Gemini G.E.L.: Art and Collaboration,* exh. cat. (Washington, D.C.: National Gallery of Art; New York: Abbeville Press, 1984), p. 20.

9. Baro, *Anni Albers,* p. 10.

10. This print was commissioned for the 1982 Chicago International Art Exposition, and the image was also reproduced, with the addition of text, as a poster for the art fair.

11. Fine, *Gemini G.E.L.,* p. 127. See also "Catalog of Prints, 1950–1970," in Diane Waldman, *Ellsworth Kelly: Drawings, Collages, Prints* (Greenwich, Conn.: New York Graphic Society, 1971), p. 251.

12. Kenneth Tyler, conversation with author, May 21, 1985.

13. E. C. Goossen, *Ellsworth Kelly,* exh. cat. (New York: Museum of Modern Art, 1973), p. 45.

14. Ibid.

15. Reproduced in Waldman, *Ellsworth Kelly,* p. 75.

16. Ellsworth Kelly, conversation with author, October 30, 1985.

17. Reproduced in John Coplans, *Ellsworth Kelly* (New York: Harry N. Abrams, 1972), pl. 101.

18. See Fine, *Gemini G.E.L.,* pp. 140–41.

19. Reproduced in Patterson Sims and Emily Rauh Pulitzer, *Ellsworth Kelly: Sculpture,* exh. cat. (New York: Whitney Museum of American Art, 1982), p. 79.

20. "Interview: David Whitney and Michael Heizer," in *Michael Heizer/Dragged Mass Geometric,* exh. brochure (New York: Whitney Museum of American Art, 1985), n.p.

21. "Interview: Julia Brown and Michael Heizer," in Julia Brown, ed., *Michael Heizer: Sculpture in Reverse,* exh. cat. (Los Angeles: Museum of Contemporary Art, 1984), p. 18.

Pop, Post-Pop, and Beyond

Elizabeth Armstrong

Among those artists associated with the Pop movement, Richard Hamilton, Roy Lichtenstein, Claes Oldenburg, Malcolm Morley, and David Hockney have made prints at Tyler Graphics Ltd. While these five artists have very different sensibilities, they share an overriding interest in the imagery of popular culture and the techniques of the mass media. It is hardly surprising, then, that they gravitated toward the reproductive medium of printmaking, especially its most commercial forms, lithography and silk screen. In Lichtenstein's words, "Pop looked like printed images, . . . and putting the printed images back into print was intriguing."[1] Indeed, printmaking was a natural extension of their art.

In the view of some critics, the English artist Richard Hamilton is the founding father of Pop Art, or at least its first theorist. As early as 1957 he committed his views to writing, describing Pop Art, in a now-famous statement, as "Popular (designed for a mass audience), transient (short-term solution), expendable (easily forgotten), low cost, mass produced, young (aimed at youth), witty, sexy, gimmicky, glamourous, big business."[2] While these were characteristics the media could use to describe this brash new art phenomenon, Hamilton's description was meant more broadly; it was actually a definition of commercial mass culture.[3] A year earlier he had incorporated a number of media quotations into a remarkable collage, *Just What Is It That Makes Today's Homes So Different, So Appealing?* (p. 122), a seminal work in the Pop idiom. He arranged its components, carefully clipped from popular magazines and newspapers, to represent a living-room interior inhabited by a muscle man and a female stripper. This unusual pair, presented as the ideal modern consumers, appear against a background richly stocked with appliances and other goods.

The presence of *POP* on the lollipop in Hamilton's small collage was one of the first uses of the word that would come to be the movement's designation.[4] The collage was also prophetic in that it utilized the comic strip as a fine-art image—five years before Roy Lichtenstein made his first comic-strip painting. The primary significance

of Hamilton's *Just What Is It*, however, was its use of the mass media—printed material from newspapers and magazines—as a vital source of imagery. Hamilton has long been concerned with the suggestive powers of the mass media—with its success in conditioning the public to accept a "flat, retouched, color separation world" as reality.[5]

Hamilton's interest in the visual aspects of popular culture also led to his thorough examination of the printmaking media, which he studied at the Slade School of Fine Art, London, between 1948 and 1951.[6] By the 1960s the versatile technique of screen printing had become his preferred medium, as it had for a number of other artists of his generation.[7] A major advantage of this process lay in its use of photographically prepared stencils that allowed revisions to be made quickly and simply. For Hamilton, who used photography as both subject and technique, the medium was ideal.

During the 1960s Hamilton's manipulation of photographic processes became increasingly complex as he combined photographic images with hand-drawn passages and abstract planes of transparent and opaque color. In prints such as *I'm Dreaming of a White Christmas*, 1967 (p. 123), he created environments rife with spatial ambiguities. In

Richard Hamilton
Just What Is It That Makes Today's Homes So Different, So Appealing? 1956
collage
10¼ x 9¾
Collection Kunsthalle Tübingen, Sammlung Zundel

this print, what appears to be a reproduction of a film still of Bing Crosby is juxtaposed with details of an interior that appears to be painted. In fact, Hamilton has inverted our expectations: the "film still" is really a drawing, and painterly-looking passages such as the window behind Crosby were taken directly from the film.[8]

Since the 1970s Hamilton has moved away from media paraphrases to investigate individual styles, gestures, and techniques in more traditional interiors, landscapes, and still lifes. Working at Atelier

Crommelynck, Paris, in 1973–74, Hamilton used a traditional still-life subject, a bouquet of flowers, to pursue these experiments. Perversely, perhaps, he set out to produce by manual means an etching with the characteristics of a commercially made reproduction. This involved the use of four etching plates printed in four colors, superimposing yellow, magenta, cyan blue, and black to create a full range of colors. In his typically thorough fashion, Hamilton made another still life, *Flower-Piece A,* this time using collotype and screen printing. Working with E. Schreiber and Frank Kicherer in 1974 in Stuttgart, Germany, he again explored the concept of reproducing commercial color in a fine-art print.

Fascinated by the differing temperaments of various techniques, Hamilton traveled to Tyler Graphics to try out the still-life image in lithography. In *Flower-Piece B,* 1976 (p. 126), his intention was to draw four litho stones to parallel the four plates used for the color etching done with Crommelynck. Finding the stones inadequate to print a full tonal range, Hamilton decided to make multiple printings of different densities in the same colors from each of the stones. Fifteen separation proofs document the lengthy printing process required to make such a lithograph by hand (see pp. 124–25).

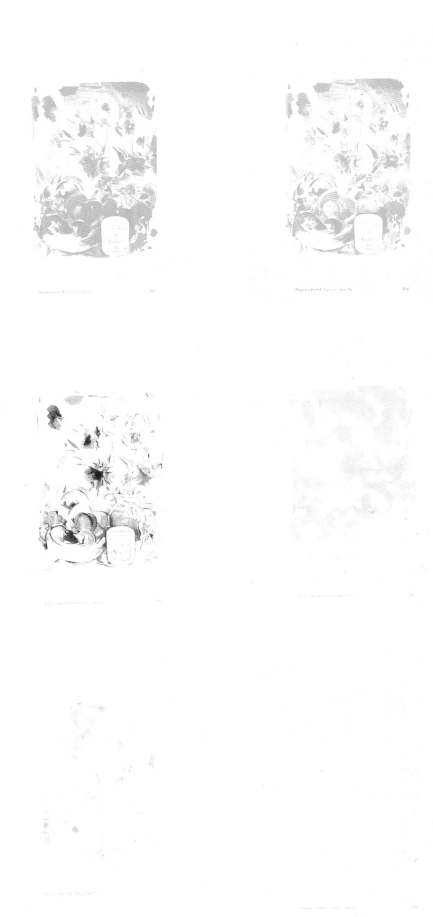

Richard Hamilton
separation proofs for
Flower-Piece B 1976
lithograph on paper
25½ x 18¾ each
Collection Walker Art
Center, Minneapolis
Tyler Graphics Archive

For Kenneth Tyler, working with Hamilton was comparable to working with one of his most skilled printers, and the project stimulated the highest level of technical performance. But the process of making *Flower-Piece B* was more than an exercise in printmaking. While the work attests to the artist's fascination with technique, it also reflects his

love of irony and mordant humor. The roll of toilet paper placed in front of his depiction of fruit and flowers is typical of his response to superficial beauty. Seeking historical sources for his compulsion to defile a sentimental cliché, Hamilton notes the still-life convention of placing, often in the lower right of a composition, a memento mori (an insect, a crab, a skull)—"some sinister motif which suggests that life is not all prettiness and fragrance."[9] On another level the contrast between the

Richard Hamilton
Flower-Piece B   1976
lithograph on Arches
Cover paper
25⅝ x 19¾
Collection Walker Art
Center, Minneapolis
Tyler Graphics Archive
(Tyler 219:RH1)

roll of toilet paper and the flowers recalls the controversy over low and high art that flared up in the early days of Pop. Toilet paper is the ultimate "popular ... expendable ... low cost, mass produced" product. As such, it is also a foil for the romanticism often associated with the still-life form.[10]

Richard Hamilton
Flower-Piece B,
Crayon Study 1976
lithograph on Arches
Cover paper
25⅝ x 19¾
Collection Walker Art
Center, Minneapolis
Tyler Graphics Archive
(Tyler 221:RH3)

While working at Tyler Graphics, Hamilton produced another Flower-Piece (p. 127) using a crayon instead of a brush. With this relatively subtle change in technique, he created an image with a strikingly different feel. The individual qualities of the various printmaking processes continue to absorb this cerebral artist, and the prints he has made with Tyler reflect his ongoing fascination with the nature of representation.

Roy Lichtenstein's appropriation of the comic-book style for paintings—complete with flat primary colors and simulated benday dots—inevitably brought him to an exploration of printmaking. He published his first prints in this style in 1963, just two years after he developed his hallmark style of painting. Like the paintings, these prints are derived from cartoons, newspaper ads, and other commercial sources.

Lichtenstein's exploration of the relationship between art and the mass media coincided with the emergence of a new generation of critics, led by Susan Sontag, who challenged the once-sacred distinction between high and low art. Well aware of how the media freely appropriated the

symbols and vocabulary of high culture, Lichtenstein inverted the process. Choosing commonplace objects with particular cultural and emotional resonance—such as engagement rings and cherry pies—he transformed them into prints and paintings that capitalized on advertising's use of streamlined single-object pictures. In the process he drained the images of specific associations, focusing attention on style and form.

More than his paintings, Lichtenstein's prints reveal his meticulous way of working and his immersion in formal refinements that result in a more mechanical effect. "In my paintings I can try to make things 'perfect,' but I can't because I'm not that skillful," he has said. "The paintings, in spite of me, have a certain handmade look, but in prints, you can achieve that sense of perfection."[11]

Roy Lichtenstein
Sandwich and Soda,
from Ten Works/Ten
Painters 1964
screenprint in blue and
red on white plastic
20 x 24
Collection Walker Art
Center, Minneapolis
Art Center Acquisition
Fund, 1965

During the 1960s Lichtenstein often used commmercial printing techniques, especially silk screen and offset lithography, to achieve an unmodulated, industrial look. He also experimented with new materials in his prints, particularly plastics. In 1964 he produced his first plastic silk screen, *Sandwich and Soda* (p. 128), and he went on to manipulate the optical effects of Rowlux, a type of plastic that catches light in moirélike patterns.[12]

Lichtenstein's prints, which are usually derived from his paintings, often pursue a subject through a series of subtle variations. Working at Tyler Graphics in 1975, Lichtenstein began a series based on the Entablature theme that he had been exploring in painting since 1971. He perceived these mass-produced friezes of architectural ornament as abstractions in their own right. At Tyler Graphics he further refined the Entablature paintings into prints (see pp. 129–30), developing a variety of configurations using their essential, geometric elements. In addition

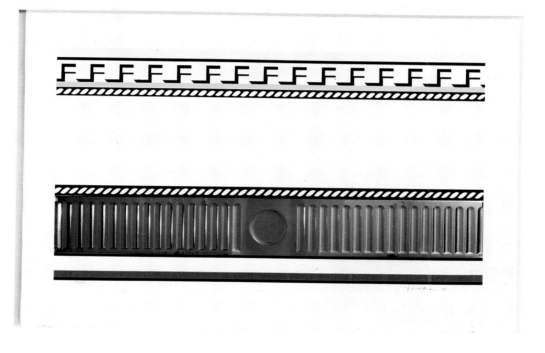

to his customary primary colors, Lichtenstein also employed a range of uncharacteristic colors, combining golds, silvers, and grays with post-modern aquas and pinks.

Lichtenstein wanted the Entablature prints literally to reflect light. This desire led to prolonged research by Tyler Graphics into the development of three-dimensional foil elements. The print workshop, in consultation with industrial technicians, searched for a way to emboss foil paper without destroying it. Before they were through, a variety of machined, cast, and etched metal parts had been custom-made for the embossing dies, which simulated the bas-relief images in the series. Through trial and error the workshop produced its most technically complex prints to date, combining screen printing, lithography, and collaged metallic foil with deep embossing. Ironically, Lichtenstein's

Roy Lichtenstein
Entablature I 1976
screenprint, collage, embossing on Rives BFK paper
29¼ x 45
Collection Walker Art Center, Minneapolis
Tyler Graphics Archive
(Tyler 334:RL2)

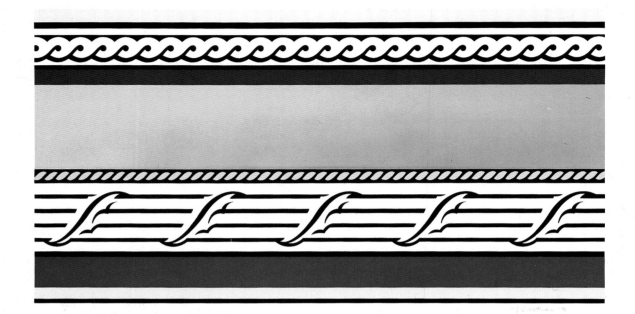

Entablatures required extensive manual manipulation, particularly in the fabrication of the special printing elements needed to create highly precise, mechanical-looking prints.

In 1979 Lichtenstein began work on a group of prints using Surrealist and Native American art as source material. *American Indian*

Roy Lichtenstein
American Indian Theme III 1980
woodcut on Suzuki handmade paper
35 x 27
Collection Walker Art Center, Minneapolis
Tyler Graphics Archive
(Tyler 348:RL16)

(opposite, top)
Roy Lichtenstein
Entablature IV 1976
screenprint, collage, embossing on Rives BFK paper
29¼ x 45
Collection Walker Art Center, Minneapolis
Tyler Graphics Archive
(Tyler 337:RL5)

(opposite, bottom)
Roy Lichtenstein
Entablature X 1976
screenprint, lithograph, collage, embossing on Rives BFK paper
29¼ x 45
Collection Walker Art Center, Minneapolis
Tyler Graphics Archive
(Tyler 343:RL11)

Theme III (p. 131) combines Daliesque lips with American Indian motifs such as the simplified, totem-pole eye of Northwest Coast art, the stylized imprint of a bear paw, and a cactus. Personal associations that one might bring to this imagery are diffused by Lichtenstein's mannered style and his usual touches of wit—in this case the cartoon eyebrow and the teardrop reflection in the pupil of the eye. In *American Indian Theme IV* (p. 120), a large, grimacing face, at once horrific and

Roy Lichtenstein
Figure with Teepee
1980
etching, engraving on
Lana paper

24¼ x 21
Collection Walker Art
Center, Minneapolis
Tyler Graphics Archive
(Tyler 353:RL21)

Roy Lichtenstein
*Head with Feathers
and Braid* 1980
etching, aquatint,
engraving on Lana
paper

24 x 19¾
Collection Walker Art
Center, Minneapolis
Tyler Graphics Archive
(Tyler 352:RL20)

humorous, confronts the viewer. It is a picture of a plywood mask, with the small square eyes, the gaping cross where the nose should be, and the jagged, downturned mouth all seemingly cut out with a jigsaw.

The use of the mask exemplifies the impersonation that is central to Lichtenstein's art: his real intentions are hidden behind the comic facade. He has said that "part of the intention of Pop Art is to mask its intentions with humor."[13] On one level his transformation of a sacred mask indicts the kitsch quality that many contemporary Native American art objects and curios have acquired. His use of wood-grain patterns suggests the material of the original mask but gives it the simulated quality of plywood instead. At the same time, the stylized wood grain refers to the material from which the printed image—a woodcut—was made. Yet Lichtenstein heavily varnished the wood so that no traces of the actual grain are evident in the print. With customary zeal, the artist relishes the use of artifice and double entendre.

Several months after starting the six American Indian Theme woodcuts, Lichtenstein returned to Bedford to begin work on a second series of six prints using the same motif but a different technique. These etchings are much closer in size and feel to the artist's sketches and studies for his paintings. Oddly animated cartoonlike figures (see pp. 132–33) replace the iconic presences in the larger American Indian Theme prints. In contrast to the aggressive plywood mask of *American Indian Theme IV,* for instance, the etched profile of *Head with Feathers and Braid,* 1980, reveals not a grimace but the few remaining teeth in an aging mouth. While many of the woodblocks for the American Indian Theme series had been cut by printers at Tyler Graphics according to the artist's specifications, Lichtenstein drew directly on the etching plates. His customarily solid blocks of red, blue, and black are replaced by sketchy areas of softer colors such as pale yellow and pink. The slightly irregular, handmade feel of these new prints is distinctly different from the hard-edged, commercial quality of Lichtenstein's graphic work of the 1960s and 1970s, and their looser style parallels the vulnerable character of the new imagery.

Shortly after finishing the etchings, Lichtenstein worked on several woodcuts pulled at Tyler Graphics in 1981. Most of the blocks for these prints had been carved in 1978 by artisans in Ahmadabad, India, and were made of teak. Leaving the wood unvarnished, Lichtenstein allowed the natural wood-grain patterns to be prominent in the prints. The still-life themes explored in these works are similar to those found in Lichtenstein's early Pop drawings and paintings. In his early work he had contrived a new kind of still life in which items from office-supply catalogues, to take one example, were treated as subjects equal in worth to the genre's traditional fruit and flower arrangements. During the 1970s Lichtenstein transformed some of these still lifes into sculptures, which retained the flat, two-dimensional quality of his paintings and prints. The sculptures look like Lichtenstein drawings floating in space, anchored only by the artist's characteristic black outlines.

Roy Lichtenstein
Lamp 1981
woodcut on natural
Okawara handmade
paper
25 x 18¼
Collection Walker Art
Center, Minneapolis
Tyler Graphics Archive
(Tyler 360:RL28)

Roy Lichtenstein
Goldfish Bowl 1981
woodcut on natural
Okawara handmade
paper
25 x 18¼
Collection Walker Art
Center, Minneapolis
Tyler Graphics Archive
(Tyler 362:RL30)

The sculptures, in turn, became the source for the three woodcuts made at Tyler Graphics in 1981. *Lamp* (p. 135), with the simplified, forceful lines of commercial art, is closely related to Lichtenstein's early office still lifes, a theme he revived in paintings made in 1976. *Picture and Pitcher,* a simple image that makes overt use of a clichéd verbal pun, is more in the vein of his "cubist" still-life paintings of the early

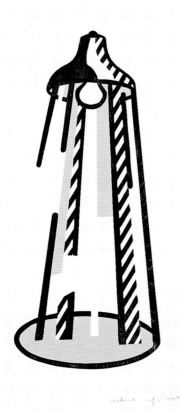

1970s.[14] The third woodcut, *Goldfish Bowl* (p. 135), is one of many images in which Lichtenstein refers to the influence of Henri Matisse, especially the French artist's compositional sense and bold use of color, line, and pattern. While this particular image directly quotes Matisse's 1911 painting *Goldfish,* it is unmistakably Lichtenstein's.

As simple as jigsaw puzzles, these woodblock prints are antithetical to the multimedia Entablatures, with their high-tech polish, and they exemplify Tyler Graphics's ability to accommodate an artist's divergent technical needs. Different as they are, both series reflect Lichtenstein's remarkably consistent approach to art. These refined distillations of everyday objects reveal his continued interest in the play between realism and abstraction and epitomize his emphatic style.

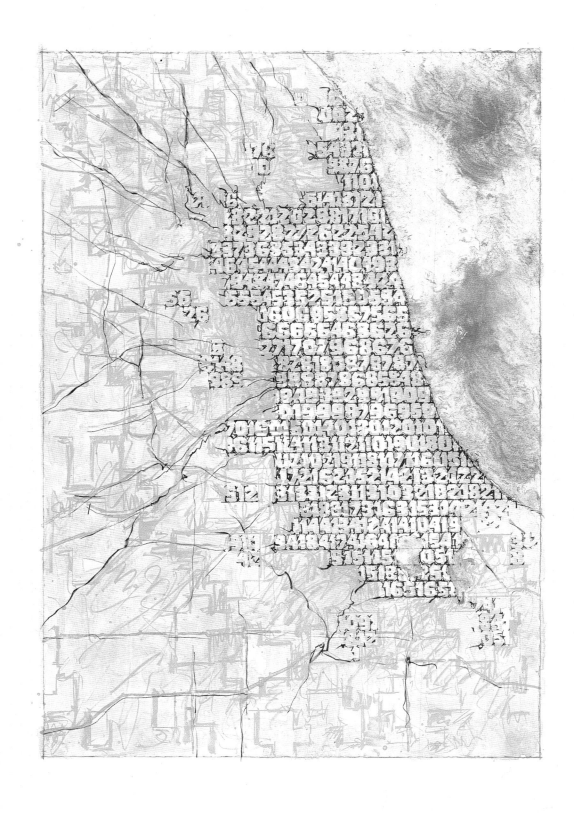

Claes Oldenburg has freely traversed the boundaries between sculpture, drawing, printmaking, and performance, cross-fertilizing these activities in an ever-evolving process in which the ideas that appear in his early work continue to metamorphose into a variety of forms today. The print he worked on at Tyler Graphics in 1976–77, *Chicago Stuffed with Numbers* (p. 136), recalls his soft sculptures of the 1960s, particularly works such as *Soft Calendar for the Month of August* and *Soft Manhattan I—Postal Zones,* the latter a soft canvas map of Manhattan divided into interlocking zip-code areas. The more immediate sources for the print, however, are drawings such as *Map of Chicago Stuffed with Soft Numbers* (p. 138), made by the artist while he was in Chicago in 1963 in conjunction with a happening called *Gayety,* which took place at the University of Chicago. Oldenburg subtitled the happening *Map of the City* and structured the space according to landmarks on the map of Chicago (see p. 138). In the drawing he used the boundaries of the city's metropolitan area to contain a mass of soft, inflated-looking numbers.

Maps function for Oldenburg as ground plans for the construction of his own world of images, a place where reality and imagination intermingle.[15] Everyday objects—food, furniture, tools—are transformed into the unfamiliar through the use of unexpected scale and materials. Since the early 1960s Oldenburg has infused these forms with new associations, especially characteristics of the human body, giving them a life of their own.

For Oldenburg, "if an idea is not set down immediately, the *form* of it is lost."[16] His images generally appear first as working sketches, which reveal the facility of his draftsmanship. Oldenburg continually returns to these sketches as source material for more finished drawings and sculptures. Working with Tyler at Gemini G.E.L. in 1968, he first used his sketches as the basis of his printmaking activity. In these lithographs, simply titled Notes, Oldenburg enlarged objects or parts of the body to a colossal scale and then set these "monuments" in real or imagined sites.

A vignette in one of the Notes features buildings in the city of Los Angeles in the form of colossal letters. As Oldenburg wrote in the accompanying text, "A city is all words—a newspaper, an alphabet." He suggested making buildings out of the letters of the word that described the building's function: "Arguments about how a building should look would be reduced to arranging these huge letters."[17] In another print made at Gemini a few years later, *The Letter Q as a Beach House, with Sailboat,* 1972 (p. 139), Oldenburg enlarged and inverted the letter Q, transforming it into a modernist monolith in a beachfront setting. Throughout the early 1970s Oldenburg made graphic and sculptural variations of his *Good Humor Bar*—one of the earliest plaster objects he made for the *Store* (1961–62)—filling it with letters of the alphabet. "Swollen letters," he later wrote, "signify the affluence that advertises a good store."[18]

Claes Oldenburg
Chicago Stuffed with Numbers 1977
lithograph on Arches
Cover paper
47½ x 30½
Collection Walker Art Center, Minneapolis
Tyler Graphics Archive
(Tyler 477:CO1)

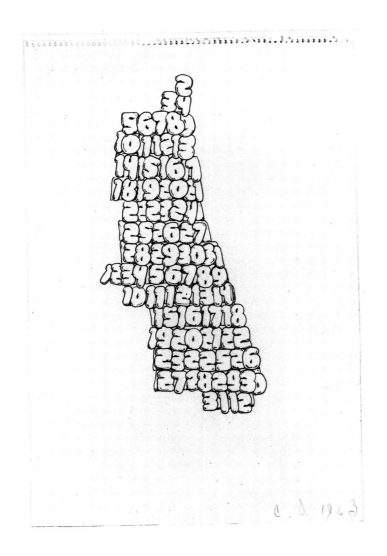

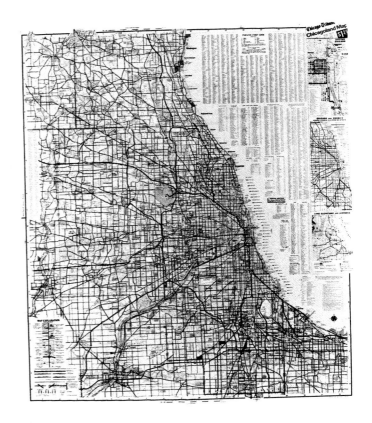

Working at Tyler Graphics in 1976, the artist returned to his musings about inserting characters into the landscape. Instead of using letters, he superimposed digits onto a map of Chicago. Instead of portraying the city as an alphabet, he defined it as street numbers, zip codes, and phone exchanges. The print, *Chicago Stuffed with Numbers*, was commissioned by the Art Institute of Chicago, where both Oldenburg and Tyler had studied in the 1950s. Expanding on his 1963 drawing *Map of Chicago Stuffed with Soft Numbers*, Oldenburg added outlying areas of the city, including the highways that feed into Chicago. These orange and red lines are like major arteries supporting the heart of the city. In contrast to the crayonlike quality of these areas of the lithograph, the massive abstract form of Lake Michigan, made from a lithographic wash and mezzotint stencil, hovers uncomfortably above the map-city. This ambiguous relationship between figuration and abstraction is found in much of Oldenburg's work, and *Chicago Stuffed with Numbers* is a graphic manifestation of the continuum that marks the artist's evolution. Intimately related to his work in other media, made at other times, it embodies the intersection of reality and imagination at the core of Oldenburg's art.

Claes Oldenburg
Map of Chicago Stuffed with Soft Numbers 1963
ink on paper
12 x 9½
Collection of the artist

"Chicagoland Map," published by the *Chicago Tribune*
Courtesy of Claes Oldenburg

(opposite)
Claes Oldenburg
The Letter Q as a Beach House, with Sailboat 1972
lithograph on Arjomari paper
39 x 29½
Collection Walker Art Center, Minneapolis
Gift of Kenneth E. Tyler, 1984

Malcolm Morley's work reveals him to be an astute observer and forecaster of art-historical transformations. Born in London in 1931, he attended the Royal College of Art from 1954 to 1957. He shared with many artists of his generation an early interest in work by Mark Rothko, Willem de Kooning, and other American abstract artists whose paintings he saw at the Tate Gallery in the 1950s. Shortly after he moved to the United States in 1958, he met Barnett Newman, who continued to influence him throughout his abstract period.

By the mid-1960s, however, Morley began making superrealist paintings that anticipated the photorealist movement. He derived his images from printed material—color postcards, travel brochures, and calendars—often including a white border around the image that called attention to its printed source.[19] Morley transferred imagery from his sources to the canvas with the aid of a grid technique similar to that used during the Renaissance. The systematic process of working on small sections of the composition, arbitrarily imposed by the grid, emphasized the abstract elements of painting, and Morley has stressed the importance of this compositional method in enabling him to concentrate on color and gesture.[20]

The use of images from contemporary life, undoubtedly affected by the ideas of such artists as Richard Hamilton, briefly aligned Morley's work with the Pop Art movement. His early paintings, such as the image of middle-class vacationers on a pleasure cruise in *On Deck*, 1966 (p. 141), share the ambivalence projected by much Pop Art in regard to its subject matter, for the intention of the painting might be seen as an implicit critique of the vacationers pictured in its image.

In the early 1970s Morley moved away from the use of found photographs and other printed matter as sources for his paintings, and his work appeared increasingly restless. He overlaid once-serene views of ocean vessels with a cacophony of disjointed images animated by lively brushwork. Intentionally chaotic and abrasive compared to the cerebral and refined reductionist sculpture and painting being done by his contemporaries during this period, Morley's compositions betray his struggle to create works of an entirely independent character. Rejecting prevalent formal trends, Morley attempted to discover a personal mode of expression outside the confines of avant-garde conventions. This resulted in his development of a more expressive style. As with his figurative subject matter, he had already begun to paint in a style that would be widely revived in the late 1970s in the guise of Neo-Expressionism.

Not surprisingly, given his self-critical and art historically astute appraisal of the art of his time, Morley's imagery underwent yet another metamorphosis in the late 1970s, when he began to produce rich, painterly views of animals in nature. Working in such places as Florida, Greece, and the south of France, he made drawings and watercolors on site. He continued, nonetheless, to use the grid technique, employing

Malcolm Morley
On Deck 1966
Magnacolor on
Liquitex ground on
canvas
83¾ x 63¾
Collection Metropol-
itan Museum of Art,
New York
Gift of Mr. and Mrs. S.
Brooks Barron, 1980

the new drawings and watercolors as source materials for paintings and prints. In a number of lithographs that Morley began during his first visit to Tyler Graphics in 1981, however, he abandoned the grid and worked directly on smooth sheets of acetate rather than lithographic plates or stones. He attacked these pristine surfaces with colored inks, applied with brushes, sponges, rags, and even his fingers. The resulting images have a vigorous, allover painterly quality that recalls his early interest in Abstract Expressionists such as de Kooning.

In *Devonshire Cows,* 1982 (p. 142), Morley portrays several brown-and-white Guernseys with such furious abandon that their forms, recognizable at the left, dissolve into amorphous abstractions at the

Malcolm Morley   46¼ x 34⅜
Devonshire Cows   Collection Walker Art
1982   Center, Minneapolis
lithograph on Rives   Tyler Graphics Archive
BFK paper   (Tyler 377:MM4)

Malcolm Morley
Devonshire Bullocks
1982
lithograph on Rives
BFK paper

47¾ x 35
Collection Walker Art
Center, Minneapolis
Tyler Graphics Archive
(Tyler 376:MM3)

Malcolm Morley
Beach Scene 1982
lithograph on Arches
88 paper
38¼ x 51⅛
Collection Walker Art
Center, Minneapolis
Tyler Graphics Archive
(Tyler 374:MM1)

right. The top half of this print, like that of its companion, *Devonshire Bullocks* (p. 143), is all clouds and sky, reflecting Morley's interest in certain British landscape traditions. Although his acid colors are characteristically Pop, Morley's exuberant depictions of nature may be compared to the tumultuous brushwork of J. M. W. Turner's seascapes and John Constable's cloud studies. Morley's largest print from Tyler Graphics, *Beach Scene* (p. 144), bursts with activity on all fronts, encompassing beach, ocean, and sky. Innumerable bathers with colorful umbrellas populate the beach, sails flutter on the water, and over it all looms a threatening sky. Morley has captured the intensity of light just before a storm, infusing the scene with a sense of drama that again recalls Turner.

In several prints Morley's usual intensity borders on the over-wrought. The subjects named in prints such as *Goat* and *Fish* (p. 145) are lost in a sea of vehement finger markings, frenzied brush strokes,

Malcolm Morley
Fish 1982
lithograph on Pur
Charve Nacre
handmade paper
26 x 39
Collection Walker Art
Center, Minneapolis
Tyler Graphics Archive
(Tyler 378: MM5)

and energetic spatterings. Morley's uninhibited immersion in his subject matter and style inspires the observer to draw parallels between the purely sensual aspects of making art and the physical wonders of constantly transforming nature. Morley has explained his visceral relationship to his subjects: "I like all my paintings to come out of what I've actually seen and experienced in one way or another. In a sense, they're about being in the physical, phenomenological, manmade world and then retreating from it."[21] Working at Tyler Graphics, at a far remove from the sites where he first sketched these scenes, he recaptured a sense of adventure in nature that parallels a sense of constant and unpredictable change intrinsic to his work.

As a young student at the Royal College of Art, London, from 1959 to 1962, David Hockney was part of the second wave of British artists who promoted the Pop aesthetic. In the early 1960s, when Richard Hamilton's ideas permeated the college, a younger generation began to embrace the imagery of consumer society in their art. While Hockney

lacked the Pop artists' interest in the specific iconography and methodology of the media, his art drew from the emancipated life-style of the period, which was promoted by popular culture.

Hockney's absorption in printmaking started while he was still in college, when he discovered that etching was well suited to his facility with line. The linear quality of the medium encouraged his interest in storytelling, and he soon began his first major series of prints. A Rake's Progress (see p. 146), published by Editions Alecto in 1963, is an autobiographical tale tracing his first visit to New York in 1961. Like William Hogarth's eighteenth-century work of the same title, Hockney's series uses satire to moralize about a young rake—in this case, however, openly referring to his own homosexuality and the temptations of contemporary life.

A Rake's Progress epitomizes Hockney's unique style of this period, in which he juxtaposed passages of self-conscious abstraction with realistically rendered figures, and diagrammatic objects with well-defined, volumetric ones. The portfolio also reflects the impact of the United States on the young artist. His initial visit in 1961 was followed

David Hockney
Receiving the Inheritance 1961–63
etching, aquatint on Barcham Green handmade paper
19⅝ x 34⅜
Collection Walker Art Center, Minneapolis
McKnight Acquisition Fund, T.B. Walker Acquisition Fund, Clinton and Della Walker Acquisition Fund, 1984

(opposite)
David Hockney
Picture of a Pointless Abstraction Framed under Glass 1965
lithograph on Rives BFK paper
30 x 20
Collection Walker Art Center, Minneapolis
Art Center Acquisition Fund, 1967

H.P. VI/XXXV

David Hockney

two years later by a trip to the West Coast, and early in 1964 he made Southern California his second home. His work immediately incorporated the palm trees and swimming pools, the vivid light and color of the California landscape, so inspiring after the "Gothic gloom," as Hockney has described it, of northern England. But his response to California was not without pointed commentary as he simultaneously reveled in and deflated the subject at hand. In a suite of prints made shortly after moving to California, A Hollywood Collection, 1965, he gibed style-conscious collectors seeking prestige through art. The six prints in the series present a smorgasbord of images: a still life, a landscape, a portrait, a nude, a street scene, and an abstract painting. This last work, *Picture of a Pointless Abstraction Framed under Glass* (p. 147), summarizes Hockney's ironic attitude toward pure abstraction during this period. It also exemplifies the basic Pop tenet that an artist can choose any subject, even mediocre painting, and make it the subject of his own art.

The prints in A Hollywood Collection were among the first produced at Gemini Ltd. Tyler had met Hockney when the artist was at Tamarind, and they worked together a number of times at Gemini G.E.L. throughout the 1970s. In 1973 Hockney's preoccupation with portraiture led to a series of lithographs including a portrait of Tyler entitled *The Master Printer of Los Angeles* (p. 12) and one of Celia Birtwell, a close friend and frequent model of the artist's. These portraits reflect the increasingly realistic nature of Hockney's work in the late 1960s and the early 1970s, a time when he was using photographs as a major source for his images.

In his portraits of Tyler and Birtwell, set in the workshop, the working proofs of another group of prints, the Weather Series, can be seen hanging in the background (see p. 12). Distinctly different from the naturalistic portraits of his friends, the prints in the Weather Series pay tribute to Japan, which Hockney had visited for the first time in 1971. *Sun, Rain, Mist, Lightning, Snow,* and *Wind* were based more on Japanese art than on the country's weather. In *Rain,* Hockney dripped liquid tusche down the stone to depict puddles of rainwater in a delightfully graphic suggestion of wetness that brings subject and technique into perfect harmony.

Later in 1973 Hockney was invited to work in Paris on a portfolio in homage to Pablo Picasso, who had died in April of that year. Working with Picasso's extraordinary etching printer, Aldo Crommelynck, Hockney learned sugar-lift and color etching techniques that had been perfected for the older artist.[22] The experience also seems to have rekindled Hockney's longtime passion for Picasso's work. Several years later he began a set of drawings inspired by the Wallace Stevens poem "The Man with the Blue Guitar," 1937, which was itself inspired by Picasso's painting *The Old Guitarist,* 1903. Hockney went on to produce a set of twenty etchings, The Blue Guitar, 1976–77 (see p. 148), that draws on the lessons of the Spanish master—especially his limitless

David Hockney
Discord Merely Magnifies 1976–77
etching, aquatint on Inveresk paper
18 x 20¼
Collection Walker Art Center, Minneapolis
Gift of Robert and Janet Sabes, 1986

ability to borrow and create new styles—and uses printmaking techniques devised by Crommelynck for Picasso.[23] At this time Hockney was struggling to free himself from the strictures imposed by photography, and he found these prints a welcome release for his imagination.

Other important outlets for Hockney's inventiveness were provided in the 1970s by several commissions to design sets for the opera. It was after the completion of *The Magic Flute* for England's Glyndebourne Festival Opera in 1978 that Hockney, in between projects, accepted a long-standing invitation to visit Tyler at his new print workshop in Bedford Village. Although unwilling to commit to making a series of prints, Hockney agreed to join his friend for dinner one night. By the end of the evening, he was so intrigued by Tyler's new experiments with paper pulp that he extended his visit. Hockney stayed on to create the Paper Pools, iconic images of one of his favorite subjects, which are discussed elsewhere in this volume (see "Paperworks at Tyler Graphics").

During the long visit to create the Paper Pools, Hockney also began work on a series of lithographs on that theme. A fitting expression of his prolonged fascination with the illusion of surface, these eleven prints all show the same view of a pool, each with slight variations on the water's surface (see p. 151). In this series, which is about looking *on* water versus looking *through* it, Hockney returned to his fascination with transparent surfaces: "I'd always been interested in drawing transparency or drawing what goes on under the surface of water because, actually, if you see any pattern at all on top of water, it's only on the surface. . . . So your eye has to go through two levels: it's the actual surface, and then you can see the other lines drawn which represent another level. So the eye keeps moving in between the two levels, and it was that that interested me."[24] Here the different ways of seeing water in a pool are intimately bound up with the process of making a print: ten of the lithographs are the result of alterations and additions to the first one. This print—the one in which it is easiest to see through the water's surface to the bottom—is also the simplest in terms of technique (it was printed from one plate in one color). In a later image four additional printings from plates and stones—and a second color—divert attention from the pool's depth to the movement of water and shadows on its surface. Hockney challenges the viewer's eye to move from the surface to the background, capturing something of the actual experience of viewing light refracted by the water's surface.

Hockney returned to Tyler Graphics in 1979 to continue work on the pool lithographs and to make a series of portraits. As usual, the artist's models were friends who sat for him in Tyler's studio. These portraits have an improvisational feeling, as if Hockney were consciously trying to loosen up. In many of these lithographs he worked with a brush and a liquid tusche that offered little resistance to his marks. The feeling of spontaneity that characterizes these prints recalls the work of the French modernists—especially Matisse and Raoul Dufy—which

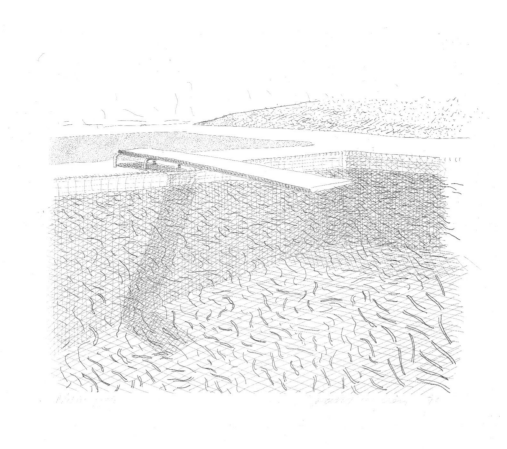

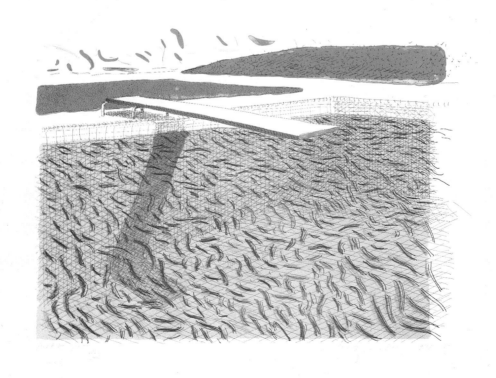

David Hockney
*Shoes. Kyoto,
Feb. 1983* 1983
photographic collage
44 X 39
Courtesy of David
Hockney

(opposite)
David Hockney
*Views of Hotel Well
III* 1985
lithograph on TGL
handmade paper
48½ x 38½
Collection Walker Art
Center, Minneapolis
Tyler Graphics Archive
(Tyler 282:DH69)

Hockney was studying in preparation for another theater project, the Metropolitan Opera's triple bill of French modernist works collectively titled *Parade*.

Between 1981 and 1983 Hockney made very few paintings or prints, but he took thousands of photographs and began to create numerous photocollages (see p. 152). These compositions led directly to new ideas that he has explored since 1983 in drawings, paintings, and, in particular, prints. Among the most intriguing of his new works is a series started at Tyler Graphics in 1984.

Hockney based a number of these prints on his drawings of a small hotel in Acatlán, Mexico, that he and Tyler visited. In preparation for making the prints, Tyler provided Hockney with a special sketchbook of transparent Mylar and acetate sheets and crayons custom-made for

David Hockney
*Hotel Acatlán: Second
Day* 1985
lithograph on TGL
handmade paper

two sheets: 28¾ x 76
Collection Walker Art
Center, Minneapolis
Tyler Graphics Archive
(Tyler 283:DH70)

155

the project. By isolating each of his colors on separate transparent sheets of the sketchbook—simulating, in effect, the color separation process required by lithography—Hockney was able to visualize the final prints even as he worked on his initial sketches. Upon returning to Tyler Graphics, Hockney relied not only on his sketches, which had meanwhile been proofed by Tyler, but also on photographs and on his memory of walking through the spaces of the Mexican courtyard. Like the earlier photocollages, these new images force the viewer's eye to move rapidly around the picture in order to take in all its elements. In prints such as *Views of Hotel Well III*, 1985 (p. 153), Hockney makes use of multiple perspectives. Here the eye is drawn diagonally in opposite directions, up the red walkways toward the distant blue doors at either side of the picture. At the same time, the print creates a sense of reverse perspective. While the center portion of the image—where we see the hotel's well with its red brick arch—is further removed from the viewer than the tables and chairs in the foreground, the center seems to loom out, sweeping the viewer into its vortex. Hockney's sensational use of color in the prints further activates the eye. In *Hotel Acatlán: Second Day*, 1985 (pp. 154–55), the vivid reds, yellows, pinks, and aquas of the hotel's courtyard are as vibrant as colors lit by the bright Mexican sun.

Hockney spent vast periods of time working on this series, which includes twenty-nine lithographs. In addition to the scenes of the Mexican hotel, these include a number of interior views as well as several portraits. In *The Perspective Lesson*, 1985 (p. 157), a humorously didactic print, Hockney emphasizes his rejection of Western conventions of perspective. Beneath the crossed-out image of a chair rendered with one-point perspective, he depicts a second chair using a different perspective. Hockney's goal in the series is not just to reject conventional perspective but also to employ multiple perspectives within each work.

The playfulness found here and in other interior scenes is replaced by a more sustained exploration of space, movement, and time in the portraits. Hockney presents his subjects from various perspectives and distances. In his picture of Gregory Evans, *An Image of Gregory*, 1985, he divides the portrait into halves, underscoring the separation of body and mind. The bottom half, encompassing the bulk of Evans's body, suggests the sitter's physical being, his restless movement as he posed for the artist. The top half focuses on Evans's head, which Hockney fractures as if seen from two viewpoints—a clear tribute to Picasso's dual-sided Cubist heads.

In *An Image of Celia*, 1986 (p. 158), Hockney acknowledges his own movements as he worked on the picture as well as his model's. Again, the fragmented image is reminiscent of Picasso's Cubist portraits, and like the Cubists, Hockney uses collage elements to reorder space and suggest elapsed time. Working on the print over a period of several years, he also allowed real time to inform the picture. By placing a portion of another print, *Red Celia*, 1985 (a special printing of it was done specifically for use in *An Image of Celia)*, next to a newer, frontal

David Hockney
*The Perspective
Lesson* 1985
lithograph on gray
HMP handmade paper
30 x 22
Collection Walker Art
Center, Minneapolis
Tyler Graphics Archive
(Tyler 284:DH71)

rendering of his subject's face, Hockney accosts the viewer with an unusually aggressive portrait. Duplicating the forms of his sitter's arms and legs and extending portions of the boldly patterned background right into the hand-painted frame, Hockney sets the image in motion.

Since the 1960s Hockney has been searching for new approaches to perspective. Before rejecting artistic conventions entirely, he had thoroughly explored, indeed exhausted, their use in his paintings based on photographs, of the 1970s. Today, using photographs as a tool rather than a subject, Hockney has forsaken photographic realism for a pictorial

space that he considers much closer to the way we experience the world. The recent prints made at Tyler Graphics indicate the depth of his new interests. That Hockney's recent evaluations of space and perspective have been freely explored in the print medium testifies to Tyler's gifts as a printer and publisher. It was at his encouragement that the series was begun, and he then offered Hockney the complete resources of his workshop. Based on a long history of stimulating collaborations, Hockney and Tyler have developed an unusually symbiotic working arrangement that has yielded many of the touchstones by which contemporary printmaking is judged.

Notes

1. *Roy Lichtenstein: Graphic Work, 1970–1980,* exh. brochure (New York: Whitney Museum of American Art, Downtown Branch, 1981), n.p.
2. Richard Hamilton to Alison and Peter Smithson, January 16, 1957, in Richard Morphet, introduction to *Richard Hamilton,* exh. cat. (London: Tate Gallery, 1970), p. 31.
3. Ibid.
4. The British critic and curator Lawrence Alloway coined the term *Pop Art* as early as 1956, but it was not until the early 1960s that the movement took on a recognizable, coherent identity.
5. John Loring, "Not Just So Many Marvelously Right Images," *Print Collector's Newsletter* 4 (November–December 1973): 98.
6. Hamilton has written in detail about his own printmaking. See Richard Hamilton, *Collected Words, 1953–1982* (London: Thames & Hudson, 1982), pp. 84–110.
7. To name a few, R. B. Kitaj, Eduardo Paolozzi, and Joe Tilson in England, and Robert Rauschenberg and Andy Warhol in America.
8. Richard S. Field, *Richard Hamilton: Image and Process, 1952–1982,* exh. cat. (London: Tate Gallery, 1983), p. 38.
9. Hamilton, *Collected Words,* p. 100.
10. Kristine Stiles makes this point in correspondence with the author, December 1, 1985. In reference to Hamilton she writes, "I'll never forget how he told me that putting the toilet paper in *Soft pink landscape,* he saved himself from his own sentimentality when confronted with doing a beautiful landscape painting."
11. Roy Lichtenstein, in Ruth Fine, *Gemini G.E.L.: Art and Collaboration,* exh. cat. (Washington, D.C.: National Gallery of Art; New York: Abbeville Press, 1984), p. 192.
12. Diane Waldman, *Roy Lichtenstein: Drawings and Prints* (Lausanne: Publications I.R.L., 1970), p. 215.
13. Bruce Glaser, "Oldenburg, Lichtenstein, Warhol: A Discussion," *Artforum* 4 (February 1966): 22.
14. The designations "office" and "cubist" are among those used by Jack Cowart to describe Lichtenstein's thematic approach. See Jack Cowart, *Roy Lichtenstein, 1970–1980,* exh. cat. (Saint Louis: Saint Louis Art Museum; New York: Hudson Hills Press, 1981).
15. Coosje van Bruggen, *Claes Oldenburg: Mouse Museum/Ray Gun Wing,* exh. cat. (Cologne: Museum Ludwig, 1979), p. 34.
16. Claes Oldenburg, in Barbara Rose, *Claes Oldenburg: Notes,* publisher's brochure (Los Angeles: Gemini G.E.L., 1968), n.p.
17. Claes Oldenburg, in Barbara Haskell, *Claes Oldenburg: Object into Monument,* exh. cat. (Pasadena, Calif.: Pasadena Art Museum, 1971), p. 81.
18. Claes Oldenburg, *Claes Oldenburg: The Alphabet in L.A.,* exh. brochure (Los Angeles: Margo Leavin Gallery, 1975), n.p.
19. Michael Compton, *Malcolm Morley: Paintings 1965–82,* exh. cat. (London: Whitechapel Art Gallery, 1983), p. 75.
20. See Les Levine's interview with Morley, "Dialogue: Malcolm Morley," in *Cover* 1 (Spring–Summer 1985): 28–31.
21. Malcolm Morley, in "Expressionism Today: An Artists' Symposium," *Art in America* 70 (December 1982): 68.
22. Marco Livingstone, *David Hockney* (New York: Holt, Rinehart & Winston, 1981), p. 119.
23. Ibid., p. 192.
24. David Hockney in dialogue with Kenneth Tyler, Clifford Ackley, chair, Museum of Fine Arts, Boston, October 10, 1984, transcript, p. 8.

Frank Stella at Bedford

Richard H. Axsom

[Caravaggio] communicates the anxiety and urgency inherent in the mechanics of pictorial expression, yet makes these mechanics perform miracles. Dare we ask for more?

—Frank Stella[1]

Frank Stella's first full-dress print retrospective in 1982 was a revelation for many familiar with his paintings but unsuspecting of the scope and achievement of his printmaking.[2] In active collaborations with Gemini G.E.L., Petersburg Press, and Tyler Graphics Ltd., he had produced nearly two hundred editions since 1967. The exhibition traced the artist's gradual broadening of interests from the early lithographic drawings and screenprints to the later mixed-media prints, with their intricate blending of processes. Most clearly divulged by the retrospective was Stella's serious and persistently experimental approach to printmaking. The successful appropriation of printmaking to the ambitious visual discourses associated with his painting revealed Stella to be a major maker of prints, a *peintre-graveur* of the highest order.

It is ironic, given the esteem accorded the prints, that Stella has had reservations about printmaking. He has hesitated over what he has seen as the visual weakness of the medium. The technical innovations of his prints, so notable an aspect of their development, have been spurred by his aspirations to resolve this problem and by a desire to involve them in the formal and expressive absorptions of the paintings. There are few artists whose prints and paintings share such a profound relationship between the technical processes of their making and their poetics. Kenneth Tyler of Tyler Graphics, in his long-standing role as technical collaborator for Stella's art making, has facilitated this fundamental reciprocity.

Unlike other artists who may be indebted to a number of print workshops and master printers, Stella has had a nearly exclusive bond to Tyler. Three quarters of his graphic work has been printed and published with Tyler. Central to these collaborations has been the

Frank Stella
Talladega Three II
1982
relief print on
hand-colored TGL
handmade paper
66 x 52
Collection Walker Art
Center, Minneapolis
Tyler Graphics Archive
(Tyler 559:FS18)

continuous search for solutions to the often demanding technical problems posed by Stella's prints. The experimental edge fostered by their technical ambitiousness has distinguished the Tyler-Stella affiliation. Tyler has said that "Stella did more than anyone else to blast a hole in the traditional tools and aesthetics of printmaking."[3]

In spring 1967 Tyler, then master printer at Gemini G.E.L., invited Stella to make lithographs. The issue of the first session was the Star of Persia Series and Black Series I (see p. 163). Over the next six years, Stella, in periodic visits to Los Angeles, undertook nineteen projects with Tyler at Gemini, creating ninety editions in all.[4] Before leaving Gemini in 1974, Stella completed the Eccentric Polygons (see p. 163) and *York Factory II*. These works signaled an important shift in his handling of print media. The single-color rendering of the earlier prints was complicated by overprinting, a basic, traditional procedure that plays upon cumulative effects of multiple plates, but one that Stella had only begun to explore. Although overprinting paralleled his contemporaneous investigation of transparent color washes in his painting, the freely crayoned line of the Eccentric Polygons and *York Factory II* as well as the noodled drawing of the lithographic crayon in many of the early prints were formative influences in the development of a new calligraphic style in the paintings.[5] These last prints at Gemini accompanied the single most radical break in Stella's painting career, the emergence in 1974 of the etched and painted metal-relief constructions: three-dimensional vehicles for exuberant brushwork that marked an explosive break with the flat, shaped canvases and precise geometries of the earlier work. The year 1974 was pivotal. The first metal-relief paintings appeared; the Eccentric Polygons were published; Tyler moved to the East Coast and opened Tyler Graphics Ltd.; and Stella began his first project at Tyler's new workshop, the Paper Reliefs.

Tyler's collaborations with Stella at Bedford Village have taken their special character from the continuous relationship the two men have enjoyed since the mid-1960s. Tyler has always sought to know, in the most intelligent sense, the art of those artists with whom he collaborates. He has stated the wish "to always have my foot in the studio, so to speak, the private studio of the artist, to have a better knowledge there and understanding of the artist so I could make a different kind of graphic in my workshop."[6] One important reason for Tyler's going east was to keep better track of artists' studio work. With few exceptions, those with whom he has collaborated are clustered in and around New York. Physical proximity to them permits the type of intensive, extended project to which Tyler is drawn and which is made prohibitive if artists must travel long distances. The nearness of the printmaking resources at Bedford Village has had its effect on Stella. The facilities at Tyler Graphics and a lithography shop established with Petersburg Press on the first floor of his own residence in 1973 have allowed the artist more intimate and sustained contact with his printmaking than was possible at Gemini G.E.L.

Frank Stella
Bethlehem's Hospital
1967
lithograph on
Barcham Green paper
20⅛ x 25 1/16
Collection Walker Art
Center, Minneapolis
Gift of Kenneth E.
Tyler, 1985

Frank Stella
Effingham 1974
lithograph, screenprint
on Arches paper
17½ x 22½
Collection Walker Art
Center, Minneapolis
Purchased with the aid
of funds from Mr. and
Mrs. Miles Q.
Fiterman and the
National Endowment
for the Arts, 1975

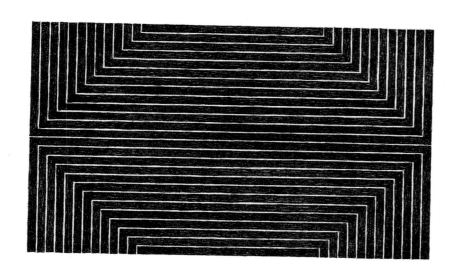

While Stella is at Bedford, Tyler's assistance is, in part, similar to what he offers other artists who visit the workshop.[7] He orchestrates the physical making of the prints from preparation and processing of print elements and paper to proofing and editioning. He participates directly, supervises the active collaboration of extraordinarily dedicated and gifted shop printers, and oversees outside involvements with industry. And yet the creative rhythms of Tyler and Stella are patently distinctive. Tyler claims that "there is no model for collaboration, no given pattern. Each artist demands a certain style from me and I have to try to make it available on short notice." Tyler's working relationship with Stella is nearly effortless given their experience together and, of course, their compatibility. Both are quiet workers in the studio. Mutual respect for each other's habits and Tyler's understanding of Stella's art make for intuitive exchanges. Tyler has joked that they need only mumble to get things done in the studio. The two men are also a felicitous match because of their mutual passion for fabricating things. Stella's art is technically advanced. His love of technology, his curiosity about new materials, his ceaseless looking and tinkering all mirror Tyler's enthusiasms. Tyler's eagerness to help and his technical bend-of-mind make him the ideal collaborator for Stella.

Tyler's activities with Stella are not limited to the work spaces of Bedford. Less known is the fact that Tyler has long been the technical adviser for the relief paintings. His role of consultant and processing agent dates back to 1969, when he introduced Stella to Tompkins Tooling Industries, one of many outside collaborators for Gemini, who would produce the wood-relief variants and Tri-Wall supports of the Polish Village Series, 1970–73. Tompkins Tooling also fabricated the 1975–76 Brazilian Series metal paintings and the first six metal-relief constructions for the Exotic Bird Series, 1976–78, the balance of which were made at the Hexcel Corporation in Casa Grande, Arizona.[8] In collaboration with Hexcel, Tyler invented Tycore, a thick cardboard that was developed to make models for the metal-relief paintings. Hexcel was also responsible for patenting a design of honeycomb aluminum that has served as the core support for a number of the latter.

By the late 1970s, having used other sources nearer New York to alleviate the inconvenience of long-distance consulting and shipping, Stella and Tyler had moved their activities to the Swan Engraving Company in Bridgeport, Connecticut,[9] primarily because Swan was the only shop with the capacity for producing artwork on magnesium, the facing for the honeycomb aluminum that Stella had come to prefer. During the 1980s Swan Engraving, under Tyler's and Stella's supervision, has cut, etched, and assembled the metal-relief paintings. Stella has thus consolidated his art making to the golden triangle of Manhattan, Bridgeport, and Bedford, to the spaces of home, painting studio, print workshop, and factory, where, he has said, he spends his life.[10]

Tyler's relationship to the relief paintings has given him a rich understanding of Stella's art. It has provided a privileged basis for

assistance to Stella's printmaking, one that Tyler had sought deliberately. As he has said, "It all fits together. Outside collaboration with the original art in the artist's studio puts another ingredient into the collaborative act. It is because we collaborate on two fronts, printmaking and painting, that it gets mishmashed together." Stella's projects at Bedford, which include sets of paperworks and multiples, are outgrowths of his relief paintings. The 1975 Paper Reliefs, a series of editioned cast-paper pieces, were a postscript to the relief versions of the Polish Village paintings. The mixed-media Playskool bronzes of 1983, an editioned group of metal reliefs, were smaller-scaled variants of the wood Playskool Series. The first graphic work per se was derived from the Exotic Bird paintings, which resulted in the Exotic Bird lithograph-screenprints, 1977, and the four hand-colored screenprints, 1979. A second painting series, the Circuits, was the basis for what has been Stella's most extensive print project to date, the separate but related Circuits, Swan Engravings, and Journals, which variously blend intaglio, relief printing, screen printing, and lithographic processes. Forty-four prints in all, the Circuits-related editions were produced between 1981 and 1985.

When Stella began his first project with Tyler at Bedford, he was in the midst of executing the Brazilian paintings (see p. 165). The etched-metal surfaces of this series carried bright, transparent washes and energetic line work. These effects had been approximated, as noted earlier, in the Eccentric Polygons prints. The next series, the Exotic Birds, furthered Stella's new baroque exuberance with deeper and more

Frank Stella
Botafogo #9   1975
painted aluminum
86 x 130
Collection the
Corcoran Gallery of
Art, Museum Purchase
with the aid of funds
from the Richard King
Mellon Foundation
and the National
Endowment for the
Arts, 1976

open relief, more saturated color, and etched and textured surfaces strewn with ground glass. In the wake of these new interests, could the prints keep up? Textured three-dimensional surfaces and sparkly color are hard to duplicate in printmaking. Postponing the making of a print series, Stella fashioned a cast-paper one, the Paper Reliefs (see pp. 208–9). Helping to initiate a new concern among American artists for handmade and cast paper, the Paper Reliefs also genuinely reflected directions in Stella's own art. Like their counterpart shapes in the Polish Village Series, the Paper Reliefs were three-dimensional and collaged. But they were also more textured and mottled as a result of hand-painting on the coarse, often wet surfaces of the unsized paper. Tyler feels that "materials are always a sign" for Stella and that returning to the same surface does not challenge him sufficiently. After the Brazilian and Exotic Bird paintings and the Paper Reliefs, Stella did not return to the superflat print on even, mould-made paper.

The Exotic Bird prints (see p. 167) undertook the challenge leveled by the metal-relief paintings and cast-paper pieces in their multiple layerings of screen printing and lithography. As a result of Stella's first use of liquid tusche, lithographic washes were introduced that duplicated the transparent sheets of color in the metal-relief paintings.[11] The reflective, gritty surfaces of the pulverized glass in the latter were captured in the prints with commercial Glitterflex, which—together with screen-printed gloss varnishes and thick deposits of inks—gave the prints their tangible and sumptuous surfaces. The expansive drawing, which required large sheets of paper, was deliberately transferred from the paintings. Stella has said that the big scale of the prints was prompted by his interest in emulating the broad arm gestures necessary for applying paint on the metal-relief constructions.[12]

Large scale was also a distinct issue in the hand-colored screenprints (see p. 168), which continued to mine the imagery of the Exotic Bird paintings and attained their physical size. Inasmuch as the five-by-seven-foot dimensions of the prints equaled the outside perimeter of the "3x" scale variant of the paintings (i.e., they were three times the size of the maquette), drawing in the prints and 3x paintings was identical in expressive gesture. The Tycore paper panel for the screenprints was closely related to the making of the paintings, since it had been conceived by Tyler to provide durable three-dimensional models for the relief paintings. But it was also adaptable for printing, painting, watercoloring, and matting. Available in five-by-seven-foot sheets, it could be placed on a large honeycombed screen-printing bench, which Tyler had designed for other work of Stella's at Bedford, and loaded with inks.[13] The decision to hand-paint the Tycore prints was made at a later stage in the project as an expedient to get certain color saturations finally seen by Stella as unobtainable with screen printing alone. In evidence here is Stella's pragmatic approach to resolving problems and the priority the image took over any allegiance to a given medium for its own sake. The thick screen-printed inks on the Tycore support, the oil coloring

Frank Stella
Puerto Rican Blue Pigeon 1977
lithograph, screenprint on Arches 88 paper
33⅞ x 45⅞
Collection Walker Art Center, Minneapolis
Tyler Graphics Archive
(Tyler 549:FS8)

Frank Stella
Steller's Albatross 1977
screenprint, lithograph on Arches 88 paper
33⅞ x 45⅞
Collection Walker Art Center, Minneapolis
Tyler Graphics Archive
(Tyler 553:FS12)

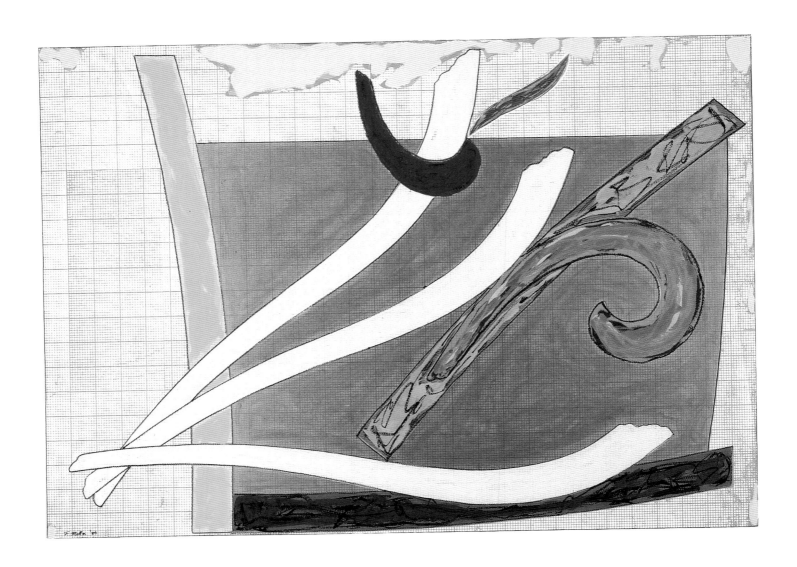

Frank Stella
Bermuda Petrel 1979
screenprint, stencil,
hand-colored, on
Tycore panel
61¾ x 85½ x ⅝
Collection Walker Art
Center, Minneapolis
Tyler Graphics Archive
(Tyler 554:FS13)

stick, and the Glitterflex of the completed work testify to the technical and conceptual influence of the paintings on the prints. Without the example of the metal-relief paintings, as well as the Paper Reliefs, it is doubtful that Stella would have arrived at the particular surfaces of the four Tycore editions, which augured new directions in the prints.

The Circuits prints (see pp. 160, 173, 180–82) and the Swan Engravings (see p. 175) were Stella's first excursion into intaglio and relief printing. Material left over from the fabrication of the Circuits paintings (see p. 169), as well as material discovered by the artist, provided the starting point for these separate but related series. The looping shapes and arabesques of the Circuits prints were derived from shapes in the Circuits paintings. The skeins of lines in each print were based on incised patterns left on wood backing boards during the cutting

out of flat metal shapes for the paintings. As a mechanical routing machine with a laser head cut a shape from the magnesium sheet, the backing board beneath caught the outline, which was burned into the wood. Used again and again, the boards accumulated superimposed contours. These boards, at one fortuitous moment, struck Stella as potential woodblocks that might be rolled and printed.[14] They were, and in this fashion the Circuits prints began. After Stella saw a backing board whose routed designs interested him, an impression on Mylar was pulled from the board and used as a core design over which further Mylar sheets were placed and drawn upon for additional line work and crayoned washes. The sum total of the Mylar sheets for a single image was used for the fabrication of etched magnesium plates and additional blocks. The finished prints are thus intricate amalgams of residual contours from the metal-relief paintings and newly conceived artwork.

Frank Stella
Pergusa 1981
mixed media on etched
magnesium
98 x 125 x 28
Courtesy M. Knoedler
& Co., Inc.

As the laser head cut out the shapes for the Circuits paintings, metal shapes were left over. These unused pieces were never discarded. Kept back for possible later projects, they became the basis for the collaged metal plates from which the Swan Engravings were pulled. Gathered, and in some instances re-etched, these shapes, in addition to etched and newly snipped forms and discarded commercial magnesium plates found by Stella at the Swan Engraving factory, were butted, fitted, and affixed to plywood backings. The finished collaged plates, consisting of between six and fifty irregularly shaped magnesium pieces, were inked and wiped for intaglio and relief printing. In a number of the prints the exposed outside margins of the plywood were rolled and printed as borders.

Stella's use of discovered and altered material in the Circuits prints and the Swan Engravings elaborates upon the history of the *objet trouvé* as initiated by Marcel Duchamp and Pablo Picasso. Much of the found material was Stella's own: the leftover metal from the Circuits paintings that was kept back for potential reuse. The routed backing boards used for relief printing were a serendipitous discovery. One category of found material, however, was indeed true scrap: the discarded plates for tablecloths and other commercial products that Stella happened upon at Swan, even tusche jars whose rims were traced and etched on the plates. Collectively, these objects were a priori elements that Stella decided would make art. They were drawn together, however, in a context of art making that still contained invented forms. What is noteworthy is the assertive presence of the found object and recycled material at this point in Stella's development. Although there are precedents in his work for both the use of discovered material and the recycling of his own art,[15] the Circuits prints and Swan Engravings represent the artist's first thoroughgoing manipulations of the *objet trouvé*.

The use of the found object as developed in the Circuits and the Swan Engravings was immediately appropriated in the metal-relief constructions. The Playskool bronzes incorporated actual objects such as bowling pins, plastic hose, and metal clamps into assemblages of cast bronze, honeycomb aluminum, and wood (see p. 171). The South African Mine, 1982–83, and Malta paintings, 1983–84, were the result of Stella's interest in using residual magnesium skins from the Circuits paintings as he had for the Swan Engravings. For these new series, Stella was prompted to use leftover material rather than throwing it away by his desire to get away from making the relief paintings in stages: from drawings to maquettes to specially manufactured honeycombed panels, which were faced, etched, and painted. He wanted to invent something on the spot and see where it took him. The approach had worked in the prints, and in the wake of the Circuits prints and Swan Engravings, it succeeded in the new paintings.

Stella's decision to work with intaglio and relief printing was not motivated by his wish to complete his exploration of the major print media (thus far he had considered only lithography and screen printing).

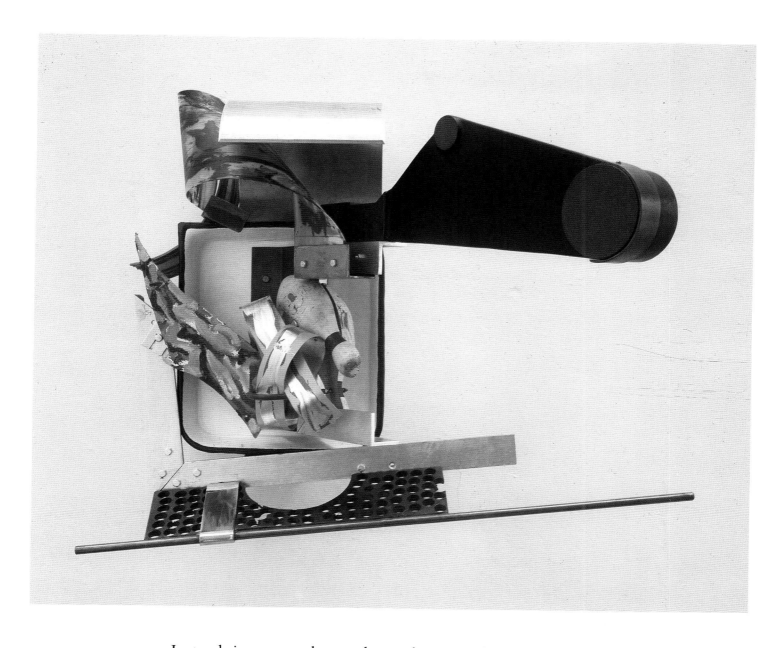

Frank Stella
Playskool Sink 1983
patinated cast bronze,
fabricated aluminum,
plastic, steel hose
hanger, cut wooden
bowling pins, plastic
and metal bracket,
hand-colored
31 x 36 x 29
Courtesy Tyler
Graphics Ltd.
(Tyler 581:FS40)

Instead, in yet another exchange between the prints and the paintings, Stella's exploration of intaglio and relief printing grew out of his discipline of brushing, etching, wiping, and painting the magnesium skins of the metal-relief paintings and from the printing potential of the wood backing boards. If the traditions of etching, engraving, and woodcut are invoked in the Circuits and Swan Engravings, Stella's response to them was unorthodox and did not proceed from a self-conscious notion of making a "good" etching or woodcut.

In certain instances Stella left intact the grained surfaces of wood-block elements in the Circuits and Swan Engravings, which, when rolled with ink, produced flat color grounds and borders. Blocks were also cut with irregular cross-hatchings to create negative line work that picked up the color it was printed over. Unlike the preparations for a traditional woodcut, there was little carving of actual shape in the block. The etched plates, which for *Pergusa Three* in the Circuits Series were embedded

in the blocks, did not resemble or produce traditional etchings. Stella drew and painted directly on a magnesium plate with a stop-out tusche or had his designs photographically transferred. The designs were raised in relief, not incised, after the plate was immersed in an acid bath—the identical method for the embossing of designs on the magnesium surfaces of the paintings. These deeply etched plates, known in the commercial printing industry by the terms *letterpress* and *linecut*, can also be engraved by a mechanical routing tool that incises designs directly into the plate. In most instances plates were relief-printed, but a number of them, particularly for the Swan Engravings, were variously rolled and wiped for both intaglio and relief effects.[16]

The printing elements for the Circuits and Swan Engravings are

Frank Stella
woodblock #2 for
Pergusa Three 1982
wood, magnesium-
plate insert
Collection Walker Art
Center, Minneapolis
Tyler Graphics Archive

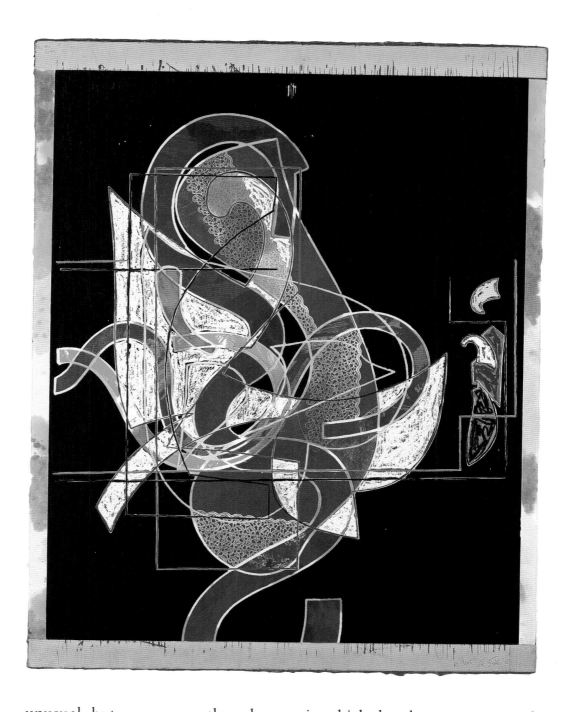

Frank Stella
Pergusa Three 1983
relief, woodcut on
hand-colored TGL
handmade paper
66 x 52
Collection Walker Art
Center, Minneapolis
Tyler Graphics Archive
(Tyler 575:FS34)

unusual, but no more so than the way in which the plates were treated with ink or how—and on what paper—they were printed. All aspects of these prints defy conventional expectations. For example, in the preparation of the metal collaged plates for the printing of the Swan Engravings, the inking and wiping of the plates were critical. All projecting and recessed surfaces were first rolled and inked. Surfaces might remain inked or be variously freed of ink by means of hand-blotting, Q-tips, sandy blocks, newsprint, tarlatans, and rags. The complex nuances of texture and color—for example, the false impression of aquatint—were introduced by extremely sophisticated and time-consuming wiping techniques. The immense variety of plate tone was not built into the plate; it was achieved through the fingers.[17]

Paper for Stella is an active ingredient, not a neutral substrate. The thick cotton-fiber paper, handmade at Tyler Graphics, was a crucial element in permitting the intricately inked plates and blocks to be printed for the Circuits prints and the Swan Engravings. If impressions had been made on conventional mould-made paper, most of the inked plate would not have taken. In the quest for color-saturated and textural surfaces, the Circuits and Swans were not printed on a conventional etching press. To drive as much ink as possible into the sheets of paper, without ink spurting out under the lateral pressures of an etching press, a platen press was used, whose vertical pressures allowed great amounts of ink to be laid in without smearing.

If the printer's subject, so to speak, of the Swans was the wiping of a single color, black, for tonal complexity, the subject of the Circuits was the layering of color on colored paper. The paper for a number of the Circuits prints was color-stained with liquid dyes while still wet to create varying border treatments or multicolor Dalmatian patterns. The colored paper provided a material layer of pigment upon which to build printing inks, but, as importantly, it was an underlayer of color that was exposed and concealed in a series of overprintings with print media.

Stella's and Tyler's free use of print media and processes—the rules broken in creative plate preparation, inking, and press and paper selection—produced two print series of astonishing spatial complexity and depth of color. The visual strength of the Circuits prints and Swan Engravings is practically unequaled in the history of printmaking. Robert Hughes aptly described the Circuits prints as taking on a "stiff, congested richness like mosaic or embossed hide, invoking a Byzantine degree of ceremonial excess."[18] It is, indeed, the dense materiality of these prints that most dramatically established their technical significance for the recent course of contemporary printmaking. The patent difference between Stella's prints and traditional ones is *surface*. The tactile appearance of the Bedford prints was achieved through multiple interactions of paper, mixed media, and the charging of paper until it was ink-saturated. Traditional prints are flat; Stella's adamantly are not.

In his paintings Stella has always desired a spatial dynamism, an activated space he has recently likened to that carved out by the human figure in old master paintings. Opticality of color and form achieved a quavering space in his shaped canvases of the 1960s and 1970s. In making these effects three-dimensional in the relief paintings of the later 1970s and 1980s, Stella so animated space that it was literally thrust at the viewer by means of jutting shapes. The assembly of these shapes has steadily become more open and projective in each new series. Although he admits that space is not the subject of his art but a means to expressiveness, Stella implies in his theoretical statements that its articulation in his metal-relief paintings offers a way out of what he perceives to be an impasse in modernist abstraction.[19] This concern has also affected the course of the recent prints, in which Stella has addressed the issue of space with a comparable fervor and intelligence.

The varied textures of ink-charged paper in the Circuits and the noticeably debossed areas of the Swans lend the prints subtle sculptural effects. A peculiarity of printing inks also contributes to an attainment of heightened optical qualities. Layers of ink constitute a thinner film of color than layers of viscous artist's paint, which produce a thicker, more inert curtain of pigment.[20] Intricate overprintings of ink on paper arguably allow drawing and shape a special elusiveness not permitted by paint on flat surfaces. If variform space in the metal-relief paintings can then be approximated in the prints through texture and the properties of printer's inks, it is also stylistically gained by a specific handling of form. In the Circuits and the Swan Engravings, Stella recapitulated the ambiguous spaces of Cubism. Spatial uncertainty in the Swans is established in the play between the tautly locked irregular shapes and the febrile drawing contained within each shape. The transparent, opaque, and translucent forms of the Circuits prints, interpenetrating and eliding in indeterminate positions, also recall the iridescences of Cubist form. In progressive proofs for *Pergusa Three,* the deliberate attainment of these effects is apparent. A shimmering oscillation of appearances is established not only by the intricately braided forms but also by webs of color-changing lines, loosely crayoned shapes, and the impress of wood grain. Spatial activation in the prints, although a two-dimensional fiction, is as lively as it is in the paintings, which, in contrast, rely on manipulations of literal, three-dimensional shapes.

The Bedford prints have been persistently experimental. But traditional notions of the print have never willfully been trifled with. Stella's prints are born of three central factors: a desire to achieve the strongest resolution of a pictorial idea as it is refracted through the properties of the print media, an instinctive curiosity about materials, and the wish to visit upon the prints the ambitions of his paintings. Just as Tyler has been an ideal collaborator for the technical realization of the prints, he also has been a firsthand witness to the attitude Stella has taken toward the enterprise of making prints. According to Tyler, "Stella tackles problems that are not easy. They are demanding, and he pulls them off. But I also see the risk taking: the color that may kill the other color, the drawing that may not work. But he goes ahead anyway. Frank never loses his enthusiasm for finding, for discovery. I like that. I like that in anybody. I particularly like that in a collaborator of any sort, especially in something called printmaking. It's a missing ingredient in a lot of life you experience. Frank never disappoints me." The technical significance of Stella's Bedford prints for the history of printmaking is considerable. The radical expansion of materials and the unconventional handling of print media and processes have contributed toward bringing the print squarely in line with the distinctive tendency of twentieth-century painting and sculpture to explore new materials and methods. In this respect, Stella's achievement in his printmaking is a genuine direction in his art, inasmuch as the paintings have always stretched the acceptable limits of media (commercial enamels, metallic paints, epoxy paints, fluorescent alkyds, wood, cardboard, felt, and ground glass) and supports (the shaped canvas and metal-relief construction).

The example set by Stella in his attitudes toward the print has been as important for other artists as the prints themselves. His impatience with the canonical world of printmaking frees the print to become something new. Risk taking is declared a bona fide instigator of creativity. And the print may draw the best from modern technology without being compromised. In his refashioning of how prints look, Stella has also loosened the hold of traditional print terminologies and documentation. Conventional technical descriptions of his later prints have become increasingly less revelatory as uses of, and extended interactions between, media, inks, elements, and paper have become more complex. Most significantly, by refusing to approach printmaking as an endeavor peripheral to the course of mainstream art, Stella has demonstrated that the print can be as viable a vehicle for elevated artistic concerns as the *genre noble,* painting.

The Bedford prints have, as Meyer Schapiro said of Arshile Gorky's paintings, "the grace of art" in being "beautifully made."[21] The material basis of all art contributes to meaning. The technical and physical dimension of Stella's prints and paintings is no exception. But its distinction lies in the extent to which it actively constitutes subject and provokes meaning. This we sense with our knowledge of Stella's working habits and, it will be argued, in his imagery. For Stella, the creative processes of tinkering, testing, putting together, correcting, recycling, and redoing are not means alone, as they are for most artists, but expressive ends in themselves. The focus of Stella's abstraction is the generation of form, the act of making.

A sense of continuous processing pervades Stella's art: the processing of a pictorial idea within a single series, the reprocessing of previous solutions into a new series. Series develop with an apparent logic from one to the next and follow a continuous line of elaboration.[22] As a series clears new ground, it, in turn, offers new sets of possibilities upon which the next series may be predicated. These transformations take place within a special system of shapes and designs. Imagery has always been derived from measuring and form-making tools (see p. 180). Straightedge and protractor engendered the purely abstract compositions of the 1960s and early 1970s. Since the Exotic Bird Series of the 1970s, however, additional devices have been introduced— T squares, French and flexible curves, templates, and pantographs—and the entire miscellany of drafting tools more explicitly depicted. The persistence of these objects, of their implied use in creating abstract form as well as their overt representation, establishes an iconography with significant thematic ramifications. As used in industry and in the architect's studio, drafting implements create plans for things to be made. For Stella, they are the means by which his abstract art is created, yet this is an art highly connotative in its delineation of generating and

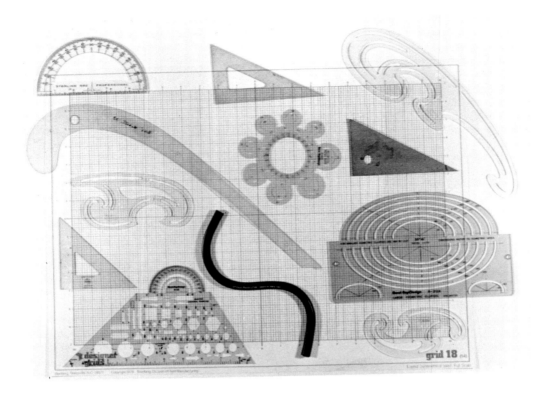

generated forms. The print or the painting portrays, in a figurative sense, what made it; the image appears to have created itself.

Stella's inclusion of graph-paper patterns also enhances a sense that an image is in the process of being realized. First used in the prints, then later borrowed for the metal-relief paintings, graph paper is at once a reference to the draftsman's table and to a method by which Stella's drawings are squared up for enlargement. The concept of the maquette is another conceit. The steps involved in making a metal-relief painting include models or maquettes—smaller, experimental versions that lead to the final work. A given metal-relief painting is often replicated in different sizes, which may comprise a "maquette" version and larger versions graduated in scale according to specific ratios. Stella brings into the realm of the finished painting the activities of the artist's preliminaries. The processes of *making* have a critical resonance in Stella's art, an art that in both the painting and print studios comes into being through distinct progressive stages and that is intensely collaborative because of the high degree of mechanical fabrication and technical assistance required. In this respect, Stella's enterprise of making art resembles that of the Renaissance studio, or better, factory, with its array of master painter, apprentices, and journeymen.

The artist's preoccupation with making has punctuated the history of modern art. Precedent was set in the pasted-together collages of Picasso and Georges Braque, in which disjunctive insertions of everyday materials and the printed word called attention to the fact that the work of art was an artificial concoction, not a seamless illusion of reality. In American art an emphasis on the act of creation has been pronounced

Drafting tools, including assorted triangles, protractors, and French curves.

since World War II. Existential and mystical significance was ascribed to Jackson Pollock's rapid applications of flung and poured paint, which—instead of the completed canvas—were conceived in the early critical literature as the locus of the work of art. The free linearities of Pollock's drip-and-spatter paintings were in fact related to the automatic line of the Surrealists, which tapped and transcribed unconscious sources of creativity. The development of a postpainterly abstraction in the early 1960s, with Stella's Stripe paintings at the center of critical debate, was first explicated in formalist language. Stella's art was described in terms of "deductive structures" of composition and "literalness" of materials and support as the means by which the work of art acknowledged itself as a thing made: an autonomous object, not a depiction of something. During the later 1960s and early 1970s new directions in abstraction, represented by the conceptually based art of Sol LeWitt and Dorothea Rockburne, led to form that was generated by preconceived, task-oriented instructions. The emergence of a post-Minimalist sculpture at the same time revealed a focus, most emphatic in the work of Robert Morris, Richard Serra, and Jackie Winsor, on process. The act of handling materials and making became a paradigm for sculpture.

The only contemporary American artist who approximates in his activities the character of Stella's persistent involvement with process is Jasper Johns, whose paintings and prints have explored the reworking of motifs through time and different media and whose iconography has included the form-making devices and cicada cross-hatching that have been read as cryptic emblems of the artist's marks. For Stella and Johns, as for Bertolt Brecht, "the showing must be shown." The essential generative identity of Stella's prints and paintings, however, has a distinctive tenor. Imagery is composed of two competitive visual systems. One instills order; the other, disorder. The stabilizing system is composed of precise edge and geometric form, an implied product of the form-making tools whose everyday function is the drafting of clearly delineated shapes. In opposition to this rational syntax are elements of disarray: complex geometries that fool the eye, shapes that act up; imprecise edges and scrawled calligraphies; color choices and juxtapositions that set up precarious agreements, resulting in opticalities that unravel any sense of order. Finally, there is Stella's indeterminate and fluctuating space.

The two components of Stella's art, distinct from each other in their qualities, recall the traditional critical designations of "Florentine line" and "Venetian color." These two terms refer to stylistic orientations that have been, with few exceptions, mutually exclusive in Western art since the Renaissance: line and its associations with clarity and the intellect; color and its associations with painterly form and the intuitive. Stella combines them. In the seventeenth century Nicolas Poussin integrated the two, but his distinct contours always contained the energies of his astringent color choices. The dialectic in Stella's art between line and color is different. The deliberate confrontation of precise, clean line and amorphous, bright color asserts acute and

unresolved tensions. Color and those elements considered disintegrative always have the upper hand, a slight edge in the argument. Ordering impulses are jeopardized. Stella reverses Paul Cézanne, in whose landscapes there is an emergent order; chaotic light and color are rationalized. Cézanne's art sublimates; Stella's subverts.

These interactions of forms alone, in which order clashes with disorder, have taken on a poetic resonance in Stella's prints and paintings, particularly since 1976, and have created their own archetypal tensions. Abstract patterns pit precision against spontaneity. As ordering and disordering elements are brought together but held in parities that threaten to disintegrate at any moment, imagery seems forever to be resolving itself. Forms spontaneously appear to remake themselves.

Frank Stella
Imola Three I   1982
relief, engraving on
TGL handmade paper
66 x 52
Collection Walker Art
Center, Minneapolis
Tyler Graphics Archive
(Tyler 565:FS24)

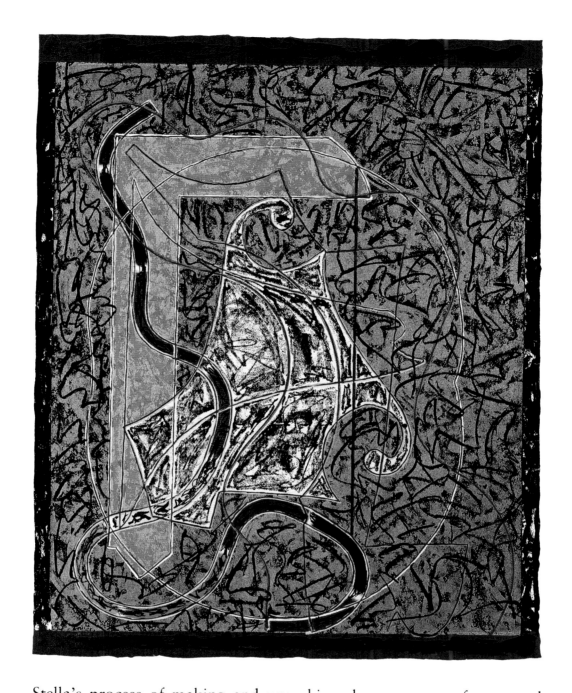

Frank Stella
Imola Three II 1984
relief, woodcut on
hand-colored TGL
handmade paper
66 x 52
Collection Walker Art
Center, Minneapolis
Tyler Graphics Archive
(Tyler 602:FS61)

Stella's process of making and unmaking shapes an art of perpetual change. This dynamic, operative in single prints and paintings, is further enhanced by the fact that he has always worked in series. A pictorial idea is explored in a set of varied but related works. The Tyler Circuits and the Swan Engravings, in addition to presenting the artist's world of opposing forces caught in precarious balance, achieve the most ambitious serialization to date in the prints, not simply in their extended number but also in the subtle changes afforded single prints in their own set of variations. The Circuits stand in a generalized relationship to one another by the repetition of centered skeins of lines and plays with borders. A single image like *Imola Three I* (p. 180) is altered in *Imola Three II* (p. 181), where the linear configuration is maintained

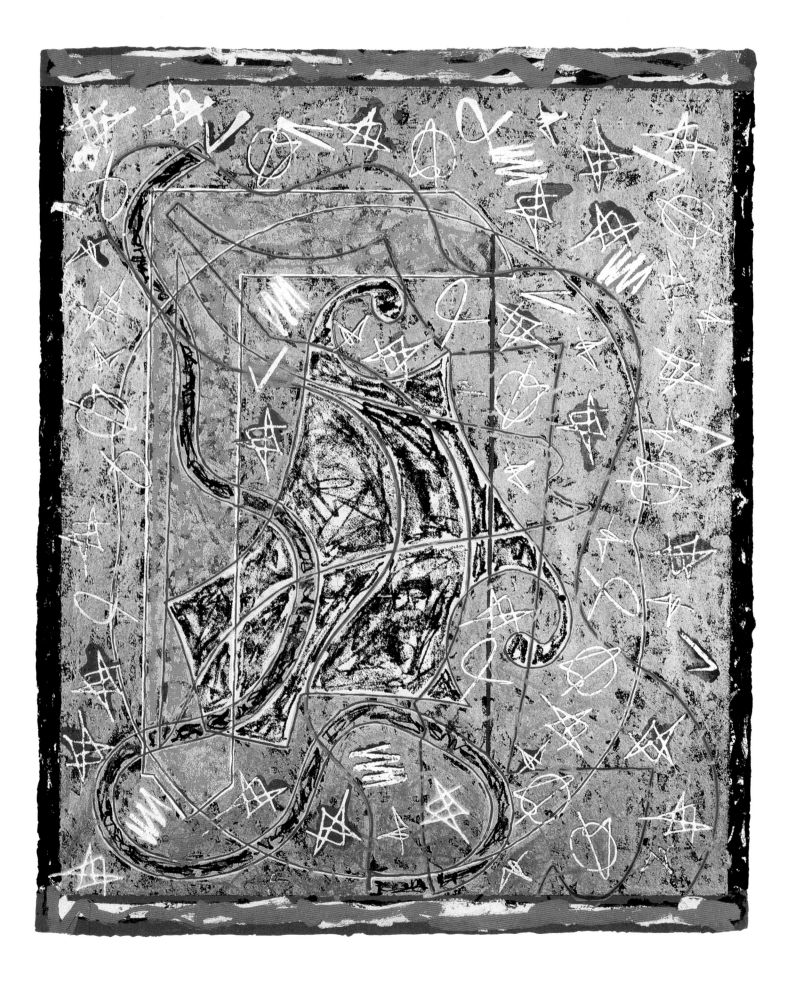

but all else changes: color, markings, and the prominence of certain shapes. *Imola Three II* is more tightly varied in *Imola Three II, State I* (p. 182): linear configuration, borders, and color markings of major shapes remain constant from one print to the other, but border colors, background graffiti, border markings, and the colors and segmentation of the large serpentine shape change.[23] A print's imagery may be amended in a new version by additional color inkings, wipings, and new plates, which are often the consequence of variant trial and color trial proofs that catch the artist's eye. State prints themselves multiply. In order to complicate the original plate and paper, for example, Stella trailed the black-and-white *Swan Engraving Circle I* and *Swan Engraving Circle II* with ten multicolor state editions.

Inasmuch as Stella's print series are related to painting series, any given print series further develops the serialized imagery of the paintings. The prints advance the visual arguments of the paintings in another medium, with its own capabilities for refiguring the image. Serialization is taken to new levels of complexity in the Circuits and Swan Engraving series. If transformation is central to Stella's art, these series best reveal an important aspect of the print for him: its potential within the context of its own processes and traditions for variation. The systems of permutation that are operative in each single print from the Circuits and Swan Engraving series are expanded in the serialization of imagery. A prodigious inventiveness characterizes these series as prints multiply dizzyingly. Nothing remains fixed. Seriality intensifies the tensions found within each image. Generated in time as one moves from print to print are the emotional overtones of serialization distilled by Lawrence Alloway in his choice of the words "transformation, destruction, and reconstruction."[24] Metamorphosis in the Circuits and Swans is aggressive. Protracted serialization italicizes the vulnerable quality of each print by swelling its context of volatility.

The continuous transformation of pictorial idea, the physical reminders of fabrication in the Circuits and the Swan Engravings, the draftsman's tools, the *perpetuum mobile* of ordering and disordering: at stake are metaphors of creativity itself. The prints are a species of self-portrait; the traditional Western theme of the artist's studio is evoked. This subject, as presented in Jan Vermeer's *Allegory of the Art of Painting,* has long been a vehicle for the dignifying of the painter's craft and the celebration of the creative act. Its treatment has become increasingly autobiographical and idiosyncratic in the modern period. Henri Matisse's lyrical *Red Studio*, with its gathering of the artist's own works, or Johns's iconic Savarin can imagery, a cogent parallel to Stella's iconography in its clustered artist's brushes, articulate the theme in visual plays upon the artist's act of representing the world. In Stella's art the finished work simultaneously registers allusions to the physical act of creating and also to its expressive issue: highly connotative works of abstraction. What we see is the artist Frank Stella's, and no one else's, invention: his personal world of the imagination, his act of rendering

Frank Stella
*Imola Three II,
State I* 1984
relief, woodcut,
stencil, screenprint on
hand-colored TGL
handmade paper
66 x 52
Courtesy Tyler
Graphics Ltd.
(Tyler 603:FS62)

it visible. Stella is the magician whose sleight of hand with tools and materials conjures up fantastic illusions out of mere printer's inks and papers. The poetics of his art, however, extend past the making of abstract metaphors of creativity alone. The forms we see resolving before us are allusive in shape and in title. They generate content and emotionalized fictions that lie beyond a world of self-contained, pure form.

The deciphering and relevance of Stella's titles have never been simple matters. Formalist criticism has dismissed them as literary adjuncts. Stella's titles, however, lend new levels of meaning to his imagery. The titles veil the work with dimensions of autobiography, history, geography, and political event. Implications are often concealed beneath unfamiliar-sounding words. The titles direct one's reading of the image: color it, poeticize it. They yield other sensuous dimensions. Such titles as *Puerto Rican Blue Pigeon, Inaccessible Island Rail,* and *Steller's Albatross* from the Exotic Bird Series have their own wit and outlandish charm. A raucous and resplendent aerie is called forth in which French curves are visual puns for bright plumage. Without their titles the prints are captivating enough; with them a new, more complicated world of perceptions opens up. The birds in question are extinct. Their blithe spirits and eccentric beauty have not so much been portrayed as poignantly memorialized. The ironic titling of the Exotic Bird Series is repeated in the Swan Engravings, whose titles are derived from a mundane reference to the factory where they were, in part, produced and from formal descriptions of imagery—color, composition, sequence number. Yet, independent of any objective function, the title "Swan Engraving" is lyrical, conjuring up, perhaps, some *raffiné* Symbolist portfolio. This particular suggestiveness, however, is rudely countered by the aggravated tensions of black and white, which, in *Swan Engraving Square II,* are apocalyptic. The titles accentuate an explosiveness that Tyler likens to "shattered glass." Shape and title combine—do not stand apart—to provoke meaning.

Of all the Stella series, the Circuits are, however, the most complex in their interactions of title and image. The exotic names of the Circuits prints—Talladega, Estoril, Imola, and Pergusa—identify Grand Prix and stock-car racing tracks.[25] Many of Stella's series titles derive from specific biographical contexts: here, the artist's fascination with racing and cars.[26] The titles and the careening skeins of lines elicit associations with the literal appearance and psychological feel of a racing course. The prints gain more specific meaning from the titles, but meaning is potentially figurative.[27] A circuit is a closed circular or curved path, the complete traversal of which requires returning to the same starting point. Stella's Circuits are not simple ones; they have no start or finish. As much as speeding-car circuits, they are labyrinths. The oblong, intertwined configurations of each Circuits print dominate a vertical sheet. Within a flattened, shallow space, they are relatively centered and frontal; that is, we do not look at the web of lines from an angle but square on. The visual presentation of the image in these particular ways—flattened and centered—is iconic.

The Circuits prints, then, are icons. Our relationship to them is direct and confrontational. We are placed in a position, as Joseph Masheck has written of abstract painting in general, of "the direct purveying of some elemental motif for our apprehension."[28] The elemental motif is the labyrinth. The calligraphic line of the labyrinth calls to mind Arabic script and the initial and carpet pages of Hiberno-Saxon illumination.[29] In its spontaneity and fluidity, Stella's autographic line, like the automatic line of Surrealism, suggests a primal and formative language. Although the magisterial emblems of the Circuits are not specific reproductions of either Christian or Moslem holy texts, they are imbued, like ancient writings, with transcendental mystery. The ambiguously interlaced configurations evoke sacred monograms and pictographs, their complexities not dissimilar from Christian initials and Islamic phrases that name deity as infinite and unknowable. The unresolved tensions and paradoxes of the interlaces are made emblematic. For the subject of our modern veneration is ambiguity itself. Indeterminacy is raised to the status of the mythic. The Circuits prints reaffirm abstraction's potential for dense levels of connotation and meaning.

Modern art, like modern science and philosophy, attempts to sort out how we understand the world. Frank Stella's prints and paintings rest on the traditional epistemological basis of abstraction, the lofty pursuit of addressing the nature of experience. Formalist exegesis alone cannot explain an art whose maker has stated: "Painting is always better the more it can account for, the more it's like the totality of what we know."[30] Making sense of and mythologizing experience is Stella's real enterprise. It is analogized in his art by acts and images of fabrication. In his recent theoretical statements, Stella has said much of Michelangelo da Caravaggio's formal renewal and elaboration of Renaissance space. But given his own attraction to the expressiveness of process, so clearly evident in the work he has done with Tyler, Stella's goal in making art transcends formalism and gives us other reasons for his fascination with the seventeenth-century Italian master. Or so he has hinted: "[Caravaggio's] realism extends to more than the successful portrayal of his subjects. He has the ability to make the act of making a picture so real that the paint appears fresh. We can feel the painting being painted. We can feel the painting coming to life. We can feel the red oil paint turning into spurting blood."[31] Caravaggio's gain is also Stella's.

Notes
1. Frank Stella, "On Caravaggio," *New York Times Magazine*, February 3, 1985, p. 71.
2. *Frank Stella: Prints, 1967–1982* was co-organized by the University of Michigan Museum of Art, Ann Arbor, and the American Federation of Arts, New York.
3. Richard H. Axsom, *The Prints of Frank Stella: A Catalogue Raisonné, 1967–1982*, exh. cat. (New York: Hudson Hills Press in association with the University of Michigan Museum of Art, Ann Arbor, 1983), p. 35.

4. For a discussion of Stella's work at Gemini G.E.L., see ibid., pp. 13–17, and Ruth E. Fine, *Gemini G.E.L.: Art and Collaboration* (Washington, D.C.: National Gallery of Art; New York: Abbeville Press, 1984), pp. 54–61.

5. Axsom, *Catalogue Raisonné,* p. 31.

6. Unless otherwise noted, Kenneth Tyler's remarks quoted in this essay were made in conversation with the author, November 1, 1984, and July 11, 1985, Bedford Village. The author wishes to express his sincere gratitude to Mr. Tyler for the generous donation of his time during which a multitude of questions were answered and invaluable insights provided. The author also acknowledges Barbara Delano, assistant to Mr. Tyler, whose frequent clarifications of documentation were indispensable to the preparation of this text.

7. There are periods during which Tyler and Stella work together, with shop assistants in attendance and actively participating. Private time in the workshop allows Stella to sort things out and present requests to Tyler for resolution before he returns for the next session. Stella's time away from Bedford gives him needed perspective on work in progress and also gives Tyler and his staff the opportunity to work out problems, the solutions to which may necessitate any number of experimental approaches.

8. Philip Leider, *Stella since 1970,* exh. cat. (Fort Worth, Tex.: Fort Worth Art Museum, 1978), p. 17.

9. In 1974 Stella had several Brazilian Series pieces made in steel that he wished to have etched. While collaborating with Swan Engraving on the making of plates and negatives for the Bedford workshop, Tyler saw Remington guns being etched. He then made arrangements for Swan Engraving to etch Stella's steel works. The attempt was inconclusive, and no other projects were undertaken in Bridgeport until the later 1970s.

10. Caroline Jones, "Spaces and the Enterprise of Painting," *Harvard Magazine* 86 (May–June 1984): 47.

11. The Exotic Bird Series was the first print project Tyler made at Bedford on a flatbed offset lithography press. Offset was adopted increasingly during the 1970s for advantages gained over stone lithography in general dependability and facility of use.

12. Axsom, *Catalogue Raisonné,* p. 31.

13. Tyler designed the large bench and had it built to accommodate the screen printing of twelve-foot canvases for Stella, an experimental effort that was discontinued.

14. The first block was printed in February 1982. An Estoril image was printed in black on lathed-up paper borrowed from an ongoing project being done by Robert Zakanitch. No available shop paper was large enough.

15. Color trial proofs for the Star of Persia Series, 1967, were cut up and used to create the V Series, 1968. Plates from the Polar Co-ordinates for Ronnie Peterson, 1980, were fragmented and used again in Shards, 1982. In the development of the relief paintings, the first inclusion of everyday materials occurred in a set of maquettes for the Indian Bird Series, 1977–78, for which, because certain materials were unavailable to the artist during a sojourn in India, flattened pop cans with their logos showing were used.

16. The only historical precedents for this type of element and printing are William Blake's metal-relief prints and Stanley William Hayter's experiments with simultaneous printing from relief and intaglio surfaces. But Stella's and Tyler's work was not undertaken in a self-conscious emulation of the past. The Circuits and the Swan Engravings developed from Stella's paintings. In scale and elaboration, the prints are utterly different from anything that came before.

17. Printers Rodney Konopaki and Bob Cross were responsible for the demanding edition printing of the Swan Engravings and *Talladega Three I.* It is a tribute to their abilities that Stella entrusted the critical wiping of the plates to them. Half a day of shop time was entailed in the inking of a single Swan plate. After each impression was pulled, the plate was then cleared of ink and prepared once again.

    Many of the printers at Tyler Graphics are often entrusted with crucial aspects of printing and fabrication. They are active collaborators on shop projects. Intentionally trained by Tyler to assume almost any task, they stand apart in their versatility from traditional printers who specialize in a particular process. For example, Steve Reeves and Tom Strianese were responsible for the proofing and edition printing of the Circuits and also for the papermaking. Professional competence and excellence have made Cross, Konopaki, Reeves, Strianese, and Roger Campbell, Pete Duchess (at the Swan Engraving Company), Lee Funderburg, and Duane Mitch indispensable contributors to the long-term Circuits and Swan Engravings projects. Although no longer at Tyler Graphics, John Hutcheson, Kim Halliday, and Todd Johnston, who collaborated with Stella and Tyler on the Exotic Bird Series and the hand-colored screenprints, should also be mentioned.

18. Robert Hughes, *Frank Stella: The Swan Engravings,* exh. cat. (Fort Worth, Tex.: Fort Worth Art Museum, 1984), p. 7.

19. Stella has argued persuasively for the centrality of space as depicted and periodically reinvented by the painter, particularly in the case of Caravaggio's illusionistic projection of space and human action into the viewer's sphere. But Stella has never confused his formal terms with the expressivity of his art: "Space is part of the spirit of the thing, but it's secondary. The aim of art is to create space. You must have space in printing and you must have space in painting. The question of space is an inherent one, not the subject matter" (Judith Goldman, *Frank Stella: Fourteen Prints with Drawings, Collages, and Working Proofs,* exh. cat. [Princeton, N.J.: Art Museum, Princeton University, 1983], p. 16). For Stella's recent comments on this issue, see Jones, "Spaces and the Enterprise of Painting," p. 47; Stella's Charles Eliot Norton Lectures, given at Harvard University in 1983–84, published in Frank Stella, *Working Space* (Cambridge: Harvard University Press, 1986); and Stella, "On Caravaggio," p. 71.

20. Stella has commented upon the differences in media: "Print ink is irredeemably different from oil and acrylic art pigments. The quality of multiple layers of ink is very different from multiple layers of pigment" (Goldman, *Frank Stella,* p. 15).

21. Meyer Schapiro, "Arshile Gorky," in *Modern Art, Nineteenth and Twentieth Centuries: Selected Papers* (New York: George Braziller, 1979), p. 182.

22. An exclusively aesthetic reading of continuity between series is provocatively qualified by Carter Ratcliff's supposition that Stella's reprocessing of imagery reflects the strategies of American corporate marketing. See "Frank Stella: Portrait of the Artist as an Image Administrator," *Art in America* 74 (February 1985): 94–107.

23. Involved in the state prints, as in the "variations," are new color inkings and wipings and new plates, not reworkings of original print elements alone, which constitute the technical definition of the traditional state print. But such definitions are beside the point when the distinctions made in the use of the term *state print* are visual and not purely technical. The relationship between the original print and its state print is defined by the closeness of the variation.

24. Lawrence Alloway, "Systemic Painting," reprinted in *Minimal Art: A Critical Anthology,* ed. Gregory Battcock (New York: E. P. Dutton, 1968), p. 56. This essay formed the introduction to the exhibition catalogue *Systemic Painting* (New York: Solomon R. Guggenheim Foundation, 1966). Given the development during the 1970s of a poststructuralist art criticism that addressed the generation of meaning on levels other than the purely visual, Alloway's challenge to formalism was prescient. His essay concludes: "Formal analysis needs the iconographical and experiential aspects, too, which can no longer be dismissed as literary except on the basis of an archaic aestheticism."

25. Estoril is located in Portugal, Imola in Italy, Pergusa in Sicily. Talladega is a stock-car track in Alabama.

26. There is a history of racing as a theme in Stella's prints and paintings. In the Race Track Series of the early 1970s, titles name horse-racing tracks in Southern California and Mexico—Del Mar, Los Alamitos, Agua Caliente. Stella has followed horse racing and Grand Prix racing for years. In the 1970s he traveled in Europe with the BMW team, and in 1976 he painted a BMW stock car with Stella grids and French curves. His interest in racing brought him into contact with Ronnie Peterson, the Swedish Grand Prix race driver, whose death at Monza in 1978 provided a motive for the print series Polar Co-ordinates for Ronnie Peterson, a series that was conceived, as much of Stella's art has been, as a tribute.

27. The artist's own comments about the titles of the series corroborate the idea of a resonant set of meanings for the Circuits prints that is not limited to the automotive. Originally, Stella had considered "Race Circuits" but abandoned it for "Circuits" because the single-word title was more ambiguous (conversation with author, Knoedler Gallery, New York, October 1981).

28. The relationship of abstraction and the icon has been astutely explored by Joseph Masheck, an American critic who has argued for the inherently spiritual basis of modern abstraction. See his collected writings on the subject in *Historical Present: Essays of the 1970s* (Ann Arbor, Mich.: UMI Research Press, 1984), pp. 143–228. In keeping with the visual strategies of the Byzantine or Russian icon, intended by church doctrine to establish a transcendental realm apart for veneration, abstraction sustains an "aura of the sacred." Masheck has further observed that abstraction, in both its geometric and painterly modes, was evolved by two Russian painters, each with documented fascinations for the icon: Kasimir Malevich and Wassily Kandinsky. The iconic qualities of early abstraction were compatible with the theosophical content claimed by the early abstractionists.

29. Stella's junior-year essay at Princeton was on Hiberno-Saxon manuscript illumination. The relationship between this interest and the Protractors has previously been observed by William S. Rubin in *Frank Stella,* exh. cat. (New York: Museum of Modern Art, 1970), pp. 146, 155.

30. Jones, "Spaces and the Enterprise of Painting," p. 46.

31. Stella, "On Caravaggio," p. 60.

A History of Papermaking

Leonard B. Schlosser

The making of paper by hand, in any commercial sense a romantic throwback to the bygone age of handcrafts, has now become an accepted part of the aesthetics of contemporary art, and the work of Kenneth Tyler as printmaker and papermaker stands at the forefront of that development. The use of paper as an integral part of the art object, rather than simply as a carrier of the image, did not originate with Tyler; nor is it his alone, as the recent proliferation of paperworks by others testifies.

Professionally handmade paper has provided interesting—sometimes exciting—printmaking substrates, and some artists have learned the papermaker's craft for use in creating their own images. Tyler is among the few, however, to offer papermaking by hand as an on-premises tool to extend the reach of the artist within the printmaking shop. His particular use of paper is important to the development of contemporary art, for he has broadened the artist's vocabulary by treating paper as essential to the printmaking process.

Although the traditional papermaking process has remained basically unchanged in his hands, Tyler has adapted preexisting techniques to the contemporary idiom, combining technical virtuosity with unceasing innovation. The history of paper and the development of papermaking techniques have been part of Tyler's integration of papermaking into his work. His insatiable curiosity, along with a mechanical instinct rarely encountered in the art world, has led him along new paths, always guided by elements from the past. For example, in his 1973 project with Robert Rauschenberg at the Moulin à Papier Richard de Bas in France, he used "cookie-cutter" papermaking molds or templates of galvanized metal to define the images (see p. 190). These were an outgrowth of the stencils used in Japanese papermaking, which he had encountered during a visit to Osaka. Oriental paper, in fact, has provided inspiration for him, although his papermaking techniques are more often Western in origin. Knowledge of the differences between the two traditions is basic to an understanding of Tyler's accomplishments.

Kenneth Tyler pouring colored pulp into a mould for a multicolored sheet for the Kenneth Noland Handmade Paper Project, 1978.

For the first fourteen hundred–odd years of its use, paper was entirely a writing material, and only after A.D. 1450 did it become the carrier of images and printed words in a European sense. The origins of paper in China during the first century A.D. are documented in later Chinese texts, and modern findings by Western explorers and Chinese investigators have confirmed the existence of paper a few years before the birth of Christ. Paper, as distinguished from other earlier flexible writing substrates (leaves, bark, papyrus), is formed from a suspension of fibers in water (see p. 191). The fibers are deposited onto a sievelike carrier (called a mould), from which the water drains away, leaving the fibers in the form of a wet mat that is then removed and dried (see

p. 192). In the Chinese method the damp, limp sheet of paper would be brushed onto a smooth board (or, in later times, a smooth, heated tile surface) and permitted to dry completely. One side, consequently, was rougher than the other, the smooth side being the one touching the board or tile.

Fiber for the earliest Oriental papers varied from the linen or hemp of China to the kozo (paper mulberry, *Broussonetia papyrifera*) of Japan, where papermaking began in the early seventh century. Until the nineteenth century, Oriental papers were most often made of fibers obtained from the plant's stalk or bark by a cooking and maceration process. Both the raw material and the process changed in about A.D. 1250, when paper came to Europe, where it was made from rags. Distinctly different from the Oriental product, Western paper is harder, with a more compact surface.

The traditional writing methods of the East and West differ as much as their papers. In the East, densely pigmented ink of carbon black was

Kenneth Tyler and Robert Rauschenberg positioning a galvanized metal image mold for *Link*, from Rauschenberg's Pages and Fuses. Richard de Bas paper mill, Ambert, France, 1973.

removed from the surface of an ink block by brush and water. In the West, a sharpened goose quill was used to apply ink made of lampblack suspended in water and mixed with ox gall for easy flow. Writing with quills predated the use of paper in the West and may have had some influence upon the earliest Western paper, but in any case it is certain that Western writing technique could not have been adapted to the typical soft, absorbent Eastern paper, so admirably suited to the brush.

By the thirteenth century the cloth or split bamboo moulds of the East had given way to the typical Western mould made of brass wire, the primary tool of hand papermaking, which is still used today when paper is made by hand in the European tradition. The mould is a strong

and rigid frame, made more rigid by transverse ribs that must endure long and repeated immersion in water without warping. Over the frame a screen of some type is stretched tight to prevent sagging. From the time of the earliest European papermaking until the 1760s, this screen was composed of closely spaced wires, usually parallel to the length of the mould, and sewn at right angles every inch or so to its supporting ribs. The closely spaced lengthwise wires are called "laid" wires, and the marks caused by them in the paper, seen when it is held up to the light, are called "laid" lines. The more widely spaced translucent marks caused by the crosswise wires sewn over the ribs are called "chain" marks. The basic construction of the mould frame and ribs, all of wood (usually mahogany for the frame and a white wood for the ribs), is the same in modern hand moulds, but modern materials permit a wider choice of metal screening.

In the late eighteenth century, when machine-drawn wire had replaced the handmade product and when power looms permitted the weaving of wire cloth for screening, the "wove" mould was invented by John Baskerville, the famed printer of Birmingham, England. This revolutionary development was accomplished by stretching woven wire cloth over the mould frame, replacing the unidirectional laid wires. Since the water now drained through the holes of the screen rather than through longitudinal channels, there was no discernible pattern of translucent lines, and the surface of the paper was likely to be considerably smoother. Papermaking in the Tyler shop has utilized both types of Western moulds as well as Oriental ones in order to achieve specific effects in sheet thickness and surface.

Tyler first came to papermaking in search of a new kind of colored surface, to be developed somehow by the addition of dyes, pigments, or papermaking fiber before the printing process. His experiment with Rauschenberg at Ambert was the first of many attempts to apply color to the surface of handmade paper. The application of colored pulp as pure form continued in Ellsworth Kelly's Colored Paper Images, 1976 (see pp. 194–95, 212–13), in which the two-dimensionality of the print is belied by the modeling of the colored pulp, which the artist poured onto the wet surface of the white background paper in the process of papermaking. The work, done in collaboration with Tyler and paper-makers John and Kathleen Koller, inevitably resulted in a bleeding of the colored portion of the prints that was atypical of Kelly's hard-edge style. Moving from there to David Hockney's 1978 Paper Pools (see pp. 196–97, 219–21, 240) was a logical step: in them, pulp was applied to define natural, rather than abstract, forms for the first time, a process made possible by outlining with "cookie cutters" (which Hockney called "biscuit cutters").

The heavy, relatively unmodeled application of the colored pulp in the Hockney works presented new problems. After removal from the mould by the process called *couching*, paper had always been pressed as the second step in water removal, drainage through the mould having

Steve Reeves and Tom Strianese of Tyler Graphics couching a sheet of newly made paper, 1986.

Steve Reeves and Tom Strianese removing a large mould from the couching table, 1986.

been the first. The process of couching is of European origin (the word comes from the French *coucher*, "to lay"). To facilitate the pressing of water from the newly formed sheets, the sheets are transferred, one by one, from the mould to felts. The vatman hands the mould to the coucher, who turns it over and with a rocking motion deposits the sheet onto the topmost of a pile of felts. As he turns to the vatman to hand him back the now empty mould, the vatman hands him another carrying

Ellsworth Kelly spooning colored pulp through a plastic image mold during proofing for edition standard of *Colored Paper Image XXI*, HMP paper mill, Woodstock, Connecticut, 1976.

Ellsworth Kelly
*Colored Paper Image
XIII* 1976
colored, pressed paper
pulp
32¼ x 31¼
Collection Walker Art
Center, Minneapolis
Tyler Graphics Archive
(Tyler 309:EK16)

David Hockney
Steps with Shadow,
Paper Pool 2 1978
colored, pressed paper
pulp
50½ x 33½
Collection Walker Art
Center, Minneapolis
Tyler Graphics Archive
(Tyler 237:DH2)

(opposite, top)
David Hockney,
Lindsay Green, and
Kenneth Tyler
applying colored pulp
using straight metal
strips, for *A Large
Diver*, driveway
adjacent to TGL paper
mill, 1978.

(opposite, bottom)
David Hockney
applying colored pulp
with a turkey baster
through a galvanized
metal image mold, for
Steps with Shadow,
TGL paper mill, 1978.

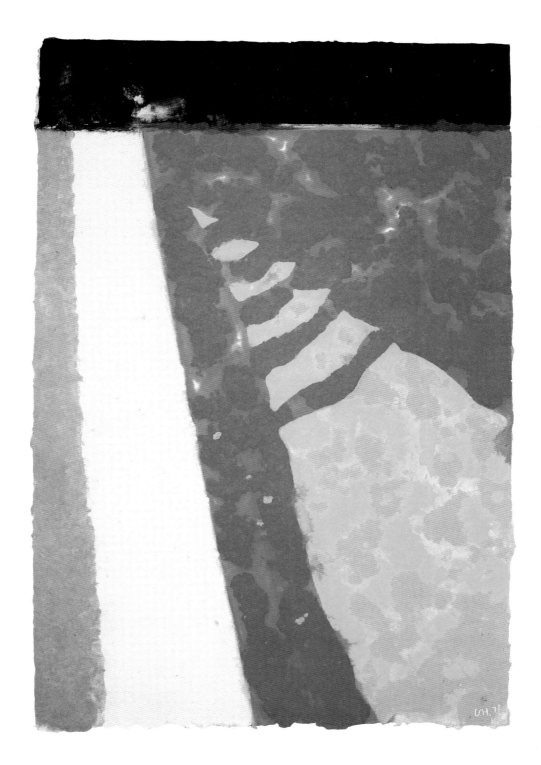

a newly formed sheet, and during this pass, the third member of the papermaking team places another felt on top of the one supporting the last sheet. Once the pile of alternating sheets of paper and felts (the "post") has built up to some height, it is hauled off to a press, where mechanical or hydraulic pressure is applied to it to remove water. The post is removed from the press, reversed sheet by sheet, and pressed again. The sheets may then be sized before being dried either by being hung over ropes in a loft or by the newer method of applying warm air. Pressing Tyler's works was far more complicated than this traditional process, for it required maintaining colored images on the surface of the sheet. It also required, in the Hockney project, application of pressure to an unusually large sheet.

The question of scale became increasingly important to Tyler as yet another stimulant to the artist's creative process. Sheet size in handmade paper had always been limited by the strength required to pull the mould straight up from the vat of pulp and water, fighting the accompanying suction. Papermakers in the West developed powerful arms since one man normally handled the mould alone, even for oversized sheets (such as those made in the early 1800s for the Audubon double elephant folio—40 by 26¾ inches). In Japan and other Eastern countries pulley systems were customarily used to help lift large moulds.

Tyler knew that there was a precedent for making oversize sheets and that hydraulic presses large enough to squeeze water out of them existed in other industries; it was simply a matter of using his own mechanical ingenuity to adapt preexisting tools to make ever-larger sheets of paper. Moulds for the Tyler shop had to be specially fabricated on a scale never seen before in Western hand papermaking, and vats had to be constructed to accommodate these huge wooden frames, which were lifted by two or more people, sometimes with mechanical help (see p. 199). It was Tyler's continual experimentation that enabled Hockney to work comfortably on his Paper Pools on a scale never before possible.

While exploring the definition of images by colored pulp alone, as in the Rauschenberg, Kelly, and Hockney projects, Tyler also attempted to develop a printable, applied-color surface. His earlier approach, used in his work with Ronald Davis in 1975 and with Stanley Boxer from 1976 to 1979, had been to superimpose the printed image on paper with colored surface areas made by his "cookie-cutter" mold technique. Tyler soon began experimenting with couching a formed sheet of colored paper onto another base sheet, again a process with a precedent, this time in Oriental papermaking. Having begun to use this technique as early as 1974 with Robert Motherwell's *The Stoneness of the Stone,* Tyler expanded it in Kenneth Noland's Handmade Paper Project of 1978 (see pp. 215, 217), in which a laid sheet of one color was couched onto a wove sheet of another color, and then the completed sheet was printed. The Noland pieces involved another new element: they utilized paper made from traditional Japanese fibers on traditional Japanese moulds (in some cases Western moulds were used to form the sheets).

Electric hoist, harness, and metal frame to assist papermakers in lifting large, heavy moulds from the vat.

Steve Reeves and Tom Strianese removing fifty-two-by-sixty-six-inch mould from vat using an electric hoist. Paper is for Frank Stella's *Pergusa Three Double*, TGL paper mill, 1983.

Making a thin, yet strong sheet from the Japanese kozo or gampi (a wild shrub, *Wikstroemia canescens*, whose inner bark is a prized papermaking fiber in Japan) appealed to Tyler. He obtained from Japan quantities of the raw plant fiber, which he prepared for papermaking. The Noland pieces are further complicated by the inclusion of bits of colored wool fiber. The problems of producing a printable sheet of such a compound nature—laid couched on wove, Oriental couched on Western fiber, both with inclusions—can hardly be imagined. The success of the Noland project is testimony to Tyler's ability to join his resources and ingenuity with Noland's creative effort in the type of partnership Tyler has always sought—one in which the printer does not become the dominating partner.

Prior to the Noland project and in the midst of his continuing early work with colored surface, Tyler published Frank Stella's Paper Reliefs (pp. 208–9), his only major publication in which paper was formed three-dimensionally and fabricated elsewhere. Stella designed the moulds on which John Koller made the paper, but the actual papermaking was carried out by Koller in his shop. Despite their aesthetic success, the finished high-relief images, which were collaged by Koller and painted individually by Stella, are now regarded by Tyler as something of a dead end in papermaking terms. His subsequent work with paper led Tyler away from relief and toward two-dimensionality, but with ever more complicated colored surfaces and ever-expanding scale.

Tyler's desire for improved ink receptivity has led to constant experimentation with fiber treatment, sizing materials, pressing, and all the other variables of the papermaking process in order to provide a printing surface of superior quality. When demand for paper soared with Johannes Gutenberg's invention of printing from movable type around 1450, its characteristics began to change. By 1500 printing paper had begun to be distinguished from writing paper, the former requiring absorbency for oil-base ink and the latter requiring a hard surface, achieved by "sizing" with glue or gelatin, to prevent the spread of water-base writing ink. The advent of engraving and etching techniques required far more refinement and consistency of surface from sheet to sheet, and within each sheet, than had writing, typographic printing, or the printing of images from woodblocks. As the craft of papermaking spread from country to country in Europe, some papers were sought after for their whiteness (this was before the days of chemical bleaching), others for their stiffness, their surface qualities, or their printability.

Because the smoother, more absorbent Oriental papers could not stand the stress of being dampened and then run through a rolling press, early nineteenth-century printers glued them to a Western base sheet. When it was printed and glued down at the same time (chine collé), China paper provided a smooth, ink-receptive surface, especially ideal for the reproduction of the finest lines of intaglio plates. Tyler has adopted various approaches using this method, either in white or in color, especially in some of the prints by Robert Motherwell and in

Motherwell's book *El Negro*. Tyler has always been concerned with printability, and while he is certain that that is best achieved by the use of freshly made paper from his own shop, he has nevertheless resorted from time to time to the dry collé method, rather than to the wet application of another sheet in the papermaking process itself. The visual effects are different as well, both because of the more sharply defined area of collé and the simultaneous printing and gluing that takes place in that process, as opposed to the softer, more textured surface of the wet application.

Tyler is well aware that there is nothing inherently wrong with machine-made paper—especially the mould-made product—and he has often used it. But the limitations of size and, more important, of color and surface have turned him toward handmade paper and, in more recent years, toward his own production. Almost half of the editions made in his Bedford studio between 1974 and 1985 were printed on handmade paper, and Tyler estimates that more than ten thousand sheets have been made in his own shop. All are larger than twenty-two by thirty-five inches, and about a third of the production has been made on his largest moulds, particularly the paper used for Stella's Circuits. The high average weight of Tyler's sheets, not to mention their complexity, precludes any quantitative comparison with commercial handmade paper.

With the production of the first of Stella's Circuits, Tyler accomplished a long-sought goal. He and Stella had determined that the heavily printed surface should have underlying areas of color in the paper itself. To fabricate paper that would have a varicolored surface, be larger than any sheet the Tyler shop had yet produced, and be able to stand the strain of repeated passes through the printing press was perhaps the greatest challenge the Tyler papermakers had faced, but they met it successfully.

Tyler's papermaking has been revolutionary precisely because he has stuck to the simple essentials of hand papermaking while using modern technology and a modern artistic viewpoint to draw more from the process than might at first appear possible. While Tyler's papermaking techniques are little different from those of the eighteenth century, his innovations in the use of applied colored surfaces represent a unique contribution to printmaking when integrated with his development of large-scale printed images. Tyler's concern with permanence, too, is typical of his modern approach within the confines of this ancient craft. He has scrupulously used acid-free materials and nonfugitive dyes so that longevity has not fallen prey to experiment and innovation.

In his papermaking, as in his printing, Tyler's objective has always been to expand the creative arsenal of the artist without permitting the process itself to dominate. Tyler's ventures into papermaking have transcended the merely novel to become a means of expression integrated into the printmaking process itself.

Paperworks at Tyler Graphics

Ruth E. Fine

Given Kenneth Tyler's absorbing interest in the technology and materials of printing, it is not surprising that the physical properties of paper have engaged his imagination and efforts. For example, a search for large sheets was spurred by Robert Rauschenberg's seventy-two-inch-high *Booster,* 1967 (p. 16). Tyler sought papers with a neutral pH that would last for centuries, rather than a cheaper, nonarchival product. Working with manufacturers here and abroad, he was able to meet these special needs. By 1969 a commercially produced French sheet, Special Arjomari, was available to carry the eighty-nine-inch-high images of *Sky Garden* and *Waves,* from Rauschenberg's Stoned Moon series.

Many people were instrumental in aiding Gemini's paper research, which was supported in part by a grant from the National Endowment for the Arts. Tyler established connections with paper manufacturers and distributors in the United States and Europe, including Larry Hardy of Crown Zellerbach and Vera Freeman of Andrews Nelson Whitehead. It was through Hardy that he made a connection with the S. D. Warren Company's facilities in Westbury, Maine. Tyler worked closely with them, testing papers for many factors, making paper in the lab, and "deviling up" some ideas that led, for example, to the use of Warren's Lowell paper for Frank Stella's V Series, published by Gemini a year after *Booster.* Tyler also worked closely with the Rochester Paper Mill in Rochester, Michigan, where neutral-pH papers were created on a Fourdriniers paper machine to have some of the characteristics of mould-made paper. From this experimental project a waterleaf paper named Roleaf was developed for Josef Albers's 1971 White Embossings on Gray. The project also produced a neutral rag board that became a mill product called Gemini rag board. Tyler was eager to have the great French mill Arjomari-Prioux participate in his programs. Problematical was the fact that at the time the minimum production possible was a ton of pulp, far too much for Gemini's needs.[1] However, Tyler maintained a close working relationship with Elie d'Humières, the director for fine arts papers at Arjomari-Prioux.

Robert Zakanitch
Straightback Swans II
1981
colored, pressed paper pulp
four sheets: 85 x 70
Collection Walker Art Center, Minneapolis
Tyler Graphics Archive
(Tyler 620:RZ34)

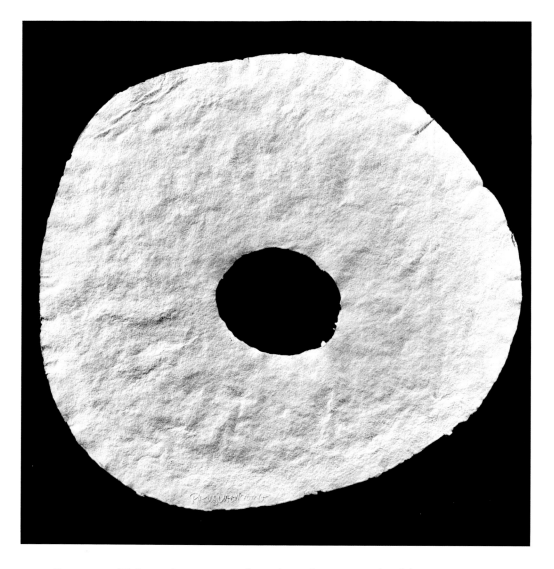

By 1969 Tyler's interest in handmade papers had been aroused. As a guest artist at the Cranbrook Academy of Art in Bloomfield Hills, Michigan, he spent time talking with Laurence Barker about papermaking and observed the mill Barker had set up. As a result of this encounter, a pure white paper was produced at the school from old diapers, especially for Roy Lichtenstein's *Modern Head #2* and *Modern Head #3*, which were published by Gemini the following year. Also during this trip, Tyler met John Koller, then a student of Barker's, who later set up the HMP paper mill in Woodstock Valley, Connecticut, only a few hours' drive from Tyler's present workshop.

Handmade papers remained on Tyler's mind. In 1970 he was in Japan for the Osaka world's fair, where Claes Oldenburg's *Giant Ice Bag—Scale A,* produced by Gemini, was featured at the entrance to the United States pavilion. On a side trip to Kyoto the printer encountered brilliantly dyed papers airing on clotheslines. Immensely impressed by their beauty, he "was convinced that rich color could be incorporated into Western papermaking."[2] A few years later he had an opportunity to find out. With assistance from Vera Freeman and Elie d'Humières,

Robert Rauschenberg
Page 2 1974
natural-fiber
handmade paper
22 x 22
Collection Walker Art
Center, Minneapolis
Gift of Mr. and Mrs.
Miles Q. Fiterman;
purchased with the aid
of funds from the
National Endowment
for the Arts

Robert Rauschenberg
Link 1974
natural-fiber
handmade paper, with
embedded screen-
printed tissue
25 x 20
Collection Walker Art
Center, Minneapolis
Gift of Mr. and Mrs.
Miles Q. Fiterman;
purchased with the aid
of funds from the
National Endowment
for the Arts

Gemini was able to rent a week's mill time at the Moulin à Papier Richard de Bas in Ambert, France. The plan was to go there with an artist and work with Marius Peraudeau and his staff. Choosing the artist was easy: Robert Rauschenberg, in Tyler's opinion, was "the only artist at that time who had enough information in terms of handmade and mould-made papers and who was an on-the-spot kind of image-inventor."

Rauschenberg, ripe for the challenge, created his Pages and Fuses. The five Pages (see p. 204) are monochrome works of austere elegance made from variously proportioned mixtures of two types of rag pulp (one unbleached and dark gray, the other bleached white). The six Fuses (see p. 205), by contrast, are marked by the vivid colors of fine Swiss dyes, eccentric shapes, and the bounteous collage of images

Rauschenberg persistently offers in his art. For the Fuses, the images were screen-printed in California and shipped to France to be laminated into the pulp as it was formed. While the Pages and Fuses are not the earliest examples of an artist's employing the pulp medium, the high visibility of Rauschenberg's art combined with the sheer beauty of these pieces undoubtedly helped spark the widespread interest in working with pulp that soon developed.[3] In addition, for Tyler, the project initiated the concept of using "cookie-cutter" templates to form paper-pulp shapes, which became increasingly complex in later projects such as David Hockney's Paper Pools.

Pages and Fuses was one of Tyler's last projects at Gemini, but it was only the first of his many important collaborations with artists working with paper. In establishing Tyler Graphics Ltd., Tyler wanted to set up a paper mill in addition to installing equipment immediately for all of the printing processes. He was eager to work with artists who might respond to this exceedingly diverse material, and his collaborations with them have been among his great accomplishments. Tyler's own paper mill was completed in 1978. Before that, however, he completed projects in paper with Ronald Davis, Frank Stella, and Ellsworth Kelly, working with John and Kathleen Koller at their HMP mill in Connecticut.

The Davis project came first, and it involved printing as well as work in pulp. Davis's keen interest in materials and specialized processes was familiar to Tyler from earlier collaborations at Gemini. For example, in Davis's Cube Series, 1970, offset lithographs were mounted on plastic with a Mylar overlay, creating shaped, shiny, layered pieces that were part print, part object. Paper pulp became another means of achieving expressive surfaces with spatial implications. The new images were composed of planar and geometric structures, defining—and defined by—the fluctuating activity surrounding them. The scale is elusive: toylike objects in a galactic space. A sectioned plastic template of pinwheels, diamonds, and panels of color was placed on a newly formed, wet sheet of paper to establish the structures of Davis's printed pulp pieces. Pigmented pulps were then spooned into the individual sections. As in printing, variant trial sheets were produced prior to final decisions on the precise nature and distribution of colors. The wetness of both the base sheet and the pulps created a softness at the edges of the colored shapes, a softness that is both mirrored and countered by an image that was printed from a copper plate onto the pulp understructure after it was dry. In Bent Beam (p. 207), for example, the copper plate was worked in both aquatint and etching, and the fluid quality of the colored pulp is echoed by the aquatint splotches. Together they challenge the linear geometry of the velvety etched lines that establish a taut structure.

By 1979 Tyler had a far greater menu of possibilities to offer artists who came to Bedford Village to work in paper pulp. Working there again in that year, Davis planned images to be printed on specially made multicolor sheets (see pp. 100–101). In them, dense, opaque colors are

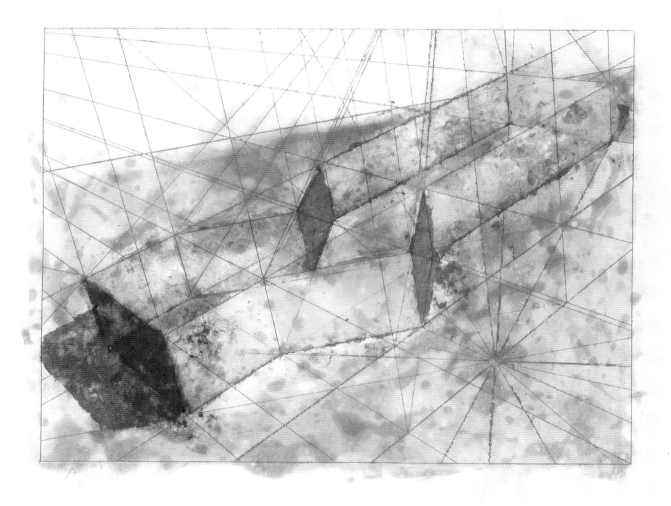

Ronald Davis
Bent Beam 1975
aquatint, etching on
hand-colored HMP
handmade paper
20 x 24
Collection Walker Art
Center, Minneapolis
Tyler Graphics Archive
(Tyler 165:RD4)

worked in lithography and screen printing. Shapes are tightly contained.
The variegated pulp base sheets are especially rich in comparison with
the sheets in Davis's earlier project.

Frank Stella's sumptuous cast Paper Reliefs also were executed at
HMP (see pp. 208–9).[4] Six groups of pieces were completed. Five are
in "editions" of twenty-six unique variants, plus proofs, including two
sets of trial proofs for each made from impenetrable, brown-black pulp.
The sixth structure, *Bogoria (VI),* exists in a total of only eight examples.
The configurations stem from Stella's 1970–73 Polish Village Series, the
artist's first painting series to employ relief elements. After the Paper
Reliefs were formed over the three-dimensional brass-screening and
mahogany moulds, every one was individually collaged and painted,
using casein paints, watercolors, and dyes. The collage layers, generally
on the highest surfaces, incorporate various sheets of handmade paper,
also from the HMP mill. These altered the surfaces of the planes, affecting

Frank Stella
Olyka (III)   1975
paper-pulp relief,
collage, hand-colored
26 x 21½ x 1¾
Collection Walker Art
Center, Minneapolis
Tyler Graphics Archive
(Tyler 544:FS3)

Frank Stella
Kozangrodek (II)
1975
paper-pulp relief,
collage, hand-colored
26 x 21½ x 1¾
Collection Walker Art
Center, Minneapolis
Tyler Graphics Archive
(Tyler 543:FS2)

the receptivity of the paint that was applied later. Some collage sheets in themselves gave color to surfaces. Where paint was applied, one color was often placed over another, the colors underneath remaining visible at the edges of forms. Evidence of this layering provokes further awareness of the constructed evolution of the pieces. The colors altered the spatial structures; texture was also a crucial element in this regard. Both factors have had reverberations in Stella's more recent prints. (For a discussion of Stella's investigation of pigmented papers at Tyler Graphics, see "Frank Stella at Bedford.")

Tyler's last collaboration with the Kollers at HMP was Ellsworth Kelly's Colored Paper Images.[5] This was also the first Tyler Graphics project worked entirely in paper pulp, and it was Kelly's first experience with the medium. "I was intrigued with the idea of another way of putting color to paper and think of the Colored Paper Images series as wet collages which are a cross between painting and collage."[6] Kelly completed twenty-three Colored Paper Images (see pp. 212–13); *Nine Colors* (p. 211) was issued as well. All were formed from pigmented paper pulps laid on a newly made, wet base sheet. By this time Tyler had done considerable experimentation with ways of coloring pulp. In addition to colored rags, powdered pigments, water-base paints, and various dyes, he was also using acrylic gouaches. One of these, Flashe, was the main source of color for the pulps Kelly used. The images were produced in varying editions of between nine and twenty-four, but—as with Stella's cast Paper Reliefs—referring to them as editioned works is a bit of a misnomer. Each of Kelly's pieces is unique, in this case because of variation that occurred as part of the working process.[7]

The schemes of the Colored Paper Images are similar to those explored in Kelly's paintings and prints: horizontal or vertical bands; squares within squares; two triangles, diagonally disposed, base to base, to form a square; an arc or a parabola, set congruent to a color that may function as a field or as a shape (if the arc or parabola is seen as field) or—together with the arc or parabola—as form with no field. These images present us with questions as to what, exactly, we are seeing. The mottled surfaces resulted both from the characteristics of individual pigments and from the manner in which batches of colored pulp of different tonal values were mixed together to make new ones. The less mixing, the more mottling. The effect is an unusual, almost translucent quality. To make the Colored Paper Images, areas of pulp were separated by plastic or wooden strips. In the finished pieces the sense of the strips is evoked by the white bands of the base sheets seen between the fields of color.

Numerous trial proofs were necessary before the desired color solutions were achieved, and trial studies were made to explore format as well. In particular, the relationship of the color-form and the ground was radically altered, evidence of one of Kelly's principal concerns: "I have wanted to free shape from its ground and then to work the shape so that it has a definite relationship to the space around it; so that it

Ellsworth Kelly
Nine Colors 1977
colored, pressed paper
pulp
30 x 30
Collection Walker Art
Center, Minneapolis
Tyler Graphics Archive
(Tyler 319:EK26)

Ellsworth Kelly
*Colored Paper Image
V* 1976
colored, pressed paper
pulp
46½ x 32½
Collection Walker Art
Center, Minneapolis
Tyler Graphics Archive
(Tyler 300:EK7)

Ellsworth Kelly
*Colored Paper Image
VII* 1976
colored, pressed paper
pulp
46½ x 32½
Collection Walker Art
Center, Minneapolis
Tyler Graphics Archive
(Tyler 302:EK9)

has a clarity and a measure within itself of its parts (angles, curves, edges, amount of mass); and so that, with color and tonality, the shape finds its own space and always demands its freedom and separateness."[8] These powerful Colored Paper Images—some quiet, almost somber, others extremely vivid—reveal two aspects of Kelly as a colorist: sometimes immersed in black and white and, in his sculpture, exploring the natural surfaces of woods and metals; at other times exploring primary-color relationships and finishing his sculpture with brilliant enamel.

Kenneth Noland's desire to work on a larger scale than HMP could accommodate motivated Tyler to complete his own mill, equipped with moulds and raw materials for making both Oriental and Western sheets. Noland is one of the few artists collaborating at Tyler Graphics who had worked elsewhere with paper pulp. A painter (he also has made sculpture) with no interest in printmaking, Noland was introduced to papermaking in 1976, working with Garner Tullis at the Institute of Experimental Printmaking, first in Santa Cruz, California, and later in San Francisco. His affinity for the process was instant, and in 1977 he set up his own paper mill, Gully Paper, in North Hoosick, New York; when he moved to South Salem, New York, in 1979, he established the Kitchawan paper mill there. In 1978, however, from April through August, Noland worked in Bedford Village, collaborating with Tyler and papermaker Lindsay Green.[9] They completed five series of works: Circle I, Circle II, Horizontal Stripes (groups I through V and group VII), Diagonal Stripes, and Pairs. Altogether these include more than three hundred unique images.

For Noland, "papermaking is a way of drawing—not like a sketch, leading to a larger work in kind—but as a practice medium . . . such as drawing or watercolor or working with plaster or clay."[10] The specific properties of pulp that allow color to be *of* rather than *on* a surface are particularly sympathetic to Noland's art. As a painter he has been involved with staining unprimed canvas—allowing pigment to soak into and become a part of the fabric, often leaving large areas unpainted. In working with pulps, this unity of image and object is an immediate one, the essence of Noland's approach. Although he remains uninterested in printmaking per se, the Circle I and Circle II pieces and group V in the Horizontal Stripes are structured by monoprint additions in lithography or in lithography and screen printing. And Noland brushed some papers with transparent dyes. In number, placement, and color, these printed and brushed elements are unique to each work, and all of the pieces are remarkably subtle and elegant.

The Roman-numeral designations in Noland's Horizontal Stripes (see p. 215) group pieces by the general placement of their bands. The works are composed of two to six layers of colored pulp, and within a given structure the effects of color create considerable differentiation in mood and space. Formal aspects are varied: edges of stripes (some dissolving, some razor sharp), surface modulations (some of the pieces

Kenneth Noland
*Horizontal Stripes
I-7* 1978
colored, pressed paper pulp
53 x 32
Collection Walker Art Center, Minneapolis
Tyler Graphics Archive
(Tyler 466:KN229)

are smooth and monochromatic; others are fluid, changing, marked by flecks of brightly colored wools, threads, and small pieces of paper; and still others are subtle and harmonious in their color relationships or dynamic and surprising in their juxtapositions). Some areas are rich and dense, while others appear as if veils had been placed one on top of another to form them. In fact, in six works a layer of cotton gauze modifies the colors beneath it and adds a clearly defined physical, as distinct from visual, texture.

In many sheets the base layer is almost entirely covered, and its color, when it can be seen, quietly enhances those added to mask it. Individual pulp bands may be internally varied in physical density, with openings that expose contrasting colors below. Strong horizontality pushing at the edges of vertical formats is a characteristic of most of the series. However, in some—for example, *Horizontal Stripes I-7* (p. 215)—the horizontal thrust is countered within the central field as an atmospheric space is constructed by soft vertical divisions.

Noland's Diagonal Stripes—some horizontal in format, others vertical—are composed of seven layerings of diverse colored pulps in parallel bands on a base sheet. The base layer varies in color from piece to piece. Visually as well as physically, it locks in the bands of color, which mesh with it. After a plastic template with divisions for the stripes was placed atop the wet base sheet, Noland "pushed and patted colored pulp. Using his hands, he sometimes smeared pulp to create a ragged edge or poured water over the pulp, causing color to ooze and bleed into the sheet."[11] These bleeds from the stripes often merged with the base layer, interrupting the clear divisional structure.

In the Circle I (see p. 217) and Circle II series, as in the Diagonal Stripes, some works are horizontal and others vertical. The concentric-rings format focuses activity intensely. The pieces are relatively small,[12] and they are delicate both in the actual weight of the sheets and in the visual weight of their coloration. Embroidery hoops were used as molds for the pulp. Edges are often subtle and always crucial: pulp edges are softer than the printed edges, and they evoke the "feel" of some of Noland's stained canvases of the late 1950s. Overprinting altered the pulp colors, often forming secondary bands and edges that are barely discernible.

Both Oriental and Western papers were made especially for Noland's paper project, the only one to date that called for Oriental pulp to be made at Tyler Graphics. Since the sheets made from Oriental fibers were formed on a laid mould and the Western sheets were formed on a wove mould, this scheme provided a basic difference in the textures of the two papers, establishing an extremely subtle surface where the overlay is apparent. The Oriental sheets, laminated as a top layer, physically hold the rings of pulp, colored-paper chips, wool, and colored threads to the base sheet, modifying tonalities—again, the veil. Noland's paper pieces masterfully confront one of the key dilemmas of modernism: "The question we [Noland and Morris Louis] always discussed was

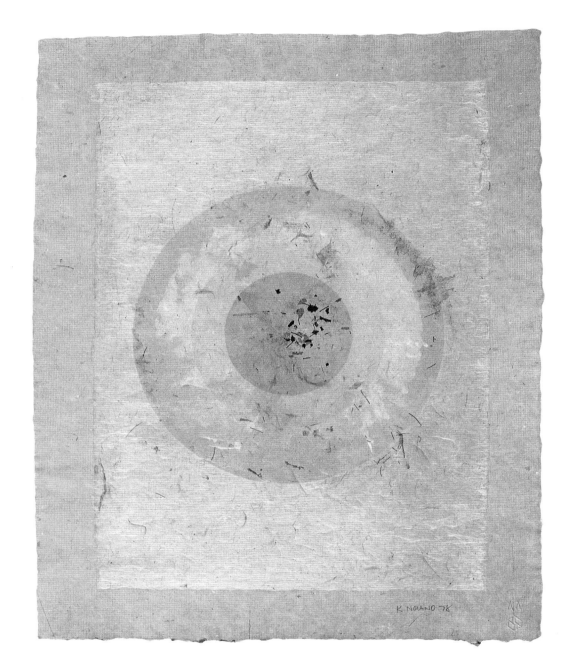

what to make art about. . . . We wanted the appearance to be the result of the process of making it—not necessarily to look like a gesture, but to be the result of real handling."[13]

The fluid nature of paper pulp may seem most appropriate for abstract works such as Kelly's or Noland's. However, Tyler challenged this notion with his very next papermaking project, David Hockney's Paper Pools, 1978. The artist has given us his own account of how he entered reluctantly into the odyssey that led to this spectacular series. His prime purpose in visiting Bedford Village was to tell Tyler that he, Hockney, was en route to California to paint, a solitary activity, and that he didn't wish to embark on a collaborative venture just then.[14] Tyler, however, always eager to share his enthusiasms and fully aware of Hockney's love of new media, showed him some of the work recently completed in the shop. Among the pieces were several made by Kelly and Noland from colored pulp. "They were stunningly beautiful . . . [and] I said, they are very, very good, beautiful, Ken, but I'm on my way to California."[15] Tyler's seduction won out, however, and Hockney stayed in Bedford Village for forty-five days, working nonstop to form images from "mush" made out of "chewed-up rags" and water.[16]

The first of Hockney's paper pieces was a vase of flowers, one of his favorite subjects. But it didn't take long for a distinctive characteristic of papermaking—its wetness—to merge with another of his favorite motifs, the swimming pool, a stellar example of which was situated not far from the Tyler Graphics workshop. Hockney immediately recognized the "watery subject" appropriate to the process. He then made a number of trials (see p. 219) to become familiar with the possibilities of the medium: different ways of handling pulp to model form, for example, or to create edges; methods of incorporating color into the pulp and of applying it directly to an already formed pulp image; and so forth.

The Paper Pools, worked from Polaroid photographs and drawings, reflect Hockney's keen sensitivity to the ways in which changes in light and air alter what we see. There are thirty-one differently numbered Paper Pools (including the vase of flowers). Some numbers were completed in several variant versions, and many of the differently numbered ones are closely related. Onto the wet paper base Hockney poured colored pulps through "cookie-cutter" templates. Once the overall motif was in place, the templates were removed, and Hockney worked with additional colored pulps and dyes, using a variety of methods that he and Tyler developed: pulp was spooned, poured, painted, and dropped. Combs, toothbrushes, fingers, a garden hose, and the patter of the rain added textures. Liquid dyes were applied with paintbrushes, an airbrush, and a turkey baster.[17]

The earliest Paper Pools are single panels, but Hockney soon saw that "because the medium was so bold, you had to be bold in other ways. I thought the paper should be bigger."[18] To achieve this, Tyler built an outdoor slab on which six sheets of newly made paper could be placed, three across and two up. Hockney then worked all six sheets at once to form a single, cohesive image. One group of works shows the empty swimming pool, diving board directly at center, from a vantage point we might have if we were approaching along the board, about to dive in. In them the quality of the sunlight changes the appearance of the water, the poolside (defined by blue and violet shadows), and the green coloration of the foliage. Paper Pool 19, *Piscine à minuit* (p. 240), shows the pool in the blackness of night. The diving board, yellow in the daytime scenes, is black, and the steps leading into the water, of little consequence during the day, at night become an active visual element across the liquid expanse. Hockney shows us the extent to which we look *at* water during the day and *into* it at night.

In most of the Paper Pools, the pool is ours alone. Occasionally the solitude is provocatively offset by a rippling in the water—a sense

David Hockney
studies for Paper Pools
1978
colored, pressed paper
pulp
26 x 18¼ each
Courtesy Tyler
Graphics Ltd.

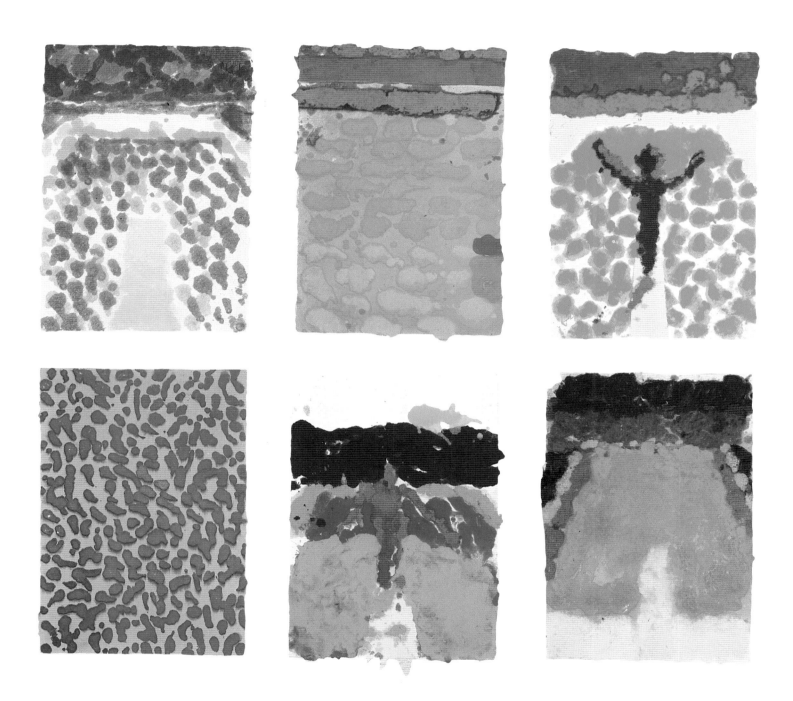

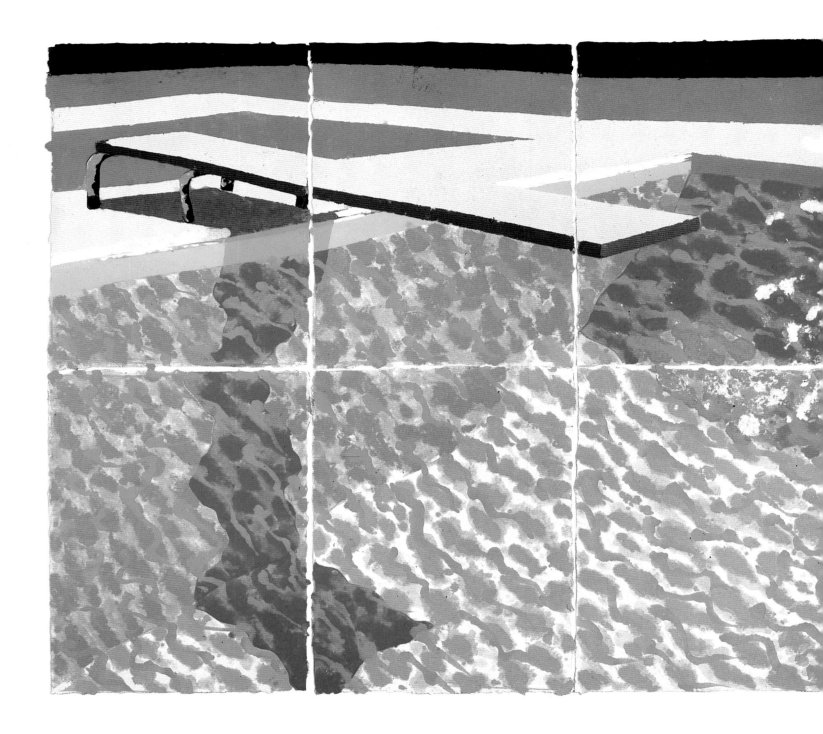

of activity that implies a swimmer someplace outside the image's edges. In a few of the pieces Hockney's friend Gregory Evans is present. Perhaps the most spectacular of all the Paper Pools, however, are those composed of twelve sheets, each laid side by side and measuring in their entirety 72 by 171 inches, among them Paper Pool 27, *A Large Diver* (pp. 220–21). The figure swimming underwater has just dived into the pool, leaving a splash of brilliant white in his wake. According to Hockney, "it took a thousand gallons of water to make one of these, which seems to me an awful lot; in a watercolour you use a cupful."[19]

David Hockney
A Large Diver,
Paper Pool 27   1978
colored, pressed paper
pulp
twelve sheets: 72 x 171
Collection San
Francisco Museum of
Modern Art, T.B.
Walker Foundation
Fund Purchase
(Tyler 244:DH27)

In these paper-pulp projects, Tyler helped atune papermaking to the painter's urges. His own interests matched those of the artists: their concern with direct image making; their desire to find an approach to handling this unknown and unusual material; their interest in issues of color saturation and how the form of pigment alters color; the matter of texture; and so forth. In his own mill he was able to rummage around, experiment, try whatever came to mind. He was developing a large palette of dyes and colored pulps and various kinds of stenciling devices and systems for using color in a repeatable manner. When he invited artists to the shop to work with him, his hope was that each project would bring new challenges and generate new procedures. "I invited artists I thought would approach it a different way."

Robert Zakanitch came to Tyler Graphics shortly after Hockney's Paper Pools were completed. Within the next two years, Zakanitch worked in both printmaking and papermaking. Six multicolor prints in as many as thirty-two colors were completed. Five of them combined lithography, screen printing, and pochoir; the sixth used lithography and screen printing alone. Working with pigmented paper pulp, Zakanitch completed the Double Peacock Series, twenty-one unique variations, as well as a series of twenty-three one-of-a-kind pieces. Many of these are composed of multiple panels. They feature swans, geese, peacocks, and the sumptuous, overall floral patterning associated with Zakanitch's paintings.

This was the artist's first use of pigmented pulps; however, his imagery is particularly lyrical and sympathetic to the fluidity of the material. The freely worked, gestural approach that distinguishes his paintings was similarly employed with remarkable freedom. *Straight-back Swans II* (p. 202), an unabashedly romantic night scene of swans in a pond, their necks intertwined, their bodies surrounded by pink flowers and green leaves, is one of the twenty-three unique pieces. Composed on four white base sheets, the broad image areas were laid in using numerous complicated templates that Zakanitch designed (the same ones were variously combined for several of the pieces), similar in type to those used by Hockney. Zakanitch's pulp, however, was quite different—of a particularly "creamy" consistency, rather than "chunky."[20] After removing the templates, Zakanitch worked further, laying down small touches of colored pulps and dyes directly, working wet into wet with painterly ease. The piece was also enhanced by strokes and lines of direct drawing and painting, added after the sheet had been half-pressed, allowing for a slightly sharper mark to become embedded in the paper as it was further pressed and dried.

Variations in the Double Peacock Series are mainly in color. For example, birds may be gray or black, with gray or turquoise fields and pink or yellow flowers. In these variations and in several other pieces—for example, *Red Thunder* (p. 223)—Zakanitch's innovative approach to papermaking is best seen. In them the artist did away with the base sheet, pouring pulp into templates placed directly on the felts used in pressing paper, or pouring it to conform to shapes that were drawn on the felts as a guide. Areas were left free or cleared, establishing an irregular, openwork structure. This invests many of Zakanitch's paper works with a fragile quality that is held in tension with their strong, iconic character. Internally, the power of suggestion is paramount—form is never specifically articulated.

British painter Hugh O'Donnell, working in an abstract mode, has also used paper pulp in a very personal and lyrical manner. O'Donnell completed one project at Tyler Graphics, in 1983. Entitled Weapons of

Robert Zakanitch
Red Thunder 1981
colored, pressed paper pulp
backing sheet: 67 x 46
Courtesy Tyler Graphics Ltd.
(Tyler 853:RZ50)

Desire, Bedford Series, these twenty-five unique pieces in three configurations were based on O'Donnell's vigorous line drawings.[21] A galvanized metal template with divisions was placed on top of a newly formed base sheet and filled with colored pulps. After the template was removed, the artist continued to work directly with colored pulps and dyes and, for some, iridescent powder.

These dynamic compositions thrust multicolor bands (some of them resembling arrowheads or exaggerated boomerangs) in opposing directions. This gives an explosive quality to the pieces. Some shapes imply a three-dimensional form; others appear flat. This may be seen in the contrast between the essentially red and salmon colored form with purple modulations at the lower right of *III-9* (p. 224) and the

Hugh O'Donnell
III-9 1983
colored, pressed paper pulp
49⅜ x 40¼
Collection Walker Art Center, Minneapolis
Tyler Graphics Archive
(Tyler 476:HO'D19)

rich blue shape appearing to move in space behind it at its left. Specific colored pulps generally function in particular zones of the sheet. Some colors are extremely splashy in effect, while others are more locally placed. Bleeds from the pigmented pulps modulate areas outside the template image. Tyler has described O'Donnell's use of the pulp in the manner of an action painter, "throwing it, spattering it, and making very quick marks in the wet pulp as part of the papermaking process."

Another British artist, Richard Smith, has collaborated at Tyler Graphics on two projects. In 1980 he completed the Cartouche Series: one-of-a-kind objects made from cloth and handmade paper suspended with cotton twine from aluminum tubes; and in 1982 he completed seven intaglio prints with lithography as a group entitled Field and Streams (see p. 226). Printed on Arches Watercolor paper, the Field and Streams are among the few intaglio prints Tyler has printed on sized sheets. The beautifully fluid appearance of the color gradations results from Smith's exceedingly subtle use of spitbite aquatint. For the Cartouches (see pp. 9, 227), Smith layered paper pulp with fabric, creating works distinctive in their internal tension and their relation to the wall. The structure of gesture, the gesture of construction, the tension of suspension, and the nature of overlap and interruption are among the concerns of Smith's art explored in the Cartouche Series. As with his paintings suspended from rods, the tubes and the twine that attaches the fabric-paper laminate function both to define and to modify the form. Image and process are simultaneous. The activity of forming is inherent in what is formed, and the making of the pieces is part of their subject.

The Cartouches were Smith's first paper-pulp pieces, and the pulp he employed was the thinnest used at Tyler Graphics to date. He explored five formats. Three of these employ three panels, while the others are composed of two. For each piece, a layer of wet, specially dyed cotton was stretched over a newly formed base sheet of handmade paper. A sheet of colored paper was then couched onto the fabric, in registration with the base sheet below, sandwiching the fabric layer. Smith then added smaller pieces of handmade paper (both cotton and Oriental kozo fibers were used) as well as directly applying colored pulps and dyes. The resulting pictorial structures are asymmetrical in their distribution of color and shape. After pressing and drying, the laminated sheets were attached to rods, and the overlapping positioning was determined. A tight structure that seems casual resulted.

Of the Cartouches, Smith has noted, "I had thought that the process of making paper would match my formal vocabulary very closely. The pouring of pulp on the paper mould screens was a very natural process, something I found direct and right and not a substitute for a brush. The results hold the intentions. The way the pulp is poured gives direction and pulse to the paper in an equivalent of a painted surface and contrasts with the perfection of paper as it is pulled from the vat. . . . Plans could be followed, but then there was also space and time for improvisation.

Adjustments and corrections were best made by new decisions rather than restoration and niggardly improvements."[22]

The luminous surfaces retain the variations in the pulp layers: in some the thin layer of watery pulp "feels" as if it is still wet and drippy. In others, a dense, heavy layer adds weight to the structure of the object. Some of Smith's Cartouches are rich, deep, and somber; others are celebratory, like festive banners.

Tyler's involvement with objects made from paper was pushed forward again when sculptor Anthony Caro worked at the shop in 1982.

Richard Smith
Ouse 1982
aquatint, etching,
lithograph on Arches
Watercolor paper
30 x 22¼
Collection Walker Art
Center, Minneapolis
Tyler Graphics Archive
(Tyler 526:RS60)

226

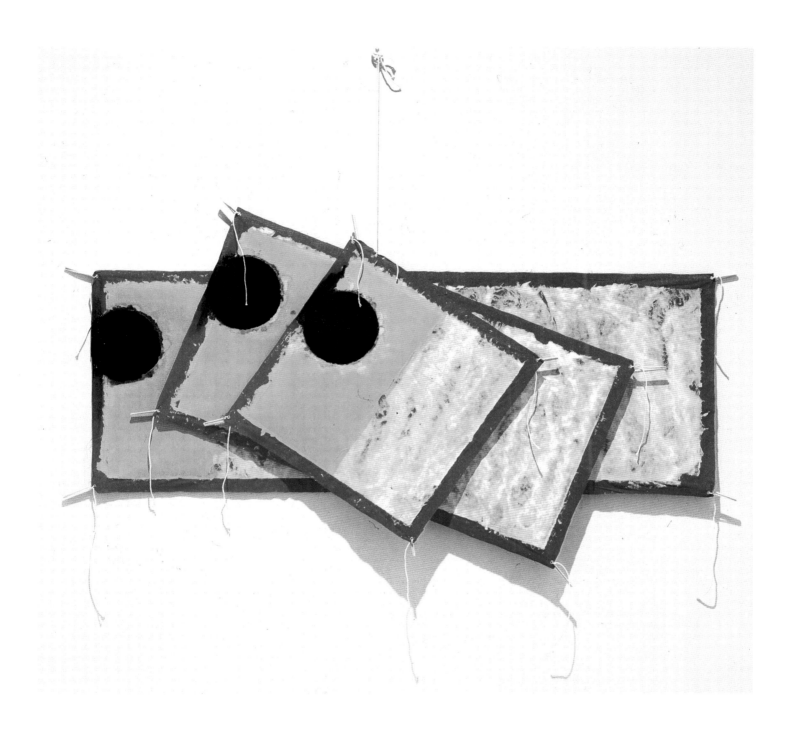

Richard Smith
Cartouche II-9   1980
colored, pressed paper
pulp; fabric;
grommets; string;
aluminum tubes
37 x 60
Collection Walker Art
Center, Minneapolis
Tyler Graphics Archive
(Tyler 518:RS24)

Earlier, in a 1978 interview, Caro had indicated: "I am interested in trying a lot of new things and going into areas I have not attempted before. I have been thinking about making some sculptures in paper."[23] At Tyler Graphics a few years later he followed through, completing 124 one-of-a-kind paper wall reliefs (see p. 228). The form is not readily associated with Caro, whose sculpture is usually freestanding, often with a clear orientation to the floor. However, by 1980–81, shortly before working on these paper reliefs, he had completed constructed wall reliefs in bronze.

Caro's paper sculptures are a departure from his use of metal, but they are about assembling, constructing, in this case, collaging—the "language of sculpture: that has to do with materials, shapes, intervals, and so on."[24] For his steel pieces, the sculptural components may be found or specially made to suit his needs. In working at Tyler Graphics, both kinds of components were employed. As a starting point for Caro, using a variety of TGL handmade papers, mould-made papers, and Tycore panels, Tyler and fellow collaborators Steve Reeves and Tom Strianese made elements of a sort associated with the sculptor's steel pieces—tubes; shaped, flat planes; undulating planes with fluid curves; folded sheets; and so on. As he worked, Caro altered these elements, moving back and forth between the Tyler Graphics artist's studio and the paper mill, making additional sculptural elements as he needed them. In fascinating contrast to his open and expansive steel pieces, the paper reliefs, small and compact, feel extremely weighty, and the layered structures are relatively closed.

Caro's paper reliefs are essentially monochromatic, employing variations of gray and white. Some are housed in four-sided wooden boxes that play a strong enclosing role; others, formed on a base, move freely into space. Caro worked many of them with pencil, crayon, and paint,

Anthony Caro
#28. *Untitled* 1982
paper sculpture,
hand-colored, on
wood on Tycore panel
24½ x 37 x 7½
Collection Walker Art
Center, Minneapolis
Tyler Graphics Archive
(Tyler 149:AC26)

using color to modify form in entirely new ways. In some instances this hand-coloring emphasizes the structure, separating it from the wall plane; in others it acts to diffuse structure by allying two or more forms and establishing additional visual connections.

Kenneth Noland equated papermaking with drawing. Caro has made a similar equation in talking of his small tabletop sculptures: "... there's something nice about their different size, their smaller size. [Making them] would be rather like drawing. I made a lot, just as one would make a lot of drawings."[25] Given this context, Caro's small paper reliefs, too, seem like highly refined, tightly constructed drawings.

Among the more elaborate of the recent projects at Tyler Graphics involving handmade paper were the collaborations with Alan Shields. Shields, like Noland, had worked with handmade paper on many projects before coming to Bedford Village, having collaborated most extensively with papermakers Joe Wilfer and William Weege in Wisconsin. Shields's work with Tyler has involved both papermaking and the use of special papers handmade elsewhere. In the early collaborations, while various sheets were used, the printing and construction methods, rather than the papermaking, were of primary importance.

A fascinating three-dimensional piece is Shields's 1978 *Box Sweet Jane's Egg Triumvirate,* produced in three configurations: *Moose Set* (p. 230), *Roosevelt Set,* and *Kool Set.* All were constructed from printed woven strips of HMP handmade paper. Before cutting, both sides of the sheets were worked in a variety of ways. Luscious, delicately modulated lithographic surfaces were juxtaposed with flat screen-printed areas and hand-stamping (using, for example, the circular erasers at the ends of pencils). Other works called for the use of both Oriental and Western papers; sewing; double-sided printing; laminations of brightly dyed papers on the versos of white sheets, the bleed-through subtly coloring areas of a printed image; combinations of several techniques, including embossed linocut, mezzotint, drypoint, and relief rolling in a single work (as in *TV Rerun, C* [p. 231]; silver leaf was a component of *TV Rerun, A*); and printed ghost images from blocks already used in Shields's endless recycling processes.

The seven prints in The Castle Window Set are layered; in each of them a sheet of paper Shields made especially for the project at the Gandhi Ashram in Ahmadabad, India, was placed over a sheet of TGL handmade. All of the Indian papers were made with window openings by a method Shields refers to as his "watermark" process, because, as for a watermark, designated parts of the sheet are thinner than its main body. These areas of the mould were blocked out, usually with paint or tape, preventing the pulp from taking hold there except as it seeped under the blockout. In this way sheets with openings or with very thin, almost transparent, membranelike areas were made. In Shields's sheets these areas—squares, circles, diamonds, and so forth—were loosely organized on a grid. In The Castle Window Set, similar shapes were repeated in the areas printed on both sheets of paper. Close looking is necessary to determine what is a shaped perforation, allowing color to show through, and what is a printed shape. Aspects of each print in the set usually appear in some other manner in the others. And for *Santa's Collar* (p. 232), printed entirely on TGL handmade, the central sheet was used as a backing sheet for the Castle Window Set editions. This sheet, which is composed of bleeds and ghosts from all seven Castle Window prints, shows how Shields, as he works, creates his own "found" materials.

For Shields's 1984 prints *Odd-Job* (p. 233), *Bull-Pen, Milan Fog,* and *Gas-Up,* making paper was again the crucial first step. A variety

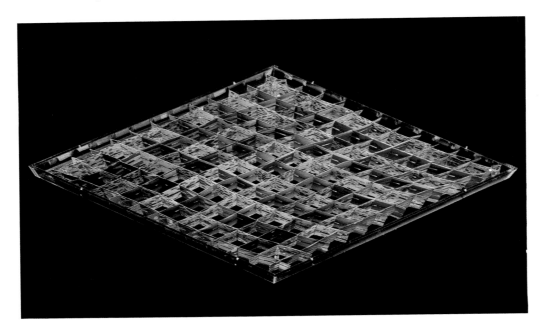

of strategies were used, among which was the watermark method described above. For other sheets, special papermaking frames were strung with twine in patterns the artist established. When the frames were dipped, pulp clung to the strings. (A committed fisherman, Shields has related this to what he sees when slip gut, a stringy seaweed, wraps itself around his fishing line.)[26] The areas between the widely spaced threads remained open, producing latticelike sheets that were cut from the frames when the pulp was fully dried. The strings that formed the grid were incorporated into the paper, giving strength to the lattices by supporting the pulp structure and adding a formal element related to the sewing thread Shields uses in much of his art (see p. 234). Some sheets were "double-dipped," using a frame with a string grid stretched on both sides.

Establishing the structures for Shields's 1984 sheets was only the first step in the papermaking process, however. Important, too, was the manner of drying: some sheets were air-dried, forming relatively thick, puffed-up, three-dimensional lattices; some were partially pressed and then air-dried, also forming dimensional elements, but of a medium thickness; and some sheets were fully pressed, forming lattices of a

Alan Shields
Box Sweet Jane's Egg Triumvirate: I, Moose Set 1978
lithograph, screenprint, stamping on cream/gray HMP duplex handmade paper
21 x 46 x 3¼
Collection Walker Art Center, Minneapolis
Tyler Graphics Archive
(Tyler 478:AS1)

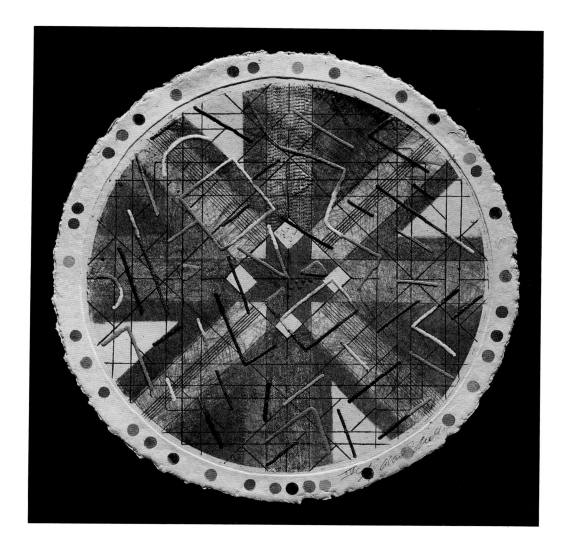

Alan Shields
TV Rerun, C 1978
linocut, mezzotint,
drypoint, stamping on
colored TGL
handmade paper
10 diameter
Collection Walker Art
Center, Minneapolis
Tyler Graphics Archive
(Tyler 488:AS11)

thickness that we would normally associate with TGL handmade paper. The dipped-string method leaves openings that are more sharply defined at their edges than those made by the watermark method. These two kinds of specially formed papers were eventually printed and then, in combination with "ordinary" handmade sheets activated by printing alone, they were layered. The sizes and shapes of the pieces evolved as the papers were combined: horizontals were juxtaposed with verticals; sheets were torn in half and used to flank another sheet. The remarkably varied surface quality established by differences in how the sheets were formed was made more evident by the richness of the printing.

For these 1984 prints, most sheets were printed several times. Two sheets were often printed simultaneously or from different sections of a single printing element. For example, by using an openwork sheet as a mask at the same time that it was being printed, the image on a second sheet laid under it was developed: the blocked-out areas of the lower sheet became an open, unprinted reflection of the configuration on the top sheet. Thus, a similar image, in positive in one place, may be found in negative in another. Or in printing a perforated sheet from a solidly inked plate or block, ink was transferred only where the paper touched

Alan Shields
Santa's Collar 1981
relief, woodcut,
linocut, aquatint,
stitching, collage on
white with straw TGL
handmade paper with
blue TGL handmade
paper border
43¼ x 36½
Collection Walker Art
Center, Minneapolis
Tyler Graphics Archive
(Tyler 505:AS28)

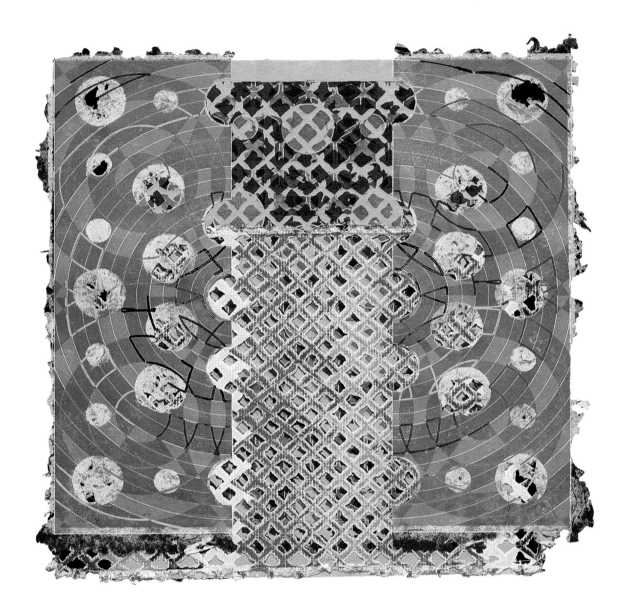

Alan Shields
Odd-Job 1984
woodcut, etching,
relief, stitching, collage
on blue TGL
handmade paper

42 x 42
Collection Walker Art
Center, Minneapolis
Tyler Graphics Archive
(Tyler 506:AS29)

Alan Shields
four paper-pulp grids
for *Odd-Job* 1984
approximately 40 x 30
each
Collection Walker Art
Center, Minneapolis
Tyler Graphics Archive

Alan Shields
copper plate and
woodblocks for
Odd-Job 1984
Collection Walker Art
Center, Minneapolis
Tyler Graphics Archive

it. Where there were perforations, no ink left the plate, and the residue was later printed on a second sheet. Shields's work is filled with ghosts, reversals, and echoes. The ghost impressions are subtle, delicate renditions of the richer first printings. Incredibly self-referential, the elements require the astuteness of a detective to sort out their sources and the interplay Shields creates among his images and forms.

Many of the metal plates and woodblocks—for example, those used for *Odd-Job* (see p. 235)—are composed of computer-generated cuts based on the artist's drawings. In many instances a jigsawlike format was used. To print the plates and blocks, the several pieces often were separated, inked in various colors, reassembled, and then printed, yielding a number of colors from one press run. Shields's palette is as active and colorful as a fiesta: reds, greens, blues, yellows, grays, and blacks, as well as variants of the primaries—rose, turquoise, ocher, and so forth. The hues are intense and dense, creating great contrast. As with the thin places and openings in the "watermarked" paper, grids were often used to structure printed color. At times there is a left-right or top-bottom color reversal. In activating surfaces, color sets up pulsating spatial tensions that are reinforced by the actual physical differences established by the layering of sheets. These complicated pieces, incorporating sewing, perforating, layering, collaging, and printing, began with papermaking, a step central to the art.

Paper, not papermaking, is central to Steven Sorman's paintings, drawings, and prints, all of which explore collage. His collaborations with Tyler during the past few years have come at an important time, just as he was about to add an explosive vigor to his elegant work. In describing the fascination of working with Tyler, he has recounted how "Ken sort of tosses materials at you and watches out of the corner of his eye to see what you'll do. He knows just when to stay away and when to show up."[27] Sorman's first sessions in Tyler's shop led to a group of fourteen monoprints, and his second project, of 1985, included both monoprints and editions, all of which incorporate several printing processes as well as direct painting. Among them is *Trees Blowing and Blowing like Arms Akimbo* (p. 237), structured by juxtapositions of TGL handmade and Oriental papers and drapery sheer, with lithography, woodcut, etching, linecut, and hand-painting. Layers of ink and strokes of paint, in themselves of great variety, were also considerably affected by the quality of the sheet. They soaked into and became a part of some and remained on the surface of others. Texture, transparency, and so forth vary considerably from one section of the collage-print to another.

Generally, Sorman works on several pieces simultaneously, one supplying elements for another. A psychological environment is established in which figurative fragments are juxtaposed with abstract elements. Carefully considered titles add to the seduction, give clues to meaning, show the artist "leaving footprints. . . . I try to construct very simply, very rationally, step by step, and I'm interested in the implications

Steven Sorman
Trees Blowing and Blowing like Arms Akimbo 1985
woodcut, etching, relief, lithograph, collage, hand-colored, on Oriental and TGL handmade papers
59 x 37
Collection Walker Art Center, Minneapolis
Tyler Graphics Archive
(Tyler 533:SS17)

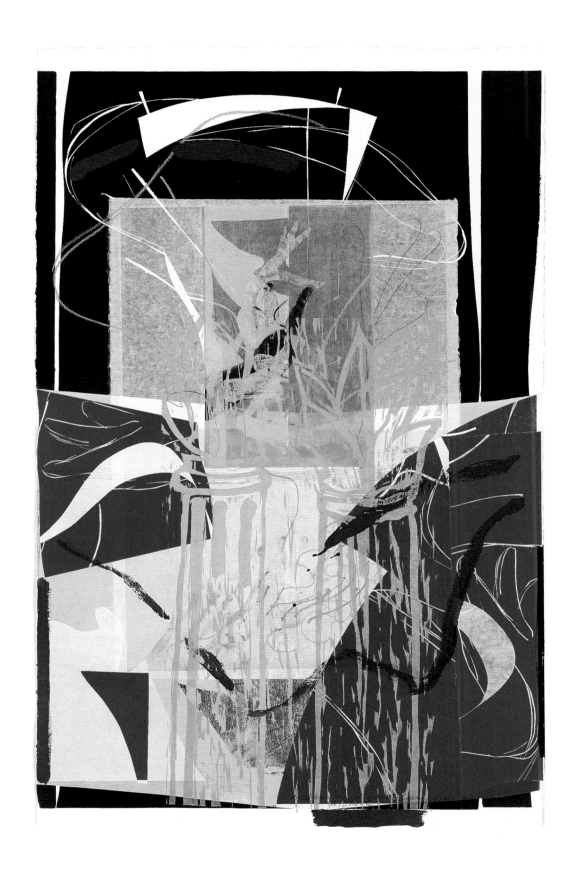

very simple methods of construction have. In printmaking, in particular, you have to think in layers, in almost cartoon sequence. You know—somebody walks into the first frame, does something in the second frame, and by the time they walk out of the fourth frame you know what's happened."[28] One has the sense that Sorman's pieces evolve as much from the substrates he uses as from his fragmented imagery—that fabrics and papers offer ideas for forms to be placed on them.

On a certain level, an involvement with paper is intrinsic to the art of the print. Tyler's commitment to studying its ramifications, however, is one of extraordinary proportions, and the artists he has worked with have understood this and have taken full advantage of his imagination and expertise. His approach to collaboration is one of both provocation and response. In anticipation of an artist's arrival, he will prepare materials that he knows the artist likes to use, but he will also set out unfamiliar materials that he thinks might be challenging, might spark new ideas or generate that special kind of energy essential to creative thought. TGL paper has made a difference to most of the artists who have worked in Bedford Village, not only the special multicolor sheets but the more standard sheets as well. Tyler is always worrying over what he might do to change his paper's surface to achieve greater ink absorption, to make it sparkle even more, to make it larger. His concern for the printing papers coupled with the great range of paper-pulp projects he has published in the past decade make apparent the extent to which paper is a key component in the Bedford Village scheme. While the concern with papermaking for printing has remained constant, however, artists' projects in paper pulp have not. In considering the use of paper pulp for art, Tyler has taken a philosophical view: "[Papermaking] is now a part of the vocabulary in a workshop, and I think that's about all you can do. Then you have to let it sleep for a while, and not abuse it. I think you can push things to the point where they get too crafty, and it's all about cooking, about deviling up something new. Then it's not about making images, and in the end that's what you really should be working for. You think about where the good image is going to come from—woodblock, lithography, paper, it doesn't matter—and you go there."

Notes

1. According to Tyler, the French papers were too acidic and had rosin sizing. The results of tests in American mills, however, demonstrated to the French papermakers that finer products could be made, and they soon manufactured some (conversation with author, June 27, 1985).

2. Ibid. Although all quotations from Tyler in this essay come from this conversation, a general understanding of Tyler Graphics and how it functions, as well as Tyler's long-standing interest in papermaking, has come from a number of conversations over several years.

3. Many exhibitions emphasizing handmade paper have been organized in recent years. Bibliographies on the subject may be found in the catalogues for several of them, including Jane M. Farmer, *Paper as Medium* (Washington, D.C.: Smithsonian Institution Traveling Exhibition Service, 1978); Janet Flint, *New Ways with Paper* (Washington, D.C.: National Collection of Fine Arts, Smithsonian Institution, 1977); Pat Gilmour and Anne Willsford, *Paperwork* (Canberra: Australian National Gallery, 1982); and Richard Kubiak, *The Handmade Paper Object* (Santa Barbara, Calif.: Santa Barbara Museum of Art, 1976). Much of the work in handmade paper has had a craftsmanlike emphasis on technique, quite contrary to the image or process orientation to handmade paper embraced at Tyler Graphics Ltd.

4. See Richard H. Axsom, *The Prints of Frank Stella: A Catalogue Raisonné, 1967–1982*, exh. cat. (New York: Hudson Hills Press in association with the University of Michigan Museum of Art, Ann Arbor, 1983), pp. 178–79.

5. For his printing projects, however, Tyler continues to use paper made by the Kollers at HMP.

6. Ellsworth Kelly, in Farmer, *Paper as Medium*, p. 41.

7. Despite their differentness from traditional graphics, paperworks immediately became a part of the print world. Often produced in collaboration with graphic workshops, they were closer to prints than anything else, and terminology used to describe them has reflected this closeness. At the time these Kelly pieces were made, the language of the print world made "varying edition" seem a more accurate category than "group of unique pieces." Such a set of paper pieces would probably be called something else today.

8. Ellsworth Kelly, *Ellsworth Kelly*, exh. cat. (Los Angeles: Margo Leavin Gallery; New York: Leo Castelli Gallery, 1984), n.p.

9. Others not mentioned here who have been involved with papermaking projects at Tyler Graphics are Anthony D'Ancona, Lee Funderburg, Kim Halliday, John Hutcheson, Rodney Konopaki, Susan Millar, and Duane Mitch.

10. Kenneth Noland, in Gerrit Henry, "Paper in Transition," *Print Collector's Newsletter* 10 July–August 1979): 84. Much of this issue is devoted to paperworks.

11. Judith Goldman, *Kenneth Noland: Handmade Papers*, publisher's brochure (Bedford Village, N.Y.: Tyler Graphics, 1978), n.p.

12. The Circle I works measure twenty by sixteen inches, and the Circle II works measure thirty-two by twenty-one inches; the Horizontal Stripes and Diagonal Stripes prints measure approximately fifty by thirty-two inches.

13. Kenneth Noland, in Kenworth Moffett, *Kenneth Noland* (New York: Harry N. Abrams, 1977), p. 39.

14. Jan Butterfield, "David Hockney: Blue Hedonistic Pools," *Print Collector's Newsletter* 10 (July–August 1979): 73–76; David Hockney, *Paper Pools*, ed. Nikos Stangos (New York: Harry N. Abrams, 1980). Both publications offer the artist's account of the project.

15. Hockney, *Paper Pools*, p. 10.

16. Butterfield, "David Hockney," p. 74; ibid.

17. Stangos, in Hockney, *Paper Pools*, p. 7.

18. Hockney, *Paper Pools*, p. 36.

19. Ibid., p. 80.

20. Kenneth Tyler's terms, in conversation with author, June 27, 1985.

21. Tyler Graphics Ltd. records show configurations I (one image), II (twelve images), and III (eight images), with four additional variations. It would seem more apt, however, to record this group in two basic configurations with five variations.

22. Richard Smith, in Richard Smith and Kenneth E. Tyler, *Richard Smith: Cartouche Series*, exh. cat. (Regina: Norman Mackenzie Art Gallery, University of Regina, 1980), p. 5.

23. Anthony Caro, in "Anthony Caro: A Discussion with Peter Fuller," in Dieter Blume, *Anthony Caro: Catalogue Raisonné*, vol. 3 (Cologne: Verlag Galerie Wentzel, 1981), p. 47.

24. Ibid., p. 33.

25. Anthony Caro, in Diane Waldman, *Anthony Caro* (New York: Abbeville Press, 1982), p. 68.

26. Much of this information about Alan Shields's processes came out of a papermaking demonstration the artist gave on April 25, 1985, at the University of Minnesota and during a gallery tour of the exhibition *Paperworks at Tyler Graphics* at Walker Art Center the following day.

27. Steven Sorman, conversation with author, April 23, 1985.

28. Ibid.; Philip Larson, "Steven Sorman: An Interview," *Print Collector's Newsletter* 11 (May–June 1980): 43.

Acknowledgments

The phrase "extended image" in the title of this publication refers to the wide scope of printmaking activity at the Tyler Graphics workshop. Made in editions, prints by their very nature extend an artist's work. Kenneth Tyler's adventurous approach to the graphic arts, in which variant editions and one-of-a-kind works are common practice, has extended our notion of printmaking as well.

The Walker Art Center is extremely grateful to Tyler for his generous assistance with this publication. Almost daily he and his staff, in particular Barbara Delano and Kim Tyler, responded to our innumerable requests for information regarding the workshop's production and the artists who have worked there. To those versatile artists, we also express our deepest appreciation. Many were called upon to provide information, and all gave willingly of their time.

I am pleased to acknowledge key support from the Luce Fund for Scholarship in American Art, a program of The Henry Luce Foundation, Inc. Major funding provided by the National Endowment for the Humanities also gave this publication important impetus from the beginning.

I extend my gratitude to the fine writers whose thoughtful essays form this book: Richard H. Axsom, Ruth E. Fine, Jack Flam, Judith Goldman, E. C. Goossen, Robert M. Murdock, and Leonard B. Schlosser. It was a privilege to work with such a knowledgeable and perceptive group of art historians. I also extend special thanks to two other colleagues, Kristine Stiles and Celeste Connor, who kindly reviewed early drafts of my manuscript.

I am particularly grateful to our editors for their careful attention to this book. Andrea Belloli reviewed early versions of *Tyler Graphics: The Extended Image;* Karen Jacobson, who also served as editor of the companion volume, *Tyler Graphics: Catalogue Raisonné, 1974–1985,* oversaw the final editing of both texts. Special thanks are due the staff of Abbeville Press as well, particularly Nancy Grubb, Dana Cole, and Sharon Gallagher, for their editorial and production assistance.

Many former and present staff members at Walker Art Center worked with me on the preparation of this book: Betsy Wright, who ably aided in securing all photographs for this volume as well as in preparing the bibliography, was of special assistance; Karen Lovaas and Mary Cutshall worked closely with Glenn Halvorson, the museum's photographer, to supply the many illustrations of prints in the collection; Nora Heimann and Sheri Stearns provided a wide range of research and administrative assistance; and Lucinda Gardner and Linda Krenzin typeset the manuscript. I thank them all for their enthusiastic participation. I also want to thank Lorraine Ferguson, the museum's graphic designer, as well as Mildred Friedman, design curator, and David Galligan, administrative director, for their help in guiding the publication on its course. I am indebted to Martin Friedman as well, for his early and crucial interest in this project.

I am, finally, grateful for the invaluable support of Daniel Boone throughout my involvement with this project.

Elizabeth Armstrong

David Hockney
Piscine à minuit,
Paper Pool 19   1978
colored, pressed paper
pulp
six sheets: 72 x 85½
Collection Walker Art
Center, Minneapolis
Gift of Mr. and Mrs.
Kenneth E. Tyler
(Tyler 243:DH19)

Selected Bibliography

General

Adams, Clinton. *American Lithographers, 1900–1960: Artists and Their Printers.* Albuquerque: University of New Mexico Press, 1983.

Antreasian, Garo Z., and Clinton Adams. *The Tamarind Book of Lithography: Art and Techniques.* Los Angeles: Tamarind Lithography Workshop in association with Harry N. Abrams, 1971.

Armstrong, Elizabeth. *Prints from Tyler Graphics.* Exhibition catalogue. Minneapolis: Walker Art Center, 1984.

Baro, Gene, and Donald Saff. *Graphicstudio U.S.F.: An Experiment in Art and Education.* Exhibition catalogue. Brooklyn: Brooklyn Museum, 1978.

Baskett, Mary Welsh. *American Graphic Workshops: 1968.* Exhibition catalogue. Cincinnati: Cincinnati Art Museum, 1968.

Beal, Graham W. J. *Artist and Printer: Six American Print Studios.* Exhibition catalogue. Minneapolis: Walker Art Center, 1980.

Castleman, Riva. *Technics and Creativity: Gemini G.E.L.* Exhibition catalogue. New York: Museum of Modern Art, 1971.

Castleman, Riva. *Prints of the Twentieth Century: A History.* London: Thames & Hudson, 1976.

Castleman, Riva. *Printed Art: A View of Two Decades.* New York: Museum of Modern Art, 1980.

Castleman, Riva. *American Impressions: Prints since Pollock.* New York: Alfred A. Knopf, 1985.

Cate, Phillip Dennis, and Jeffrey Wechsler. *The Rutgers Archives for Printmaking Studios.* New Brunswick: Jane Voorhees Zimmerli Art Museum, Rutgers, State University of New Jersey, 1983.

Eichenberg, Fritz. *The Art of the Print: Masterpieces, History, Techniques.* New York: Harry N. Abrams, 1976.

Farmer, Jane M. *Paper as Medium.* Exhibition catalogue. Washington, D.C.: Smithsonian Institution Traveling Exhibition Service, 1978.

Field, Richard S., and Louise Sperling. *Offset Lithography.* Middletown, Conn.: Wesleyan University Press, 1973.

Field, Richard S. *Recent American Etching.* Exhibition catalogue. Middletown, Conn.: Davison Art Center, Wesleyan University, 1975.

Fine, Ruth E. *Gemini G.E.L.: Art and Collaboration.* Exhibition catalogue. Washington, D.C.: National Gallery of Art; New York: Abbeville Press, 1984.

Garlock, Trisha. *Glossary of Papermaking Terms.* San Francisco: World Print Council, 1983.

Gerrit, Henry. "Paper in Transition." *Print Collector's Newsletter* 10 (July–August 1979): 83–86.

Gilmour, Pat. *Modern Prints.* London and New York: Studio Vista, 1970.

Gilmour, Pat. *Understanding Prints: A Contemporary Guide.* London: Waddington Galleries, 1979.

Gilmour, Pat. *Ken Tyler, Master Printer, and the American Print Renaissance.* New York: Hudson Hills Press in association with the Australian National Gallery, 1986.

Gilmour, Pat, and Anne Willsford. *Paperwork.* Canberra: Australian National Gallery, 1982.

Goldman, Judith. "The Print Establishment." Parts 1, 2. *Art in America* 61 (July–August, September–October 1973): 105–9, 102–4.

Goldman, Judith. *Art off the Picture Press: Tyler Graphics Ltd.* Exhibition catalogue. Hempstead, N.Y.: Emily Lowe Gallery, Hofstra University, 1977.

Goldman, Judith. "The Master Printer of Bedford, N.Y." *Art News* 76 (September 1977): 50–54.

Goldman, Judith. "Printmaking: The Medium *Isn't* the Message Anymore." *Art News* 79 (March 1980): 82–85.

Goldman, Judith. *Print Publishing in America.* Exhibition catalogue. Washington, D.C.: United States Communication Agency, 1980.

Goldman, Judith. *American Prints: Process and Proofs.* Exhibition catalogue. New York: Whitney Museum of American Art and Harper & Row, 1981.

Goodman, Calvin J. "Master Printers and Print Workshops." *American Artist* 40 (October 1976): 67–73.

Halbreich, Kathy. *Paper Forms: Handmade Paper Projects.* Cambridge: Hayden Gallery, Massachusetts Institute of Technology, 1977.

Harvey, Donald. *Seven Artists at Tyler Graphics Ltd.* Exhibition catalogue. Athens: Trisolini Gallery, Ohio University, 1979.

Hayter, Stanley William. *New Ways of Gravure.* New York: Pantheon, 1949.

Hayter, Stanley William. *About Prints.* London: Oxford University Press, 1962.

Heller, Jules. *Printmaking Today.* New York: Holt, Rinehart & Winston, 1972.

Henry, Gerrit. "Paper in Transition." *Print Collector's Newsletter* 10 (July–August 1979): 83–86.

Hunter, Dard. *Papermaking through Eighteen Centuries.* 1930. Reprint. New York: Burt Franklin, 1971.

Ivins, William M., Jr. *How Prints Look.* 2d ed. Boston: Beacon Press, 1960.

Ivins, William M., Jr. *Prints and Visual Communication.* Cambridge: Harvard University Press, 1968.

Johnson, Una E. *American Prints and Printmakers*. Garden City, N.Y.: Doubleday, 1980.

Kase, Thelma Green. "The Artist, the Printer, and the Publisher: A Study in Printmaking Partnerships, 1960–1970." Master's thesis, University of Missouri, 1973.

Kubiak, Richard. *The Handmade Paper Object*. Exhibition catalogue. Santa Barbara, Calif.: Santa Barbara Museum of Art, 1976.

Long, Paulette, ed. *Paper—Art and Technology*. San Francisco: World Print Council, 1979.

Mayor, A. Hyatt. *Prints and People: A Social History of Printed Pictures*. New York: New York Graphic Society, 1971.

Meyer, Susan E. "The Revolution in Paper." *American Artist* 41 (August 1977): 33–49.

Phillips, Deborah C. "Artist and Printer: A Coincidence of Sympathies." *Art News* 80 (March 1981): 100–106.

"Printing Today: Eight Views." Panel discussion between Pat Branstead, Chip Elwell, Alexander Heinrici, Jack Lemon, Bud Shark, Judith Solodkin, Kenneth Tyler, and Jeff Wasserman, October 30, 1982. *Print Collector's Newsletter* 13 (January–February 1983): 189–200.

Riggs, T. A. *Two Decades of American Printmaking: 1957–1977*. Exhibition catalogue. Worcester, Mass.: Worcester Art Museum, 1978.

Robison, Andrew. *Paper in Prints*. Exhibition catalogue. Washington, D.C.: National Gallery of Art, 1977.

Rubin, David S. *Paper Art*. Exhibition catalogue. Claremont, Calif.: Lang Art Gallery, Scripps College, 1977.

Saff, Donald, and Deli Sacilotto. *Printmaking: History and Process*. New York: Holt, Rinehart & Winston, 1978.

Saft, Carol. *Artist and Printer: Printmaking as a Collaborative Process*. New York: Pratt Graphics Center, 1981.

Schlosser, Leonard, and Kenneth E. Tyler. *Paper and Printmaking Glossary*. Privately printed, 1978.

Stasik, Andrew, ed. "Toward a Broader View and Greater Appreciation of America's Graphic Artist: The Printmaker, 1956–1981." *Print Review* 13 (1981): 24–37.

Studley, Vance. *The Art and Craft of Handmade Paper*. New York: Van Nostrand Reinhold, 1977.

Tully, Judd. "Paper Chase." *Portfolio* 5 (May–June 1983): 78–85.

Walker, Barry. *The American Artist as Printmaker*. Exhibition catalogue. Brooklyn: Brooklyn Museum, 1983.

Watrous, James. *A Century of American Printmaking, 1880–1980*. Madison: University of Wisconsin Press, 1984.

Webb, Sheila. *Paper: The Continuous Thread*. Exhibition catalogue. Cleveland: Cleveland Museum of Art, 1982.

Zigrosser, Carl, and Christa M. Gaehde. *A Guide to the Collecting and Care of Original Prints*. Sponsored by the Print Council of America. London: Crown Publishers, 1965.

Anni Albers

Albers, Anni. *On Designing*. New Haven, Conn.: Pellango Press, 1959.

Albers, Anni. *On Weaving*. Middletown, Conn.: Wesleyan University Press, 1965.

Baro, Gene. *Anni Albers*. Exhibition catalogue. Brooklyn: Brooklyn Museum, 1977.

Buzzard, Marion L. *Anni Albers: Prints and Drawings*. Exhibition catalogue. Riverside: University Art Gallery, University of California, 1980.

Weber, Nicholas Fox. "Anni Albers and the Printerly Image." *Art in America* 63 (July–August 1975): 89.

Weber, Nicholas Fox. *Anni Albers: Triangulated Intaglios*. Publisher's brochure. Bedford Village, N.Y.: Tyler Graphics, 1976.

Weber, Nicholas Fox, Mary Jane Jacob, and Richard S. Field. *The Woven and Graphic Art of Anni Albers*. Exhibition catalogue. Washington, D.C.: Smithsonian Institution Press, 1985.

Josef Albers

Albers, Josef. *Interaction of Color*. New Haven, Conn.: Yale University Press, 1963.

Albers, Josef. *Josef Albers: White Line Squares, Series II of Eight Lithographs*. Publisher's brochure. Los Angeles: Gemini G.E.L., 1967.

Bucher, François. *Josef Albers: Despite Straight Lines, an Analysis of His Graphic Constructions*. 2d ed. Cambridge: MIT Press, 1977.

Geldzahler, Henry. *Josef Albers at the Metropolitan Museum of Art*. Exhibition catalogue. New York: Metropolitan Museum of Art, 1971.

Geldzahler, Henry. "Josef Albers (1888–1976): Homage to Man the Maker." *Art News* 75 (May 1976): 76.

Goldstein, C. "Teaching Modernism: What Albers Learned in the Bauhaus and Taught to Rauschenberg, Noland, and Hesse." *Arts Magazine* 54 (December 1979): 108–16.

Hunter, Sam, Hugh M. Davies, Peter P. Morrin, Mary Laura Gibbs, and Niel A. Chassman. *Josef Albers: Paintings and Graphics, 1917–1970.* Exhibition catalogue. Princeton, N.J.: Art Museum, Princeton University, 1971.

Miller, Jo. *Josef Albers: Prints, 1915–1970.* Exhibition catalogue. Brooklyn: Brooklyn Museum, 1973.

Museum of Modern Art. *Josef Albers: Homage to the Square.* Exhibition catalogue. New York: International Council of the Museum of Modern Art, 1964.

Nordland, Gerald. *Josef Albers: The American Years.* Exhibition catalogue. Washington, D.C.: Washington Gallery of Modern Art, 1965.

Rowell, M. "On Albers's Color." *Artforum* 10 (January 1972): 26–37.

Spies, Werner. *Albers.* New York: Harry N. Abrams, 1971.

Tyler, Kenneth E., Josef Albers, and Henry T. Hopkins. *Josef Albers: White Line Squares.* Exhibition catalogue. Los Angeles: Los Angeles County Museum of Art in association with Gemini G.E.L., 1966.

Weber, Nicholas Fox. *Josef Albers: Never Before.* Publisher's brochure. Bedford Village, N.Y.: Tyler Graphics, 1976.

Anthony Caro

Bannard, Walter D. "Caro's New Sculpture." *Artforum* 10 (June 1972): 59–64.

Blume, Dieter. *Anthony Caro: Catalogue Raisonné.* 5 vols. Cologne: Verlag Galerie Wentzel, 1981 (vols. 1–4), 1986 (vol. 5).

Forge, Andrew. "Interview with Anthony Caro." *Studio International,* no. 171 (January 1966): 6–9.

Fried, Michael. "Anthony Caro and Kenneth Noland: Some Notes on Not Composing." *Lugano Review* (Summer 1965): 198–206.

Masheck, Joseph. "Reflections on Caro's Englishness." *Studio International,* no. 188 (September 1974): 93–96.

Rubin, William. *Anthony Caro.* Exhibition catalogue. New York: Museum of Modern Art, 1975.

Waldman, Diane. *Anthony Caro.* New York: Abbeville Press, 1982.

Whelan, Richard, Clement Greenberg, John Russell, Phyllis Tuchman, and Michael Fried. *Anthony Caro.* New York: Penguin Books, 1974.

Ronald Davis

Elderfield, John. "New Paintings by Ron Davis." *Artforum* 9 (March 1971): 32–34.

Fried, Michael. "Ronald Davis: Surface and Illusion." *Artforum* 5 (April 1967): 37–41.

Kessler, Charles. *Ronald Davis: Paintings, 1962–1976.* Exhibition catalogue. Oakland: Oakland Museum, 1976.

Larsen, Susan C. "Imagine a Space, a Form, a World: The Paintings of Ron Davis." *Art News* 79 (January 1980): 102–8.

Lippard, Lucy. "Perverse Perspectives." *Art International* 11 (March 20, 1967): 28–33, 44.

Marmer, Nancy. "Ron Davis: Beyond Flatness." *Artforum* 15 (November 1976): 34–37.

Rose, Barbara. "Abstract Illusionism." *Artforum* 6 (October 1967): 33–37.

Tyler Graphics Ltd. *Ronald Davis.* Publisher's brochure. Bedford Village, N.Y.: Tyler Graphics, 1975.

Von Baeyer, Hans Christian. *Finity/Infinity: The Art of Ronald Davis.* New York: New York Academy of Sciences, 1985.

Helen Frankenthaler

Alloway, Lawrence. "Frankenthaler as Pastoral." *Art News* 70 (November 1971): 66–68, 89–90.

André Emmerich Gallery. *Helen Frankenthaler: Monotypes and Drawings on Proofs.* Exhibition catalogue. New York: André Emmerich Gallery, 1981.

André Emmerich Gallery. *Helen Frankenthaler Monotypes.* Exhibition catalogue. New York: André Emmerich Gallery, 1982.

Ashton, Dore. "Helen Frankenthaler." *Studio,* no. 170 (August 1965): 52–55.

Battcock, Gregory. "Helen Frankenthaler." *Art and Artists* 4 (May 1969): 52–55.

Elderfield, John. "Specific Incidents." *Art in America* 70 (February 1982): 100–106.

Frankenthaler, Helen. "The Romance of Learning a New Medium for an Artist." *Print Collector's Newsletter* 8 (July–August 1977): 66–67.

Goldman, Judith. "Painting in Another Language." *Art News* 74 (September 1975): 28–31.

Goossen, E. C. "Helen Frankenthaler." *Art International* 5 (October 1961): 76–79.

Goossen, E. C. *Helen Frankenthaler*. Exhibition catalogue. New York: Whitney Museum of American Art, 1969.

Krens, Thomas. *Helen Frankenthaler Prints: 1961–1979*. Exhibition catalogue. New York: Harper & Row, 1980.

Nemser, Cindy. "Interview with Helen Frankenthaler." *Arts Magazine* 46 (November 1971): 51–55.

Rose, Barbara. "Helen Frankenthaler." *Artforum* 7 (April 1969): 28–33.

Wilkin, Karen. *Frankenthaler: Works on Paper, 1949–1984*. Exhibition catalogue. New York: Solomon R. Guggenheim Museum, 1984.

Nancy Graves

Balken, Debra Bricker. *Nancy Graves: Painting, Sculpture, Drawing, 1980–1985*. Exhibition catalogue. Poughkeepsie, N.Y.: Vassar College Art Gallery, 1986.

Carmean, E. A., Linda L. Cathcart, Robert Hughes, and Michael Edward Shapiro. *The Sculpture of Nancy Graves: A Catalogue Raisonné*. New York: Hudson Hills Press in association with Fort Worth Art Museum, 1987.

Cathcart, Linda L. *Nancy Graves: A Survey, 1969–1980*. Buffalo: Albright-Knox Art Gallery, 1980.

Channin, Richard. "Nancy Graves: Map Paintings." *Art International* 18 (November 15, 1974): 26–27, 62.

Heinemann, Susan. "Nancy Graves: The Paintings Seen." *Arts Magazine* 51 (March 1977): 139–41.

Richardson, Brenda. "Nancy Graves: A New Way of Seeing." *Arts Magazine* 46 (April 1972): 57–61.

Russell, John. "New Prints by Nancy Graves." *New York Times,* September 16, 1977.

Tyler Graphics Ltd. *Nancy Graves*. Publisher's brochure. Bedford Village, N.Y.: Tyler Graphics, 1977.

Wasserman, Emily. "A Conversation with Nancy Graves." *Artforum* 9 (October 1970): 42–47.

Richard Hamilton

Field, Richard S. *The Prints of Richard Hamilton*. Exhibition catalogue. Middletown, Conn.: Davison Art Center, Wesleyan University, 1973.

Field, Richard S. *Richard Hamilton: Image and Process, 1952–1982*. Exhibition catalogue. London: Tate Gallery, 1983.

Gilmour, Pat. "Richard Hamilton." In *Contemporary Masters: The World Print Awards,* pp. 23–36. San Francisco: World Print Council, 1983.

Gilmour, Pat. "Symbiotic Exploitation or Collaboration: Dine and Hamilton with Crommelynck." *Print Collector's Newsletter* 15 (January–February 1985): 193–98.

Hamilton, Richard. *Collected Words, 1953–1982*. London: Thames & Hudson, 1982.

Hamilton, Richard. *Richard Hamilton Prints: A Complete Catalogue of Graphic Works, 1939–83*. Stuttgart: Edition Hansjörg Mayer in association with Waddington Graphics, London, 1984.

Knox, George. *Richard Hamilton: Graphics*. Vancouver: Vancouver Art Gallery, 1978.

Loring, John. "Not Just So Many Marvelously Right Images." *Print Collector's Newsletter* 4 (November–December 1973): 98–100.

Morphet, Richard. *Richard Hamilton*. London: Tate Gallery; Eindhoven: Stedelijk van Abbemuseum, 1970.

Perry, A. "Richard Hamilton Graphics, 1979." *Artmagazine* 10 (February–March 1979): 37–40.

Russell, John. *Richard Hamilton: Prints, Multiples, and Drawings*. Manchester: Whitworth Art Gallery, 1972.

Russell, John. *Richard Hamilton*. Exhibition catalogue. New York: Solomon R. Guggenheim Museum, 1973.

Russell, John. *Drawings and Graphics: Richard Hamilton*. Exhibition catalogue. Grenoble: Musée Grenoble, 1977.

Stedelijk Museum. *Catalogue of Prints and Multiples by Richard Hamilton*. Exhibition catalogue. Amsterdam: Stedelijk Museum, 1971.

Stedelijk Museum. *Richard Hamilton: Paintings, Pastels, Prints*. Exhibition catalogue. Amsterdam: Stedelijk Museum, 1976.

Michael Heizer

Brown, Julia, ed. *Michael Heizer: Sculpture in Reverse*. Exhibition catalogue. Los Angeles: Museum of Contemporary Art, 1984.

Cowart, Jack. *Currents 7: Michael Heizer*. Exhibition catalogue. Saint Louis: Saint Louis Art Museum, 1980.

Crone, Rainer. "Prime Objects of Art: Scale, Shape, Time: Creations by Michael Heizer in the Deserts of Nevada." In *Perspecta 19: The Yale Architectural Journal,* pp. 14–35. Cambridge: MIT Press, 1982.

Dreyfuss, John. "Levitated Mass." *Bomb* 6 (May 1983): 66–67.

Felix, Z., E. Jooster, and Michael Heizer. *Michael Heizer*. Exhibition catalogue. Essen: Museum Folkwang, 1979.

Gruen, John. "Michael Heizer: 'You Might Say I'm in the Construction Business.'" *Art News* 76 (December 1977): 96–99.

Heizer, Michael. "The Art of Michael Heizer." *Artforum* 8 (December 1969): 32–39.

Heizer, Michael. "Point of View." *Image* 8 (April 1971): 2.

Hutchinson, Peter. "Earth in Upheaval." *Arts Magazine* 43 (November 1968): 19–21.

Linker, Kate. "Michael Heizer." *Artforum* 21 (May 1983): 100–101.

Müller, Grégoire. "Michael Heizer." *Arts Magazine* 44 (December 1969): 42–45.

Selz, Peter. "New Work: Michael Heizer." *Arts Magazine* 55 (February 1981): 20–22.

Tomkins, Calvin. "Onward and Upward with the Arts: Maybe a Quantum Leap." *New Yorker,* February 5, 1972, pp. 42–67.

Whitney Museum of American Art. *Michael Heizer/Dragged Mass Geometric.* Exhibition brochure. New York: Whitney Museum of American Art, 1985.

Zimmer, William. "Heizer's Circles." *Soho Weekly News,* May 26, 1977.

David Hockney

Bailey, Anthony. "Profiles: Special Effects." *New Yorker,* July 30, 1979, pp. 35–69.

Baro, Gene. "The British Scene: Hockney and Kitaj." *Arts Magazine* 38 (May–June 1964): 94–101.

Baro, Gene. *David Hockney: Prints and Drawings.* Exhibition catalogue. Washington, D.C.: International Exhibitions Foundation, 1978.

Bowness, Alan, and Martin Friedman. *London: The New Scene.* Exhibition catalogue. Minneapolis: Walker Art Center, 1965.

Brighton, Andrew. *David Hockney Prints, 1954–77.* Exhibition catalogue. Nottingham, England: Midland Group Gallery in association with the Scottish Arts Council and Petersburg Press, 1979.

Butterfield, Jan. "David Hockney: Blue Hedonistic Pools." *Print Collector's Newsletter* 10 (July–August 1979): 73–76.

Friedman, Martin. *Hockney Paints the Stage.* Minneapolis: Walker Art Center; New York: Abbeville Press, 1983.

Geldzahler, Henry. "David Hockney: An Intimate View." *Print Review* 12 (1980): 36–50.

Geldzahler, Henry. "Hockney Abroad: A Slide Show." *Art in America* 69 (February 1981): 126–41.

Glazebrook, Mark. *David Hockney: Paintings, Prints, and Drawings, 1960–1970.* Exhibition catalogue. London: Whitechapel Gallery, 1970.

Gosling, Nigel. "Things Exactly as They Are." *Horizon* (November 1977): 46–51.

Haworth-Booth, Mark. *Hockney's Photographs.* Exhibition catalogue. London: Arts Council of Great Britain and Hayward Gallery, 1983.

Hockney, David. *The Blue Guitar: Etchings by David Hockney Who Was Inspired by Wallace Stevens Who Was Inspired by Pablo Picasso.* London: Petersburg Press, 1978.

Hockney, David. *David Hockney by David Hockney.* Edited by Nikos Stangos. London: Thames & Hudson, 1976; New York: Harry N. Abrams, 1980.

Hockney, David. *Paper Pools.* Edited by Nikos Stangos. New York: Harry N. Abrams, 1980.

Hockney, David. *David Hockney: Photographs.* Exhibition catalogue. London and New York: Petersburg Press in association with Centre Georges Pompidou, Paris, 1982.

Livingstone, Marco. *David Hockney.* New York: Holt, Rinehart & Winston, 1981.

Pillsbury, Edmund. *David Hockney: Travels with Pen, Pencil, and Ink.* Exhibition catalogue. London: Petersburg Press, 1978.

Tyler Graphics Ltd. *David Hockney: Twenty-three Lithographs, 1978–80.* Publisher's brochure. Bedford Village, N.Y.: Tyler Graphics, 1980.

Weschler, Lawrence. "The Art World: True to Life." *New Yorker,* July 9, 1984, pp. 60–71.

Weschler, Lawrence. *Cameraworks: David Hockney.* New York: Alfred A. Knopf, 1984.

Ellsworth Kelly

Axsom, Richard H. *The Prints of Ellsworth Kelly.* New York: Hudson Hills Press, 1987.

Baker, Elizabeth C. *Ellsworth Kelly: Recent Paintings and Sculpture.* Exhibition catalogue. New York: Metropolitan Museum of Art, 1979.

Coplans, John. *Ellsworth Kelly.* New York: Harry N. Abrams, 1972.

Debs, Barbara Knowles. "Ellsworth Kelly's Drawings." *Print Collector's Newsletter* 3 (September–October 1972): 73–77.

Geldzahler, Henry. "Interview with Ellsworth Kelly." *Art International* 8 (February 1964): 47–48.

Goossen, E. C. *Ellsworth Kelly.* Exhibition catalogue. New York: Museum of Modern Art, 1973.

Kelly, Ellsworth. *Ellsworth Kelly.* Exhibition catalogue. Los Angeles: Margo Leavin Gallery; New York: Leo Castelli Gallery, 1984.

Ratcliff, Carter. "Ellsworth Kelly's Spectrum of Experience." *Art in America* 69 (Summer 1981): 98–101.

Rose, Barbara, and Ellsworth Kelly. *Ellsworth Kelly: Paintings and Sculpture, 1963–1979*. Exhibition catalogue. Amsterdam: Stedelijk Museum, 1979.

Sims, Patterson, and Emily Rauh Pulitzer. *Ellsworth Kelly: Sculpture*. Exhibition catalogue. New York: Whitney Museum of American Art, 1982.

Tuchman, Phyllis. "Ellsworth Kelly's Photographs." *Art in America* 62 (January–February 1974): 55–61.

Tyler Graphics Ltd. *Ellsworth Kelly: Colored Paper Images*. Publisher's brochure. Bedford Village, N.Y.: Tyler Graphics, 1976.

Waldman, Diane. *Ellsworth Kelly: Drawings, Collages, Prints*. Greenwich, Conn.: New York Graphic Society, 1971.

Roy Lichtenstein

Alloway, Lawrence. "Roy Lichtenstein." *Studio*, no. 175 (January 1968): 25–31.

Alloway, Lawrence. *Roy Lichtenstein*. New York: Abbeville Press, 1983.

Coplans, John. *Roy Lichtenstein*. Exhibition catalogue. Pasadena, Calif.: Pasadena Art Museum, 1967.

Coplans, John. "Lichtenstein's Graphic Works: Roy Lichtenstein in Conversation." *Studio International*, no. 180 (December 1970): 263–65.

Coplans, John, ed. *Roy Lichtenstein*. Documentary Monographs in Modern Art. New York: Praeger Publishers, 1972.

Cowart, Jack. *Roy Lichtenstein, 1970–1980*. Exhibition catalogue. Saint Louis: Saint Louis Art Museum; New York: Hudson Hills Press, 1981.

Glaser, Bruce. "Oldenburg, Lichtenstein, Warhol: A Discussion." *Artforum* 4 (February 1966): 20–24.

Gruen, John. "Roy Lichtenstein: From Outrageous Parody to Iconographic Elegance." *Art News* 75 (March 1976): 39–42.

Hamilton, Richard. "Roy Lichtenstein." *Studio*, no. 175 (January 1968): 20–24.

Kuspit, Donald B. "Pop Art: A Reactionary Realism." *Art Journal* 36 (Fall 1976): 31–38.

Kuspit, Donald B. "Lichtenstein and the Collective Unconscious of Style." *Art in America* 67 (May–June 1979): 100–105.

Morphet, Richard. *Roy Lichtenstein*. Exhibition catalogue. London: Tate Gallery, 1968.

Rose, Barbara. *Roy Lichtenstein: Entablature Series*. Publisher's brochure. Bedford Village, N.Y.: Tyler Graphics, 1976.

Rose, Bernice. *The Drawings of Roy Lichtenstein*. Exhibition catalogue. New York: Museum of Modern Art, 1987.

Tuchman, Phyllis. "Pop Interviews with George Segal, Andy Warhol, Roy Lichtenstein, James Rosenquist, and Robert Indiana." *Art News* 73 (May 1974): 24–29.

Waldman, Diane. *Roy Lichtenstein*. Exhibition catalogue. New York: Solomon R. Guggenheim Museum, 1969.

Waldman, Diane. *Roy Lichtenstein: Drawings and Prints*. Lausanne: Publications I.R.L., 1970.

Zerner, Henri. *The Graphic Art of Roy Lichtenstein*. Exhibition catalogue. Cambridge: Fogg Art Museum, Harvard University, 1975.

Joan Mitchell

Ashbery, John. "An Expressionist in Paris." *Art News* 64 (April 1965): 44–45, 63–64.

"Is Today's Artist with or against the Past?; Part 2, Answers by: David Smith, Frederick Kiesler, Franz Kline, Joan Mitchell." *Art News* 57 (Summer 1958): 41.

Nochlin, Linda. "Joan Mitchell: Art and Life at Vétheuil." *House and Garden*, November 1984, pp. 193–98, 226–38.

Rose, Barbara. *Joan Mitchell: Bedford Series*. Publisher's brochure. Bedford Village, N.Y.: Tyler Graphics, 1981.

Sandler, Irving H. "Joan Mitchell." In *School of New York: Some Younger Artists*, edited by B. H. Friedman. New York: Grove Press, 1959.

Schneider, Pierre. "From Confession to Landscape." *Art News* 67 (April 1968): 42–43, 72–73.

Tucker, Marcia. *Joan Mitchell*. Exhibition catalogue. New York: Whitney Museum of American Art, 1974.

Xavier Fourcade, Inc. *Joan Mitchell: New Paintings*. Exhibition catalogue. New York: Xavier Fourcade, 1976.

Xavier Fourcade, Inc. *Joan Mitchell: New Paintings*. Interview with Yves Michaud. Exhibition catalogue. New York: Xavier Fourcade, 1986.

Malcolm Morley

Compton, Michael. *Malcolm Morley: Paintings, 1965–82.* Exhibition catalogue. London: Whitechapel Art Gallery, 1983.

Kertess, Klaus. "Malcolm Morley: Talking about Seeing." *Artforum* 18 (Summer 1980): 48–51.

Kramer, Hilton. "Expressionism Returns to Painting." *New York Times,* July 12, 1981, pp. 1, 23.

Kramer, Hilton. "The Malcolm Morley Retrospective." *New Criterion* 2 (September 1983): 71–74.

Levin, Kim. "Malcolm Morley: Post Style Illusionism." *Arts Magazine* 47 (February 1973): 60–63.

Levine, Les. "Dialogue: Malcolm Morley." *Cover* 1 (Spring–Summer 1985): 28–31.

Loring, John. "The Plastic Logic of Realism." *Arts Magazine* 49 (October 1974): 48–49.

Lucie-Smith, Edward. "The Neutral Style." *Art and Artists* 10 (August 1975): 6–15.

Nadelman, Cynthia. "New Editions: Malcolm Morley." *Art News* 81 (April 1982): 106.

Pace Prints. *Malcolm Morley: Prints and Process.* Exhibition brochure. New York: Pace Prints, 1986.

Seitz, William C., "Real and the Artificial: Painting of the New Environment." *Art in America* 60 (November–December 1972): 58–72.

Tatransky, Valentin. "Morley's New Paintings." *Art International* 23 (October 1979): 55–59.

Robert Motherwell

Armstrong, Elizabeth, and Jack Flam. *Robert Motherwell: The Collaged Image.* Exhibition catalogue. Minneapolis: Walker Art Center, 1985.

Arnason, H. H. *Robert Motherwell.* 2d ed. New York: Harry N. Abrams, 1982.

Ashton, Dore, and Jack Flam. *Robert Motherwell.* Exhibition catalogue. New York: Abbeville Press in association with Albright-Knox Art Gallery, 1983.

Brooke Alexander, Inc. *Robert Motherwell: Selected Prints, 1961–74.* Exhibition catalogue. New York: Brooke Alexander, 1974.

Carmean, E. A., Jr. *The Collages of Robert Motherwell: A Retrospective Exhibition.* Exhibition catalogue. Houston: Museum of Fine Arts, 1972.

Carmean, E. A., Jr., ed. *Robert Motherwell: The Reconciliation Elegy.* Geneva: Editions d'Art Albert Skira; New York: Rizzoli International Publications, 1980.

Colsman-Freyberger, Heidi. "Robert Motherwell: Words and Images." *Print Collector's Newsletter* 4 (January–February 1974): 125–29.

Flam, Jack. *Robert Motherwell: Drawings.* Exhibition catalogue. Houston: Janie C. Lee Gallery, 1979.

Flam, Jack. *Robert Motherwell/El Negro.* Publisher's brochure. Bedford Village, N.Y.: Tyler Graphics, 1983.

Mattison, Robert S. "Two Decades of Graphic Art by Robert Motherwell." *Print Collector's Newsletter* 11 (January–February 1981): 197–201.

McKendry, John, Diane Kelder, and Robert Motherwell. *Robert Motherwell's A la pintura: The Genesis of a Book.* Exhibition catalogue. New York: Metropolitan Museum of Art, 1972.

Motherwell, Robert. *Robert Motherwell: Prints 1977–79.* Exhibition catalogue. New York: Brooke Alexander, 1979.

Nelson, Harold, and Jean S. Tucker. *Robert Motherwell: The Collage Prints, 1968–78.* Exhibition catalogue. Saint Louis: University of Missouri, 1979.

O'Hara, Frank. *Robert Motherwell.* Exhibition catalogue. New York: Museum of Modern Art, 1965.

Rohowsky, Peter S., Deborah D. Strom, and Harry B. Titus. *Robert Motherwell: Recent Work.* Exhibition catalogue. Princeton, N.J.: Art Museum, Princeton University, 1973.

Terenzio, Stephanie. *Robert Motherwell and Black.* Exhibition catalogue. Storrs: William Benton Museum of Art, University of Connecticut, 1980.

Terenzio, Stephanie. *Robert Motherwell: Etchings 1984/85.* Publisher's brochure. Bedford Village, N.Y.: Tyler Graphics, 1985.

Terenzio, Stephanie, and Dorothy C. Belknap. *The Painter and the Printer: Robert Motherwell's Graphics, 1943–1980.* With illustrated catalogue raisonné. New York: American Federation of Arts, 1980.

Terenzio, Stephanie, and Dorothy C. Belknap. *The Prints of Robert Motherwell: A Catalogue Raisonné, 1943–1984.* New York: Hudson Hills Press, 1984.

Tyler Graphics Ltd. *Robert Motherwell: Collage Prints.* Publisher's brochure. Bedford Village, N.Y.: Tyler Graphics, 1984.

Kenneth Noland

Fried, Michael. "Recent Work by Kenneth Noland." *Artforum* 7 (Summer 1969): 36–37.

Goldman, Judith. *Kenneth Noland: Handmade Papers.* Publisher's brochure. Bedford Village, N.Y.: Tyler Graphics, 1978.

Greenberg, Clement. "Poetry of Vision." *Artforum* 7 (April 1968): 18–21.

Hess, Thomas B. "Kenneth Noland, Hesitant Prophet." *New York Magazine,* May 23, 1977, pp. 76–78.

Krauss, Rosalind E. "On Frontality." *Artforum* 6 (May 1968): 40–46.

Moffett, Kenworth. "Noland Vertical." *Art News* 70 (October 1971): 48–49, 76–78.

Moffett, Kenworth. "Kenneth Noland's New Paintings and the Issue of the Shaped Canvas." *Art International* 20 (April–May 1976): 8–15, 28–30.

Moffett, Kenworth. *Kenneth Noland.* New York: Harry N. Abrams, 1977.

Noland, Kenneth. *Kenneth Noland: Recent Paperworks.* Exhibition catalogue. Durham, N.C.: Institute of the Arts, Duke University, 1983.

Tatransky, Valentin. "Kenneth Noland: As Great as Ever." *Arts Magazine* 57 (June 1983): 118–19.

Waldman, Diane. "Color, Format, and Abstract Art: An Interview with Kenneth Noland." *Art in America* 65 (May–June 1977): 99–105.

Waldman, Diane. *Kenneth Noland: A Retrospective.* Exhibition catalogue. New York: Solomon R. Guggenheim Museum, 1977.

Hugh O'Donnell

Dennison, Lisa. "Hugh O'Donnell." *Arts Magazine* 57 (February 1983): 7.

Marlborough Gallery. *Hugh O'Donnell: Recent Paintings and Drawings.* Gallery brochure. New York: Marlborough Gallery, 1982.

Marlborough Gallery. *Hugh O'Donnell: Recent Work.* Gallery brochure. New York: Marlborough Gallery, 1987.

Rees, Ronald. *Hugh O'Donnell: Recent Work, April 1984 to April 1985.* Gallery brochure. London: Marlborough Fine Art, 1985.

Waldman, Diane. *British Art Now: An American Perspective, 1980 Exxon International Exhibition.* Exhibition catalogue. New York: Solomon R. Guggenheim Museum, 1980.

Claes Oldenburg

Baro, Gene. *Claes Oldenburg—Drawings and Prints.* New York: Chelsea House Publishers, 1969.

Bruggen, Coosje van. *Claes Oldenburg: Drawings, Watercolors, and Prints.* Exhibition catalogue. Stockholm: Moderna Museet, 1970.

Bruggen, Coosje van. *Claes Oldenburg: Mouse Museum/Ray Gun Wing.* Exhibition catalogue. Cologne: Museum Ludwig, 1979.

Bruggen, Coosje van, and Claes Oldenburg. *Claes Oldenburg: Large-Scale Projects, 1977–1980.* New York: Rizzoli International Publications, 1980.

Friedman, Martin. *Oldenburg: Six Themes.* Exhibition catalogue. Minneapolis: Walker Art Center, 1975.

Glaser, Bruce. "Oldenburg, Lichtenstein, Warhol: A Discussion." *Artforum* 4 (February 1966): 20–24.

Goldman, Judith. "Sort of a Commercial for Objects." *Print Collector's Newsletter* 2 (January–February 1971): 117–21.

Haskell, Barbara. *Claes Oldenburg: Object into Monument.* Exhibition catalogue. Pasadena, Calif.: Pasadena Art Museum, 1971.

Johnson, Ellen H. *Claes Oldenburg.* New York: Penguin Books, 1971.

Margo Leavin Gallery. *Oldenburg: Works in Edition.* Los Angeles: Margo Leavin Gallery, 1971.

Oldenburg, Claes. *Notes in Hand.* New York: E. P. Dutton & Co. in association with Petersburg Press, 1971.

Oldenburg, Claes. *Claes Oldenburg: The Alphabet in L.A.* Exhibition brochure. Los Angeles: Margo Leavin Gallery, 1975.

Rose, Barbara. *Claes Oldenburg: Notes.* Publisher's brochure. Los Angeles: Gemini G.E.L., 1968.

Rose, Barbara. *Claes Oldenburg.* Exhibition catalogue. New York: Museum of Modern Art, 1970.

Alan Shields

Ashbery, John. "Emblazoned Shields." *New York Magazine,* June 12, 1978, pp. 97–99.

Cohen, Ronny. "Paper Routes." *Art News* 82 (October 1983): 79–85.

Cohen, Ronny. *Alan Shields: Print Retrospective.* Exhibition catalogue. Cleveland: Cleveland Center for Contemporary Art, 1986.

Contemporary Arts Museum. *Alan Shields.* Exhibition brochure. Houston: Contemporary Arts Museum, 1973.

Emont-Scott, Deborah. *Alan Shields.* Exhibition catalogue. Memphis: Memphis Brooks Museum of Art, 1983.

Kelder, Diane. "Alan Shields' Things with Printmaking Techniques." *Art in America* 61 (May–June 1973): 86–88.

Pindell, Howardena. "Tales of Brave Ulysses: Alan Shields Interviewed by Howardena Pindell." *Print Collector's Newsletter* 5 (January–February 1975): 137–43.

Ratcliff, Carter. *Alan Shields.* Exhibition catalogue. Chicago: Museum of Contemporary Art, 1973.

Sims, Patterson. *Alan Shields.* Exhibition catalogue. Philadelphia: Moore College of Art, 1977.

Tyler Graphics Ltd. *Alan Shields.* Publisher's brochure. Bedford Village, N.Y.: Tyler Graphics, 1979.

Tyler Graphics Ltd. *Alan Shields: The Castle Window Set and Santa's Collar.* Publisher's brochure. Bedford Village, N.Y.: Tyler Graphics, 1981.

Richard Smith

Andersen, Wayne. *Richard Smith: Recent Work, 1972–1977: Paintings, Drawings, Graphics.* Exhibition catalogue. Cambridge: Hayden Gallery, Massachusetts Institute of Technology, 1978.

Bowness, Alan, and Martin Friedman. *London: The New Scene.* Exhibition catalogue. Minneapolis: Walker Art Center, 1965.

British Council. *Richard Smith.* Exhibition catalogue. British Pavilion, thirty-fifth Venice Biennale 1970. London: British Council, 1970.

Denvir, Bernard. "A Double Reality: The Work and Career of Richard Smith." *Art International* 14 (Summer 1970): 78–82.

Lippard, Lucy R. "Richard Smith: Conversations with the Artist." *Art International* 8 (November 1964): 31–34.

Robertson, Bryan. *Richard Smith.* Exhibition catalogue. London: Whitechapel Gallery, 1966.

Rose, Barbara. "Richard Smith: An Interview with Barbara Rose." *Studio International*, no. 190 (September–October 1975): 165–67.

Rose, Barbara. *Richard Smith: Seven Exhibitions, 1961–75.* Exhibition catalogue. London: Tate Gallery, 1975.

Seymour, Anne. "Preoccupations: Richard Smith Talks to Anne Seymour." *Art and Artists* 5 (June 1970): 18–22.

Smith, Richard. "Printing Paintings, Painting Prints." *Print Collector's Newsletter* 6 (January–February 1976): 156–57.

Smith, Richard, and Kenneth E. Tyler. *Richard Smith: Cartouche Series.* Exhibition catalogue. Regina: Norman Mackenzie Art Gallery, University of Regina, 1980.

Steven Sorman

Cohen, Ronny H. "Three Artists—Three Arguments." *Print Collector's Newsletter* 11 (May–June 1980): 37–38.

Deschamps, Madeleine. *La Peinture américaine: Les Mythes et la matière.* Paris: Denoël, 1981.

Fine, Ruth E. *Steven Sorman: Mixed Media Prints and Monotypes.* Exhibition brochure. Philadelphia: Dolan/Maxwell Gallery, 1984.

Hampl, Patricia. *Steven Sorman.* Exhibition brochure. Philadelphia: Dolan/Maxwell Gallery, 1986.

Larson, Philip. "Steven Sorman: An Interview." *Print Collector's Newsletter* 11 (May–June 1980): 42–44.

Martin, Mary Abbe. *Steven Sorman: Collage Prints and Monoprints.* Publisher's brochure. Bedford Village, N.Y.: Tyler Graphics, 1985.

Riddle, Mason. *Steven Sorman: Paintings—Monotypes—Graphics.* Exhibition brochure. Stockholm: Thorden Wetterling Galleries, 1984.

Frank Stella

Ackley, Clifford S. "Frank Stella's Big Football Weekend." *Print Collector's Newsletter* 13 (January–February 1983): 207–8.

Axsom, Richard H. *Frank Stella Prints, 1967–1982: Handbook to the Exhibition.* Exhibition catalogue. Ann Arbor: University of Michigan Museum of Art, 1982.

Axsom, Richard H. *The Prints of Frank Stella: A Catalogue Raisonné, 1967–1982.* Exhibition catalogue. New York: Hudson Hills Press in association with the University of Michigan Museum of Art, Ann Arbor, 1983.

Cook, Christopher C. *Frank Stella: From Start to Finish.* Exhibition catalogue. Andover, Mass.: Addison Gallery of American Art, Phillips Academy, 1982.

Frackman, Noel. "Tracking Frank Stella's Circuit Series." *Arts Magazine* 56 (April 1982): 134–37.

Goldman, Judith. *Frank Stella: Fourteen Prints with Drawings, Collages, and Working Proofs.* Exhibition catalogue. Princeton, N.J.: Art Museum, Princeton University, 1983.

Goldman, Judith. *Frank Stella: Prints 1967–1982.* Exhibition brochure. New York: Whitney Museum of American Art, 1983.

Hughes, Robert. *Frank Stella: The Swan Engravings.* Exhibition catalogue. Fort Worth, Tex.: Fort Worth Art Museum, 1984.

Leider, Philip. *Stella since 1970.* Exhibition catalogue. Fort Worth, Tex.: Fort Worth Art Museum, 1978.

Ratcliff, Carter. "Frank Stella: Portrait of the Artist as an Image Administrator." *Art in America* 74 (February 1985): 94–107.

Rosenblum, Robert. *Frank Stella.* Baltimore and Harmondsworth, England: Penguin Books, 1971.

Rubin, Lawrence. *Frank Stella: Paintings, 1958 to 1965: A Catalogue Raisonné.* New York: Stewart, Tabori & Chang, 1986.

Rubin, William S. *Frank Stella.* Exhibition catalogue. New York: Museum of Modern Art, 1970.

Stella, Frank. "On Caravaggio." *New York Times Magazine,* February 3, 1985, pp. 39–60, 71.

Stella, Frank. *Working Space.* Cambridge: Harvard University Press, 1986.

Tomkins, Calvin. "Profiles: The Space around Real Things." *New Yorker,* September 10, 1984, pp. 53–97.

Tyler Graphics Ltd. *Frank Stella: Paper Reliefs.* Publisher's brochure. Bedford Village, N.Y.: Tyler Graphics, 1975.

Jack Tworkov

Armstrong, Richard, and Kenneth Baker. *Jack Tworkov: Paintings, 1928–1982.* Exhibition catalogue. Philadelphia: Pennsylvania Academy of the Fine Arts, 1987.

Bryant, Edward. *Jack Tworkov.* Exhibition catalogue. New York: Whitney Museum of American Art, 1964.

Finkelstein, Louis. "Tworkov: Radical Pro." *Art News* 63 (April 1964): 32–35, 52–54.

Forge, Andrew. *Jack Tworkov: Fifteen Years of Painting.* Exhibition catalogue. New York: Solomon R. Guggenheim Museum, 1982.

Gula, Kasha Linville. "The Indian Summer of Jack Tworkov." *Art in America* 61 (September–October 1973): 62–65.

Kingsley, April. "Jack Tworkov." *Art International* 18 (March 20, 1974): 24–27.

Plous, Phyllis. *Jack Tworkov: Recent Paintings and Drawings.* Exhibition catalogue. Santa Barbara: University Art Galleries, University of California, 1977.

Talalay, Marjorie, and Tom E. Hinson. *Jack Tworkov: Recent Paintings and Drawings, 1968–1975.* Exhibition catalogue. Cleveland: New Gallery, 1975.

Tuchman, Phyllis. "An Interview with Jack Tworkov." *Artforum* 9 (January 1971): 62–68.

Tucker, Marcia. *Jack Tworkov: Recent Paintings.* Exhibition brochure. New York: Whitney Museum of American Art, 1971.

Tworkov, Jack. "Notes on My Painting." *Art in America* 61 (September–October 1973): 66–69.

Robert Zakanitch

Goldin, Amy. "Pattern and Print." *Print Collector's Newsletter* 9 (March–April 1978): 10–13.

Jensen, Robert, and Patricia Conway. *Ornamentalism: The New Decorativeness in Architecture and Design.* New York: Clarkson N. Potter, 1983.

Kardon, Janet. *Robert Zakanitch.* Exhibition catalogue. Philadephia: Institute of Contemporary Art, University of Pennsylvania, 1981.

Morrin, Peter, and Jean E. Feinberg. *Content in Abstraction: The Uses of Nature.* Exhibition catalogue. Atlanta: High Museum of Art, 1983.

Perreault, John. "Issues in Pattern Painting." *Artforum* 16 (November 1977): 32–36.

Perreault, John. "The New Decorativeness." *Portfolio* 1 (June–July 1979): 46–50.

Rickey, Carrie. "Decoration, Ornament, Pattern, and Utility: Four Tendencies in Search of a Movement." *Flash Art,* no. 90/91 (June–July 1979): 19–30.

Weber, Bruce. *A Collaboration: Patsy Norvell and Robert Zakanitch.* Exhibition catalogue. West Palm Beach, Fla.: Norton Gallery and School of Art, 1982.

Index

Reproduction Credits

Courtesy Mr. and Mrs. Harry W. Anderson
p. 98

Courtesy Art Institute of Chicago
pp. 47 (right), 48

Richard H. Axsom
p. 178

Marabeth Cohen,
courtesy Tyler Graphics Ltd.
p. 192

Courtesy Corcoran Gallery of Art
p. 165

Betty Fiske,
courtesy Tyler Graphics Ltd.
p. 194

Gianfranco Gorgoni/Contact Press
pp. 114, 116

Gianfranco Gorgoni,
courtesy Tyler Graphics Ltd.
p. 190

Lindsay Green,
courtesy Tyler Graphics Ltd.
pp. 188, 196 (bottom), 252; back
cover (top)

Courtesy David Hockney
p. 152

Courtesy Ellsworth Kelly
p. 109 (bottom)

Courtesy M. Knoedler & Co., Inc.
p. 169

Courtesy Kunsthalle Tübingen,
Sammlung Zundel
p. 122

Courtesy Metropolitan Museum
of Art
pp. 41 (left), 141

Courtesy Museum of Modern Art,
New York
p. 82

Don Myer,
courtesy San Francisco Museum
of Modern Art
pp. 220–21

Courtesy National Gallery of Art,
Washington, D.C.
p. 64

Courtesy Claes Oldenburg
p. 138

Eric Pollitzer,
courtesy Peter Palumbo
p. 111

Prudence Cuming Associates Ltd.
p. 123

Jill Sabella,
courtesy Tyler Graphics Ltd.
p. 196 (top); back cover (bottom)

Courtesy Seattle Art Museum
p. 99

Steven Sloman,
courtesy Tyler Graphics Ltd.
title page, pp. 36, 57, 68, 72, 85, 171, 182,
191, 199 (top), 223

Kenneth Tyler,
courtesy Tyler Graphics Ltd.
p. 199 (bottom)

Courtesy University Art Museum,
University of New Mexico, Albuquerque
p. 96 (top)

Walker Art Center
pp. 6, 9, 10, 12, 16, 33, 38, 41 (right), 45,
47 (left), 50, 51, 54–56, 58, 61, 62, 69, 71,
73, 74, 76, 79–81, 84, 86–88, 91–93,
95–97, 100–104, 106, 107, 109 (top), 110,
112, 115, 117, 118, 120, 124–33, 135, 136,
139, 142–48, 151, 153–55, 157, 158, 160,
163, 167, 168, 172, 173, 175, 180, 181,
195, 197, 202, 204, 205, 207–9, 211–13,
215, 217, 219, 224, 226–28, 230–35, 237,
240; front cover

Courtesy Xavier Fourcade, Inc.
p. 75